Instructor's

to Accompany

ECONOMICS
Third Edition

Roger Arnold
California State University
San Marcos

Prepared by

Bryan W. Taylor, II
California State University
Los Angeles

West Publishing Company
Minneapolis/St. Paul   New York   Los Angeles   San Francisco

Photo Credit: ©Jody Dole/The Image Bank and ©Benn Mitchell/The Image Bank

WEST'S COMMITMENT TO THE ENVIRONMENT

In 1906, West Publishing Company began recycling materials left over from the production of books. This began a tradition of efficient and responsible use of resources. Today, 100% of our legal bound volumes are printed on acid-free, recycled paper consisting of 50% new paper pulp and 50% paper that has undergone a de-inking process. We also use vegetable-based inks to print all of our books. West recycles nearly 27,700,000 pounds of scrap paper annually—the equivalent of 229,300 trees. Since the 1960s, West has devised ways to capture and recycle waste inks, solvents, oils, and vapors created in the printing process. We also recycle plastics of all kinds, wood, glass, corrugated cardboard, and batteries, and have eliminated the use of polystyrene book packaging. We at West are proud of the longevity and the scope of our commitment to the environment.

West pocket parts and advance sheets are printed on recyclable paper and can be collected and recycled with newspapers. Staples do not have to be removed. Bound volumes can be recycled after removing the cover.

Production, Prepress, Printing and Binding by West Publishing Company.

 TEXT IS PRINTED ON 10% POST CONSUMER RECYCLED PAPER    Printed with **Printwise** Environmentally Advanced Water Washable Ink

ISBN 0–314–09034–7

Contents

MICROECONOMICS

THE WORLD ECONOMY

Preface

This *Instructor's Manual* is intended to accompany Roger A. Arnold's *Economics* (West Publishing, 3rd Edition, 1996). It follows the same organization of the text, and it is directed at instructors using this text. The goals of this instructor's manual are to assist instructors in familiarizing themselves with the material in and the organization of the text; to highlight the important concepts in each chapter in order to aid in the preparation of lectures; to provide suggested answers to the questions at the end of each chapter; and to provide lecture supplements which can be used for in-class discussions. Each chapter of the *Instructor's Manual* is divided into several sections which are designed to help instructors to prepare their in-class lectures and generate class discussion:

- **Overview** -- This is a brief introduction to the chapter. It is also designed to give the instructors an idea of how this chapter relates to other chapters in the text;

- **Chapter Objectives** -- This section lists the most important subjects for the chapter, and it describes the subjects in terms of goals which your students should achieve by the end of the chapter in order to understand the material which is covered;

- **Key Terms** -- This is a list of new terms which appear in the chapter. Students should know the meaning of each of these terms, and be able to provide examples or applications of these ideas. Most of these terms are highlighted in the Chapter Outline (with either **boldface** or *italics*) to remind the instructor to emphasize these terms;

- **Chapter Outline** -- This is an annotated outline of the chapter which summarizes the important ideas in each section of the chapter. This provides the instructor with a ready-made outline of each chapter, highlighting the important concepts and terms, referring to exhibits in the text, and making suggestions for how to use the special features which are included in the text to generate in-class discussion;

- **Answers to Chapter Questions** -- This section provides suggested, though not always definitive, answers to the "Questions and Problems" at the end of each chapter. Many questions are thought questions and can have numerous answers depending upon one's experience and views. The goal is to get students to think and to apply the concepts in the chapter, not to memorize the "correct" answer; and,

- **Lecture Supplements** -- Instructors who want to apply economic concepts to contemporary, real-world events, but lack the time to search through back issues of magazines and journals will find this section useful. Each chapter provides three to four articles from readily available magazines and journals which look at economic problems individuals and firms are currently facing. Most articles are relatively short, can be read in class, and cover topics which are either controversial or immediately applicable to students' lives. Too often students get so caught up in trying to understand the theoretical concepts that they don't spend enough time learning how to apply these concepts to the real world. The suggested readings are designed to solve this problem.

You should not hesitate to share the materials in this *Instructor's Manual* with your students. Many students have told me that they find economics the most difficult course which they take in college. The reason for this is that economics can be abstract, there is a lot of new vocabulary to learn, and students often find it difficult to relate economic theories and terms to the real world. Of all the professors whom I had in college, only one gave me an outline of the class and shared his lecture notes. But I was always indebted to him for doing this because instead of trying to quickly summarize in my notes what he was saying before I lost track of his next statement, I already had his notes written down. Now I could concentrate more on his lecture, and less on taking notes. Sharing these materials also applies to the answers to the chapter questions, the lecture supplements, or other sections of this Instructor's Manual. If this helps your students to understand the material in the text and to think like an economist, both you and your students will benefit.

I would like to thank Theresa O'Dell, senior developmental editor at West Publishing, for her professional, dedicated assistance and patience in helping me to produce this *Instructor's Manual*. Her comments were always useful and instructive, and she was always there to help me when I had questions or problems. I would also like to thank Roger Arnold for his feedback and guidance in writing the *Instructor's Manual*. Of course, I am responsible for the final product, and all of its contents. I would appreciate any feedback from instructors who are using this manual in order to improve future editions.

Bryan W. Taylor II
California State University
Los Angeles
November 1995

Chapter Conversion Table

This Instructor's Manual is written and organized to accompany Roger Arnold's *Economics*, Third Edition; however, only minor adjustments are required in order to use it in conjunction with *Macroeconomics* and/or *Microeconomics*. The Table below gives the chapter number in the split editions which correspond to each chapter in the *Economics* text. The Chapter Conversion Table provides the chapter for the *Economics* text in the first column, the chapter title in the second column, the corresponding chapter numbers (where appropriate) for *Macroeconomics* in the third column and *Microeconomics* in the fourth column.

Economics	Chapter Title	Macroeconomics	Microeconomics
1	What Economics Is About	1	1
2	Fundamentals of Economic Thinking	2	2
3	Supply, Demand, and Price	3	3
4	Three Economic Goals and Three Economic Measurements	4	—
5	Aggregate Demand and Aggregate Supply: In the Short Run	5	—
6	AD-AS in the Long Run and the Self-Regulating Economy	6	—
7	Economic Instability: A Critique of the Self-Regulating Economy	7	—
8	Fiscal Policy	8	—
9	Money and Banking	9	—
10	The Federal Reserve System	10	—
11	Money and the Economy	11	—
12	Monetary Policy	12	—
13	Expectations Theory and the Economy	13	—
14	Economic Growth: Resources, Technology, and Ideas	14	—
15	International Impacts on the Economy	15	—
16	Taxes, Deficits, and Debt	16	—

CHAPTER 1

What Economics is About

Chapter 1 begins our journey into the world of economic analysis. The student is introduced to economics as a way of thinking -- a set of techniques used to observe, analyze, and identify problems and their possible solutions. The chapter begins with five questions about economics which serve to offer both insight and motivation to beginning students. The chapter next looks at three fundamental concepts: scarcity, choice, and opportunity cost. It then turns to the role that theory plays in economic analysis, a discussion of theory "testing" and, finally, the distinction between normative and positive economics. The appendix to Chapter 1 covers working with graphs -- teaching the student how to read a graph, as well as how to derive the slope of both a line and a curve, and introducing the student to bar graphs, pie charts, and line graphs.

■ CHAPTER OBJECTIVES

Upon completing this chapter and Appendix A, your students should be able to:

- explain what economics is and what economists study;

- describe the relationship between scarcity and choice;

- name and identify the different types of resources which economists analyze;

- know what it means to think like an economist;

- explain the concept of opportunity cost;

- see the importance of making decisions at the margin;

- understand why economists construct theories, and identify some basic errors in economic thinking;

- distinguish between positive and normative economics, as well as between microeconomics and macroeconomics;

- rationalize, for themselves, the study of economics;

- read and interpret simple two-dimensional (X-Y) graphs, as well as bar graphs, pie charts, and line graphs;

- calculate the slope of a line and of a curve; and,

- understand and interpret pie charts and bar charts.

1

■ KEY TERMS

- scarcity
- economics
- economic analysis
- utility
- good
- disutility
- bad
- land
- labor
- capital
- entrepreneurship
- rationing device

- opportunity cost
- decisions at the margin
- total revenue
- theory
- abstraction
- fallacy of composition
- *ceteris paribus*
- positive economics
- normative economics
- microeconomics
- macroeconomics

■ CHAPTER OUTLINE

I. **WHAT IS ECONOMICS?** -- Economics is defined as the science of how individuals and societies deal with the fact that wants are greater than the limited resources available to satisfy those wants. The definition introduces several key concepts in economics which are discussed in more detail in this chapter.

   A. **Scarcity** -- The first key principle in economic analysis is that resources, such as time, land, labor, and the like, are in limited supply. Scarcity means that our wants outstrip the limited resources available to satisfy those wants at any point in time. Scarcity is the basic economic problem confronting all individuals and societies. For this reason, economics is defined as *the science of how individuals and societies deal with the fact that wants are greater than the limited resources available to satisfy those wants.*

   B. **What Do Economists Study?** -- Although most economists study problems relating to prices, interest rates, inflation, exchange rates, and so on, their inquiries can also lie in the fields of crime, war, law and other areas. The reason that economics can apply to traditionally non-economic areas is that economists apply the **economic way of thinking** to these fields of study. Economists study these areas because they believe that their analysis can help people in these fields improve their understanding of those areas of life. This leads to the next question.

   C. **What Is an Economic Way of Thinking?** -- Everybody has their own approach to understanding and interpreting the world around them. A political scientist might look at someone who is poor and wonder why they don't exercise their political power more effectively; a sociologist might study the social conditions which influence that person's behavior; a psychologist might wonder how their poverty affects their mental health. Each social scientist would view this individual from a different perspective. Economists try to explain the process of how resources are allocated and what determines the prices that allocate resources. As explained below, economists have a certain way of viewing the world, and one way of understanding this point of view, which is referred to as the *economic way of thinking* is to watch how an economist goes about solving economic problems.

   D. **Why Study Economics?** -- The primary reason for studying economics is to solve real-world economic problems. Three benefits of studying economics are

1. **Economics can be used to alleviate social problems** -- such as poverty, as Alfred Marshall tried to do.

2. **Economics can help people to understand the world around them** -- and that process of understanding can be a reward in and of itself.

3. **Economic ideas shape political and social decisions and the laws which affect us everyday** -- a fact which Keynes pointed out. Each congressional and presidential election poses one set of economic ideas against another. The economists who originally put forward those ideas are influencing your life, so it is important to understand what economists think!

E. **Why Study Economics in the 1990s?** -- The 1990s are a period of unprecedented change in which economic ideas are shaping your life every day. Whether it be economic change in Russia, Eastern Europe and China, free trade agreements such as NAFTA or GATT, changes in interest rates, prices, or exchange rates, all of these economic changes will affect your daily life. Economic change is pervasive, and understanding not only why these changes occur, but how they impact your life should be of great importance to you. Moreover, economic change is reshaping and shrinking the economic world. Not only are foreign goods increasingly available in the United States, but economic change in other countries can directly influence our own economy. A recession in Europe will decrease demand for American imports. Economics and business are becoming the international language today. Don't you think you should understand this international language?

II. **Thinking Like an Economist** -- The principle problem in economics is limited resources and unlimited wants. The result is scarcity.

A. **Defining Economic Goods** -- Economic goods can be viewed in three different ways, in terms of their utility, whether they are tangible, and the types of resources which are used to produce those goods.

1. **Goods** -- A good is anything from which individuals receive utility, or happiness.

2. **Bads** -- A bad is anything from which individuals receive disutility, or unhappiness, such as pollution and garbage. Presumably, no rational individual will voluntarily consume a bad.

3. **Tangibility** -- Goods are tangible if they can be touched (such as a car) or are intangible if they are a quality or a feeling (such as friendship).

B. **Resources** -- The production of all goods and services requires the input of some *resources*, or *factors of production*. Economists typically divide these productive factors into four categories: *land*, *labor*, *capital*, and *entrepreneurship*.

1. **Land** -- includes *all* natural resources, such as minerals, forests, water, and unimproved land.

2. **Labor** -- the physical *and mental* talents that people contribute to the production process.

3. **Capital** -- consists of produced goods that can be used as inputs to further production, such as machinery, tools, buildings, and the like.

4. **Entrepreneurship** -- refers to the unique talent that some people have for organizing inputs into the production of goods and services and to search for new business opportunities and ways of improving existing processes.

C. **Scarcity Produces Rationing** -- Because wants are unlimited and resources are limited, our needs will never be met. So how are we to decide who gets these limited resources? One solution is to create a means of allocating or rationing the resources which exist. This is the purpose of prices. When you purchase a good, you are giving up your own resources (money) in order to obtain that good. The price determines how much you have to give up, and rations ensures that only those who are willing to give up a sufficient amount of their own resources will receive the good.

D. **Scarcity Creates Competition** -- Because goods are limited, individuals compete to obtain the goods which are available, and studying this competitive process is what an economist does.

1. **Economists want to know how people compete with one another.** Individuals must compete with one another in order to obtain scarce resources. Certainly price is a very important allocative mechanism, but other factors such as influence, laws, government, charm and so on can influence the allocation of resources. Economists want to study all rationing devices to understand why they are used and how they are used.

2. **Economists want to know why people make the decisions they do**. Why are students willing to devote years to schooling? Obviously, to get a better job, but an economist would want to determine whether this investment was a productive one.

E. **Opportunity Cost** -- Another important concept is that choice implies opportunity cost. Opportunity cost is defined as the value of the best alternative foregone when a decision is made. Several examples can be given.

1. **Pizzas** -- Suppose I spend $10 to buy a pizza. If I hadn't bought the pizza, my second choice would have been to use the money to buy a CD. Since I chose to buy the pizza, the opportunity cost of that choice would be the value I would have received from buying the CD. Because I was forced to choose (by having a limited supply of funds to spend at present), I incurred an opportunity cost. Therefore, we may ultimately say that scarcity implies opportunity cost.

2. **The Revolutionary War** -- Another example of opportunity cost can be seen in the revolutionary war. The British army faced the problem of desertion, so the army's solution was to have them wear bright red uniforms. Unfortunately, this had an opportunity cost. The red uniforms made them an easy target to shoot at during the war. The red uniforms may have decreased the number of deserters, but they increased the number of casualties.

3. **Big Macs** -- A third example of opportunity costs is what a person gives up in terms of leisure in order to consume a good which they buy, such as a Big Mac. The opportunity cost of work is leisure, so when you buy something, you might want to measure the cost of that good in terms of how much leisure you gave up in order to buy that good. If a computer costs $2000 and you earn $10 an hour, then the cost of the computer is 200 hours of leisure. Opportunity cost also allows us to compare costs between different countries. On average, someone living in New York must work 15 minutes to be able to buy a Big Mac, but someone living in Tokyo has to work 30 minutes.

4. **Small-town Friendliness and Large-Town Indifference** -- Opportunity costs can also explain why people seem to be friendlier in small towns than in large cities. In a large city, there are many opportunities which are competing for individuals' time, not only in terms of jobs which are available, but also in terms of leisure activities. Because these opportunities are not as widely available in small towns, people are more likely to spend time making friends.

F. **Thinking In Terms of What Would Have Been** -- Another aspect of the *economic way of thinking* is to try to understand what would have been if a certain event had not happened and to measure the opportunity cost of that event. The interstate highway system can provide a couple examples.

   1. **What if the interstate highway system did not exist?** -- People would still be able to travel across the country (they certainly did so before the 1950s); however, it would be more costly to do so. Asking how much more costly travel would have been is exactly the type of question an economist would ask.

   2. **The interstate highway system was not free.** It was paid for with tax dollars. An economist would ask, "If the interstate highway system had not been built, how would people have spent the money?" In other words, what was the opportunity cost? Did the benefits exceed the costs? This is the economic way of thinking!

G. **Thinking in Terms of Costs and Benefits and Decisions Made at the Margin** -- When economists study individuals' decisions, they study their decisions at the margin, they study the additional cost or benefit which that person has. Economists refer to these as the *marginal costs* and the *marginal benefits* of their decision. The reason for studying decisions at the margin is that it is the trade-off between marginal benefits and marginal costs which shape economic decisions. By how much will an additional hour of studying raise my grade? If the store opens an hour earlier, how much will revenues increase by? If I hire this person, how many more goods will they be able to produce?

H. **Thinking in Terms of Unintended Effects** -- Life doesn't always go as we expect or hope. Sometimes the choices we make can produce the opposite result of what we had intended. This happens in economics as well. What if the government raises the minimum wage to a level higher than what you are currently earning? Initially you would be happy, but what if your employer told you he could no longer afford to pay you at the higher wage rate, and he had to lay you off? In this case, you would definitely *not* benefit from the government's new law. Economists want to understand why the results in the real world are often different from what people wanted to happen. The book provides a couple examples of unintended effects:

   1. **Gun Bounties** -- If the government pays people to turn in their guns, no questions asked, in order to reduce crime, some people may steal guns to get the gun payment, creating crime.

   2. **Seat Belts** -- If the government requires people to wear seat belts to reduce injuries when auto accidents occur, individuals may not drive as safely figuring that if they did have an accident, they probably would not get hurt. Although fewer injuries may occur when there is an accident, there might be an increase in the number of auto accidents.

I. **The book identifies six ways that students can think like an economist:**

   1. **Analyze scarcity and its effects.**

   2. **Look at the opportunity costs of economic decisions.**

3. **Try to determine what would have been if the event you are analyzing had not occurred.**

4. **Measure the benefits and costs of your actions.**

5. **Analyze decisions in terms of their marginal impact.**

6. **Try to determine the unintended effects of actions which take place.**

III. ECONOMISTS BUILD AND USE THEORY

A. **The Uses of Theory** -- Everyone uses theories, or models, to explain things they observe, and to predict the future. The focus of most theories is not abstract or esoteric. In fact, most theories are attempts to explain observable facts like "when an apple separates itself from its tree, it falls down." A theory is built on (only) the critical factors that the theorist believes affect the observed fact. Thus, in order to explain why apples fall down, we would first find out what factors might be critical to this outcome, and then build a theory explaining how these factors affect the outcome.

B. **Abstraction: Getting More for Less** -- Because we focus only upon a limited number of variables, we are reducing reality to a simplified explanation, such as: "Apples fall from trees due to the effect of gravity." By so simplifying, we leave out a great deal of specific information, such as how far any given apple will fall and whether or not it will fall straight, but we answer the basic question -- and that is the goal of theory-building.

C. **Parts of a Theory**

1. **Variables** -- **Variables** are *magnitudes that can change*, or *take on different values*, such as the height of any individual chosen from a crowd, or the temperature on a given day. Variables are the most basic elements of a theory, and are what we use to explain our observed outcome and/or predict the future.

2. **Assumptions** -- Every theory must make some basic assumptions about the nature of reality. For example, before we set out to explain the falling apple problem, we assumed we were talking about conditions on the Earth, rather than the Moon.

3. **Hypotheses** -- A **hypothesis** is a *conditional statement specifying how two or more variables are related*. Typically, it follows the "if-then" form -- for example, "If there is gravity, and no other body is acting to impede gravity, then an apple will fall when separated from its tree."

4. **Predictions** -- Predictions are statements that logically follow from the assumptions and hypotheses of the theory. For example, based upon the assumption that we are on earth, and the hypothesis that, "if there is gravity, and no other body is acting to impede gravity, then an apple will fall when separated from its tree," I may predict that if I pull an apple off its tree and let go, it will fall to the earth. This is not a statement of fact, it is a prediction.

D. **Formulating and Testing Theories: The Scientific Approach** -- The approach typically used in building, testing, and refining economic theories, as illustrated in Exhibit 1-1. The **Economics in the Media** insert entitled "Jerry Seinfeld Builds a Theory, George Tests It Out" provides a good example of applying theory-building and theory-testing to a non-economic situation. Formulating and testing theories follows six discernible steps:

1. **Decide on what it is you want to explain or predict.**

2. **Identify the variables that you believe are important to what you want to explain or predict.**

3. **State the assumptions.**

4. **State the hypothesis.**

5. **Test the theory by comparing its predictions against real-world events.**

6a. **If the evidence supports the theory, then no further action is necessary (though continued monitoring and assessment is wise); but,**

6b. **If the evidence rejects the theory, then either formulate a new theory or amend the old theory, in terms of its variables, assumptions, and/or hypothesis.**

E. **Judging Theories** -- There is no universally-accepted means of judging theories. It is important to realize that most theories will be somewhat "unrealistic" because they use abstraction -- that is, they will exclude some facts/viewpoints, in order to concentrate upon those factors viewed as most essential. Many people would argue that any theory should be evaluated "in context." That is, if we accept the underlying assumptions, is the theory a good predictor/explanation of reality. Others, including Nobel laureate Milton Friedman, argue that how "realistic" the assumptions of a theory are is unimportant, what matters is how well it works. Still others argue that the most important consideration is the logical soundness of the theory's assumptions and hypotheses.

F. **Errors in Economic Thinking** -- While there are many possible mistakes that might be made in economic analysis, some stand out as likely enough and important enough to justify a special discussion.

   1. **Association vs. Causation** -- Association does not imply causation. Two events may be **associated** because they happen in close proximity to each other, perhaps even with great frequency. For example, the Moon is often shining during the 3 A.M. "red-eye" express from New York to Los Angeles. However, **causation** implies that one observed event is responsible for the other taking place. Clearly, while the Moon often shines during the airplane flight, we cannot argue that the Moon shines because of the airplane flight.

   2. **The Fallacy of Composition** -- Another common error in economic analysis is the so-called **fallacy of composition** -- t*he belief that what is good for an individual (or part of the whole) is necessarily good for the group (or the whole).*

   3. **The *Ceteris Paribus* Condition** -- A mistake that is often made in assessing economic theories is blaming them for not taking this or that into account. It is important to realize that most economic theories -- indeed, most theories of any nature -- implicitly or explicitly utilize the ceteris paribus condition. From the Latin, *ceteris paribus* means "all other things held constant." It is used in a theory to separate out the effects of that which we want to observe from that which we do not.

G. **Normative Economics vs. Positive Economics** -- **Normative** economics attempts to determine *what should be*, while **positive** economics addresses *what is*. While the former is quite interesting, we will focus our attention upon the latter. However, bear in mind that, with some issues, it is almost impossible to completely separate the two. And, even where you choose to make a decision "based upon morality," positive economics may still assist you in deciding the best way to pursue your normative goal.

H. **Microeconomics and Macroeconomics** -- While most economic issues defy simple classification, for pedantic purposes we distinguish between **microeconomics** -- *the study of human behavior and choices as they relate to relatively small units, such as the individual, the firm, the industry, or a single market* -- and **macroeconomics** -- *the study of human behavior and choices as they relate to either highly aggregated markets or the economy as a whole.* The important thing to realize is that the real distinction is not so much one of issues, for there are very few issues that are "purely microeconomic" or "purely macroeconomic." Rather, the distinction is one of approach -- given a particular problem, do we choose to approach it from the "micro" level, or from the "macro" level? And, based upon that answer, we then choose the appropriate tools, and set to it.

IV. **ECONOMICS AND THE INTERNET** -- This section is designed to help you and your students use the Internet to improve your understanding of economics. Each chapter provides useful addresses which can be used gain access to information and user groups which discuss economic issues. The first chapter describes the basic components of the Internet.

A. **Welcome to the Internet** -- The Internet is a collection of computer networks which exchange information with one another. As with most things, practice is the best way of getting to understand the Internet and its services.

B. **Electronic Mail** -- allows Internet users to communicate with one another via a computer. Both individuals need e-mail accounts and addresses.

C. **Usenet Newsgroups** -- are electronic "bulletin boards" that allow discussions on a variety of topics. Before sending messages to a Usenet newsgroup, you should familiarize yourself with its topics to make sure your messages are appropriate and not redundant.

D. **Discussion Lists** -- are sent directly to your e-mail account. They advise members on current topics of discussion.

E. **File Transfer Protocol** -- is a means by which one computer transfers information or files to another computer using a standard set of commands. All the sites given in this book are anonymous FTP sites allow any user to download data from that site.

G. **Gopher** -- is a program that allows a user to access information through a series of menus. This makes access to the Internet and the World Wide Web easier.

H. **World Wide Web** -- allows access to FTP sites, Gopher sites and Hypertext Transfer Protocol sites. HTTP sites allow users to click bold-faced words in the text to move to other documents which relate to that topic.

I. **Internet Addresses** -- FTP, Gopher and HTTP sites have a particular address which must be used to access them.

J. **Internet Etiquette** -- Emoticons can be used to express emotions. A list of emoticons can be found in the last chapter.

V. **APPENDIX A: WORKING WITH GRAPHS** -- Appendix A covers the usage of graphs in economics, and some basic information to assist the student in reading and interpreting them.

A. **HOW TO READ GRAPHS** -- The primary purpose for using graphs in economic analysis is to study the relationship between two variables. Exhibits 1A-1 and 1A-2 demonstrate the range of possibilities.

   1. **Inversely-Related Variables** -- Two variables are said to be **inversely** (or *negatively*) **related** if the value of one variable increases as the value of the other variable decreases. The graph of this relationship would be a *downward-sloping line*, as shown in Exhibit 1A-1.

   2. **Directly-Related Variables** -- Two variables are said to be **directly** (or *positively*) **related** if the value of one variable increases as the value of the other variable increases, and decreases as the value of the other variable decreases. The graph of this relationship would be an *upward-sloping line*, as shown in Exhibit 1A-2a.

   3. **Unrelated Variables** -- Two variables are said to be **independent**, or *unrelated*, if the value of one variable is not systematically affected by a change in the value of the other variable. The graph of such a relationship would be a straight line, perpendicular to the axis of the variable in question. [See Exhibits 1A-2b and 1A-2c]

B. **Slope of a Line and of a Curve** -- It is often important to know how much one variable changes when the other variable changes. The slope of the graph can tell us this. The **slope** of a graph is *the ratio of the change in the variable on the vertical axis* (the "rise") *to the change in the variable on the horizontal axis* (the "run").

   1. **The Slope of a Line** -- To find the slope of a line, take any two points A and B on the line, and find the difference between the value of the X-variable at A and at B -- this is the "change in X," or X. Then, find the difference between the value of the Y-variable at A and at B -- this is the "change in Y," or Y. Then, to find the slope of a line, all you have to do is divide the change in Y by the change in X, that is:

$$\text{Slope} = \Delta Y / \Delta X.$$

   2. **The Slope of a Curve** -- To find the slope of a curved line at a given point, first draw a straight line tangent to the curve at that point, then take the slope of the tangent line (as described above). [See Exhibit 1A-3]

C. **Special Graphs in Economics**

   1. **The 45° Line** -- The **45°-line** is a straight line that bisects the intersection of the vertical and horizontal axes. It has the unique property that any point on the (45°) line has the same value on both the horizontal and vertical axes. [See Exhibit 1A-4]

   2. **Pie Charts** -- A *pie chart* is used to demonstrate how the parts of a whole are distributed. [See Exhibit 1A-5]

   3. **Bar Graphs** -- Bar graphs are also used to convey relative magnitudes, but have the advantage that they may be used to compare *anything*, not just the distribution of some whole. [See Exhibit 1A-6]

   4. **Line Graphs** -- Line graphs, or "trend lines" as they are often called, trace the value of a single variable over a period of time, and may be used (as their secondary name suggests) to spot trends. [See Exhibit 1A-7] Two or more line graphs may be displayed together, in order to show relative trends, or to demonstrate a "gap," such as the budget deficit, which is shown in Exhibit 1A-8.

■ ANSWERS TO CHAPTER QUESTIONS

1. The United States is considered a rich country because Americans have an abundance of goods and services to choose from. How can there be scarcity in a land of abundance?

The key to this question is understanding the economic definition of scarcity. Although some people may understand scarcity as a temporary shortage of a good, or some people being able to have their essential needs met, the economic definition of scarcity is that at a zero price, demand exceeds supply. And this definition applies to most of the goods which people consume. The reason is that wants generally exceed the resources available to meet those desires and the result is scarcity.

2. Give two examples for each of the following: (a) an intangible good, (b) a tangible good, (c) a bad.

There are numerous examples which could be provided for any of these definitions. (a) Intangible goods are those which have no concrete existence. Friendship is an example. Being intangible does not mean that they cannot have a price. Friendship, love, sunsets are all intangible goods for which people are willing to give up resources; however, it is more difficult to mass-produce intangible resources and quality often plays an important role in the value of these goods.

(b)   Tangible goods are concrete goods which can be exchanged and reproduced more easily than intangible goods. One way of comparing tangible and intangible goods is to compare an economics lecture with a videotape of the lecture. The lecture itself is an intangible service while the videotape of the lecture would be a tangible good which could be traded; however, both are scarce resources which have a price.

(c)   Bads are goods which provide negative benefits. Examples might be pollution, the noise produced by planes taking off at an airport, or the smell a skunk produces--unless you are a female skunk.

3. What is the difference between resource labor and resource entrepreneurship?

Resource labor refers to applying skills which individuals have in order to produce economic goods. Resource entrepreneurship refers to creatively discovering new ways to produce goods, new ways to organize the allocation of resources, or introducing new goods which previously did not exist in the marketplace. Entrepreneurship increases economic productivity and takes risks. For these two reasons, successful entrepreneurship receives a higher return than labor. An individual who creates and sells a new form of software is an entrepreneur; the person who oversees the machines which produce the software is a laborer.

4. Explain the link between scarcity and each of the following: (a) choice, (b) opportunity cost, (c) the need for a rationing device, (d) competition.

(a)   Because individuals have limited resources and unlimited wants, they will have to choose between the different goods which they have the opportunity to consume.

(b)   In choosing between different goods, individuals face an opportunity cost. When they decide to choose one good (go to a baseball game), they give up the opportunity to consume another good (see a movie).

(c)   Because wants exceed resources, some method for allocating scarce resources is necessary. Although there are many rationing devices, the most common one used in economic transactions is the price mechanism which defines how much of one resource (money) you must give up in order to obtain another resource.

(d)   Because resources are limited, people compete with one another both to obtain the resources they need to purchase the limited resources, and to get the resources which are available. This process is called competition.

5. Is it possible for a person to incur an opportunity cost without spending any money? Explain.

Yes. An opportunity cost occurs when an individual gives up any resource when they make a choice. An example would be leisure time. When students study for an exam, the opportunity cost is the time they could have spent watching a movie or listening to Pearl Jam. Of course, not studying for the exam could also have an opportunity cost--flunking the course.

6. Discuss the opportunity costs of attending college for four years. Is college more or less costly than you thought it was? Explain.

Most students will probably find that the opportunity cost of college is significantly higher than they thought it was before they ever entered this class, but will probably make the mistake of assuming that every alternative that they give up should be considered an opportunity cost of attending college and therefore once they have been exposed to the notion of opportunity cost the are liable to overestimate it. In fact, the opportunity cost of any choice is the value of the next best alternative that is sacrificed to make that choice. And it's important that the student realize that only the next best alternative constitutes a choice foregone, therefore the opportunity cost of attending college is not all of the leisure and all of the income and all of the other activities that could have been done independently instead of going to college. The opportunity cost of attending college is only those activities that could have been undertaken jointly -- that could have been "consumed" at the same time and not conflicted with one another.

Suppose, for example, that Susie decides to attend a small, private university where the cost of going to school, including tuition, room and board, and other necessary expenditures is approximately $22,000 per year. In most students' minds and in the minds of most laymen who have not been exposed to economics or who have forgotten what they've been exposed to, the cost of going to college is $22,000. But that is not the case. In addition to the $22,000 that must be paid out in order for Susie to attend school, there are other costs that she is going to have to incur. Suppose that the best alternative use of her time would be for Susie to take a job paying $25,000 a year as a legal secretary for a hometown law firm. In this case then, the opportunity cost of going to college is clearly more than the $22,000 that has to be paid. It must also include the $25,000 that Susie is not earning, the income foregone by not going to college. Are there other opportunity costs involved? If Susie is forced to give up part of her leisure time as a result of going to college, time that she could have enjoyed if she had simply taken the job, then the opportunity cost of going to college is even greater than the $22,000 that must be paid for tuition, room and board and the cost of living and the $25,000 that is income foregone. It's important to realize, however, that Susie could not have taken several different jobs at one time, nor could she have spent an entire year relaxing in leisure and worked for a year and made $25,000 and gone to Africa for a year to take a job with the Peace Corps. Only those alternatives that could have been undertaken simultaneously without conflicting with one another would be considered the true opportunity costs of attending college.

7. Explain the relationship between changes in opportunity costs and changes in behavior.

To the extent that opportunity costs determine behavior, by identifying those activities and goods that are "worth" making "sacrifices" for and those that aren't, as opportunity costs change so will a rational consumer's assessment of the various options facing her. For example, suppose that Becky, a high school graduate, is currently working as a model, earning $25,000 per year and that, in order to go to college she would have to cut back on her modeling, reducing her annual income to $10,000. Further, suppose that tuition, books, and fees at the college of Becky's choice total $15,000 per year. In deciding whether to quit modeling full-time and go to college, Becky is faced with balancing a present opportunity cost of $30,000, ceteris paribus, against the future benefits of a college education. Now, suppose that Becky earns a scholarship which will reduce her tuition, books, and fees bill to $5,000 per year, thus reducing her present opportunity cost to $20,000. While this may not change Becky's mind (she may have already decided to accept the present burden for the future benefit), such a change in opportunity cost would certainly weigh in favor of going to college.

8. Economists say that individuals make decisions at the margin. What does this mean?

When economists say that individuals make decisions at the margin, they are referring to the fact that individuals consider the additional (marginal) benefits of their actions and the additional (marginal) costs of their actions. If the marginal benefits exceed the marginal costs, they proceed with the action. If the marginal costs are greater than the marginal benefits, then they do not carry out the action. For example, in studying, students would compare the marginal cost of studying an additional hour with the marginal benefits. At some point, this relationship turns negative and a student will stop studying.

9. A layperson says that a proposed government project simply costs too much and therefore shouldn't be undertaken. How might an economist's evaluation be different?

The layperson is only looking at the cost of the project and not considering the benefits. An economist would consider both the marginal costs and the marginal benefits of the project. For example, the interstate highway system in the United States has cost a lot of money, but it has also provided a lot of benefits. Consequently, the United States has introduced an interstate highway system because the benefits of the system exceed the costs. On the other hand, the Apollo project which sent men to the moon was suspended after a handful of flights because many people perceived that the marginal costs of sending men to the moon was exceeding the marginal benefits.

10. A change in X will lead to a change in Y; the predicted change is desirable, so we should change X. Do you agree or disagree? Explain.

Assuming that the relationship between X and Y had been accurately measured, and that the relationship did not change, then the change in X would be desirable; however, several caveats should be recognized. First, the relationship could have been misspecified. Important factors which also influence Y, perhaps more strongly than X, could have been ignored in the analysis. It might be more efficient to change these other factors rather than X. Some logical explanation of why the relationship between X and Y which occurs, should be developed before proceeding. Second, the relationship between X and Y can change over time. You don't want to commit the fallacy of confusing correlation with causation. You can reduce the probability of this error by developing a logical explanation of why X will lead to a change in Y

11.   **Which of the following statements would Milton Friedman agree with and why?**

Statement 1: The theory does not work because its assumptions are false.
Statement 2: The assumptions are false because the theory does not work.

Friedman would agree with statement 2 and disagree with statement 1. He would disagree with the first statement because he doesn't believe a theory should be judged by its assumptions, which is what statement 1 implies. For Friedman, a theory could work (predict accurately) as long as the assumptions are sufficiently good approximations for the process at hand. If, however, the theory does not work (statement 2), Friedman would argue that the assumptions are not "sufficiently good approximations . . ." In short, Friedman emphasizes the accuracy of a theory's predictions and not the degree of realism of its assumptions; therefore, he would not toss out the assumptions of a theory until he was sure the theory didn't work. This is the ordering expressed by statement 2.

12. Why do economists prefer to say that the evidence *supports* the theory instead of the evidence *proves* the theory is correct?

The primary reason why economists say that the evidence *supports* the theory rather than that the evidence *proves* the theory is that the set of data which was used to analyze the relationship between the two variables may have excluded data which provided evidence against the theory. For example, if you asked people in Washington D.C. (whose residents tend to favor the Democratic party) whom they were going to vote for in the presidential election and based your conclusion on this evidence alone, you would predict that the Democratic presidential candidate would win. However, by excluding portions of the country where the Democratic party was not widely supported, you would have found evidence for your theory, but you would not have proven it.

13. Theories are abstractions from reality. What does this mean?

The world is very complex. Whenever there is an economic change, such as a decline in the value of the dollar, there are thousands of factors which contributed to this change. It would be impossible to measure the impact of each factor on the value of the dollar and be able to predict how the value of the dollar would change given the changes in the thousands of variables which influenced the dollar. Economists have to simplify, so they concentrate on the primary factors which influence the dollar. By ignoring many of the minor factors which influence an economic variable (the change in the value of the dollar), economists abstract from reality, but they do so to better understand the world around them.

14. Think of three examples that illustrate that association is not causation.

Everyday life is full of examples suggesting that causation and association are not the same thing. Tom takes the 5:30 train home from work. By the time he reaches his house in the suburbs, it is 6:45 and it is dark. There is clearly an association here. When he gets on the train it is light, when he gets off the train it is dark. But is there causation? Causation implies that one variable causes another, that getting off the train causes it to be dark. This is simply not the case.

Another example. Tony goes to the grocery store approximately once a month and buys a head of lettuce. About every three months Tony notices that the price has risen since the last time that he has been to the grocery store. The two events are clearly related. When Tony goes to the grocery store the price that he pays for a head of lettuce rises. But is there causation? That is, does the price of lettuce rise because Tony goes to the grocery store? Unless Tony buys thousands of heads of lettuce at one time, the answer is probably no. The price of lettuce does not rise because Tony goes to the grocery store, it's only that Tony notices the price of lettuce has risen already when he does go to the grocery store. There is association, but not causation.

A final example relates the behavior of the stock market and the Superbowl. Over 90% of the time when the team from the National Football Conference has won the Superbowl, the stock market moved up during the year. There is clearly an association between these two variables, but why should there be a causation? There shouldn't be. The probable reason for the association is that NFC teams tend to be stronger than AFC teams and consequently are more likely to win the Superbowl. Similarly, the stock market moves up in more years than it moves down, hence the association.

15. Think of three examples that illustrate the fallacy of composition.

Perhaps the clearest example is student grades. While an individual student may do better in terms of applying to graduate school or getting a certain job if she makes an "A" in economics, if every student taking this class made an "A," and employers and admissions committees knew that every student had done so, the "A" would be much less valuable.

A second example would be the pricing of airline tickets. If one airline lowers their prices, they may be able to take business away from other airlines and increase their profits, but if every airline lowered their prices, no airline would be able to take business away from the other airlines and increase their market share and profitability. If all airlines lower their prices, the net result could be a decrease in profitability. What was true for one airline, was not true for all airlines.

For a third example, assume that the President of the United States gave you $5000. You would clearly be better off. But if the President of the United States gave everybody $5000, the benefits would be eliminated through the resulting inflation. What was true for one person, was not true for everybody.

16. Why would economists assume "all other things are constant," or "nothing else changes," when, in reality, some other things may change?

Economists assume that all other things are constant to simplify their analysis of the world. By doing this you can concentrate on the relationship of two variables. There are thousands of factors which influence economic variables such as inflation or unemployment; however, it might prove very difficult to accurately determine how all of these variable change simultaneously and how inflation or unemployment reacts to all of these changes. It is simpler to look at each variable in order to see how that one variable affects the dependent variable. Will an increase in the money supply, by itself, cause an increase or a decrease in the inflation rate? Once the relationship between each independent variable and the dependent variable have been analyzed, then you could see how changes in several variables simultaneously would influence the dependent variable.

17. What is the difference between positive and normative economics? Between macroeconomics and microeconomics?

Positive economics refers to facts. The unemployment rate is currently 5.8% Normative economics refers to opinions. The unemployment rate in the United States is too high, and the government should make an effort to lower the unemployment rate. Positive economics refers to what is, and normative economics refers to what should be. As far as possible, economics tries to keep its analysis positive.

Macroeconomics deals with those variables which affect everyone in the economy simultaneously. Examples would be government fiscal and monetary policy, the value of the dollar, interest rates, and so forth. Microeconomics deals with individuals and firms and how they interact in markets. Examples would be monopolies, factor markets, indifference curves, and so forth.

■ ANSWERS TO APPENDIX QUESTIONS

1.   What type of relationship would you expect between the following: (a) hot dogs and hot dog buns, (b) the price of winter coats and sales of winter coats, (c) the price of personal computers and the production of personal computers, (d) sales of toothbrushes and sales of cat food, (e) number of children in a family and the number of toys in a family.

(a) Hot dogs and hot dog buns being complementary goods, a concept discussed in Chapter 3, one would expect the quantity of hot dog buns to be directly related to the quantity of hot dogs, ceteris paribus. (b) Quantity demanded for normal goods being inversely related to price, another concept from Chapter 3, one would expect the quantity of winter coats sold to be inversely related to the price of winter coats, ceteris paribus.   (c) Quantity supplied of normal goods being positively related to price, again Chapter 3, one would expect the production of personal computers to be positively related to the price of personal computers, ceteris paribus. (d) One would expect no discernable relationship between sales of cat food and sales of toothbrushes -- air freshener, perhaps, but not toothbrushes. (e) Ceteris paribus, one would expect that the more children in a family, the more toys -- that is, the two should be positively related.

2.   Represent the following data in bar graph form.

Year	U.S. Money Supply ($ Billions)
1985	620.1
1986	724.5
1987	750.0
1988	787.1
1989	794.6
1990	827.2
1991	899.3
1992	1,026.6
1993	1,131.2

3.   Plot the following data and specify the type of relationship between the two variables. (Place "price" on the vertical axis and "quantity purchased" on the horizontal axis.)

Price of apples ($)	Quantity Demanded of apples
0.25	1000
0.50	800
0.70	700
0.95	500
1.00	400
1.10	350

Clearly, the two variables are inversely related -- that is, the higher the price of apples, the lower the quantity of apples demanded.

4.   **In Exhibit 1A-4a, determine the slope between points B and C.**

Recall that the slope of a line on a graph is the ratio of the change in the variable on the vertical axis (the "rise") to the change in the variable on the horizontal axis (the "run"), or slope = Y / X. In Exhibit 1A-1a, the value of X at point B is 20, and at point C is 30; thus, from B to C, X increases by 10. The value of Y at point B is 30, and at point C, Y = 20; therefore, from B to C, Y decreases by 10. Putting it together, the slope of the line between points B and C is -10/10, or -1.

5.   **In Exhibit 1A-4b, determine the slope between points A and B.**

Using the same methodology as described above, the slope between points A and B = +2.

6.   **What is the special characteristic of a 45° line?**

16

The special characteristic of a 45° line is that any point on it is equidistant from both the horizontal and vertical axis -- or, in layman's terms, at any point on the 45° line the values of X and Y are equal.

7.   What is the slope of a 45° line?

The slope of a 45° line is always +1.

8.   When would it be preferable to illustrate data using a pie chart instead of a bar chart?

A pie chart is a convenient way to illustrate values that, when added together, equal a whole. Thus, while both pie charts and bar graphs can be used to show magnitudes, pie charts are preferable when the values being graphed are percentages -- such as the allocation of the federal budget or the location of world oil reserves.

9.   Plot the following data and specify the type of relationship between the two variables. (Place "price" on the vertical axis and "quantity supplied" on the horizontal axis.)

Price of apples ($)	Quantity supplied of apples
0.25	350
0.50	400
0.70	500
0.95	700
1.00	800
1.10	1000

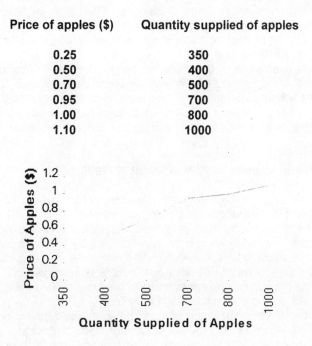

The variables are positively, or directly, related -- that is, when the price of apples rises, the quantity of apples supplied also rises.

■ LECTURE SUPPLEMENTS

"The Word Processor is Ticking," *The Economist*, 335 (7909), April 8, 1995, p. 61

This article is short enough that you could copy it and have students read it in class, but it raises a lot of questions about opportunity costs and can help to teach students the *economic way of thinking* which is emphasized in this chapter. The article will also prove appealing because it discusses new technologies and deals with something students encounter in their own lives-- using word processors at the computer lab.

The article discusses the problems Microsoft faces in offering site licenses for its Excel software. The question is, How should Microsoft charge firms (and colleges) for the site licenses which allow multiple individuals to use their software? The college will try to estimate how many licenses are needed. If the college buys too many licenses, it is wasting money, but if it buys too few, then some students will not be able to access the software when they need it because all of the licenses are being used. What if some users have signed on to Excel, but then go out to get a cup of coffee, and leave their machine on while they are gone? Even though they are not using the software, they are preventing others from using it.

The solution? Metering usage of word processors and spreadsheets so that a computer keeps track of each keystroke which is used to enter words and/or data is an alternative. This way users will not have to worry about not having access to the software, and the college will not have to worry about paying too much for unused licenses. Of course, in order to make this system effective, the cost of metering the usage of software programs must be low. Microsoft must consider the marginal cost of keeping track of the keystrokes which are used against the marginal benefit of collecting additional fees.

The purpose of this example is to get students to think about the opportunity costs that exist and the trade-offs that must be made for a service which they use every day. Get your students to find out how the school pays for their site licenses, and ask them if they have ever had difficulty gaining access to word processors, spreadsheets, Lexis/Nexis or other programs. Now, something that your students took for granted has become an economic problem.

"For Love or Money?" *The Economist*, 335 (7915), April 20, 1995, p. 78

This article can prove an interesting topic for discussion, and might be a good way of approaching the *economic way of thinking*. Since economics looks at trade-offs, opportunity cost, marginal decisionmaking and so forth, some students might wonder why individuals would carry out altruistic actions in which they seemingly receive no benefit. Why do people do volunteer work? Why do some people make sacrifices for individuals they may have never met before? Why would someone die for a cause for which the individual cost is extremely high? Why is some behavior, "outside the market?" Why do migrants travel to the United States and virtually live in poverty so they can send all their money back to their family?

As the article points out, some seemingly altruistic behavior could have a selfish side to it. Individuals may visit their grandparents not only out of love for them, but out of a hope that they will inherit some money. Such analysis is probably too simplistic. The authors point out that parents may take their children to see the grandparents in part to teach their children. If children see their parents looking after their own parents, it is hoped that the children will do the same when they become parents and a new generation exists.

Whether individuals consciously think out these reasons for what they do is a matter of debate. The article points out that most behavior is a combination of both altruism and a self-calculus, and altruism can be its own reward. Groups which cooperate together and altruistically support one another may be more successful than individuals who are selfish. Both nature and nurture may combine to encourage humans (and animals) to be altruistic.

The purpose of this discussion is to get students to think why they make the choices they do. Since most economic decisions which are discussed in the book "coldly" relate marginal benefits against marginal costs, students might wonder about cases where they do not consciously think about the costs and benefits. This will show them that even when they are acting selflessly to help others, in one way or another, they may be making an economic calculation without realizing it.

"More and More Jails Are Charging Inmates for Their Incarceration," *The Wall Street Journal*, **132 (43), March 3, 1995, p. 1, column 1.**

As with the other articles, this one is designed to help your students begin thinking about problems from an economic point of view, and hopefully, generate some controversy and discussion as well. As the article points out, it costs society over $20,000 a year to incarcerate a convicted criminal. In California in 1995, the state spent more money on incarcerating criminals than it did on education (this figure, of course, ignores what municipalities spent on education). This brings up an important question. Should taxpayers pay for the individuals while they are in prison, or should criminals be required to pay for part of their incarceration.

According to the article, about half the states have enacted laws permitting room-and-board charges. Some federal prisoners, such as Washington D.C. Mayor Marion Barry, have had to pay for their incarceration ($10,000 to be exact). So when Kathleen Hawk, Director of the Federal Bureau of Prisons says that "prison space is a scarce and costly resource," she means it. For example, one prison charges up to $40 per day for room and board, $3 to see a nurse, $5 to see a doctor, $2 for a haircut, and $100 for busting up one of the new porcelain toilets in the cells. In prison, individuals' opportunity cost of time is very low, and they may get a haircut simply because they are bored. Charging them might make them think about the marginal cost of getting a haircut.

In short, incarcerated individuals use up society's resources. Should they pay for them? Should taxpayers foot the bill? Which "services" should the prison charge for and which should they not charge for? Should people be charged according to their ability to pay, i.e. charging rich prisoners more than poor prisoners?

There are many economic issues here concerning choice, scarcity, decisions at the margin, opportunity costs, the allocation of resources, and so forth. This is certainly an article about which many people will have an opinion which will help to open up the discussion and get your students to think like an economist.

CHAPTER 2

Fundamentals of Economic Thinking

Chapter 1 began our study of the basics of economic analysis. Chapter 2 continues the task, introducing the student to such concepts as marginal choice, efficiency, economic growth, and exchange through the construct of the production possibilities frontier (PPF). Not exactly a "tools of economics" chapter, instead we look at basic premises which underlie the economic analysis presented in the text -- that, in essence, form the "economic way of thinking" referred to in Chapter 1.

■ CHAPTER OBJECTIVES

Upon completing this chapter, your students should be able to:

- use a *production possibilities frontier* to demonstrate the concepts of efficiency, scarcity, resource specialization, and opportunity cost;

- distinguish between constant and increasing opportunity costs, and show how these relate to the shape of the production possibilities frontier;

- state and explain the law of increasing opportunity costs;

- understand the *efficiency criterion*; and,

- identify three economic questions which every society must ask and answer for itself.

■ KEY TERMS

- production possibilities frontier (PPF)
- technology
- law of increasing costs
- efficiency
- inefficiency
- efficiency criterion

■ CHAPTER OUTLINE

I. **EFFICIENCY** -- Efficiency is, at one time, both the primary goal and the primary strength of the market system. While there are several types of efficiency, here we will focus upon *efficiency in production*, or **productive efficiency**. We say that an economy is *efficient* (with respect to productive efficiency) if it is *producing the maximum possible output, given available resources and technology*.

   A. **Production Possibilities Frontier (PPF)** -- The **production possibilities frontier** is a graphical construct that shows *all possible output combinations for a particular economy at a particular point in time, given its resource and technology constraints*. In this section, we will construct the PPF; in the following section, we will discuss several important economic concepts which can be studied using the PPF.

      1. **Getting Grade in College and a Production Possibilities Frontier** -- This example is designed to illustrate to students how the production possibilities frontier works using an example they are familiar with. Students have a limited amount of time to study, so if they choose to spend an hour studying economics, assuming a fixed amount of study time, they give up an hour which they could be using to studying sociology. This, of course, is an opportunity cost. Consequently, their economics grade will improve at the expense of their sociology grade. If students were able to increase their study time, this would increase the resources which are put into the productive process. As a result, the students "grade possibilities curve" would shift out enabling them to make higher grades in all of their classes.

      2. **Constant Opportunity Costs between Goods: The Straight-Line PPF** -- There are, essentially, two possible shapes for a two-good, or one-good-vs.-all-other-goods, PPF. The first possibility is a PPF which demonstrates a constant trade-off between goods. In such a case, the PPF is a straight, downward-sloping line, such as is presented in Exhibit 2-3a.

      3. **Changing Opportunity Costs between Goods: The Bowed-Outward PPF** -- Under most circumstances, there is not a constant trade-off between goods, for reasons which we will discuss shortly. If this is true, then the PPF will be a convex (bowed outward), downward-sloping line, demonstrating that the cost of producing one good rises as more of the good is produced. Exhibit 2-4a shows such a PPF.

   C. **Economic Concepts Illustrated by the PPF** -- The production possibilities frontier is a great teaching tool, for it demonstrates a number of important economic concepts.

      1. **Scarcity** -- The PPF is a downward-sloping line which always connects at both the horizontal and vertical axes. In so doing, it forms a "finite" frontier, clearly demarcating that which is "attainable" from that which is not, given current resources and technology. Like the principle of scarcity, the PPF implies that some things are attainable and some things are unattainable, at present. [See Exhibit 2-3]

      2. **Choice** -- Within the attainable region, society must choose the combination of goods it wishes to produce from the thousands of possible combinations. The issue of choice is illustrated in *The Global Economy* feature; "Life on the Frontier -- Production Possibilities Frontier, That Is." How much of GDP countries devote to health care, food, the military, education, and other outputs depends on political goals, the level of development, and other factors.

3. **Opportunity Cost** -- As we move from one point to another on, or within, the frontier, we can see the opportunity cost of any such move as the amount of one good that we must sacrifice to gain more of the other good. As the book illustrates in the "Blue Jeans, Rock 'n' Roll, and the Berlin Wall" *Economics In Our Times* feature, the Soviet Union placed too many resources in the military during the cold war relative to the number of consumer goods which its citizens wanted. As long as the Soviet economy expanded, the government was able to satisfy both the military and consumers, but once the economy stagnated and the PPF failed to expand outward, discontent became inevitable.

4. **Law of Increasing Opportunity Costs** -- *When resources are specialized, increased production of one good comes at increased opportunity costs* -- that is, as the production of one good increases, the (opportunity) cost of producing that good rises faster and faster. This is what gives most PPFs their convex curvature. As we said before, when there is not a constant trade-off between goods, the PPF will be bowed outward (convex). The reason for both a non-constant trade-off between goods and an outwardly-bowed PPF is the same: resource specialization. The book provides two examples to illustrate the law of increasing costs.

   a. **The Armed Services** -- When the United States had a draft during World War I, World War II, the Korean war and the Viet Nam war, individuals were drafted into services regardless of their earning power in the civilian sector. The opportunity cost of serving in the war to someone with a degree from Harvard was a lot higher than the opportunity cost to someone who had not graduated from high school. During the civil war, individuals were allowed to have others serve in their place, and there was an active market for hiring individuals to serve in the army; however, this practice was perceived as being unfair, and thereafter, the opportunity cost of serving in the armed services was not factored into the drafting process.

   b. **Home Improvement** -- Swedish men spend more time on home improvements than men in the United States. The probable reason? Marginal tax rates are very high in Sweden compared to the United States. In the United States, men are more likely to work additional hours and use the additional pay to hire someone to do the work for them than is true in Sweden because the person who is hired must be paid with after-tax income.

5. **Economic Growth** -- A given PPF only applies to the economy in question at one point in time. As resource availability and/or technology improve, the PPF will shift outward, as is shown in Exhibit 2-6. Similarly, a decrease in available resources and/or decline in technology will shift the PPF inward. One result of economic growth has been that farmers have become more efficient. A smaller number of farmers can feed the same number of people, reducing both the absolute number and relative number of farmers in the United States. Economic growth can make everyone happy, as the book illustrates in the example of politicians. If economic growth occurs, the economic pie gets larger, and instead of Conservatives and Liberals fighting over the servings which are currently available, by increasing the size of the economic pie, everyone can get more of what they want.

6. **Efficiency** -- We noted earlier that an economy is said to be efficient (in production) if it is producing the maximum output possible given its resources and technology. The PPF provides an excellent device for assessing efficiency. In order to determine whether or not a given output combination is efficient, all we need do is check to see if that point is on the PPF. By definition, all points on the PPF are the maximum attainable output, given existing resources and technology. Therefore, all points on the PPF are, by definition, efficient, while any point within the frontier is, also by definition, inefficient. [See Exhibit 2-8]

7. **Unemployed Resources** -- When the economy is not producing the maximum output with its available resources and technology, output will occur at a point within the PPF. This is illustrated by point F in Exhibit 2-8.

D. **The Efficiency Criterion** -- In evaluating the efficiency of an economy's production, as well as economic policies, programs, and institutions, economists consider the following question: *Will an alternative arrangement of resources or goods make at least one person better off without making anyone else worse off?* If so, then the economy (or whatever) is not operating at optimum efficiency. If not, then efficiency has been attained.

II. **THREE ECONOMIC QUESTIONS** -- Every society must, in some way or another, ask itself, and answer, the following questions. The answers to these questions will often both reflect and explain the economic structure of that society. The market, politics, sociological factors, psychology, and other non-economic variables can affect how these questions are answered.

A. **What Goods Will Be Produced?**

B. **How Will Goods Be Produced?**

C. **For Whom Will Goods Be Produced?**

III. **ECONOMICS ON THE INTERNET** -- This chapter provides the addresses of some of the most important Internet sites for economic information, including the Sam Houston State University Gopher and the University of Michigan Gopher. Information on the Veronica research tool is also provided.

■ ANSWERS TO CHAPTER QUESTIONS

1. **How would each of the following affect the U.S. production possibilities frontier: (a) an increase in the number of illegal aliens entering the country; (b) a war; (c) the discovery of a new oil field; (d) a decrease in the unemployment rate; (e) a law that requires individuals to enter lines of work for which they are not suited?**

(a) *Ceteris paribus*, an increase in the number of illegal aliens entering the country will increase the available productive human resources of the economy; therefore, the PPF should shift outward, as is shown in Exhibit 2-6. (b) A war would remove individuals, capital, and potentially resources, from the productive process; therefore, *ceteris paribus*, the PPF would shift inward. (c) The discovery of a new oil field would represent an addition to the country's resources; therefore, the PPF would shift outward. (d) A decrease in the unemployment rate would be represented by movement from a point inside the PPF to another point closer to or on the frontier, such as from point F to point D, in Exhibit 2-8. (e) Such a law would decrease the productive efficiency of labor, thereby moving the economy from a point on or inside the frontier to another point further inside the frontier.

2. In the past, the more time Jill has spent studying, the higher the grades she has earned. Last week she had more time to study, but her grades remained constant. Does it follow that her courses are getting harder?

The invalid assumption here is that Jill apportioned her spare time to studying and leisure activities in the same proportions as she had used prior to the increase in her free time. If Jill had three extra hours to study, but spent the three hours at a movie, then there is no reason why her grades should improve.

3. Explain why disagreements and disappointments are natural in a world characterized by scarcity

In a world of scarcity, choices create opportunity costs. When individuals work together, they will inevitably disagree about how resources should be allocated. One political group may want to spend more money on prisons, and another group might want to spend more money on education. Since the money cannot be spent on both simultaneously, disagreement results. Whoever loses the disagreement will be disappointed. Similarly, if you want to go to a movie Friday night and a friend wants to go to a rock concert, disagreement results and one person will be disappointed when their preference is not chosen.

4. Suppose the economy can produce cars and computers only. Write out six attainable combinations of the two goods, holding the opportunity cost (between the two goods) constant at something other than 1 for 1. Draw the production possibilities frontier.

There are endless possible combinations which students might imagine. For illustrative purposes, substitute "cars" for "television sets" in Exhibit 2-5. The key is for the student to realize that a constant trade-off between goods yields a straight-line PPF.

5. Suppose the economy can produce cars and computers only. Write out six attainable combinations of the two goods in which you represent the law of increasing opportunity costs. Draw the production possibilities frontier.

As with the previous question, there are endless possible combinations which students might imagine. Again, for illustrative purposes, substitute "cars" for "television sets" in Exhibit 2-2. The key is for the student to realize that a non-constant trade-off between goods yields an outward-bowed, or convex, PPF.

6. Explain how the following can be represented in a production possibilities framework: the finiteness of resources implicit in the scarcity condition, choice, and opportunity cost.

Scarcity is illustrated by the existence of the frontier itself -- were it not for limited resource availability, there would be no limit on a country's ability to produce. Choice is illustrated by the variety of possible combinations of output along any given frontier -- there is not one optimum combination, but rather a set of efficient choices. Opportunity cost is represented by the slope of the frontier.

7. What condition must hold before the production possibilities frontier is bowed outward? a straight line?

In order for a nation's PPF to be bowed outward, resources must be somewhat specialized, such that the law of increasing opportunity costs holds. With specialized resources, additional units of a good can only be produced at increasing opportunity costs. In order for a nation's PPF to be a straight line, there must be complete interchangeability of resources, with no specialization, such that the law of increasing opportunity costs does not apply.

8. Give an example to illustrate each of the following: (a) constant opportunity costs; (b) increasing opportunity costs.

Constant opportunity costs occur when increasing the output of a good, does not cause society to have to give up more and more resources in order to produce that good. Although at some point, increasing opportunity costs will occur, over some level of output, constant opportunity costs could prevail. For example, if the college has a $20 million budget, and each class costs the school $25,000, then the school can offer 800 classes during the year. If the school got a $500,000 grant, it might be able to offer another 20 classes if its costs did not increase, perhaps because there were unemployed professors ready and willing to work at the going wage rate Increasing opportunity costs occur when society has to give up more and more of one resource in order to obtain another resource. If the school had received a $2 million grant and wanted to offer more classes, the college might hire the readily available professors and still not have met the demand for classes. In order to hire additional teachers, the school would have to hire individuals who had a higher opportunity cost.

9. Why are most production possibilities frontiers (for goods) bowed outward, or concave?

Most production possibility frontiers are concave because of the law of increasing opportunity costs which says that as society devotes more resources to the production of a given good, the opportunity cost of producing that good will increase. The reason for this is that the most efficient resources will be used to initially produce that good. Only as those resources are used up, will society employ less productive resources. Farmers will plant wheat in Kansas before they plant wheat in Alaska or Nevada.

10. Which is cheaper for the country as a whole: (1) the draft, or (2) voluntary service? Explain your answer.

The correct answer to this question depends upon the opportunity cost of serving in the armed forces. With voluntary service, those individuals who have the lowest opportunity cost of serving in the armed forces will sign up. A draft might force brain surgeons to spend most of their time scrubbing floors. However, you should also consider the cost of hiring inductees, and the willingness of individuals to join the armed forces. During war time, if there were voluntary service, a high probability of death would make the opportunity cost of joining the army very high for anyone. During peace time, voluntary service might be the most efficient answer, but during war time a draft might be the most efficient answer. In short, the answer depends upon the opportunity cost!

11. Within a PPF framework, identify the cost of unemployment.

The presence of unemployment would prevent society from producing on the production possibilities frontier because society would not be able to fully employ its available resources. Consequently, the cost of unemployment would be that society would produce inside the production possibility frontier, reducing its production possibilities.

12. Within the PPF framework, explain each of the following: (a) a disagreement between a person who favors more domestic welfare spending and one who favors more national defense spending; (b) an increase in the population; and (c) a technological change that makes resources less specialized.

(a) This first question merely deals with choices among possible output combinations along a frontier representing total government spending. For illustrative purposes, substitute "domestic welfare spending" for "cars" and "national defense spending" for "television sets" in Exhibit 2-8. The person favoring more welfare spending would prefer point D or E, while the person favoring more defense spending would prefer point A or B. (b) As discussed before, an increase in population, ceteris paribus, will shift the PPF outward, as from PPF_1 to PPF_2 in Exhibit 2-7. (c) A technological change that makes resources less specialized will reduce the opportunity cost of switching production from one good to another; therefore, the production possibility frontier will become less bowed-outward -- i.e., more like Exhibit 2-3b and less like Exhibit 2-4b.

13. Some people have said that the Central Intelligence Agency (CIA) regularly estimates (a) the total quantity of output produced in the Soviet Union and (b) the total quantity of civilian goods produced in the Soviet Union. Of what interest would this information, or the information that perhaps could be deduced from it, be to the CIA? (Hint: Think in terms of a PPF.)

Imagine a PPF which shows possible output combinations for civilian goods and military goods. If the CIA had an accurate estimate of total output of all goods and total output of civilian goods, it could estimate the total output of military goods by subtracting the latter from the former. If it then plotted civilian-military output combinations over time, it could estimate the productive capacity of the Soviet economy during that time period.

14. Suppose the United States can produce the following efficient combinations of cars and tanks.

26

Possible Combinations

	A	B	C	D	E
Cars (in millions)	0	10	20	30	40
Tanks (in thousands)	60	55	45	30	0

a. Are there constant or increasing opportunity costs associated with tank production?

Opportunity costs are increasing as tank production increases.

b. Draw the production possibilities frontier based on the data in the table.

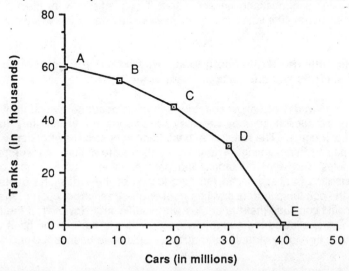

c. Suppose there is a change in technology that allows the United States to produce more tanks with the same resources, but does not allow it to produce more cars with the same resources. Draw and label the new PPF in relation to the old PPF.

Such a situation would be represented by an outward-rotation of the frontier from the point representing the maximum quantity of cars -- here, point E. The new frontier would be PPF$_2$.

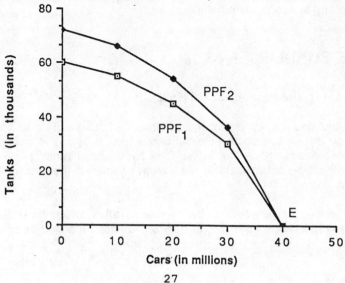

27

14. Suppose a nation's PPF shifts inward as its population grows. What happens, on average, to the material standard of living of the people? Explain your answer.

It would tend to decrease. The economy, as a whole, would have less goods and services to go around, and would be distributing them to more people. Consequently, each person would get less and less.

15. "A nation may be able to live beyond its means, but the world cannot." Do you agree or disagree? Explain your answer.

Yes. By importing the production of other countries, especially on credit, one nation can provide its citizens more goods and services than it can efficiently produce with its own resources. However, barring the introduction of interplanetary trade, the world cannot do so.

16. Country A currently has tariffs and quotas. How would you go about determining whether a policy of tariffs and quotas is efficient or inefficient.

The purpose of foreign trade is to allow countries to export goods for which they have a low opportunity cost of production so they can pay for imports for which they have a high opportunity cost of production. The result is a "consumption possibilities frontier" which shows what society is capable of consuming. You could compare the nation's consumption without the tariffs and quotas and with the tariffs and quotas. If the country had been on its consumption possibilities frontier prior to the introduction of the tariffs and quotas, but was consuming inside the consumption possibilities frontier after the introduction of the tariffs and quotas, then you could conclude that the quotas were inefficient. However, if the introduction of the tariffs and quotas allowed the country to move closer to the consumption possibilities frontier or onto it, then the policy of tariffs and quotas would have been efficient.

17. Use the PPF framework to explain something in your everyday life (that was not mentioned in the chapter).

There are innumerable possible answers to this question. One possibility might be for a student who has a choice between living on campus and a student who lives at home. Living on campus saves commuting time which can be devoted to studying which will enable the student to push out his or her "grade possibility curve."

■ LECTURE SUPPLEMENTS

"The End of the Line," *The Economist*, 336 (7923), July 15, 1995, p. 61

This article is included to get your students to think about the law of increasing opportunity costs. The article is primarily about the difficulties Intel is facing in making each new generation of semiconductor chips, but it also talks about the increasing opportunity costs society has faced in the past in building the railway system in the United States in the nineteenth century.

During the nineteenth century, the number of miles of railway which the United States had doubled every decade for sixty years. At this point, the nation reached its saturation point.

"Laying rails was too expensive to justify connecting smaller towns; people simply did not need track everywhere."

The same story is beginning to apply to semiconductor chips. Chips have doubled their power every two years, and this doubling has occurred 15 times already. Intel and other companies are beginning to run into two sets of problems. First, there are physical limits to how small transistors can be made. Atoms may be small, but even they take up some space. Second, and more importantly for this class, the cost of building new plants to create the new chips is rising. Gordon Moore, one of the founders of Intel, is quoted as saying "What has come to worry me most recently is the increasing cost....This is another exponential." So even computers face the law of increasing opportunity costs!

"Israel Moves to Build Tighter Economic Ties to Its Arab Neighbors," *The Wall Street Journal*, August 3, 1995, page 1 column 1.

This article can be used to illustrate the trade-offs which society faces between public and private goods. As Israel and its Arab neighbors begin to make peace with one another, neither will need to spend as much money on the military as was true in the past. The advent of peace will allow Israel and its Arab neighbors to choose a new point on its production possibilities frontier, one that favors more private goods and fewer military goods. The benefit of this article is that it provides exact details on how this process of moving from one point on the production possibilities curve to another takes place.

The article also discusses how "economic power" is replacing "military power." Beyond this, there are a number of topics which can be discussed. This can lead to a discussion of the "peace dividend." Make sure that students see that there are two benefits coming from the peace dividend. First, there is a reallocation of resources from military to consumer goods, a movement along the PPF. Second, increases in economic efficiency can push out the PPF through the more efficient use of resources, trade opportunities with Arab countries, and the reallocation of research and development away from military goods to economic goods where marginal costs are more important.

"As Millions of Chinese Try to Get Rich Quick, Values Get Trampled," *The Wall Street Journal*, 132 (85), May 2, 1995, page 1, column 1.

The purpose of this article is to get students to think about the three economic questions society faces of what goods to produce, how to produce those goods, and for whom the goods will be produced? In making its transition from a centralized, planned economy to a decentralized market economy, China is making many changes. Under planned communism, the state decided what would be produced, where individuals worked, where individuals could live, and so forth. The state answered the three economic questions and gave little choice to individuals. In relying more on the market, the state is playing a smaller role in answering these three economic questions in China. The article points out some of the economic and non-economic problems that China faces in finding a new way of answering these three economic questions.

Since the article talks about the impact of the market economy on Chinese values and selflessness, this article might be a useful follow-up to the article quoted in Chapter 1 on altruism. One purpose of introducing this article in class is to show students that the society faces trade-offs and opportunity costs when it chooses how to answer these three fundamental questions. Was life better in a China in which people were poorer, but there was less crime? Do your students agree with Xiao Guochang who says both "It's better to be free," and "My job's more important than my family?" Greater personal freedom and higher incomes can have a cost: more crime and greater financial uncertainty. Get your students to discuss these trade-offs.

"The Price of Imaging Arden," *The Economist,* 333 (7892), December 3, 1994, p. 80.

This article is designed to make students think about opportunity costs and apply them to goods which are not traded in the market. The article poses the question, how do you place a value on the environment? In 1990, the United States is estimated to have spent $130 billion complying with environmental laws. Was it worth it? Everyone wants to have a clean environment, but the economic question is, how much are people willing to pay for a clean environment? If you restrict cutting timber, people lose jobs and the price of wood-based products go up. If you restrict farmland to restrict excessive farming, the price of crops will increase. If you limit the number of dams to help salmon swim upstream, you raise electricity costs. Most people will support cleaning up the environment, but few will think about the costs.

One solution is to compare property values when environmental laws are passed with the values which existed before the laws were passed. This way you can get a measure of how much the environmental laws cost. Similarly, you could calculate the number of jobs that are lost and the additional cost of resource that people have to pay. But as the article points out, this evaluation would look at the costs, but ignore one of the important benefits. Individuals may receive personal benefits just from knowing that pristine forests exists and that Yellowstone is a wonderful place they can vacation to, even if they never go there. How do you measure this?

Some people may pay for these benefits by sending contributions to organizations which fight for environmental causes, but the authors suggest that if you ask people specific questions about how they value resources, you may be able to get a fairly accurate answer. Nevertheless, the article points out the problems with this methodology. Specifically, many people were willing to spend about the same to save 2000 birds as to save 2 million. In other words, many individuals were not thinking at the margin. They put a value on saving the environment, but did not think about the environment in terms of marginal costs and benefits. Let's hope your students do.

CHAPTER 3

Supply, Demand, and Price

Chapter 3 begins our discussion of one of the cornerstones of economics: supply and demand analysis. In this chapter, the author focuses on the theory of consumer demand and of supply, describing to the student the basics of supply and demand, the importance of understanding these concepts, and the various factors which affect the decisions of consumers and producers. The theory portion of the chapter concludes by combining supply and demand in the market, introducing the concepts of equilibrium and disequilibrium, and discussing the consequences of surpluses and shortages. The rest of the chapter provides applications for the theory of supply and demand introduced in this chapter. In particular, the chapter focuses on restrictions which are placed upon the free market -- specifically, price floors and price ceilings -- and their effects. Finally, Chapter 3 includes several examples of supply and demand at work, applying supply and demand to freeway congestion at rush hour, student parking, ticket scalping, and expensive wines.

■ CHAPTER OBJECTIVES

Upon completing this chapter, your students should be able to:

- state the laws of demand and supply;

- clearly distinguish between a *change in quantity demanded (supplied)* and a *change in demand (supply)*;

- understand why demand curves slope downward and supply curves slope upward;

- explain how equilibrium price and quantity are determined in a *market*;

- describe how the market tends to remedy *surpluses* and *shortages*;

- define a *price ceiling* and a *price floor* and identify some "real world" examples of each type of control;

- understand the effects of price ceilings and price floors on markets; and,

- explain the problems of freeway congestion, common water, expensive wines, and student parking.

■ KEY TERMS

- market
- demand
- law of demand
- demand schedule
- demand curve
- normal good
- inferior good
- substitutes
- complements
- own price
- supply
- law of supply

- surplus (excess supply)
- shortage (excess demand)
- equilibrium price (market-clearing price)
- equilibrium quantity
- disequilibrium price
- disequilibrium
- equilibrium
- price ceiling
- tie-in sale
- price floor
- supply curve
- supply schedule subsidy

■ CHAPTER OUTLINE

I. **MARKETS AND THE CIRCULAR FLOW** -- A *market* is any arrangement by which people exchange goods and services (including money). Market transactions have two "sides" -- those who wish to buy (*demand*) and those who wish to sell (*supply*). Economists divide the market into product markets for outputs and resource markets for inputs. Individuals participate in both by selling their labor supply in resource markets in order to obtain money which can be used to buy goods offered for sale in the product markets. The relationships between firms and consumers in the product and resource markets are represented in the circular flow diagram which is illustrated in Exhibit 3-1.

II. **DEMAND** -- Demand revolves around the concept of a purchaser's willingness and ability to buy a particular good/service. We distinguish between *quantity demanded* -- the amount of a good that individuals are willing and able to buy at a particular price at a particular time -- and *demand*, which is the quantity demanded at all prices during a specific time period.

A. **The Law of Demand** -- The *law of demand* holds that *as the price of a good rises, the quantity demanded of a good falls, and as the price of a good falls, the quantity demanded of the good rises, ceteris paribus.* That is, the price of a good and the quantity demanded of that good are inversely related, ceteris paribus.

B. **Representing Demand**

1. **The Demand Schedule** -- a numerical tabulation of the quantity demanded of good X at different prices. [See Exhibit 3-2a]

2. **The Demand Curve** -- the graphical representation of the relationship between the quantity demanded of good X and the price of good X. [See Exhibit 3-2b]

C. **The Individual and Market Demand Curves** -- An *individual demand curve* represents the price-quantity demanded combinations for a single buyer, such as Smith or Jones. The *market demand curve* represents the price-quantity demanded combinations for all buyers of a particular good. It is the summation of all of the individual demand curves for a particular item. [See Exhibit 3-3]

D. **Determinants of Demand** -- Common sense, as well as economic theory, tell us that the price of a good (its *own price*) affects the demand for that good. We will address this further, later in the chapter. However, there are other non-price determinants of demand which deserve our attention.

1. **Income** -- As a person's income rises, his or her ability to purchase a given good also rises; as income falls, ability to purchase falls. However, demand requires both ability and *willingness* to buy. The actual effect of a change in income on demand depends upon whether the good in question is considered *"normal"* or *"inferior"* by the consumer.

    a. **Normal Goods** -- A ***normal good*** is one that is consumed voluntarily, and for which *demand will rise as income rises, and fall as income falls.* In this most prevalent case, an increase in income will shift the demand curve to the right, and a decrease will shift the demand curve to the left. [See Exhibit 3-4]

    b. **Inferior Goods** -- An ***inferior good*** is one that is consumed due to economic circumstances, and for which *demand will fall as income rises, and rise as income falls.*

2. **Preferences** -- People's preferences affect their willingness to buy a good at any given price. *A change in preferences in favor of a good will increase demand* (shift the demand curve to the right). *A change away from the good will do the opposite.*

3. **Prices of Related Goods**

    a. **Substitutes** -- Two goods are considered ***substitutes*** if they satisfy similar needs or desires, such as butter and margarine. *If the price of a good rises, the demand for its substitute(s) will rise, if the price of a good falls, the demand for its substitute(s) will fall.* [See Exhibit 3-5a]

    b. **Complements** -- Two goods are ***complements*** if they are consumed jointly, such as hamburger meat and hamburger buns. *If the price of a good rises, the demand for its complement(s) will fall, if the price of a good falls, the demand for its complement(s) will rise.* [See Exhibit 3-5b]

4. **Number of Buyers** -- The demand for a good in a particular area is related to the number of buyers in that area. *If the number of buyers increases, demand will increase* (shifting the demand curve to the right). *If the number of buyers decreases, demand will fall* (shifting the demand curve to the left).

5. **Price Expectations** -- Finally, expectations about future price movements will affect consumer demand. *If prices are expected to rise, current demand will increase. If prices are expected to fall, current demand will decrease.*

E. **Change in Demand vs. Change in Quantity Demanded** -- A *change in demand* refers to a shift in the demand curve brought about by a change in any of the non-price determinants of demand mentioned above. [See Exhibit 3-6a] A *change in quantity demanded* refers to a movement along a single demand curve in response to a change in the *own price* of the good. [See Exhibit 3-6b]

III. **SUPPLY** -- Supply revolves around the concept of a producer's willingness and ability to provide a particular good/service. *Quantity supplied* is the amount of a good that producers are willing and able to sell at a particular price at a particular time, and *supply* is the quantity supplied at all prices during a specific time period.

    A. **The Law of Supply** -- The *law of supply* holds that *as the price of a good rises, the quantity supplied of a good rises, and as the price of a good falls, the quantity supplied of the good falls, ceteris paribus.* That is, the price of a good and the quantity demanded of that good are directly related, ceteris paribus.

    B. **The Supply Curve** -- The *supply curve* is the graphical representation of the relationship between the quantity supplied of good X and the price of good X. In many cases, the supply curve is *upward-sloping*, indicating that quantity supplied will increase as price increases. [See Exhibit 3-8] However, in some cases the supply curve is vertical, suggesting that supply is fixed regardless of price. The reason for such a situation may be because it takes time to produce additional output, such as the theater example in Exhibit 3-9a, or because no more of the good can be produced -- as in Exhibit 3-9b.

    C. **The Individual and Market Supply Curves** -- An *individual supply curve* represents the price-quantity supplied combinations for a single producer, such as Brown or Alberts in Exhibit 3-10a. The *market supply curve* represents the price-quantity supplied combinations for all producers of a particular good. It is the summation of all of the individual supply curves for a particular item. [See Exhibit 3-10b].

    D. **Determinants of Supply** -- Much like demand, there are a number of factors that affect supply.

        1. **Prices of Relevant Resources** -- All goods and services require resources -- inputs such as labor, capital, land, etc. -- in their production. *If the price of an input rises, the supply curve of good X will shift to the left*, indicating that less will be produced at any given price. *If the price of an input falls, the supply curve of good X will shift to the right.*

        2. **Technology** -- In Chapter 2 we said that an *advance in technology* refers to the ability to produce more output with a fixed amount of resources. Under such circumstances, the per-unit cost of production falls, *shifting the supply curve to the right*.

        3. **Number of Sellers** -- The supply of a good in a particular area is related to the number of sellers in that area. *If the number of sellers increases, supply will increase* (shifting the supply curve to the right). *If the number of sellers decreases, supply will fall* (shifting the supply curve to the left).

        4. **Price Expectations** -- *If the price of a good is expected to be higher in the future, producers may cut back on current production* in order to sell more at the high price in the future (i.e., supply curve shifts left). *If prices are expected to fall, current production will increase*, shifting the supply curve to the right.

        5. **Taxes and Subsidies** -- *Some taxes increase per-unit costs, leading to a leftward shift in the supply curve for the affected good(s). Some subsidies reduce per-unit costs, leading to a rightward shift in the supply curve for the affected good(s).* Removing the tax or subsidy in question would, logically, have the opposite effect.

6. **Government Restrictions** -- *Quotas, licensing, and other efforts to restrict supply will shift the supply curve to the left* (and possibly make them vertical over some or all of the relevant range). *Removing/relaxing such restrictions will increase supply*, leading to a rightward shift in the supply curve.

E. **Change in Supply vs. Change in Quantity Supplied** -- A *change in supply* refers to a shift in the supply curve brought about by a change in any of the non-price determinants of supply mentioned above. [See Exhibit 3-12a] A *change in quantity supplied* refers to a movement along a single supply curve in response to a change in the own price of the good. [See Exhibit 3-12b]

IV. PUTTING SUPPLY AND DEMAND TOGETHER

A. **Supply and Demand: The Auction Model** -- The notion of supply and demand that has been handed down through the years functions much like an auction. As Exhibit 3-13 and the corresponding discussion in the text relate, buyers and sellers "bid" prices up and down until the quantity supplied at a particular auction price exactly equals the quantity demanded at that same price. There is one price at which quantity supplied equals quantity demanded, and the market is always working toward that point.

B. **Equilibrium** -- That blissful price, where quantity supplied just equals quantity demanded, is called the *equilibrium (or "market-clearing") price*, and the general condition is called *equilibrium* (identified by the point "E" in Exhibit 3-14).

C. **Disequilibrium** -- Any price at which quantity supplied and quantity demanded are not equal is a *disequilibrium price*, and the general condition is called *disequilibrium*.

1. **Surplus/Excess Supply** -- If the *quantity supplied at a given price is greater than the quantity demanded at that price*, a *surplus* exists, and the market price must be lowered in order to eliminate any "excess" supply. [In Exhibit 3-13, a surplus exists at $6.00, $5.00, and $4.00.]

2. **Shortage/Excess Demand** -- If the *quantity demanded at a given price is greater than the quantity supplied at that price*, a *shortage* exists, and the market price must rise in order to eliminate any "excess" demand. [In Exhibit 3-13, a shortage exists at $1.25 and $2.25.]

3. **Moving to Equilibrium** -- *If a surplus exists, price must fall* in order to entice additional demand and reduce quantity supplied until the surplus is eliminated. [See Exhibit 3-14] *If a shortage exists, price must rise* in order to entice additional supply and reduce quantity demanded until the shortage is eliminated. [See Exhibit 3-14]

D. **Applications of Supply and Demand**

1. **Romanee-Conti Wine** -- This wine, though only dating back to 1990, costs $800 a bottle or $8 a sip. Why? The high quality of the wine creates a high demand for it, and only a few hundred bottles of the wine exist. Combine high demand and a low supply, and the result is a high price.

2. **Endangered Species and the Price of Water** -- Demand for water is increasing, but the supply of water to meet this demand is constant or even declining, not necessarily because of lower rainfall, but because increased protection of endangered species has reduced the

amount of water available for consumption. Increasing demand and decreasing supply will produce a higher price.

3. **Ticket Scalping** -- Ticket scalping can exist only if the promoters of the event initially sell their tickets for less than the equilibrium price. An economist would ask, why is a business willing to sell their tickets for less than the public is willing to pay, reducing their own profits? There are two possible answers. One is that the seller may not know the equilibrium price prior to pricing the musical concert or Broadway play. Second, trying to wring the last penny out of every customer through high pricing might create ill will toward the producer or uncertainty over the prices of future concerts which could ultimately reduce demand.

4. **Supply and Demand on a Freeway** -- Although individuals pay no money when they use freeways, they do pay in other ways. During rush hour, trips take longer, and drivers "pay" for their trip by having to "spend" more time on the freeway. One solution to this problem would be to charge cars which use freeways during the rush hour. As shown in Exhibit 3-17, authorities could find what price would clear the freeway market during rush hour and enable commuters to get to their jobs (or homes) faster. Critics argue that charging tolls would reduce but not solve the problem, that the tolls would hurt the poor, and that freeways should be publicly and not privately managed.

5. **Student Parking** -- Demand for parking at colleges is highest between 8 A.M. and 2 P.M., sometimes causing students to be late. Possible solutions? Charge more for parking between 8 A.M. and 2 P.M than at other times, or rent individual spaces to students.

E. **Changes in Equilibrium Price and Quantity** -- Equilibrium price and quantity are determined by the interaction of supply and demand. A change in supply, or demand, or both, will necessarily change the equilibrium price, quantity, or both, unless the change in supply and demand perfectly offset one another so that equilibrium remains the same (highly unlikely). Exhibit 3-16 illustrates eight different cases of changing equilibrium price and/or quantity.

V. **PRICE CONTROLS** -- The free market is not always allowed to operate freely, thus restricting the ability of price to properly execute the tasks we just discussed. There are two principal forms of price control: *price ceilings* and *price floors*.

A. **Price Ceilings** -- A ***price ceiling*** is a *government-mandated maximum price above which legal trades cannot be made*. If the price ceiling is set below the "natural" equilibrium price for the market in question, any or all of the following may arise:

1. **Shortages** -- *At any price below equilibrium, the quantity demanded will exceed the quantity supplied, thus a shortage occurs.* [See Exhibit 3-18] Furthermore, the natural tendency of the market to correct for the shortage by raising price is thwarted by the ceiling, thus any shortage will likely be sustained.

2. **Fewer Exchanges** -- At any price other than the equilibrium price, the quantity sold will always be the lesser of quantity supplied and quantity demanded, since you cannot sell what won't be bought, nor can you buy what is not for sale. *As long as the supply curve is not vertical, the quantity of goods sold will be less with a ceiling than would have been true at the equilibrium price.*

3. **Nonprice Rationing Devices** -- Since a price ceiling creates a shortage, and price is no longer capable of fully rationing the distribution of the good, nonprice rationing devices, such as "first-come-first-served" or ration stamps, will likely develop.

4. **Buying and Selling at a Prohibited Price** -- Price ceilings often give rise to *black markets*, as well. Consumers who are willing to pay a price above the ceiling, in order to be assured of getting the good, can arrange illicit transactions.

5. **Tie-in Sales** -- Price ceilings also often prompt the use of *tie-in sales*, where *one good may be purchased only if another good is purchased with it.* For example, in order to evade rent control, many landlords require potential tenants to rent furniture (uncontrolled price) along with their (price controlled) apartment.

B. **Price Ceilings and the Distortion of Incentives and Information** -- Price ceilings distort normal economic incentives, often prompting consumers to prefer higher prices to lower prices, if the lower price carries with it all of the potential disruption of a price ceiling. Furthermore, price ceilings distort information, by making the availability of the price-controlled good seem greater than it actually is, since low price is supposed to be an indicator of relatively greater availability.

C. **Price Floors** -- A *price floor* is a *government-mandated minimum price below which legal trades cannot be made.* If a price floor is set above the equilibrium price, the following two effects arise:

1. **Surpluses** -- *At any price above equilibrium, the quantity supplied will exceed the quantity demanded, thus a surplus occurs.* [See Exhibit 3-19] Furthermore, the natural tendency of the market to correct for the surplus by lowering price is thwarted by the floor, thus any surplus will likely be sustained.

2. **Fewer Exchanges** -- At any price other than the equilibrium price, the quantity sold will always be the lesser of quantity supplied and quantity demanded, since you cannot sell what won't be bought, nor can you buy what is not for sale. *As long as the demand curve is not vertical, the quantity of goods sold will be less with a floor than would have been true at the equilibrium price.*

3. **The Minimum Wage Law** -- The *minimum wage* is a government-mandated floor on the price for labor. If the minimum wage is above the equilibrium wage in the labor market, a surplus of labor occurs, resulting in an excess supply of labor and lower actual employment than would be the case at the equilibrium wage. [See Exhibit 3-20]

VI. **ECONOMICS ON THE INTERNET** -- This section shows how you can use the University of Michigan Gopher to access price data from the Department of Commerce data files.

■ ANSWERS TO CHAPTER QUESTIONS

1.   True or false? As the price of oranges rises, the demand for oranges falls *ceteris paribus*. Explain your answer.

False. There is a big difference between the terms *demand* and *quantity demanded*. Quantity demanded refers to the amount of a good consumers are willing and able to buy at a particular price. Demand refers to the demand curve, depicting the quantity demanded at all possible prices. The statement holds that a change in the price of oranges can shift the demand curve for oranges. In fact, while a number of factors may shift the demand curve, a good's *own price* is <u>not</u> one of them. The only thing that own price can change is quantity demanded. This change is represented by a movement along the existing demand curve.

2.   "The price of a bushel of wheat was $3.00 last month and is $3.70 today. The demand curve for wheat must have shifted rightward between last month and today." Discuss.

Not necessarily. Both supply and demand determine price. It is possible that price rose due to a rightward shift in the demand curve for wheat [see Exhibit 3-16], but it is also possible that the price rose due to a leftward shift in the supply curve of wheat [see Exhibit 3-16]. A number of different combinations of supply and demand changes can raise price, and the suggested explanation is only one of them.

3.   "Some goods are bought largely because they have 'snob appeal.' For example, the residents of Palm Beach gain prestige by buying expensive items. In fact, they won't buy some items unless they are expensive. The law of demand, which holds that people buy more at lower prices than at higher prices, obviously doesn't hold for Palm Beachers. In short, the following rule applies in Palm Beach: high prices, buy; low prices, don't buy." Discuss.

Maybe Palm Beachers do buy only expensive items, but this only means that they have a *preference* for expensive items -- perhaps because there is some "snob appeal" associated with the item. The law of demand does not rule out such a preference. The relevant question is whether Palm Beachers buy more or fewer high-priced items as these items prices rise even further, ceteris paribus. That is, even though they may all prefer $45,000 Lexus LS400s to $25,000 Mazda 929s, will they continue to buy even more Lexuses if their price rises to $50,000? If the law of demand holds true, the answer should be "No."

4.   "The price of T-shirts keeps rising and rising, and people keep buying more and more. T-shirts must have an upward-sloping demand curve." Identify the error.

This problem was discussed in Exhibit 3-7. People can observe higher prices and higher sales, but the higher prices do not cause the higher sales. Look back at Exhibit 3-7a. Price is higher at B than at A, as is quantity demanded. Does this mean the demand curve is upward sloping? Not at all. Point A is on one demand curve, and Point B is on another.

5.   Predict what would happen to the equilibrium price of marijuana if it were legalized.

The production, sale, and purchase of marijuana are presently illegal. Some people probably do not buy marijuana at present because it is illegal. We would expect the legalization of marijuana to increase the number of buyers, shifting the demand curve to the right. Using the same logic, we would expect the number of sellers to increase, shifting the supply curve to the right, as well. If the demand curve for marijuana shifts rightward more than the supply curve shifts rightward, the equilibrium price of marijuana rises. If the demand curve shifts rightward by less than the supply curve shifts rightward, then the equilibrium price of marijuana would fall. Many people feel that legalization would likely increase supply by more than it increases demand, causing equilibrium price to be lower than at present.

6. Compare the ratings for television shows with prices for goods. How are ratings like prices? How are ratings different from prices? (Hint: How does rising demand for a particular television show manifest itself?)

Television ratings are similar to prices in that they reflect consumer demand for the product. That is, if consumers like the show, the ratings will most likely be high, if consumers do not like the show, ratings will likely be low. Furthermore, only those who can afford to watch the show are counted in the ratings, thus ratings reflect both the willingness and, to some extent, ability to "consume" television.

The most striking departure lies in the fact that ratings do not translate into a price to be paid by the television consumer. For instance, it doesn't cost any more to watch "The Simpsons" than it does to watch re-runs of "Mr. Ed" on Nick at Nite. The interesting twist is that those ratings do affect the price to advertisers of hawking their wares to the viewing public, but the viewer is not directly affected. (It might also be interesting here to consider cable television and pay-per-view events.)

7. Do you think the law of demand holds for criminal activity? Do potential criminals "buy" less (more) crime, the higher (lower) the "price" of crime, *ceteris paribus*? Explain your answer.

Except for genuine sociopaths and persons whose mental capacity is either temporarily or permanently impaired, a reasonable argument can be made that many criminals -- and certainly "professional" criminals -- take into account the likelihood of being caught and punished when they decide whether to commit a given crime. Given that assumption, if we consider the expected punishment -- that is, the likelihood of being punished multiplied by the cost of punishment to the would-be criminal -- to be the "price" of crime, it seems reasonable that the greater the perceived cost, the less crime most criminals will "buy."

8. Many movie theaters charge a lower admission price for the first show on weekday afternoons than for a weeknight or weekend show. Explain why.

If theater owners are rational, then it must be because they perceive a surplus of seats for early shows. There are two reasons. First, the physical number of available viewers is lower, because much of the viewing public is working or in school during the early show -- thus, the number of buyers is lower than at "prime" times. Second, those potential viewers who are available at the early show are likely to have less money to spend, since a large portion of them would probably be either children or non-wage earners -- thus, the income level of the average potential viewer is low. Both of these causes suggest that the quantity of seats supplied will greatly exceed the quantity of seats demanded at the full ticket price. Therefore, a rational theater owner faced with a surplus of seats does the only logical thing: he/she cuts the price.

9. **The money price of driving on a freeway is always the same--zero. Is the (opportunity) cost always zero, too? Explain your answer.**

Although driving on freeways does not use up any financial resources, it does use up another important resource--time. Many workers, and students, will try to adjust their work hours in order to reduce the amount of time they have to spend on the freeway so they will have more free time to do what they want.

10. **Think about ticket scalpers at a rock concert, a baseball game, or an opera. Might they exist because the tickets to these events were originally sold for less than the equilibrium price? Why? In what way is a ticket scalper like and unlike your retail grocer, who buys food from a wholesaler and turns around and sells it to you?**

For a scalper to be successful, there must be a shortage of tickets at the time of the "scalping." For such a shortage to happen, it may well be that the tickets were sold at a price below equilibrium, and a rational scalper is simply helping the market to "clear" by raising price until available supply exactly equals demand at that price.

Setting aside the issue of whether or not scalping is illegal where you live, the answer to the second question partially depends upon your definition of a "scalper." If a scalper is, essentially, a middleman who purchases tickets in bulk and then resells them at whatever price the market will bear, then a scalper is not that different from a retail grocer. If a scalper is someone who purchases tickets for his own use, changes his mind, and then tries to "unload" them, then the parallel to a grocer is harder to make. And, if a scalper is someone who comes about her tickets in some "shady" fashion, the parallel is, again, hard to make -- even though the scalper may see herself in much the same way as the "legitimate" middleman.

11. **How might you go about determining the equilibrium toll on a freeway at a particular time of day?**

Price is determined by two factors: supply and demand. To determine the proper toll, you would need to look at both of these. First, you would want to see what the marginal cost would be of supplying alternatives to freeways, such as rail, buses, and so on. Second, you could do market research to see how individuals would respond to different levels of fees imposed on travel. By doing this you could estimate the shape of the supply and demand curves and approximate the equilibrium price. After this had been done, the price could be periodically readjusted to reflect changes in supply and demand.

12. **Many of the proponents of price ceilings argue that government-mandated maximum prices simply reduce producers' profits and do not affect the quantity supplied of a good on the market. What must the supply curve look like before a price ceiling does not affect quantity supplied?**

It must be vertical, as in the figure below. Notice that even though the quantity supplied is 100 units at the equilibrium price and price ceiling, the quantity demanded is more than 100. Thus there is a shortage at the price ceiling.

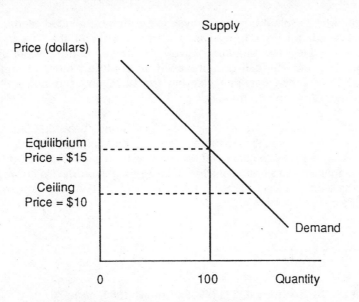

Price (dollars)

Supply

Equilibrium
Price = $15

Ceiling
Price = $10

Demand

0   100   Quantity

13. The minimum wage hurts some unskilled workers because it prices them out of the labor market. For example, if the minimum wage is $4.25 per hour and employers are only willing to pay a person $2.90 per hour, that person cannot legally be hired. Since the minimum wage largely applies to unskilled workers, would you expect all unskilled workers to argue against the minimum wage?

Not all unskilled workers would necessarily dislike the minimum wage. First, the minimum wage doesn't hurt all unskilled workers, it only hurts some of them. For example, suppose the market is in equilibrium as in the diagram below. There are N_1 one persons working. Now suppose the minimum wage is imposed. The number of unskilled workers working falls to N_2. However, the workers who do not lose their jobs because of the minimum wage (N_2) are now earning $4.25 an hour instead of $2.90 an hour. In short, some unskilled workers are earning more because of the minimum wage, and some unskilled workers end up not working because of the minimum wage (N_1 - N_2 lose their jobs if we start at the equilibrium wage).

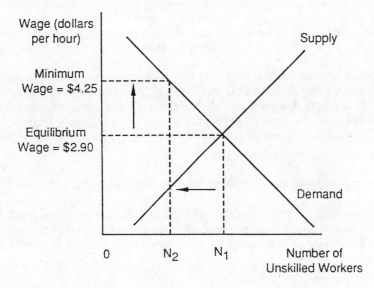

Wage (dollars
per hour)

Supply

Minimum
Wage = $4.25

Equilibrium
Wage = $2.90

Demand

0   N_2 N_1 Number of
Unskilled Workers

14. Some people argue that the minimum wage, by pricing many unskilled teenagers out of the labor market, causes these individuals to turn to selling drugs. After all, if a person can't get a job legally, he or she will get one illegally. The alternative is to starve. Other people disagree. They state that some teenagers would still sell drugs even if all could be hired at minimum wage – because of the monetary difference between clerking for $4.25 an hour and selling drugs for hundreds of dollars a week. What do you think?

For the minimum wage to be the culprit, it would seem that the difference between $0 and $4.25 an hour would have to be the "trigger" that causes kids to turn to crime. Given the great discrepancy between the earnings from a sub-minimum wage job and the potential earnings from a life of crime -- which, of course, must rationally be weighed against the risk and penalties of being caught, as well as any moral dilemmas -- the additional incentive created by being out of work, rather than working at a very low wage, seems negligible. Of course, that's just one opinion.

■ LECTURE SUPPLEMENTS

"Surely not rent controls?" *The Economist*, **335 (7909), April 8, 1995, page 70.**

This is a good little article on rent controls which will provide a useful supplement to the textbook's discussion of ceilings which are placed on rents. As the article points out, a recent survey of economists found out that the statement "a ceiling on rents reduces the quality and quantity of housing" was the statement with which the largest number of economists agreed from the list submitted to them. Some recent challenges by Richard Arnott of Boston College to the idea that rent controls are harmful are discussed.

Mr. Arnott differentiates between "first-generation" rent controls such as those introduced in New York City during World War II and "second-generation" rent controls which have been introduced more recently. Mr. Arnott points out that the first-generation rent controls were clearly harmful and inefficient. Mr. Arnott and other rent control revisionists argue that the housing market is less competitive than it appears to be, and since the analysis of price ceilings applies mainly to markets which are perfectly competitive, they may not apply to housing markets.

Housing is heterogeneous, and so there is no single market for housing, but thousands of markets for different types of housing. Some of these markets may be very thin giving landlords excessive market power which may enable them to charge monopolistic competitive prices for their housing. Fixing rents may reduce landlords' monopoly power rather than restrict a competitive market. Second-generation rent controls are more liberal than the first-generation type. They generally allow some increase in rents to adjust for inflation, but rarely freeze rents. Hence, second-generation rent controls may not be as harmful as economists assume.

As the article concludes; however, the reason most people favor rent controls and minimum wage laws is **not** because they think these markets are inefficient, but because they want to redistribute income to the poor. So the real question they (and your students) should ask themselves is whether this is the most efficient way of redistributing money to the poor? The answer clearly is no. Providing direct payments rather than micro-managing the housing market is a more efficient solution to this problem.

"Are You Listening?" *The Economist*, **335 (7912), April 29, 1995, page 74.**

This is an article which your students should find interesting since it talks about the music industry, and it is a good way of discussing both supply and demand as well as opportunity costs. The article discusses the increasing importance of music clubs as a source of sales for the music industry, and the decreasing importance of record shops.

On the demand side, record clubs offer cut-price club sales which enable club members to save money. Individuals who are members of clubs buy, on average, 33 CDs and cassettes a year, while non-members buy an average of 22. Half of the 33 CDs and cassettes came from record-club sales. Here is a clear example of how a decrease in price leads to an increase in the quantity demanded! On the supply side, record clubs emphasize sales of older music for which royalties are lower and margins are higher, i.e. the supply curve has shifted to the right enabling them to charge a lower price. One other consideration is that club members tend to be older than record store visitors. Is this because older listeners have a higher opportunity cost of visiting record stores?

The problem record clubs face is the high fixed costs of signing up new members. Their solution? Use record stores as a source for new members and share the profits with the record stores, a process Blockbuster Music is already using.

Richard Arnott and Kenneth Small, "The Economics of Traffic Congestion," *American Scientist*, September-October, 1994, pp. 446-455.

This would act as a nice follow-up to the section in this chapter on Supply and Demand on the Freeway. Although technical in points, it does a good job of teaching students about trade-offs and opportunity costs.

The article shows students how economists go about their trade. For example, in order to analyze the economics of traffic congestion, an economist has to figure out the cost of traffic congestion. The way this is done is to determine how much individuals would be willing to pay to reduce their travel time. Their estimate? About $8.00 an hour. This makes the annual cost of driving delays in the United States be about $48 billion, or $640 per driver. If economists can find a way of reducing traffic congestion which costs less than $8.00 per hour of traffic time, then society would be better off by making the changes which are recommended.

As the authors show, there is a paradox in reducing traffic congestion. Increasing capacity might increase congestion if the increased capacity causes more people to take a certain route. New highways may remain uncongested for only a short period of time until commuters change their travel plans. Similarly, if a city offers public transit, more people will use the public transportation which could cause a reduction in the quality of service. Those who do not use the public transportation find their roads less congested. At the new equilibrium, overall travel times might actually increase because of the external costs imposed by automobile users.

Other aspects of the economics of traffic congestion are discussed in the article. If your college is in an urban area, you might use this article to stimulate discussion and get your students to think about the cost and opportunity costs of traffic congestion, a problem they face almost every day, but like the weather, probably spend more time complaining about it than offering solutions.

CHAPTER 4

Three Economic Goals and Three Economic Measurements

This chapter discusses three economic goals which economists believe would exist in a healthy economy. In order to determine whether these goals are being met, economists have to measure these goals. This chapter details the standard measures of the price level and inflation, the unemployment rate, gross domestic product (GDP) and real gross domestic product (Real GDP). It discusses the effects of inflation on GDP, and defines unemployment, describing the way that unemployment is measured in the macroeconomy, as well as some of the shortcomings of that measurement.

■ CHAPTER OBJECTIVES

Upon completing this chapter, your students should be able to:

- list the three major macroeconomic goals of *price stability, low unemployment,* and *high and sustained economic growth;*

- compute the *consumer price index* and the *GDP deflator,* and describe their use for measuring annual inflation;

- clearly distinguish between *nominal GDP* and *Real GDP;*

- define *unemployment* and determine, given a set of conditions, whether a particular person is *employed, unemployed,* or *not in the labor force;*

- distinguish between *structural, frictional* and *natural unemployment;*

- calculate the *unemployment rate* and the *employment rate;*

- describe the four sectors of the economy: *households, businesses, government and foreign;*

- identify the four types of purchases which make up the economy: *consumption, investment, government purchases, and net exports;* and,

- define economic growth and understand the five different phases of the business cycle: *peak, recession, trough, recovery,* and *expansion.*

■ KEY TERMS

- price level
- price index
- consumer price index (CPI)
- base year
- inflation
- real income
- nominal income
- unemployment rate
- employment rate
- labor force participation rate
- frictional unemployment
- structural unemployment
- natural unemployment
- full employment
- cyclical unemployment rate
- gross domestic product (GDP)
- flow variable
- stock variable
- gross national product (GNP)
- final good
- intermediate good
- relative price
- double counting
- government transfer payments
- consumption
- gross private domestic investment
- investment
- fixed investment
- inventory investment
- government purchases
- net exports
- exports
- imports
- domestic income
- national income
- depreciation
- net domestic product (NDP)
- personal income
- disposable income
- Real GDP
- GDP deflator
- economic growth
- business cycle

■ CHAPTER OUTLINE

I. **STUDYING THE ECONOMY** -- The main reason economists study the economy is so they can figure out how it works. Just as doctors study someone's body to find out what is wrong with it so they can suggest a cure, so do economists with the economy. Though economists may disagree on how the economy works, they can agree on the desirable economic goals which the economy should aim for: *price stability, low unemployment, and high and sustained economic* growth. Just as the doctor has tools, such as a thermometer to measure the human body to see if it is well, economists have economic tools they use to measure the health of the economy. These tools are the focus of this chapter.

II. **MEASURING PRICES** -- One of the economic goals is *price stability*. But what is meant by this? It does not mean that the prices of goods never change in the economy, but that the *aggregate price level, average* prices or a *price* index remain relatively stable.

   A. **Measuring Prices** -- The **price level** is a weighted average of the prices of all goods and services. A ***price index*** provides us with a reliable estimate of the price level. Economists use two basic price indices, the consumer price index and the GDP Deflator. The consumer price index is discussed in this section.

   1. **Consumer Price Index (CPI)** -- The *consumer price index (CPI)* tracks the prices of a representative *market basket* of consumer goods. In order to estimate changes in the price level, the CPI compares the current prices of the market basket to the prices

of those goods in some **base year** -- a benchmark year which serves as the basis for price comparisons.

2. **Calculating the** CPI -- The CPI is calculated using the formula:

    $$\frac{\text{Total dollar expenditure on market basket in current year}}{\text{Total dollar expenditure on market basket in base year}} \times 100$$

    Exhibit 4-2 "walks through" the process of calculating a sample CPI. Exhibit 4-3 displays the value of the U.S. CPI for each year since 1980.

B. **Measuring Changes in Price Level** -- In order to measure inflation (or deflation) over a given time period using either the CPI or the GDP deflator, simply subtract the starting year index from the ending index, divide by the starting year index, and multiply by 100. Specifically, the *percentage change in prices* equals

$$\frac{CPI_{\text{later year}} - CPI_{\text{earlier year}}}{CPI_{\text{earlier year}}} \times 100$$

C. **The Inflation Rate** -- The **Inflation Rate** is the same as the percentage change in prices which we calculated above. Usually the inflation rate is calculated over the period of one year.

D. **How Do You Know If You're Beating (CPI) Inflation or If Inflation Is Beating You?** -- The answer is simple. Determine whether your *personal income* is growing faster than the inflation rate. If it is, then you're keeping up. In order to do this, you first have to calculate your **real income**. *Real Income* is nominal (money) income *adjusted for changes in the price level* -- that is, income measured in *constant* dollars, rather than in current dollars. Using the formula for the CPI, real income can be derived as follows:

    Real Income = [(Nominal) Income/CPI] x 100.

In order to show students how to measure this, the book gives three examples:

1. **Case 1. Keeping Up with Inflation: Real Income Stays Constant** -- In this case, both nominal income and prices increase by the same percentage causing *real income* to remain unchanged.

2. **Case 2. Not Keeping Up with Inflation: Real Income Falls** -- In this case, prices increase faster than nominal income, and *real* income falls.

3. **Case 3. More Than Keeping Up with Inflation: Real Income Rises** -- In this case, nominal income increases faster than prices causing *real income* to increase.

4. **Historical Examples** -- Two interesting applications of keeping up with inflation are provided by the book. The first shows that in *real* terms, President Clinton actually earns less income than Abraham Lincoln. The second example shows that though several recent films are the "box office champions" in nominal dollars, in real dollars, the true winner is *Snow White and the Seven Dwarfs*.

E. **The Substitution Bias In Fixed-Weighted Measures** -- When prices change, they not only affect the amount that people pay for goods, but also the amount they consume. People respond to the **relative prices** of goods. If the price of beef goes up and chicken goes down, consumers will respond by buying more chicken and less beef. One problem with fixed-weighted price measures is that they do not reflect this change in demand, and suffer from **substitution bias**. An index which does not allow for substitution bias will overstate changes in the cost of living.

   1. **Fixed-Weighted Price Index** -- In a fixed-weighted price index, the weights of the components do not change causing *substitution bias* which overstates changes in the cost of living.

   2. **Chain-Weighted Price Index** -- This index does not have substitution bias because it allows for substitutions. The chain-weighted measure replaced the fixed-weighted measure of price in December 1995, eliminating a bias which had been present in the past.

III. MEASURING UNEMPLOYMENT

A. **Who Are the Unemployed?** -- If you take the total population of the United States and subtract all persons who are (1) under 16 years of age, (2) on active military duty, or (3) institutionalized -- in prison or hospitalized (including mental hospitals) -- what is left is called the **civilian noninstitutional population**. Every member of the civilian noninstitutional population fits into one of two categories:

   1. **The (Civilian) Labor Force** -- The (civilian) labor force is that portion of the noninstitutional adult (civilian) population that is either *employed* or *unemployed*.

      a. **Employed** -- A person is **employed** if they are *currently engaged in wage/salary-paying employment, if they work at least 15 hours in a personal or family-owned business or farm, or are temporarily absent from work due to illness, vacation, strike, or bad weather.*

      b. **Unemployed** -- A person who is *not employed, but is actively seeking work*, is considered to be **unemployed**. Also included among the unemployed are persons who have been temporarily laid-off from a job to which they expect to return and persons waiting to report to a job within 30 days.

   2. **Not in the Labor Force** -- A person is not in the labor force if they are *neither working nor looking for work*. This would include persons who have voluntarily chosen not to work (in the technical sense of the word), as well as **discouraged workers** -- *people who have given up on job search because they feel they cannot find work*. [Exhibit 4-6 gives the complete breakdown of employment status]

B. **The Unemployment and Employment Rates** -- What specific measurements do we look at to gauge the levels of unemployment and employment, as well as to get a view of the overall health of the economy?

1. **The Unemployment Rate** -- the percentage of the (civilian) labor force that is unemployed. That is, the *unemployment rate* (U) equals

$$\frac{\text{Number of persons unemployed}}{\text{Number of persons in the civilian labor force}}$$

2. **The Employment Rate** -- the percentage of the civilian noninstitutional adult population that is employed. That is, the *employment rate* (E) equals

$$\frac{\text{Number of persons employed}}{\text{Number of persons in the civilian noninstitutional population}}$$

3. **The Labor Force Participation Rate** -- the percentage of the civilian noninstitutional population that is in the labor force. That is, the *labor force participation rate* (LFPR) =

$$\frac{\text{Number of persons in the civilian labor force}}{\text{Number of persons in the civilian noninstitutional population}}$$

C. **Redesigning the Household Survey** -- In January 1994, the household survey which is used to collect information on unemployment was redesigned. One important change involved one of the questions asked of women. Instead of being asked, "What were you doing most of last week, keeping house or something else?" as in the old survey, women are now asked "Last week, did you do any work for pay?" The change was made because the old question presumed that women interviewed at home were homemakers.

D. **Types of Unemployment** -- Individuals are unemployed for different reasons. The primary types of unemployment which economists separate people into include:

1. **Frictional Unemployment (U_F)** -- This refers to people who are moving between jobs. Someone may leave one computer job and get hired by another computer firm due to changes in demand. The intervening period is *frictional unemployment.* In a dynamic economy, there will always be some frictional unemployment because demand for goods is constantly changing.

2. **Structural Unemployment (U_S)** -- When demand for a good produced by different sectors of the economy changes, forcing people to make career changes, from being an automobile worker to being a computer network specialist, the result is *structural unemployment.*

3. **Natural Unemployment (U_N)** -- The sum of frictional and structural unemployment is the level of *natural unemployment* for the economy. This is thought by economists to currently be around 4.0 to 6.5 percent.

E. **Full Employment** -- Full employment does *not* mean that the unemployment rate is zero. Even in a growing economy, some frictional and structural unemployment will exist. Economists say that full employment exists when the economy is operating at its natural unemployment rate.

F. **Cyclical Unemployment (U_C)** -- The difference between the existing unemployment rate and the natural unemployment rate is the *cyclical unemployment rate.* If unemployment is currently 7% and the natural rate of unemployment is 5%, then cyclical unemployment is 2%. That is, cyclical unemployment rate (U_C) = unemployment rate (U) - natural unemployment rate (U_N).

IV. **MEASURING ECONOMIC GROWTH, BUT FIRST...** -- Just as we used a price index to measure inflation, we need a tool for measuring economic growth. The tool economists use is **real gross domestic product (Real GDP).** But first we discuss GDP.

A. **What is GDP?** -- **Gross domestic product (GDP)** is the *total market value of all final goods and services produced annually within a country's borders.* If an economy produces only 10 units at $4 per unit, then GDP equals $40. To understand how GDP is measured, you should distinguish between **flow variables** and **stock variables**.

1. **Flow Variables** -- A *flow variable* is one which can only be measured over a period of time. GDP is a flow variable because it measures how much is produced in the economy in a month, quarter or year.

2. **Stock Variables** -- A *stock variable* is one which can be measured at any point in time, but does not depend upon time for its measurement. Examples would be the money supply, or inventories.

B. **What is the Difference Between GDP and GNP?** -- **Gross national product (GNP)** is the *total market value of all final goods and services produced annually by the citizens of a country.* So GDP measures geographical output and GNP measures citizens' output. These measures could differ if a significant number of people from a country work abroad. A Mexican citizen who lives in the United States would contribute to the United States' GDP, but Mexico's GNP.

C. **"What Does Total Market Value" Mean?** -- We refer to GDP at current prices as *nominal GDP.* This is *the total market value of all final goods and services produced annually within a country's borders, evaluated at current market prices.*

D. **Why Measure Final Goods Only?** -- Why does GDP only measure *final goods* -- goods sold to their ultimate users? Why not include *intermediate goods* -- goods which are an input in the production of other goods -- as well? The answer is simple: we must count only final goods in order to avoid *double counting.* For example, if we measured the value of the seed that became the wheat *plus* the wheat that became the flour *plus* the flour that became the bread *plus* the bread, we would be overstating the total value of output, because the final good -- in this case, bread -- includes in its price the value of all intermediate goods that went into its production.

E. **What GDP Omits** -- Some exchanges are not included in GDP, such as:

1. **Certain Nonmarket Goods and Services** -- tasks which are performed without a market transaction, such as mowing your own lawn rather than hiring someone.

2. **Underground Activities, Both Legal and Illegal** -- Illegal transactions are not counted in GDP, because there is no record of them. Similarly, cash-only transactions, the bread-and-butter of the *underground economy* (see "Economics in Our Times"), are not recorded; and, while the government tries to estimate their value, they are not accurately counted in GDP.

3. **Sales of Used Goods** -- GDP measures only current output.

4. **Financial Transactions** -- Transactions that involve trading existing assets, such as stock purchases.

5. **Government Transfer Payments --** such as Social Security benefits and veterans' benefits.

6. **Leisure** -- Leisure is a good which is "consumed" by individuals just as cars, steak, and housing are consumed. However, because leisure, in and of itself, is not purchased from anyone, it is not included in GDP.

7. **Bads Generated in the Production of Goods** -- GDP measures the market value of new production, but ignores any *social costs* (e.g., pollution) which may be associated with production.

F. **GDP: Is It a Measurement of Happiness or Well-Being?** -- GDP figures measure the productive output of an economy. it says nothing about the quality of life, happiness, or well-being of individuals within that country.

G. **If a Tree Falls in the Forest, Do Economists Hear It? Or, What Is Green Accounting?** -- When a logging company cuts down a tree, this is registered as an increase in GDP, but if the logging eliminates our forests, was this an increase in output, or a depletion of assets? GDP measures the value added from converting the trees into housing, but many economists believe it should also account for the "cost" of production in reducing the nation's resources of trees. This is known as green accounting and is currently used by the U.S. Department of Commerce.

V. **Two Ways of Measuring GDP** -- Gross domestic product can be measured in two different ways. There is the expenditure approach and the income approach. Beginning at the end of 1995, GDP will be calculated as a *chain-weighted Real GDP* measure of output. The chain-weighted Real GDP measure of output divides nominal GDP by a chain-weighted price index.

A. **The Expenditure Approach** -- The macroeconomy is divided into four sectors.

1. **Household Sector** -- providers of land, labor, capital, and entrepreneurial skill to the business and government sectors; consumers of final goods produced both domestically and abroad; primary payers of taxes and primary recipients of government transfer payments.

2. **Business Sector** -- consumers of land, labor, capital, and entrepreneurial skill; providers of both intermediate and final goods to the government sector, business, and consumers both domestically and abroad; secondary payers of taxes and secondary recipients of government transfer payments.

3. **Government Sector** -- Government purchases final goods and services -- school desks, M-1 tanks, bridges, and paper clips, to name a few of thousands of examples. These *government purchases* add to the demand created in product markets by household expenditures and business investment expenditures.

4. **Foreign Sector** -- households *import* goods and services from abroad, thus diverting some of their expenditures from the (domestic) product markets to foreign economies; and, (domestic) businesses *export* some of their products to foreign economies, thus creating an additional source of demand in the product markets.

B. **Computing GDP** -- All final goods and services produced in the economy are bought by someone. Therefore, by summing the value of those expenditures, we may calculate the value of GDP. So, according to the expenditure approach:

$$GDP = C + I + G + (EX - IM).$$

C. **GDP as an Index Number** -- GDP can be expressed as an index number. If the GDP index was at 100 in 1987 and 125 in 1993, this would mean that GDP had increased by 25 percent between 1987 and 1993.

D. **The World GDP** -- In 1992, the world GDP was $25.6 trillion with the United States producing 23 percent of this total, and Japan producing 10 percent. [See Exhibit 4-9 for a comparison of World GDP and World Population by region]

E. **The Income Approach** -- All final goods and services are produced using factors of production which are paid for their efforts. By summing the value of those factor payments, and adjusting them for *indirect business taxes*, the *capital consumption allowance (depreciation)*, and a statistical discrepancy, we can find the value of GDP. **Domestic income** is the total income earned by the people and businesses within a country's borders. **National Income** is the sum of all factor payments, specifically: compensation of employees *plus* proprietors' income *plus* corporate profits *plus* rental income (of persons) *plus* net interest (interest earned *minus* interest paid). [See the Circular Flow Diagram provided in Exhibit 4-10]

1. **Compensation of Employees** -- Wages and salaries paid to employees plus employers' contributions to Social Security and employee benefit plans as well as fringe benefits make up *compensation of employees*.

2. **Proprietors' Income** -- All forms of income earned by self-employed individuals and the owners of unincorporated business is known as *proprietors' income*.

3. **Corporate Profits** -- All income earned by the stockholders of corporations, whether paid to stockholders or reinvested is known as *corporate profits*.

4. **Rental Income (of Persons)** -- Income received by individuals for the use of their nonmonetary assets (land, houses, offices), is referred to as their *rental income*.

5. **Net Interest** -- The interest income received by U.S. households and government minus the interest paid out is *net interest*.

F. From National Income to GDP: Making Some Adjustments -- To get from GDP to national income, several changes must be made. Specifically,

GDP   =   National income
-     Income earned from the rest of the world
+   Income earned by the rest of the world
+   Indirect business taxes
+   Capital consumption allowance
+   Statistical discrepancy

   1. **Income Earned from the Rest of the World, Income Earned by the Rest of the World** -- If US citizens live abroad, their income is included in GNP, but not GDP, so adjustments have to be made for these differences.

   2. **Indirect Business Taxes** -- include such taxes as sales taxes, excise taxes, and property taxes. They are not part of national income because they are not considered to be payments to a factor of production, but they are part of total expenditures.

   3. **Capital Consumption Allowance** -- Over time, capital goods are used up in the production process through natural wear, obsolescence or accidental destruction. The capital consumption allowance, or depreciation, represents these costs.

   4. **Statistical Discrepancy** -- Because GDP and national income are measured using different sets of data, a statistical discrepancy will exist.

G. Other National Income Accounting Measures -- Besides GDP and national income, there are three other measures of particular note: *net national product*, *personal income*, and *disposable income*.

   1. **Net Domestic Product** -- the value of gross domestic product *minus* the capital consumption allowance.

   2. **Personal Income** -- the amount of income, earned and unearned, actually received by individuals; personal income equals national income *plus* government transfer payments *minus* undistributed corporate profits *minus* social insurance taxes (Social Security contributions) *minus* corporate income (profits) taxes.

   3. **Disposable Income** -- the measure of an individual's actual "spending power," equals personal income *minus* personal taxes.

H. Per-Capita Macroeconomic Measurements -- Economists often prefer to "standardize" national income accounting by looking at *per-capita* statistics. Any measure can be converted into a per-capita measure simply by *dividing it by population*. For example, if GDP were $100,000 and population equals 10, then GDP per-capita would equal $10,000.

VI. REAL GDP -- In this section we show you how to compute Real GDP.

A. **Real GDP: A Simple Example** -- When nominal GDP figures are compared between different years, you cannot determine whether the increase in GDP came from an increase in the price level or an increase in output. **Real GDP** is GDP *adjusted for changes in the price level* -- that is, GDP measured in *constant* dollars, rather than in current dollars.

B. **One Way to Measure Real GDP** -- Real GDP can be measured by using the following formula

$$\text{Real GDP} = \Sigma \text{ (Current-year quantities x Base-year prices)}$$

On the other hand, GDP is measured using current-year prices. The formula for GDP would be

$$\text{GDP} = \Sigma \text{ (Current-year quantities x Current-year prices)}$$

Exhibit 4-11 provides some actual computations of Real GDP and GDP. Exhibit 4-12 shows Real GDP figures for the United States for 1990 through 1994.

C. **How To Measure the GDP Deflator** -- The **GDP deflator** measures changes in the prices of *all goods* produced in an economy during a given year. The formula for the GDP deflator is:

$$\text{GDP deflator} = (\text{GDP/Real GDP}) \times 100.$$

D. **Another Way to Compute Real GDP** -- Real GDP can also be calculated as

$$\text{Real GDP} = (\text{GDP/GDP deflator}) \times 100.$$

VII. **A Chain-Weighted Real GDP Measure** -- The same biases created by fixed-weighted price indices occur in Real GDP measurements. Beginning in December 1995, government statisticians measured Real GDP using a chain-weighted method rather than a fixed-weighted method. The *Economics In Our Times* feature, "Where did the Economic Growth Go? Or The Effect of a Change in How Real GDP Is Measured" discusses this change.

A. **Economic Growth** -- If Real GDP or per-capita Real GDP increases from one year to the next, then **economic** growth has occurred. The percentage change in Real GDP gives the economic growth rate which can be computed as

$$\text{Percentage change in Real GDP} = \frac{\text{Real GDP}_{\text{later year}} - \text{Real GDP}_{\text{earlier year}}}{\text{Real GDP}_{\text{earlier year}}} \times 100$$

B. **What Is a Business Cycle?** -- The rise and fall of GDP over time is referred to as the business cycle. The business cycle is divided up into five phases which are illustrated in Exhibit 4-13. These phases are

1. **Peak** -- This occurs when Real GDP is at a temporary high.

53

2. **Recession** -- Two consecutive quarterly declines in Real GDP is referred to as a *recession.*

3. **Trough** -- The low point in Real GDP, just before it turns up.

4. **Recovery** -- The period between the trough and the peak when Real GDP is expanding is referred to as the *recovery.*

5. **Expansion** -- Increases in Real GDP beyond the recovery refers to the *expansion.*

VIII.**ECONOMICS ON THE INTERNET** -- This section provides information on where to find unemployment data and GDP data through the University of Michigan Gopher. The gopher site for the Economic Report of the President is also provided.

■ ANSWERS TO CHAPTER QUESTIONS

1. Why do economists study the economy? What are three important macroeconomic goals or objectives?

Just as a doctor studies the human body in order to understand how it works so he can make people healthier when they are sick, economists study the economy to understand how it works in order to make the economy healthier and more efficient when it is performing poorly. The three major macroeconomic goals include price stability, low unemployment, and high and sustained economic growth.

2. Assume the market basket contains 10X, 20Y, and 45Z. The current-year prices for goods X, Y, and Z are $1, $4, and $6, respectively. The base-year prices are $1, $3, and $5, respectively. What is the CPI in the current year?

Total dollar expenditures in the base year were 10(1) + 20(3) + 45(5) = $295. Total dollar expenditures in the current year are 10(1) + 20(4) + 45(6) = $360. Therefore,

CPI $_{current\ year}$ = $\underline{\text{total dollar expenditure on market basket in current year}}$ = $\underline{\$360}$ **x** 100 = 122.03
　　　　　　　　total dollar expenditure on market basket in base year　　$295

3. If total dollar expenditures on the market basket in the current year is $400, and total dollar expenditures on the market basket in the base year is $360, what is the CPI in the current year? In the base year?

Base year CPI always is 100, by definition. The more interesting question is current CPI. Here,

CPI $_{current\ year}$ = ($400/$360) **x** 100 = 111.11.

4. Using Exhibit 4-3, compute the percentage change in prices between (a) 1980 and 1985, (b) 1988 and 1991, and (c) 1984 and 1993.

Given %ΔP = CPI ending year - CPI starting year / CPI starting year X 100 =

(a) 30.6%; (b) 15.1%; and, (c) 39.1%.

5. What does the CPI in the base year equal? Explain your answer.

The CPI in the base year always equals 100. This allows you to easily compare changes between the current year and the base year, and to compare several different economic measurements which share the base year as their starting point.

6. How do we compute the inflation rate?

The inflation rate is calculated by comparing the consumer price index in one year with the consumer price index in another year. Specifically, the percentage change in prices equals

$$\frac{CPI_{\text{later year}} - CPI_{\text{earlier year}}}{CPI_{\text{earlier year}}} \times 100.$$

7. Assume that noninstitutional population = 100 million persons; civilian labor force = 87 million persons; total population = 240 million persons; employed persons = 45 million persons. Calculate the following: (a) unemployment rate, (b) employment rate, and (c) number of persons not in the labor force.

(a) unemployment rate = 48.3%; (b) employment rate = 45.0%; and (c) number of persons not in the labor force = 13 million.

8. Why doesn't the sum of the unemployment and employment rates equal 100 percent?

The denominator of the unemployment rate is the civilian labor force, while the denominator of the employment rate is the civilian noninstitutional civilian population.

9. How does frictional unemployment differ from structural unemployment?

Frictional unemployment refers to people moving between jobs in the same industry in which they perform the same services for the two firms. Structural unemployment occurs when individuals have a career change which requires them to use new job skills in a completely different industry, moving from the auto industry to the computer industry for example.

10. What does it mean to say the economy is operating at full employment?

The economy is operating at full employment when the current unemployment rate equals the natural unemployment rate and cyclical unemployment is zero.

11. The structural unemployment rate is 3 percent, the frictional unemployment rate is 2 percent, and the (existing) unemployment rate is 7 percent. What is the cyclical unemployment rate?

The cyclical unemployment rate can be calculated as the existing unemployment rate minus the sum of the structural unemployment rate and the frictional unemployment rate. In this example, this would be equal to 7% - (3% + 2%) = 2%.

12. "I just heard on the news that GDP is higher this year than it was last year. It follows that our standard of living is higher this year than last year." Comment.

First, the statement simply refers to GDP, not Real GDP. Perhaps nominal GDP went up this year as compared to last year but only because of higher prices. Output may not have increased at all. In fact, it may have gone down. Secondly, neither nominal GDP nor Real GDP is a measurement of our standard of living, well-being, or happiness. Even when Real GDP increases, our standard of living could be declining if "bads" are associated with the increased production of goods and services.

13. Which of the following are included in the calculation of this year's GDP? (a) Twelve-year-old Johnny mowing his family's lawn; (b) Dave Malone buying a used car; (c) Barbara Wilson buying a bond issued by General Motors; (d) Ed Ferguson's receipt of a Social Security payment; (e) the illegal drug transaction at the corner of Elm and Fifth.

None is included in GDP. Review the relevant section of the chapter if you have problems.

14. Discuss the problems you see in comparing the GDPs of two countries, say, the United States, and the People's Republic of China.

One problem is different prices. If prices for similar goods differ in the two countries, then the GDP comparison will be clouded by price discrepancies. Secondly, there are numerous problems in drawing any conclusions from a comparison. For one thing, the populations are significantly different; therefore, we should take population into account. Even if we look at per-capita GDP, though, the actual distribution of income may be significantly different than it looks. Then, of course, there is the whole range of items and transactions that are excluded from GDP: nonmarket goods and services, illegal and underground transactions, used goods, etc. All of these different points are discussed to show that if we want to make "meaningful" comparisons about economic well-being, a GDP comparison is only going to be a small part of the package.

15. The manuscript for this book was typed by the author. Had he hired someone to do the typing, GDP would have been higher than it was. What other things would increase GDP if they were done differently? What other things would decrease GDP if they were done differently?

Most U.S. households still do their own housework and home and lawn maintenance. Hiring a maid, a handyman, and/or a lawn service would increase GDP. When a college student receives aid in the form of tuition waiver, it is not included in GDP; however, if the same aid had been in the form of payment for services rendered, it would be included in GDP. If people cooked more and ate out less, GDP would fall (assuming it is less expensive to cook for yourself than to eat out). If states provided "free" college education to residents, GDP would fall.

16. What is the difference between GDP and GNP?

Gross domestic product (GDP) is the total market value of all final goods and services produced annually within a country's borders. Gross national product (GNP) is the total market value of all final goods and services produced annually by the citizens of a country. So GDP measures geographical output and GNP measures citizens' output. These measures could differ if a significant number of people from a country work abroad. A Mexican citizen who lives in the United States would contribute to the United States' GDP, but Mexico's GNP.

17. Why does GDP omit the sales of used goods? Financial transactions? Government transfer payments?

Each of these transactions is omitted from GDP because they transfer existing resources from one individual to another rather than creating new goods or services for investment or consumption. The sale of used goods and financial transactions transfer ownership of existing goods. Transfer payments take tax receipts from one group of taxpayers and transfers the money to recipients of government programs.

18. A business firm produces a good this year that it doesn't sell. As a result, the good is added to its inventory. How does this inventory good find its way into GDP?

GDP is equal to C + I + G + (EX - IM), this much we know. We also know that I, or gross private domestic investment, is of two types: fixed investment and inventory investment. The good that is produced but not sold falls into the category of inventory investment. This is how it finds its way into the GDP measurement.

19. Using the following data, calculate the following: (a) gross domestic product (GDP); (b) net domestic product (NDP); (c) national income (NI); (d) personal income (PI). All numbers are in billions of dollars.

Consumption	1,149.5
Investment	400.3
Government purchases	425.3
Net exports	89.1
Capital consumption allowance	303.8
Indirect business taxes	213.3
Statistical discrepancy	4.4
Social security insurance taxes	216.5
Transfer payments	405.6

Undistributed profits	91.0
Corporate profits taxes	77.7
Personal taxes	340.0
Dividends	0.0
Compensation of employees	800.0
Income earned from the rest of the world	50.0
Income earned by the rest of the world	56.0
Proprietors' income	400.0
Rental income	145.0
Net interest	23.0

a. GDP = 1,149.5 + 400.3 + 425.3 + 89.1 = 2,064.2
b. NDP = 2,064.2 - 303.8 = 1,760.4
c. NI = 800.0 + 400.0 + (91.0 + 77.7) + 145.0 + 23.0 = 1536.7
d. PI = 1,563.7 - 91.0 - 216.5 - 77.7 + 405.6 = 1,557.1

20. Economists prefer to compare Real GDP figures for different years instead of GDP figures. Why?

If a country suffers from a high level of inflation, changes in nominal GDP could reflect changes in the price level rather than changes in output.

21. If GDP is $4322.1 and the GDP deflator is 146, what does Real GDP equal?

Real GDP equals nominal GDP divided by the GDP deflator which in this case would be $4322.1/146 x 100 equals $2960.3.

22. What is the difference between a recovery and an expansion?

Both recovery and expansion refer to increases in GDP. Recovery refers to that portion of growth in which the economy increases production to the levels it had reached prior to the recession, and expansion refers to growth beyond the cyclical highs which were attained in the previous business cycle.

23. If Real GDP is $3,445 and GDP is $5,333, what does the GDP deflator equal?

The GDP deflator can be calculated by computing nominal GDP/Real GDP x 100 which in this case would be $5,333/$3,445 x 100 equals 154.8

24. Define each of the following terms:
    a. Recession
    b. Business cycle
    c. Trough
    d. Disposable income
    e. Net domestic product

(a). Recession refers to the downturn in output which occurs after the economy has peaked.

(b). The business cycle is the up and down movements in Real GDP which occur over time.

(c). The trough is the low point in the business cycle.

(d). Disposable income is equal to personal income minus personal taxes.

(e). Net domestic product equals gross domestic product minus the capital consumption allowance, i.e. depreciation.

25. Explain the difference between a fixed-weighted and chain-weighted measure of prices.

As prices of goods increase, individuals will consume less of that good, and as prices of goods decrease, individuals will consume more of that good. A fixed-weight measure does not change the weights allotted to each component over time, but a chain-weighted index does change the weights.

26. Suppose GDP for a given year is 130.5 What does this mean?

This would mean that the GDP has increased by 30.5% from the base year.

■ LECTURE SUPPLEMENTS

"Counting the Jobless," *The Economist*, **July 22, 1995, p. 74.**

This article will provide students with a quick introduction to how different OECD countries measure the number of unemployed within their country. As they will see, countries differ in their definition of unemployed. "Unemployed" is applied to those who are actively looking for a job, but who have been unable to find one. Critics claim that *discouraged workers* who have given up looking for a job, and *involuntary part-time workers* who are working part-time because they have been unable to obtain a full-time job, should be included in the unemployment calculations.

The OECD data calculates the number of discouraged workers and involuntary part-time workers and adds them to the actual figures. Including these individuals would more than double the number of unemployed in Japan, but barely change the number of unemployed in Spain. The article draws no conclusion about which is the correct method, but ask your students whether they think these individuals should be included. Ask them how they would distinguish between discouraged and retired.

Gene Epstein, "Dueling Job-Longevity Studies: Why Do Their Findings Differ? And Which Is Correct?" *Barron's*, **June 12, 1995, p. 47**

This article raises the question of how reliable research data is. One question economists are analyzing currently is the stability of employment, i.e. are firms more likely to fire employees for downsizing or other reasons today than in the past, reducing job security? Two surveys asked individuals whether their employment situation was stable or volatile, but the two surveys came up with opposite results. One reason was the *way* the question was asked.

One survey asked "Did you have another main employer during the previous 12 months?" The other survey asked individuals, "How long have you been with your current employer?" The second question requires greater recall ability than the first question (how many months versus plus or minus 12 months), and men had a tendency to exaggerate their employment tenure. Over 10% of respondents reported their job tenure increasing by 24 months since the previous survey, when by definition, job tenure can increase by only 12 months in any year. But that raises the question of why individuals would tend to exaggerate their employment tenure more now than in the past.

The article concludes that the research by Rose (concluding that job stability has increased) seemed to be the more reliable evidence, not necessarily because the research was less susceptible to error, but because it seems to jive better with anecdotal evidence. Again, it is hoped that the article will make students think about the difficulty of getting accuracy when doing real-world economic research.

Gene Epstein, "You Won't Believe What Inflation Counters Have Discovered They've Been Doing Wrong," *Barron's*, January 9, 1995, p. 28.

This article discusses the difficulty of measuring consumer prices. The consumer price index (CPI) tends to overstate the inflation rate, and though a 0.1% difference may not seem like much, when many retirees' social security payments are tied to the CPI, that 0.1% difference can mean billions of dollars of difference to the government.

Primarily, the article points out that the CPI doesn't consider changes in quality and the impact this has on prices. For example, when a patented drug loses its patent, generic drugs replace them at a much lower price. Instead of substituting the generic drug for the patented drug in the CPI, the government continues to use the patented drug in its index, unless the patented drug is no longer available.

Another problem lies in measuring housing prices, which represent a significant portion of the CPI. Since houses are bought and sold infrequently, the Bureau of Labor Statistics uses rental prices as a proxy for housing, but how reliable is this proxy? Location is an important factor in housing prices, but rental housing may be located in different neighborhoods than houses are located in. And what if rental prices go up while housing prices go down? As above, the purpose is to help students understand the difficulties of getting accurate data.

CHAPTER 5

Aggregate Demand and Aggregate Supply: In the Short Run

Chapter 3 introduced students to the study of supply and demand, discussing the determinants of demand and supply for a particular product, graphing the demand and supply curves, and combining demand and supply analysis to study the market in and out of equilibrium. In this chapter, we follow much the same approach. Having laid the foundation for our study of the macroeconomy in Chapters 1-4, Chapter 5 develops an analytical framework upon that foundation, with which we can analyze the material in coming chapters. In this chapter, we look at the macroeconomy in the short run. We do this by looking at *aggregate demand*, deriving the *aggregate demand curve* and discussing the factors that affect it. Then we do the same for *aggregate supply*. Finally, we put aggregate demand and aggregate supply together.

■ CHAPTER OBJECTIVES

Upon completing this chapter, your students should be able to:

*   explain the downward slope of the *aggregate demand curve*;

*   identify the factors that can shift the aggregate demand curve;

*   define the *aggregate supply curve*, and identify the factors that can shift the aggregate supply curve;

*   find the *short-run equilibrium*, and explain the significance of being in and out of equilibrium; and

*   understand the relationship between changes in Real GDP and changes in the unemployment rate.

■ KEY TERMS

*   aggregate demand
*   aggregate supply
*   aggregate demand (AD) curve
*   real balance effect
*   monetary wealth
*   purchasing power
*   interest rate effect
*   international trade effect

*   wealth
*   exchange rate
*   appreciation
*   depreciation
*   M1 money supply
*   short-run aggregate supply (SRAS) curve
*   short-run equilibrium

61

■ CHAPTER OUTLINE

I. AGGREGATE DEMAND

A. **The Aggregate Demand Curve** -- As Exhibit 5-1 illustrates, the **aggregate demand (AD) curve** shows *the real output (Real GDP) that people are willing and able to buy at different price levels, ceteris paribus.*

B. **Why is the AD Curve Downward-Sloping?** -- The AD curve slopes downward because quantity demanded of GDP rises as the price level falls, and falls as the price level rises. But, why? [See Exhibit 5-2]

1. **The Real Balance Effect** -- One explanation is the **real balance (wealth) effect**, which says that, *as the price level rises, the real purchasing power of money falls, making people feel less wealthy, and inducing them to buy less goods and services; as the price level falls, the real purchasing power of money rises, making people feel more wealthy, and encouraging them to buy more goods and services.*

2. **The Interest Rate Effect** -- Related to the real balance effect, if the purchasing power of money held by households and businesses falls (because of a rise in the price level), they will have to borrow additional funds in order to complete their planned purchases (or investment, in the case of business). As more households and businesses demand credit, the interest rate rises, reducing actual borrowing, and curtailing planned consumption and investment. Thus, as the price level rises, interest rates rise, causing a decline in interest-sensitive consumption and investment spending. Similarly, as the price level falls, interest rates fall, enabling households and businesses to consume and invest more.

3. **The International Trade Effect** -- As the domestic price level rises, domestically-produced goods become relatively more expensive than foreign-made goods, both here at home and abroad. As a result, domestic consumers buy more foreign-made goods (imports rise), and foreign consumers buy fewer domestically-produced goods (exports fall). Similarly, when the domestic price level falls, domestic consumers buy fewer imports and foreign consumers buy more exports.

C. **A Change in the Quantity Demanded of Real GDP versus a Change in Aggregate Demand** -- A change in the quantity demanded of Real GDP occurs because of a change in the price level. This causes a movement along the aggregate demand curve, but not a shift in the aggregate demand curve, as illustrated in Exhibit 5-3a. A change in an economic variable other than price would be required to shift the aggregate demand curve as illustrated in Exhibit 5-3b. Here, the quantity of Real GDP changes even though price remains constant.

1. **Changes in Aggregate Demand** -- As we have just seen, a change in the price level causes a *movement along* a given AD curve. [See Exhibit 5-3(a)] What factors cause a shift from one AD curve to another? [See Exhibit 5-3(b)]. The

economy consists of four sectors (households, businesses, government and foreign), and each of those sectors buys a portion of GDP. The sum of their demands is known as *total expenditures (TE)* where

$$TE = C + I + G + (EX - IM)$$

Individuals will change their consumption due to either a change in the price level or a change in a nonprice factor. *A change in the price level will affect the quantity demanded of Real GDP, and a change in a nonprice factor will change aggregate demand.* You should also make sure your students understand the difference *between total expenditures* and *aggregate demand.* Total expenditures refer to the level of expenditures, while aggregate demand is a schedule showing different levels of aggregate demand which would exist at different price levels.

2. **What Can Shift the Aggregate Demand Curve?** -- Remember, *at a given price level, anything that changes total expenditures (TE) changes aggregate demand.* For this reason, any change in the individual components of total expenditures (C, I, G, or (EX - IM)) will change aggregate demand. If total expenditures increase, the aggregate demand curve will shift rightward; a decrease in total expenditures would cause a leftward shift in aggregate demand. Exhibit 5-4 summarizes how a change in the individual components of total expenditures affect aggregate demand.

D. **Factors That Can Change C, I, G, and EX-IM, and Therefore Can Change TE and AD** -- Exhibit 5-4 lists a number of factors that can influence consumption, investment and net exports, and thus aggregate demand. These factors include:

1. **Wealth** -- Individuals save money over time. If they were to use this wealth to purchase goods, the aggregate demand curve would shift to the right.

2. **Expectations about Future Prices and Income** -- If individuals expect higher prices or higher incomes in the future, they will increase current consumption and shift the aggregate demand curve to the right. If individuals expect lower prices or lower incomes in the future, they will decrease current consumption, shifting the aggregate demand curve to the left.

3. **Interest Rate** -- Interest rates affect both consumers and firms. Consumer durables often require financing, and a decrease in interest rates will lower the overall cost of purchasing consumer durables. If firms want to invest, they may also have to borrow money. Lower interest rates will cause consumption and investment to increase, shifting the aggregate demand curve to the right. An increase in interest rates would shift the aggregate demand curve to the left.

4. **Taxes** -- Higher taxes mean that individuals have less disposable income. The higher taxes will cut their consumption, shifting the aggregate demand curve to the left.

5. **Expectations About Future Sales** -- If firms expect sales to increase in the future, they will invest to meet this expected increase in demand. The increase in investment will shift the aggregate demand curve to the right.

63

6. **Business Taxes** -- An increase in business taxes lowers after-tax profitability causing businesses to reduce investment. The reduction in investment will shift the aggregate demand curve to the left.

7. **Foreign Real National Income** -- If foreigners have more real income, part of their increase in income will be used to purchase imports. If foreigners import more American goods, then American exports (EX) will rise. Total expenditures increase and aggregate demand shifts to the right.

8. **Exchange Rate** -- Exchange rates are the price of foreign currencies. An **appreciation** of the dollar means that the dollar has increased in price making American goods more expensive. A **depreciation** means that the dollar has decreased in price making American goods cheaper. An *appreciation* in the value of the dollar would decrease the demand for American goods and increase American demand for foreign goods. The aggregate demand curve would shift to the right. A *depreciation* would have the opposite effect.

E. **Can a Change in the Money Supply change Aggregate Demand?** -- Exhibit 5-4 does not include the *money supply*. An increase in the money supply (using the narrowest definition of the money supply--**the M1 money supply**--which includes *currency, checkable deposits, and traveler's checks*) would give consumers more money to spend. This would cause the aggregate demand curve to shift to the right. A decrease in the money supply would cause the aggregate demand curve to shift to the left.

F. **Exhibit 5-4 Is Incomplete In Another Way** -- Exhibit 5-4 includes interest rates as a factor affecting consumption and investment, but this begs the question, what causes interest rates to change? The primary factor causing a change in interest rates is a change in the demand for, and supply of credit (or loanable funds).

II. AGGREGATE SUPPLY

A. **The Short-Run Aggregate Supply Supply Curve** -- Exhibit 5-5 illustrates a *short-run aggregate supply (SRAS) curve*, showing *the real output (Real GDP) that producers will offer for sale at different price levels, ceteris paribus*. The upward slope of the curve indicates that producers are willing and able to sell more units of their goods as prices increase, and that their willingness (and, perhaps, ability) to sell falls as prices fall.

B. **Shifts in the Short-Run Aggregate Supply Curve** -- There are several important factors which will shift the SRAS curve.

1. **The Wage Rate (Labor Costs)** -- Higher wage rates mean higher costs of production. Given constant prices, higher costs reduce the profit per unit realized by producers, reducing the number of goods that producers are willing to sell at any price level. Lower wage rates lower the costs of production, raising profits per unit and, in turn, encouraging producers to supply more goods at any price level. Thus, *an increase in labor costs shifts the AS curve to the left; whereas, a decrease in labor costs will shift the AS curve to the right*. [See Exhibit 5-6]

2. **Prices of Nonlabor Inputs** -- Important nonlabor inputs such as energy, intermediate goods, land, and capital, will also have a significant impact on aggregate supply, and changes in any of these prices will result in a shift in the AS curve. *An increase in the price of any nonlabor input shifts the AS curve to the left; a decrease in the price of any nonlabor input shifts the AS curve to the right.*

3. **Productivity** -- the output produced per unit of input used, over some period of time. *Increases in the productivity of labor or any other input will shift the AS curve to the right; decreases in productivity will shift the AS curve to the left.*

4. **Supply Shocks** -- major natural or institutional changes that affect aggregate supply. Examples of *adverse* supply shocks are droughts, wars, and an oil embargo. Examples of *beneficial* supply shocks would include some major new energy discovery or exceptionally good weather. *Adverse supply shocks shift the AS curve to the left; beneficial supply shocks shift the AS curve to the right.*

C. **Putting AD and SRAS Together: Short-Run Equilibrium** -- It is important to remember that aggregate demand represents the buying side of the economy, and aggregate supply represents the selling side of the economy. Now we are about to bring these two sides together to find the short-run equilibrium for the economy.

1. **How Short-Run Equilibrium in the Economy Is Achieved** -- Exhibit 5-7 shows what happens when we combine an AD curve with a SRAS curve. The point where the two curves intersect (P_E, Q_E) is the point of **short-run equilibrium**, where aggregate quantity demanded and aggregate quantity supplied are equal. At any other price level, the economy is either in a surplus (P_1) -- in which case prices and output should fall, and consumption increase -- or a shortage (P_2) -- in which case prices and output should rise, and consumption should fall. Exhibit 5-8 shows the effects of shifting the AD and SRAS curves against one another.

2. **Changes in Real GDP and Changes in the Unemployment Rate** -- Changes in Real GDP will also affect unemployment. An increase in Real GDP will decrease unemployment, *ceteris paribus*, because more workers are needed to produce the additional output.

3. *Ceteris Paribus* **Makes all the Difference in the Relationship between Real GDP and the Unemployment Rate** -- *Ceteris paribus* is an important assumption here. If the labor force participation rate increased at the same time that Real GDP was increasing, the result could be an increase in unemployment. The *Global Economy* feature on "Life on the Frontier--Production Possibilities Frontier, That Is" also looks at changes in Real GDP.

4. **Thinking in Terms of Short-Run Equilibrium Changes in the Economy** -- Exhibit 5-9 pulls together the interaction of aggregate demand and short-run aggregate supply to determine the effect on the price level (P), Real GDP (Q) and the unemployment rate (U). For example, an adverse supply shock will shift the SRAS curve in, causing the price level to rise, Real GDP to fall, and unemployment to increase.

5. **AD-AS and the Vietnam War** -- Another example of the relationship between aggregate demand and unemployment, would be the Vietnam War. When the war escalated, the American economy was already producing at close to full output before the war began. Aggregate demand increased causing the price level and Real GDP to rise, and unemployment to fall.

D. **Does It Matter What Aggregate Supply Looks Like?** -- Up until now, we have looked at the short-run aggregate supply curve which is upward sloping. There are three other possible shapes of the aggregate supply curve.

1. **Horizontal AS Curve** -- This is shown in Exhibit 5-11a. This could occur when the economy is in a deep recession or depression and many economic resources are idle. Here, an increase in aggregate demand could increase Real GDP without increasing prices.

2. **Kinked AS Curve** -- A kinked AS curve is shown in Exhibit 5-11b. This could occur if the curve were horizontal up to the *natural* or *full-employment* level of Real GDP, and then vertical beyond that point. Beyond the kink, any increase in aggregate demand would cause the price level to increase, but not Real GDP.

3. **Three-Stage AS Curve** -- This combines the three possibilities mentioned until now and is illustrated in Exhibit 5-11c. Here the AS curve is initially horizontal due to idle resources, rises as the SRAS curve does, but reaches a vertical portion when full employment is reached. How the economy would respond to a change in Aggregate Demand would depend upon the condition of the economy.

III. **ECONOMICS ON THE INTERNET** -- Several good sources for information relating to aggregate supply and demand are provided, primarily by using the University of Michigan Gopher and the National Bureau of Economic Research.

■ ANSWERS TO CHAPTER QUESTIONS

1. Is aggregate demand a specific dollar amount? For example, is it correct to say that aggregate demand is, say, $1 trillion dollars this year?

Aggregate demand is not a specific dollar amount. It is a schedule that shows the Real GDP people are willing to buy at different price levels. Remember that along an AD curve there are many points, not just one.

2. Explain each of the following: (a) real balance effect, (b) interest rate effect, (c) international trade effect.

See Section I.B. in the outline for this chapter a detailed explanation of each of these effects.

3. Graphically portray each of the following: (a) a change in the quantity demanded of Real GDP, and (b) a change in aggregate demand.

A change in the quantity demanded is illustrated in Exhibit 5-3a of the text, and a change in aggregate demand is illustrated in Exhibit 5-3b of the text.

4. Explain the difference between total expenditures and aggregate demand. What are the four components of total expenditure?

Total expenditures are the actual level of expenditures which occur in the economy. Aggregate demand is a schedule showing the level of Real GDP at different price levels. The four components of total expenditures are consumption, investment, government purchases and net exports.

5. "The amount of Real GDP (real output) that households are willing and able to buy may change if there is a change in either (a) the price level, or (b) some non-price factor, such as wealth, interest rates, and so on." Do you agree or disagree? Explain your answer.

Agree. Both a change in the price level and changes in non-price factors could affect Real GDP; however, a change in the price level would change the quantity demanded of Real GDP, and a change in a non-price factor would cause a change in aggregate demand.

6. Explain what happens to the AD curve in each of the following cases:
   a. The interest rate rises.
   b. Wealth falls.
   c. The dollar depreciates relative to foreign currencies.
   d. Households expect lower prices in the future.
   e. Business taxes rise.

In examples (a), (b), (d) and (e), the aggregate demand curve would shift to the left, causing both Real GDP and the price level to decrease in the short run. In (c), the aggregate demand curve would shift to the right, causing both Real GDP and the price level to increase in the short run.

7. Will a direct increase in the price of U.S. goods relative to foreign goods lead to a change in the quantity demanded of Real GDP or to a change in aggregate demand? Will a change in the exchange rate that subsequently increases the price of U.S. goods relative to foreign goods lead to a change in the quantity demanded of Real GDP, or to a change in aggregate demand? Explain your answer.

In both cases, a change in aggregate demand will occur. A change in the quantity demanded of Real GDP would occur only if the price levels in both the U.S. and foreign countries changed by the same amount without any change in exchange rates. A change in relative prices or the exchange rates would cause a change in aggregate demand.

8. Explain how each of the following will affect short-run aggregate supply:
   a. an increase in wage rates
   b. a beneficial supply shock
   c. an increase in the productivity of labor
   d. a decrease in the price of a nonlabor resource (such as oil)

An increase in wages in (a) will shift the short-run aggregate supply curve to the left because the higher wage rates will cause Real GDP to be produced at a higher price level than existed before. The three remaining changes in (b), (c) and (d) would each shift the short-run aggregate supply curve to the right. As a result of these changes, the same level of Real GDP could be produced at a lower price level.

9. In the text, we distinguished between a change in the quantity demanded of Real GDP and a change in aggregate demand, but we did not distinguish between a change in the quantity supplied of Real GDP and a change in short-run aggregate supply. What do you think the difference is between a change in the quantity supplied of Real GDP and a change in short-run aggregate supply. (Hint: Which of the two refers to a movement along a given SRAS curve and which refers to a shift in the SRAS curve?)

A change in the price level would cause a movement along the SRAS, and a change in a non-price economic factor would cause a shift in the SRAS curve.

10. A change in the price level affects which of the following?
    a. the quantity demanded of Real GDP
    b. aggregate demand
    c. short-run aggregate supply
    d. the quantity supplied of Real GDP

A change in the price level would affect the quantity demanded of Real GDP and the quantity supplied of Real GDP (both (a) and (d)), but it would not change either aggregate demand or short-run aggregate supply (either (b) or (c)).

11. In the short run, what is the impact on the price level and Real GDP of each of the following:
    a. an increase in consumption brought about by a decrease in interest rates
    b. a decrease in exports brought about by an appreciation of the dollar
    c. a rise in wage rates
    d. a beneficial supply shock
    e. an adverse supply shock
    f. a decline in productivity

a. A decrease in interest rates increases autonomous consumption which shifts the AD curve rightward. Assuming SRAS is constant, the price level and Real GDP rise.
b. An autonomous decrease in exports shifts the AD curve leftward. Assuming SRAS in constant, the price level and Real GDP fall.
c. A rise in wage rates shifts the SRAS curve leftward. Assuming AD is constant, the price level rises and Real GDP falls.
d. A beneficial supply shock shifts the SRAS curve rightward. Assuming AD is constant, the price level falls and Real GDP rises.

e. An adverse supply shock shifts the SRAS curve leftward. Assuming AD is constant, the price level rises and Real GDP falls.

f. A decline in productivity shifts the SRAS curve leftward. Assuming AD is constant, the price level rises and Real GDP falls.

12. Explain why there is an inverse relationship between Real GDP and the unemployment rate, *ceteris paribus*.

An increase in Real GDP reflects an increase in the level of output. More workers are needed to produce this output, and when more workers are hired, the unemployment rate will fall, *ceteris paribus*.

■ LECTURE SUPPLEMENTS

Robert Barro, "The Aggregate Supply-Aggregate Demand Model," *Eastern Economic Journal*, Winter 1994, pp. 1-6.

Robert Barro makes some important criticisms of the aggregate supply-aggregate demand model in this article. There are a number of logical inconsistencies in the aggregate supply-aggregate demand model which brings its usefulness and applicability into question. You should read this article before going over this chapter to help you understand the underlying assumptions of the model and their validity.

Gary S. Becker, "Bedtime for Big Government," *Business Week,"* July 24, 1995, p. 22.

This article talks about increasing demand for a smaller role of the government in society, not only in the United States, but in France, Brazil, South Africa and other countries. The reason for including this article is not necessarily to debate the proper size of government, but to make students think how these changes will affect aggregate demand and aggregate supply.

Downsizing government also means less demand, as anyone in the defense industry in southern California has found out during the past five years. In the *short run*, reducing the size of government means lower total expenditures by society and will shift the aggregate demand curve to the left. Real GDP falls as does the price level. Is this good?

Presumably, the reason for these changes is that the private sector can provide some services more efficiently than the government, and government regulation reduces efficiency. By reducing the size and regulatory powers of government, in the long run, aggregate supply will shift to the right, increasing Real GDP and lowering the price level. This is good. But as southern California has found out, reaching that long run may take longer than was anticipated.

The real point of this exercise is to get students to think of political policies in terms of the macroeconomy and how these changes affect aggregate supply and aggregate demand.

Andy Zipper, "And Now, the Bad News," *Barron's*, December 5, 1994, pp. 33-39.

Chapter 5 introduces consumption as one of the four basic components of total expenditures. This article will get students to think about the composition of consumption from an intergenerational point of view. Consumption comes not only from earned income, but from savings and wealth. Someone who is 30 will be relying primarily upon current income for their consumption, but someone who is 80 will rely primarily upon their accumulated wealth.

Individuals dissave when they are young (paying for college, housing, cars, kids), save when they are middle-aged (once the "fixed costs" of life have been paid for, and they have to start saving for retirement), and dissave again when they retire. Ask your students to think how changing age distributions affect consumption.

As the article points out, the redistribution of wealth which will occur when the baby boomers' parents pass on has affected their consumption and saving habits. One study found that baby boomers can expect to inherit *$10.4 trillion* from their parents. That would pay for a lot of consumption, and reduce baby boomers' need to save.

In fact, the actual inheritances of the baby boomers will probably be a lot smaller than anticipated. Moreover, boomers save about half of what their parents saved and can expect more sluggish wage growth than their parents received. And what if boomers' parents are so inconsiderate as to live longer than anticipated and take more vacations than planned, reducing the amount of inheritance which they leave?

Should boomers save more than they are currently saving? What impact will this have on consumption? On savings? Does it make a difference whether parents or boomers spend the wealth? What effect does the expectation of inheritance have on consumption and saving? As always, get your students to think about economic issues and go beyond the theoretical constructs to real world problems and issues.

CHAPTER 6

AD-AS in the Long Run and the Self-Regulating Economy

Chapter 5 introduced us to aggregate demand and short-run aggregate supply, showing how these concepts can be used to determine the short-run equilibrium within the macroeconomy. This chapter uses the aggregate demand-aggregate supply framework to analyze the behavior of the economy in the long run. After this has been done, the chapter analyzes the concept of the self-regulating economy which is advocated by some economists.

■ CHAPTER OBJECTIVES

Upon completing this chapter, your students should be able to:

- understand the concepts of the *natural unemployment rate* and *Natural Real GDP*;

- identify the three states of the economy: *long-run equilibrium, recessionary gap and inflationary gap*;

- explain how the economy responds when it is in a *recessionary gap* or an *inflationary gap*;

- use the *institutional and physical production possibilities frontiers* to analyze the constraints on and the potential output capabilities of the economy; and

- use the aggregate demand/long-run aggregate supply framework to analyze the behavior of the economy in the long run.

■ KEY TERMS

- Natural Real GDP
- full-employment Real GDP
- potential output
- recessionary gap
- long-run aggregate (LRAS) curve

- inflationary gap
- self-regulating economy
- long-run equilibrium
- laissez-faire

■ CHAPTER OUTLINE

I. **THREE STATES OF THE ECONOMY** -- The three states of the economy depend upon the relative positions of *Real GDP* and *Natural Real GDP*. **Natural Real GDP (Full-Employment Real GDP or potential output)** is the level of Real GDP which occurs when the economy is operating at its natural unemployment rate. The economy can operate in one of three possible states.

A. **One Possible State of the Economy: Real GDP is Less Than Natural Real GDP** -- *If the economy is operating at a level below the Natural Real GDP*; that is, if:

Real GDP < Natural Real GDP,

then a **recessionary gap** is said to exist. When there is a recessionary gap, buyers are demanding less than the economy is capable of producing. It is also important to note that *if Real GDP is less than the Natural Real GDP, then the unemployment rate must be higher than the natural rate of unemployment.* [See Exhibit 6-1a]

B. **Another Possible State of the Economy: Real GDP is Greater Than Natural Real GDP** -- *If the economy is operating at a level above the natural real GDP*; that is, if:

Real GDP > Natural Real GDP,

then an **inflationary gap** is said to exist. When there is an inflationary gap, buyers are demanding more output than the economy is capable of producing at normal operating rates. In such a case, the actual unemployment rate will be less than the natural rate of unemployment. [See Exhibit 6-1b]

C. **Still Another State of the Economy: Real GDP is Equal to Natural Real GDP** -- On the other hand, the economy could be in equilibrium. In this case, the economy is producing at a level of output where

Real GDP = Natural Real GDP

When this occurs, the economy is said to be in a **long-run equilibrium**. This situation is illustrated in Exhibit 6-1c.

II. **THE SELF-REGULATING ECONOMY** -- Some economists believe that the **economy is self-regulating**. This means that if the economy is in either a recessionary gap or an inflationary gap, through its own internal mechanism, the economy will return to its long-run equilibrium, producing at Natural Real GDP. Those who believe in the self-regulating economy fall into one of three economic schools of thought: *classical, new classical,* and *monetarist*. Let's see how this could occur.

A. **What Happens if the Economy Is In a Recessionary Gap?** -- In a recessionary gap, the unemployment rate is higher than the natural unemployment rate. [See Exhibit 6-2a] Some economists argue that the economy will right itself by lowering the wage rate (since there is excess unemployment), in order to push the SRAS curve rightward. [See Exhibit 6-2b] This, in turn, will lower prices and cause an increase in consumption. This process will continue until the economy reaches the long-run equilibrium point 2, where the Natural Real GDP is equal to $6,000 billion.

B. **What Happens if the Economy Is In an Inflationary Gap?** -- In an inflationary gap, the unemployment rate is lower than the natural unemployment rate. [see Exhibit 6-3a] Input costs tend to rise, shifting the SRAS leftward from $SRAS_1$ to $SRAS_2$. [See Exhibit 6-3b] Prices begin to rise, causing a reduction in consumption, shown as a leftward movement along the existing AD curve. This process continues until the economy reaches the long-run equilibrium at point 2.

III. **THE SELF-REGULATING ECONOMY: A RECAP** -- The basic idea of the self-regulating economy is that if the economy is in an inflationary gap, wage rates will rise and shift the SRAS curve to the left until the economy returns to its long-run equilibrium. If there were a recessionary gap, wage rates would fall and the SRAS curve shift to the right until the economy returned to equilibrium.

A. **How Can the Unemployment Rate Be Less Than the Natural Unemployment Rate?** -- To understand how this can occur, you have to be able to differentiate between the *physical PPF* and the *institutional PPF* (see Exhibit 6-4). The physical PPF illustrates the different combinations of goods the economy can produce given the physical constraints of (1) finite resources and (2) the current state of technology. The institutional PPF imposes a *third constraint*: institutional constraints such as minimum wage laws or price controls. If society's institutional constraints were not fully effective, the economy could operate beyond its institutional PPF and cause the unemployment rate to be less than the natural unemployment rate; however, the economy could not operate beyond the physical PPF.

B. **The Long-Run Aggregate Supply Curve** -- The **LRAS curve** *shows the real output (Real GDP) the economy is capable of supplying at different price levels, assuming wage rates and all other input costs have fully adjusted to eliminate any inflationary or recessionary gaps.* The LRAS curve is depicted as a vertical line perpendicular to the real output axis at the Natural Real GDP, as shown in Exhibits 6-1 through 6-3. It follows that **long-run equilibrium** is *the intersection of the AD curve and the LRAS curve.* [See Exhibit 6-5]

C. **Policy Implication of Believing the Economy Is Self-Regulating** -- Economists who believe that the economy is self-regulating have a simple prescription: "Economy, heal thyself." There is no need to intervene in the economy because *changes in wages and prices* will eliminate inflationary gaps and recessionary gaps. Economists who advocate this approach to macroeconomic policy are said to advocate a **laissez-faire** approach.

D. **The Natural Unemployment Rate and Policy** -- The Federal Reserve uses monetary policy (influencing interest rates and the money supply) to influence the economy. In 1994, the Fed fervently feared that the economy would soon fall below its natural unemployment rate creating inflationary pressures on the economy. To prevent this possibility, the Fed raised interest rates. The problem is that economists are not certain whether the natural unemployment rate is currently at 5%, 6% or some other level. If the Fed's perception of the natural unemployment rate was wrong, they could have unnecessarily pushed the economy into a recession. It is because of this uncertainty over the true level of the natural unemployment rate and how a misinterpretation of it could cause economic harm that economists such as Milton Friedman would prefer that the Fed not intervene in the economy.

IV. **ECONOMICS ON THE INTERNET** -- This section shows how to use the University of Michigan Gopher to access historical GDP data, and how to use the Sam Houston State University Gopher to access price data. Students will like the source page for jokes about economists.

■ ANSWERS TO CHAPTER QUESTIONS

1. What does it mean to say the economy is in a recessionary gap? An inflationary gap? Long-run equilibrium?

In a recessionary gap, Real GDP < Natural Real GDP. In an inflationary gap, Real GDP > Natural Real GDP. When Real GDP = Natural Real GDP, the economy is said to be in long-run equilibrium.

2. Describe the relationship of the (actual) unemployment rate to the natural unemployment rate in each of the following economic states: (a) a recessionary gap, (b) an inflationary gap, and (c) long-run equilibrium.

In a recessionary gap, the actual unemployment rate is greater than the natural unemployment rate; in an inflationary gap, the actual unemployment rate is less than the natural unemployment rate; and in long-run equilibrium, the actual unemployment rate equals the natural unemployment rate.

3. According to classical, new classical, and monetarist economists, what happens--step-by-step--when the economy is in a recessionary gap? What happens when the economy is in an inflationary gap?

According to classical, new classical, and monetarist economists, the economy is self-regulating. If the economy is in a recessionary gap, it will move back to its long-run equilibrium without any intervention by the government. In a recessionary gap, excess unemployment exists. This will cause wages to fall, lowering prices. The SRAS curve will shift to the right, moving along the AD curve until the economy returns to its long-run equilibrium. In an inflationary gap, unemployment is below its natural rate creating wage inflation. This shifts the SRAS curve to the left, moving along the AD curve until the economy returns to its long-run equilibrium.

4. If wage rates were not flexible, would the economy be self-regulating? Explain your answer.

Flexible wages are an essential assumption of the self-regulating economy. Without flexible wages, the SRAS would not shift in response to an inflationary gap or recessionary gap. Without this flexibility, the economy could not move back to its long-run equilibrium, and the economy would not be self-regulating.

5. **Explain how the economy can operate beyond its institutional PPF, but not beyond its physical PPF.**

The institutional PPF includes institutionally/government-imposed restrictions on economic activity, such as the minimum wage. Because the minimum wage reduces economic efficiency, it could prevent the economy from operating on its physical PPF; however, inflation could reduce the real minimum wage, allowing the economy to move closer to its physical PPF. Since the physical PPF is determined by the nation's resource endowment and technology, the economy could not operate beyond the physical PPF.

6. **Explain the importance of the real balance, interest rate, and international trade effects to long-run (equilibrium) adjustment in the economy.**

The real balance, interest rate, and international trade effects explain the downward slope of the AD curve. Each reflects how aggregate demand responds to a change in prices. For example, an increase in prices reduces the purchasing power of consumers' bank accounts and other cash-related assets. Consequently, an increase in prices would reduce aggregate demand. When the SRAS curve shifts, the price level will adjust upward or downward, and to keep the economy in equilibrium, the real balance, interest rate, and international trade effects allow the economy to move along the AD curve to the new equilibrium.

7. **Diagrammatically represent an economy in (a) an inflationary gap, (b) a recessionary gap, and (c) long-run equilibrium.**

These three situations are illustrated in Exhibit 6-1.

8. **Suppose the price level is 132, the quantity demanded of Real GDP is $4,000 billion, the quantity supplied of Real GDP in the short run is $3,900, and the quantity supplied of Real GDP in the long run is $4,300 billion. Is the economy in short-run equilibrium? Will the price level in long-run equilibrium be greater than, less than, or equal to 132? Explain your answers?**

An economy is in short-run equilibrium when aggregate demand equals short-run aggregate supply. In this example, aggregate demand ($4,000 billion) is greater than short-run aggregate supply ($3,900 billion). The economy is not in short-run equilibrium. When aggregate demand is less than long-run equilibrium, the economy is in a recessionary gap. In order to bring the economy back into long-run equilibrium, prices will have to fall. In long-run equilibrium, the price level would be less than 132.

9. **Suppose the price level is 110, the quantity demanded of Real GDP is $4,000 billion, the quantity supplied of Real GDP in the short run is $4,900, and the quantity supplied of Real GDP in the long run is $4,100 billion. Is the economy in short-run equilibrium? Will the price level in long-run equilibrium be greater than, less than, or equal to 110? Explain your answers.**

In the short run, aggregate demand ($4,000 billion) is less than short-run aggregate supply ($4,900 billion) so the economy is not in short-run equilibrium. Since aggregate demand ($4,000 billion) is less than long-run aggregate supply ($4,100 billion), the economy is in a recessionary gap. In order to bring the economy back into long-run equilibrium, prices will have to fall. In long-run equilibrium, the price level would be less than 110.

■ LECTURE SUPPLEMENTS

"The Cost of Inflation," *The Economist*, May 13, 1995, p. 78.

This chapter introduces students to how changes in aggregate supply and aggregate demand affect the economy's price level. Since economists constantly wonder about costs, this raises a natural question--what is the *cost* of inflation? This article tries to answer this question.

There are several potential costs to the economy from inflation. It hampers growth, it causes uncertainty about future prices which in turn affects decisions about consumption, saving and investment; it can redistribute income from savers to borrowers, and so forth. Most importantly, if inflation discourages savings, it will in turn discourage investment, and thus growth. A simple scatter diagram comparing inflation and growth between 1960 and 1990 shows no discernible relationship between inflation and growth.

Robert Barro's research, however, tries to give a more exact measurement. First, he tries to determine any causation, from inflation to growth or vice versa. He finds that a one percentage point increase in inflation reduces growth by 0.02 to 0.03 percentage points per year. Initially, the benefit may hardly seem worth the cost of restrictive policies designed to limit inflation; however, over a long period of time, an extra 0.10% rate of growth per year (assuming inflation is reduced from 7% to 2%, for example) can compound to create a difference in the level of per capita income. Moreover, other studies have estimated the cost of inflation as being five to ten times greater than Barro's estimates.

Should governments fight inflation? If voters perceive the costs of inflation to be high, they will demand it. This is probably why most governments are trying to reduce inflation.

"What's So Natural About the 'Natural Rate of Unemployment?'", *Challenge, July-August 1995*, pp. 52-53.

According to the Humphrey-Hawkins Full Employment and Balanced Growth Act of 1978, the government is supposed to keep unemployment in the United States to 4 percent. The government has not actively tried to push unemployment down to this level, in part because many economists estimate that the nonaccelerating inflation rate of unemployment (NAIRU) is between 5.5 and 6.5 percent. But is NAIRU (another term for the natural rate of unemployment) at this level, lower, higher? Is the NAIRU fixed, or can it change over time? Is it the same in New Jersey as it is in Utah?

The article focuses on Utah which has seen its unemployment rate fall from 6.3 percent in 1980 to 3.7 percent in 1994 (versus 7.1 percent and 6.1 percent respectively for the entire United States). The authors assert that despite the falling unemployment rate, no inflationary wage pressures have developed. Housing prices have increased, but they claim this owes more to higher population growth (Mormons have more children per family than non-Mormons) than lower unemployment.

Their conclusion? The NAIRU concept is faulty. According to the authors, "No level of unemployment can be characterized as inherently natural." Why is this important? Because government policy is influenced by perceptions of whether the economy is approaching the nonaccelerating inflation rate of unemployment. If the NAIRU is believed to be 6.5%, and the economy approaches that level, the government may cut back on spending or raise taxes to reduce inflationary pressures. But what if the real NAIRU is 5%? Then the government would be cutting its spending prematurely. This raises another question, if the government doesn't know what the true NAIRU is, and if it differs from one state to the next, should the government allow an unknown NAIRU to influence its fiscal policy?

Robert Kuttner, "The Natural Rate of Inflation Isn't Carved in Stone," *Business Week*, **June 6, 1994, p. 20.**

This article takes a similar point of view to the one above, only it applies it to the natural rate of inflation instead of the natural rate of unemployment. Students should learn why it is important whether there is a natural rate of inflation and what its level is. The natural rate of inflation influences Federal Reserve Bank policy. If the Fed believes that the inflation rate is accelerating, the Fed will tighten monetary policy, choking off investment and growth through higher interest rates and restrictive monetary supply growth. The article raises the question of whether the Fed knows what the natural rate of inflation is, whether it changes over time, and whether it even exists.

Edmund S. Phelps has found that the natural rate can change. Excessive payroll taxes can raise the natural rate of unemployment, and wage subsidies can push it down. Union behavior can also influence the natural rate. The article points out that structural differences between the United States and Europe have tended to push up the natural rate in Europe (due to unions, minimum wages, and social supports) and push it down in the United States (due to workers' reduced bargaining power and technology). On the other hand, more structural unemployment in the form of unskilled workers could push the natural rate up in the United States. If the natural rate changes, then government policy should adjust to these changes, a fact which is reflected in a quote from Labor Secretary Robert B. Reich.

CHAPTER 7

Economic Instability: A Critique of the Self-Regulating Economy

In Chapter 6, we introduced the idea of the self-regulating economy. According to classical, new classical, and monetarist economists, the economy can move back to its long-run equilibrium without direct government intervention in the market. Some economists take the opposite point of view: the economy is inherently unstable and not self-regulating. Chapter 7 looks at the *Keynesian approach to the economy.* The chapter both critiques the concept of the self-regulating economy, and introduces the Keynesian model which uses the *consumption function, total expenditures, total production, the propensity to consume and save,* and *the multiplier* to explain how the economy adjusts to disequilibrium and why the economy may be unable to get out of a recessionary gap by itself.

■ CHAPTER OBJECTIVES

Upon completing this chapter, your students should be able to:

- define *Say's law* and explain its significance to classical economic thought;

- present and comprehend Keynes's major criticisms of classical economic theory;

- compare and contrast the fundamental beliefs of classical and Keynesian economists about the stability and soundness of the market economy and its ability to achieve and maintain full-employment equilibrium;

- state the assumptions of the basic Keynesian theory;

- identify three important points which Keynes made concerning the *consumption function;*

- explain how the interaction of total expenditures and total production determine whether the economy is in equilibrium; and

- understand the *multiplier* concept and derive the simple multiplier.

■ KEY TERMS

- efficiency wage models
- Say's law
- credit market
- consumption function
- marginal propensity to consume (MPC)

- autonomous consumption
- marginal propensity to save (MPS)
- average propensity to consume (APC)
- average propensity to save (APS)
- multiplier

■ CHAPTER OUTLINE

I. **GETTING STUCK IN A RECESSIONARY GAP**

A. **John Maynard Keynes on Wage Rates** -- Keynes felt that monopoly power on the part of producers (in the product market) and labor unions (in the labor market) would prevent prices and wages, respectively, from freely adjusting downward in response to an oversupply of goods and/or labor. Consequently, aggregate supply would be unable to adjust to changes on the demand side of the economy as readily as classical economists theorized.

B. **New Keynesians and Wage Rates** -- *New Keynesian* economists follow in Keynes' footsteps, but offer new ideas of their own. They argue that firms and workers prefer long-term labor contracts because they *produce fewer labor negotiations, fewer strikes, and greater job security*. One cost of this is reduced wage flexibility. Similarly, New Keynesian economists believe that the **efficiency wage model** can also explain why wages are inflexible. Under the efficiency wage model, labor productivity depends on the wage rate paid to employees, and *a cut in wages could reduce labor productivity*. Paying a higher-than-market wage rate encourages employees to be more productive and reduces shirking.

C. **Classical Economists and Keynes on Prices** -- According to the Classical model, competition forces prices down when excess demand exists. Keynes pointed out that the structure of the economy might not be competitive enough to allow downward price flexibility, reducing the ability of the economy to be self-regulating.

D. **Is It a Question of the Time It Takes For Wages and Prices to Adjust?** -- Exhibit 7-2 shows how the wage rate and price level fall to push the economy back to its long-run equilibrium. Keynes said this would not happen, and classical economists said that it would in a relatively short period of time. But how short is short? If this adjustment process takes *five years*, as it may, the self-regulating economy provides little consolation if you are unemployed during this period of time. According to Keynes, *the economy was not self-regulating in the short run*, and for this reason, the government might need to intervene in the economy.

II. **CAN AGGREGATE DEMAND BE TOO LOW? KEYNES AND CLASSICAL ECONOMISTS** -- To understand the differences between Keynes and the Classical economists, we need to take a closer look at Classical economists' views on the economy.

A. **Classical Economists and Say's Law** -- Say's Law holds that *supply creates its own demand* -- that is, everything that is produced will be purchased; therefore, there can be no *general overproduction* or *general underproduction* of goods. The notion is that producers supply their goods in order to gain the means to purchase other goods. Thus, if the act of supplying goods is directly linked to demanding other goods, supply will create an equal amount of demand.

B. **Classical Economists and Interest Rate Flexibility** -- For Say's law to hold in an economy with money, savings must generate an equal amount of investment. In order for this to happen, the **credit market** must be able to vary the interest rate up and down in order to equilibrate savings and investment. [See Exhibit 7-3] If there is a reduction in consumption, the result is an increase in savings. Higher savings will shift the savings curve to the right, reducing interest rates. Lower interest rates will increase investment enough to *exactly offset the fall in consumption*. Using the formula for *total expenditures*:

$$TE = C + I + G + (EX - IM)$$

it can be seen that if consumption increases by 100 and investment decreases by 100, then total expenditures will remain constant.

C. **Keynes's Criticism of Say's Law in a Money Economy** -- Keynes argued that it was possible (rather obviously so, if one simply looked around) to have a general overproduction of goods resulting from savings in excess of investment. Classical theory relied upon changes in the interest rate to equilibrate savings and investment, but Keynes argued that people save and businesses invest for a number of reasons, and the interest rate is only one factor in the decision process. Specifically, Keynes saw saving as being most responsive to changes in income, and investment being most responsive to business expectations and changes in technology.

D. **The Great Depression: Explanations and World-Wide Effects** -- This *Global Economy* feature updates this debate using Christina Romer's updated analysis of the Great Depression. Her evidence (provided in Exhibit 7-13) shows that aggregate demand fell and unemployment rose in 1929-1932 compared with 1925-1928, but the question remains, why?

1. **The Keynesian Explanation** -- Keynesians argue that the cause of the depression was a sharp reduction in investment. In the 1920s, increased demand from American and European consumers combined with optimism and led to increased production. But excess capacity caused the multiplier to work in reverse producing declines in consumption and Real GDP.

2. **The Monetarist Explanation** -- Monetarists point to a sharp drop in the money supply between 1929 and 1933 which shifted the AD curve leftward. Furthermore, government policies which propped up prices and wages shifted the SRAS curve leftward. Both of these changes reduce Real GDP. Without these failures in government monetary and fiscal policies, the economy would have recovered from the Great Depression much more quickly.

III. **THE KEYNESIAN FRAMEWORK OF ANALYSIS** -- Keynes's model of the economy shows how and why the economy may not be self-regulating. To do this we must use the *income-expenditure (I-E) framework*, referred to as the *Keynesian framework*. Remember that in this

80

model, the price level is assumed to be constant, so all factors are measured in their real magnitudes.

A. **Total Expenditures and Consumption** -- *Total expenditures* is the sum of consumption, investment, government purchases, and net exports. Of these four, consumption represents the largest share, and for this reason, Keynes concentrated his analysis on consumption.

B. **Consumption** -- Keynes made three basic points about consumption and disposable income. First, consumption depends upon disposable income. Second, consumption and disposable income move in the same direction (are directly related). Third, when disposable income changes, consumption changes by less.

1. **The Consumption Function** -- We specify this relationship using the consumption function:

$$C = C_0 + MPC(Y_d),$$

where C = total consumption, C_0 represents autonomous consumption (consumption independent of disposable income), MPC (marginal propensity to consume) is a fraction between 0 and 1, and Y_d stands for disposable income.

Furthermore, since all income must be either consumed or saved, we can calculate the value of saving (S) as

$$S = Y_d - C = Y_d - (C_0 + MPC(Y_d)).$$

2. **The MPC and MPS** -- Keynes said that for every dollar increase in income, consumption would increase by less than a dollar. In Exhibit 7-6, for every dollar change in income, consumption increases by 80 cents. This is called the **marginal propensity to consume (MPC)**, and it is equal to the change in consumption brought about by a change in income. That is,

$$MPC = \Delta C / \Delta Y_d .$$

A similar concept, the **marginal propensity to save (MPS)**, is the change in saving brought about by a change in income. That is,

$$MPS = \Delta S / \Delta Y_d .$$

Finally, since we know that all income must be either consumed or saved, then any change in income must also either be consumed or saved. Therefore,

$$MPS + MPC = 1.$$

3. **The APC and APS** -- Another important concept is the **average propensity to consume (APC)**, which is the portion of income spent on consumption, or

$$APC = C/Y_d .$$

A related concept is the **average propensity to save (APS)**, which is the portion of income saved, or

$$APS = S/Y_d.$$

Again, since all income must be either consumed or saved, it follows that

$$APC + APS = 1.$$

C. **Deriving a Total Expenditures (TE) Curve** -- Total expenditures is the sum of its parts: consumption, investment, government purchases, and net exports, so let's bring these four sources of expenditures together. The different sectors are illustrated in Exhibit 7-7.

   1. **Consumption** -- Exhibit 7-7a diagrams a consumption function. Notice that the consumption function does not start at the origin, this is because we assume that C_0 has a positive value. The other important thing to catch is the slope of the consumption function -- it is equal to the MPC.

   2. **Investment** -- Investment is a much smaller and much more volatile component of aggregate demand than is consumption. Part of the reason for its volatility is the important role that (very subjective) expectations play in determining investment plans. To simplify matters, we assume for now that investment is constant. [See Exhibit 7-7b]

   3. **Government Purchases** -- Again, to simplify matters we assume that government spending is constant. [See Exhibit 7-7c]

   4. **Net Exports** -- As the world grows increasingly "smaller," it is both necessary and fitting to consider the implications of exports and imports on domestic national income. Net exports are assumed to be constant for now. [See Exhibit 7-7d]

D. **Comparing Total Expenditures (TE) and Total Production (TP)** -- Total expenditures and total production can differ from one another if businesses produce an amount of goods which differs from the amount which the four sectors of the economy buy. The dollar value of total production can be greater than, less than, or equal to totoal expenditures.

E. **Moving from Disequilibrium to Equilibrium** -- We cannot know how much of an inventory a firm will hold, but we do know that there is an optimal inventory that firms can hold. This concept leads to two cases.

   1. **Case 1: TP > TE** -- *If TP > TE, firms will involuntarily accumulate inventory.* This will signal firms that they have overproduced. Subsequently, firms should cut back on production and/or prices, which will, in turn, decrease the total value of output.

   2. **Case 2: TP < TE** -- *If TP < TE, inventories will be depleted unexpectedly.* This will signal firms that they have not produced enough. Subsequently, firms should increase production and/or prices, which will, in turn, increase the total value of output.

F. **The Graphical Representation of the Three States of the Economy in the Keynesian Framework** -- The three states of the economy are presented in Exhibit 7-8. The TP (Real GDP) curve is represented by a 45-degree line. Q_1 is representative of the case where TP > TE, and Q_2 is representative of the case where TP < TE. In the first case(Q_1), overproduction has occurred and inventories have built up, so firms cut back on production. Real GDP falls to its equilibrium at Q_E. In the second case(Q_2), inventories fall below optimal levels and firms increase production. Real GDP rises to its equilibrium at Q_E.

G. **Can the Economy Be in a Recessionary Gap and in Equilibrium, Too?** -- As shown in Exhibit 7-8, it is certainly possible for the economy to be at a point such as Q_E where the economy is producing at a Real GDP level that is less than the Natural Real GDP, but is in a recessionary gap.

H. **Going from the Keynesian Framework to the AD-AS Framework** -- Exhibit 7-10 shows how to get from the Keynesian framework to the AD-AS framework. Both 7-10a and 7-10c show the economy in a recessionary gap. The former uses the Keynesian framework, and the latter uses the AD-AS framework.

I. **The Multiplier** -- Keynes observed that changes in *autonomous expenditures* -- those expenditures independent of income -- could create even larger changes in national income. As Exhibit 7-11 shows, an upward shift in the total expenditures function results in a larger change in national income. The process is explained in Exhibit 7-12. The basic idea is that any increase in autonomous spending -- those parts of C, I, G, and (EX - IM) that are not affected by income -- generates income for the recipients of that spending. From that new income, the recipients increase their consumption. By how much will national income rise in response to an increase in autonomous expenditures? The value of the multiplier is

$$\text{Multiplier (m)} = 1/(1 - \text{MPC});$$

and, the total change in national income is equal to the multiplier *times* the initial change in autonomous expenditures. That is,

$$\Delta \text{Real GDP} = m \times (\Delta \text{ autonomous expenditures}).$$

J. **The Multiplier: One Step at a Time** -- Exhibit 7-12 explains how the multiplier works, following its path one step at a time. A $60 million increase in government spending with an MPC equal to .80 would produce successive spending increases of $48 million, $38.4 million, and so on. The net increase in autonomous government purchases would be $300 million. You might also want to use the *Economics In Our Times* feature "Spring Break Meets the Multiplier" to explain the concept to your students.

K. **The Multiplier and Reality** -- Reality demands that we make a couple of basic points about the multiplier presented here. First, the multiplier takes time to work itself out. The effect described here is not instantaneous by any means. Second, for the multiplier to continuously increase real national income as described, there must be idle resources available at each expenditure "round." Otherwise, nominal income can continue to rise, but real income will not, therefore meaning that prices must rise.

IV. ECONOMICS ON THE INTERNET -- Usenet newsgroup sites are discussed in this chapter. In particular, the address for the White House is provided which can be used to link to other Federal agencies.

■ ANSWERS TO CHAPTER QUESTIONS

1. According to Keynes, why might the economy get stuck in a recessionary gap?

Wages and prices might not be as flexible as classical economists had assumed. It could take years for the economy to adjust to a new equilibrium, leaving the economy in a recessionary gap for years before the self-regulating economy moved back to its long-run equilibrium.

2. Give two reasons why wage rates may not fall.

Keynes felt that monopoly power on the part of labor unions would prevent wages from freely adjusting downward in response to an oversupply of goods and/or labor. In addition, the existence of long-term employment contracts, even in the absence of unionization, would make wages "sticky."

3. According to New Keynesian economists, why might business firms pay wage rates above market-clearing levels?

This is the efficiency wage theory which says that lowering workers' wages might cause reductions in productivity and cause workers to shirk while on the job. If the reduction in productivity were greater than the reduction in wages, the firm would be worse off from lowering wages.

4. According to classical economists, does an increase in saving shift the AD curve to the left? Explain your answer.

According to classical economists, an increase in saving would lower interest rates which in turn would increase investment. The increase in investment would be offset by a reduction in consumption which would result from the increase in saving among individuals. The result of the two effects would be that the AD curve would not shift.

5. According to Keynes, can an increase in saving shift the AD curve to the left? Explain your answer.

According to Keynes, interest rates are not the only determinant of investment. Although higher savings would lower interest rates, it would not automatically generate an increase in investment sufficient to offset the reduction in consumption. Consequently, the AD curve could shift to the left when savings increased.

6. **What is the classical economic position with respect to (a) wages, (b) prices, and (c) interest rates?**

These are the prices for labor, goods, and capital. Since classical economists believe the economy is self-regulating, all three markets are assumed to be flexible in prices both upward and downward. Any changes in demand or supply which create a short-run disequilibrium will generate changes in wages, prices or interest rates which move the markets for labor, goods and capital back into equilibrium.

7. **Explain how to derive a total expenditures (TE) curve.**

This is illustrated in Exhibit 7-7. The total expenditures curve is the horizontal summation of the consumption, investment, government purchases, and net exports curves.

8. **Explain the ways in which consumption can increase.**

Consumption can change in one of three ways: a change in autonomous consumption, a change in disposable income (through a change in taxes), and a change in the marginal propensity to consume (which also changes the marginal propensity to save).

9. **Explain what happens in the economy if total production (TP) is greater than total expenditures (TE). Explain what happens if TE is greater than TP.**

If TP > TE, firms will involuntarily accumulate inventory. This will signal firms that they have overproduced. Subsequently, firms should cut back on production and/or prices, which will, in turn, decrease the total value of output. If TP < TE, inventories will be depleted unexpectedly. This will signal firms that they have not produced enough. Subsequently, firms should increase production and/or prices, which will, in turn, increase the total value of output.

10. **Answer the following questions:**
    a. **Suppose the MPC = .80, and that it is the same at all Real GDP levels. Suppose autonomous consumption decreases by $500. How much does Real GDP change?**
    b. **Suppose the MPS = .10, and that it is the same at all Real GDP levels. Suppose autonomous investment increases by $100. How much does Real GDP change?**
    c. **Suppose the MPC = .70, and that it is the same at all Real GDP levels. Suppose autonomous consumption increases by $500 and autonomous investment decreases by $80. How much does Real GDP change?**

a. M = 1/(1 - MPC) = 1/(1 - .80) = 5. If autonomous consumption decreases by $500, then Real GDP *decreases* by five times this amount, or $2,500.
b. M = 1/(1 - MPC), which can be written as 1/MPS. The multiplier in this problem is thus equal to 1/.10, or 10. If autonomous investment increases by $100, then Real GDP *increases* by ten times this amount, or $1,000
c. M = 1/(1 - MPC) = 1/(1 - .70) = 3.33. Autonomous consumption increases by $500, but autonomous investment decreases by $80, then the net increase in spending is $420. If autonomous spending increases by $420, then Real GDP *increases* by 3.33 times this amount, or $1,400.

11. Will an increase in, say, autonomous spending always increase Real GDP by some multiple? Why or why not?

In general, if the marginal propensity to consume is positive, an increase in autonomous spending will generate some increase in Real GDP. However, there is an exception to this rule. The result depends on whether idle resources exist or not. If no idle resources exist, complete crowding out could occur and no increase in Real GDP would result. If there are idle resources and the MPC is positive, then an increase in Real GDP will occur.

12. Diagrammatically represent an economy in a recessionary gap in the Keynesian framework and in the AD-AS framework.

This is done in Exhibit 7-10.

13. Although we did not discuss an inflationary gap in this chapter, it can be diagrammatically represented within the Keynesian framework. Please do so.

This could be done by placing Natural Real GDP (Q_N) at point Q_2 in Exhibit 7-8.

14. Classical economists assumed that wage rates, prices, and interest rates were flexible and would adjust quickly. Consider an extreme case: Suppose classical economists believed wage rates, prices, and interest rates would adjust *instantaneously*. What would this imply the classical aggregate supply (AS) curve would look like? Explain your answer.

Under this assumption, the classical aggregate supply curve would be a vertical line. Instantaneous adjustment would mean that there would never be any deviations from the natural unemployment rate or the Natural Real GDP level. Supply and demand in individual markets would quickly respond to any shifts in supply and demand eliminating recessionary gaps and inflationary gaps very quickly.

15. Suppose there is an increase in autonomous investment spending with no decline in any other spending component of total expenditures. Furthermore, suppose the multiplier is fully operable: there is a multiple increase in Real GDP equal to the change in investment spending times the multiplier. What does all this imply about the shape of the aggregate supply curve? Explain your answer.

This implies that the aggregate supply curve is upward sloping. The increase in autonomous investment spending creates an increase in Real GDP greater than the increase in autonomous investment spending. In general, the higher the value of the multiplier, the flatter the SRAS curve. The flatter the SRAS curve, the larger will be the increase in Real GDP which results from any change in aggregate demand.

■ LECTURE SUPPLEMENTS

David Wessel, Paul Carroll, and Thomas Vogel Jr., "How Mexico's Crisis Ambushed Top Minds in Officialdom," *Wall Street Journal*, July 6, 1995, p. A1.

Exploring the collapse of the peso and the subsequent downturn in Real GDP is a good way of exploring what a recessionary gap is, how it comes about, and how it evolves over time. An example like this can bring a theoretical construct such as a recessionary gap to life for your students. The article is not only useful for reminding students of what a recessionary gap is, but in detailing the interaction between the government and markets which bring about a downturn in Real GDP. What this article makes painfully clear is that governments and private investors are intimately tied to one another. Self-regulating economies on automatic pilot just do not exist in the real world.

The collapse of the peso shows how the government responds to changes in the macroeconomy can dramatically influence shifts in aggregate supply and aggregate demand, sometimes for the worse. Although in the long run, the economy may be self-regulating, in the short run, both the private and public sector may overreact or not choose the best policies pushing the economy away from equilibrium in the short run.

As the article points out, even though Mexico would have been better off devaluing in November rather than in December, because of the political transition from one administration to another, a devaluation became politically impossible. Although not mentioned in the article, more recent analysis of the Mexican peso collapse shows that it was primarily Mexican money moving out of Mexico in November that reduced Mexico's reserves, forcing the government to devalue.

When Mexico did eventually devalue in December, the response of investors triggered a collapse in the peso. Private investors made matters worse. As the article says, the Mexican crisis "demonstrates both how vulnerable nations can be to hot money and how foreign investors can be misled by a sophisticated sales pitch." Foreign investors who had placed too much faith in Mexico, now had no faith at all. Use this example to make recessionary gaps come alive to your students and get a debate going over how self-regulating the economy is.

Gene Epstein, "Sorry , Mr. Keynes: Contrary to Your Theory, Many Hourly Workers Seem Willing to Accept Pay Cuts," *Barron's*, June 5, 1995, p. 48.

Are workers willing to accept pay cuts? Are wages and prices downwardly flexible? This is the heart of the debate between Keynesians and Classical economists. This article draws on research by Ben Craig at the Cleveland Federal Reserve in a study called "Are Wages Flexible?" Craig studied census data on hourly workers between 1983 and 1986. Individuals were asked if they were paid on an hourly basis, and if so, what was the pay rate on their most recent paycheck. This enabled the Census Bureau to chart the ups and downs of pay rates over a period of several years. Since workers had to refer to their paycheck to give an answer, response bias was reduced. Both union and non-union workers were included.

The results? Surprisingly, 78% of workers surveyed had at least one pay cut during this period of time, and half accepted at least two pay cuts. Even union workers had pay cuts. Though union contracts would tie pay rates to specific positions, the position a worker filled could be changed imposing a de facto pay cut. Other factors could introduce pay cuts. Construction workers got paid more when they worked in downtown Cleveland than when they worked in the suburbs. Landscapers received lower hourly wages during the winter than during the summer.

Another surprising finding was that the frequency and size of wage cuts were positively correlated. Individuals who suffered frequent wage cuts also received larger wage cuts, when they occurred, than people for whom wage cuts were infrequent. Craig's conclusion? Wage flexibility is the norm, not the exception.

Gene Epstein, "The Rise of Replacement Workers Discourages Strikes, But Spurs Other Forms of Labor Strife," _Barron's_, May 29, 1995, p. 30

The flexibility of wages and prices depends upon the interaction of management and unions. If management is able to replace union workers with other (non-union) workers, then wages will be more flexible. This article describes current tactics management is using to win the upper hand against unions and make sure wages and hiring are flexible.

As the article points out, only about 10% of private firms are unionized now, and strikes are more infrequent among firms which are unionized. Instead of striking, many unions now favor holdouts in which workers continue on the job even after a union contract has expired, but the workers follow the letter and not the spirit of the work rules. This process can lead to slowdowns which affect productivity, but not enough to violate work rules.

Another reason for this is that firms are increasingly willing to hire permanent workers to replace striking employees, rather than hire temporary workers while the union workers are on strike. Some firms may even try to force a strike in order to hire a new set of non-unionized employees. In the 10-month strike at Firestone, management hired 2,300 workers to replace those who were on strike. The union eventually caved in. In March 1995, President Clinton issued an executive order that prohibits Uncle Sam from contracting with firms that hire permanent replacements during a strike. How effective this executive order will be remains to be seen.

How flexible wages are remains a matter of debate, but it would be hard to argue that wages are becoming more inflexible.

David Colander, "The Stories We Tell: A Reconsideration of AS/AD Analysis," The Journal of Economic Perspectives," (9) 3, Summer 1995, pp. 169-188.

Although this article may be a bit too dense for most students or classes, if you have a particularly advanced group of students, they could benefit immensely from this article. But even if you do not introduce this article directly into classroom discussion, you will find it useful to review prior to going over the aggregate demand-aggregate supply model in this and the next chapter.

It would be difficult to summarize this article in a few sentences and do justice to Colander's work, but the essence of the article is that the standard aggregate demand-aggregate supply model has a number of inconsistencies inherent in its foundations and presentations which make its use as an explanation of how the macroeconomy works questionable. Colander goes over these logical inconsistencies in detail, showing why even though the AS-AD model may appear to be the natural twin of the demand-supply model used in microeconomics, it really is not. After presenting the problems with the model, Colander offers three solutions on how to deal with the problems presented by the AS-AD model. The article can also be useful in helping you to forestall criticisms of the AS-AD which your students may raise if they perceive the inconsistencies which the model presents.

CHAPTER 8

Fiscal Policy

Government plays many roles in the economy: it regulates economic activity; it collects taxes; it spends money on goods and services, as well as transfer payments; it borrows funds in the financial markets; and, it produces goods and services, both for its own use and for the private sector. While all of these activities affect economic performance, the government's taxing and spending powers -- collectively labeled *fiscal policy* -- are probably the most important, and certainly the most often used for purposes of intentionally affecting output, prices, and unemployment. Chapter 8 begins with some basic definitions, and then follows with a discussion of demand-side and supply-side fiscal policy, addressing both the mechanics of fiscal policy and its effectiveness in stabilizing the economy.

■ CHAPTER OBJECTIVES

Upon completing this chapter, your students should be able to:

- define *fiscal policy*, distinguish between the four types of fiscal policy presented in this chapter, and give examples of each;

- compare and contrast the old-time fiscal religion, and the new fiscal religion on the appropriate way to conduct fiscal policy;

- demonstrate the mechanics of *discretionary fiscal policy* within the Keynesian framework, explaining how advocates of large government and advocates of small government would differ in their approaches;

- understand the government multiplier, and how a change in government spending affects Real GDP, both when there is no increase in taxes and when there is an equal change in taxes;

- understand the concept of *crowding out (crowding in)* and the effect of crowding out on the effectiveness of discretionary fiscal policy;

- identify the five sources of *time lags* in making discretionary fiscal policy;

- explain the new classical view on fiscal policy, budget deficits, and interest rates; and,

- describe the possible effects of changes in tax rates on aggregate supply.

■ KEY TERMS

- budget deficit
- budget surplus
- balanced budget
- fiscal policy
- expansionary fiscal policy
- contractionary fiscal policy
- discretionary fiscal policy
- automatic fiscal policy

- tax base
- balanced budget theorem
- crowding out/crowding in
- complete crowding out (in)
- incomplete crowding out (in)
- trade deficit
- marginal tax rates
- Laffer curve

■ CHAPTER OUTLINE

I. **A FEW FACTS AND DEFINITIONS**

A. **The Federal Budget: Expenditures and Tax Receipts** -- The federal budget is composed of two, not necessarily equal, parts: expenditures (G) and tax receipts or revenues (T). If expenditures > tax receipts, then a **budget deficit** is said to exist. If tax receipts > expenditures, then a **budget surplus** is said to exist. And, if tax receipts = expenditures, we have a **balanced budget**.

B. **What is Fiscal Policy?** -- *Fiscal policy refers to changes in government expenditures and taxation designed to achieve particular macroeconomic goals.* Fiscal policy is the most important economic tool available to the federal government.

1. **Expansionary Fiscal Policy** -- policy aimed at increasing AD and/or SRAS through increases in government spending and/or decreases in taxes.

2. **Contractionary Fiscal Policy** -- policy aimed at decreasing AD and/or SRAS through decreases in government spending and/or increases in taxes.

3. **Discretionary vs. Automatic Fiscal Policy** -- Any expansionary or contractionary fiscal policy move may be designed in one of two ways. **Discretionary fiscal policy** involves *deliberate changes in government spending and/or taxes* to achieve particular economic objectives. **Automatic fiscal policy**, sometimes called "automatic stabilizers," involves *changes in government spending and/or taxes that occur automatically, without any additional action.*

C. **Different Types of Fiscal Policy** -- Exhibit 8-1 illustrates the four types of fiscal policy: *discretionary expansionary*, *discretionary contractionary*, *automatic expansionary*, and *automatic contractionary*, along with examples of each.

II. **THE RISE OF DISCRETIONARY FISCAL POLICY**

A. **The Old-Time Fiscal Religion** -- Before the Keynesian revolution, the commonly accepted beliefs about fiscal policy could be summarized as follows:

1. **The Federal Budget Should Be Balanced** -- With the one exception of wartime, the budget should always be balanced; furthermore, surpluses should be run after a war to pay off the deficits incurred during the war.

2. **Increased Federal Spending Should Be Tied to Higher Taxes, So That Individuals Can Correctly Judge the True Cost of Government.**

3. **Government Spending and Taxing Powers Should Be Directed to Providing the Citizenry With Publicly Demanded Goods and Services and Should Not Be Used to Manipulate Macroeconomic Variables** -- The government's only proper role in the economy is to provide publicly-demanded goods and services that the private economy cannot, or will not, provide for itself.

B. **Discretionary Fiscal Policy Moves to Center Stage** -- According to Keynesian theory, budget deficits would be the natural response to a recessionary gap and budget surpluses the natural response to an inflationary gap. When it did not prove politically expedient to raise taxes and lower government spending to create budget surpluses, some economists began to ask if the new fiscal religion favored expansionary fiscal policy without ever introducing contractionary fiscal policy.

III. DEMAND-SIDE FISCAL POLICY

A. **How Do Changes in *G* and *T* Affect Aggregate Demand?** -- An increase in government spending would shift the aggregate AD to the *right*, while a decrease in government spending would shift the AD curve to the *left*. Contrarily, an increase in taxes would reduce consumption and investment, shifting the AD curve to the *left*; a decrease in taxes would shift the AD curve to the *right*.

B. **Fiscal Policy: A Keynesian Perspective** -- The Keynesian prescription for a *recessionary gap* (where actual output is less than full employment output) is to use discretionary expansionary fiscal policy to increase AD. The Keynesian prescription for an *inflationary gap* (where actual output is greater than full employment output) is to use discretionary contractionary fiscal policy to decrease AD. As Exhibit 8-2a illustrates, *expansionary fiscal policy shifts the AD curve to the right, raising output and the price level; while contractionary fiscal policy shifts the AD curve to the left, lowering output and the price level.* Exhibit 8-3b illustrates the case of contractionary fiscal policy.

C. **The Calculations** -- A change in either government purchases or taxes will have a measurable effect on equilibrium real output greater than the magnitude of the change itself. That is, both government purchases (G) and net taxes (T) are subject to the multiplier effect.

1. **The Expenditures Multiplier** -- A change in G, like a change in any of the other autonomous components of total planned expenditures, will change Q such that

$$\Delta \text{Real GDP} = m \text{ x } \Delta G,$$

where m = 1/(1 - MPC).

2. **The Tax Multiplier** -- A change in autonomous net taxes will also change Q by a multiple of itself. However, the formula is different. Specifically,

$$\Delta \text{Real GDP} = -\text{MPC}(m) \ \mathbf{x} \ \Delta T;$$

that is,

$$\Delta \text{Real GDP} = -\text{MPC}[1/(1 - \text{MPC})] \ \mathbf{x} \ \Delta T.$$

3. **The Balanced Budget Theorem** -- What happens if both G and T increase (decrease) by the same amount? The **balanced budget theorem** tells us that *Y will increase (decrease) by precisely the amount of the increase (decrease) in G if both G and T increase (decrease) by the same amount.* Thus, we can expand (contract) the economy without necessarily adding to our budget deficit (surplus).

D. **Crowding Out: Calling the Effectiveness of Fiscal Policy into Questions** -- How well does discretionary fiscal policy work in the "real world?"

1. **What is Crowding Out?** -- *Increases in government purchases may result in decreases in private (consumption and/or investment) spending.* This may occur for a couple of reasons. For a practical application of the concept of crowding out, see the *Economics In Our Times* feature, "What Does the Deficit Have to Do with Buying a House?"

   a. **Direct Substitution** -- Increases in government purchases may reduce the availability of goods and services for private consumption and/or investment. Thus, we are effectively substituting public consumption for private consumption.

   b. **Interest Rate Effects** -- Government borrowing to finance a deficit may raise interest rates, making it more expensive for businesses and households to borrow money, and thereby reducing the amount of private investment.

2. **How Significant is Crowding Out?** -- Crowding out may be either ***complete*** -- that is, one-for-one replacement of private spending by public spending -- or ***incomplete*** -- the reduction in private spending is less than the increase in public spending. Exhibit 8-3 illustrates the effects of an expansionary fiscal policy under the assumptions of no crowding out, incomplete crowding out, and complete crowding out. See Exhibit 8-4 for a summary of the effects of crowding out.

3. **Crowding In** -- When government spending is decreased, private spending may increase, causing national income and AD to decrease by less than would be predicted. This *crowding in* may also be either complete or incomplete.

E. **Crowding Out, the Interest Rates, and Foreign Loanable Funds** -- The extent to which private borrowing may be crowded out due to deficit borrowing will be tempered by the availability of foreign capital inflows (increases in loanable funds). If foreigners make funds available to help finance a deficit, there will be less upward pressure on the interest rate, and thus less crowding out of private borrowers. However, this may not be the whole story. The purchase of U.S. dollars (by foreigners) to provide deficit financing may drive up the value of the dollar; and, in turn, hurt our net export position. Thus, while there may be less crowding out in the financial market, there may be a reduction in net exports, thus crowding out private expenditures.

F. **The New Classical View of Fiscal Policy: Crowding Out with No Increase in Interest Rates** -- New classical economics adds another wrinkle to crowding out. The argument is that people perceive deficit (debt) financing as merely postponed taxes. Therefore, they increase savings in anticipation of higher taxes in the future. This increase in savings offsets the increase in borrowing, thus preventing a rise in real interest rates. But, the increase in savings also means a decrease in consumption, thus there is a direct substitution effect. According to the new classical economists, *as long as expansionary fiscal policy is translated into higher future taxes (which new classical economists think is likely), there will be no change in Real GDP, unemployment, the price level, or interest rates.* This process is illustrated in Exhibit 8-5.

G. **Lags and Discretionary Fiscal Policy** -- Even if discretionary fiscal policy is effective at changing Real GDP, there is another problem that must be considered: There are potentially significant *time lags* involved in the process of identifying economic problems, deciding on how to address them, getting policy through "channels," and having that policy finally take effect. The problem posed by time lags is that they may negate the effectiveness of discretionary fiscal policy by making it take effect too late. In fact, if the policy takes effect late enough, it may actually cause more problems than it solves.

1. **The Data Lag** -- the time between when a potential problem arises and when policymakers notice it.

2. **The Wait-and-See Lag** -- the time between when policymakers notice a potential problem and when they decide it is worthy of action.

3. **The Legislative Lag** -- the time it takes to get a policy action approved.

4. **The Transmission Lag** -- the time required to put a policy into effect.

5. **The Effectiveness Lag** -- Once a policy is put into effect, it takes time for the economy to respond.

D. **Crowding Out, Lags, and the Effectiveness of Fiscal Policy** -- Keynesians usually view fiscal policy as effective, meaning that there is relatively little crowding out, and lags are short. Classical economists believe fiscal policy is ineffective, meaning that there is crowding out, and lags are long.

IV. **SUPPLY-SIDE FISCAL POLICY** -- Fiscal policy effects may be felt on the supply side as well as the demand side of the economy. Supply-side fiscal policy focuses on taxation issues.

A. **Marginal Tax Rates and Aggregate Supply** -- When fiscal policy measures affect tax rates, they may affect the SRAS curve as well as the AD curve. For example, consider the reduction in the *marginal tax rate* illustrated in Exhibit 8-7. All other things held constant, *if the **marginal tax rate** (Δ tax payment / Δ taxable income) falls, short-run AS will increase. If the lower marginal tax rates are permanent, then so will be the change in AS -- that is, the long-run AS (LRAS) curve will shift to the right as well.*

93

B. **The Laffer Curve: Tax Rates and Tax Revenues** -- What happens to total tax receipts if the tax rate is decreased (increased)? While the answer may appear to be intuitively obvious, economist Arthur Laffer has developed a model of why the answer may be different than we expect.

   1. **The Laffer Curve** -- shows the relationship between tax rates and tax revenues. According to Laffer, *as tax rates rise from zero, tax revenues rise, reach a maximum point, and then fall as the tax rate continues to rise.* [See Exhibit 8-8]

   2. **The Tax Revenue Equation** -- The key to understanding Laffer's argument is the equation

      tax revenues = tax base **x** (average) tax rate,

      where the **tax base** is the total amount of taxable income.

   3. **When Revenues Rise and When They Fall** -- Exhibit 8-9 shows, *if the tax base increases by more than the tax rate falls, then tax revenues will increase; if the tax base increases by less than the tax rate falls, then tax revenues will decrease.* Tax revenues increase on the downward-sloping portion of the curve when tax rates are reduced (between points B and C), and tax revenues decrease following a tax rate reduction in the upward-sloping portion of the curve (between points A and B).

C. **Journalists, Taxes, and Perceptions** -- This *Economics In the Media* feature will help students understand the extent of the tax burden and how it has increased over time. It measures taxes in terms of days worked rather than raw dollar amounts, showing that the number of days workers work before "tax freedom" day comes has increased from 93 days in 1950 to 125 days in 1994. Nevertheless, compared to other countries, Americans pay a smaller portion of their incomes in taxes than people in most developed countries (Exhibit 8-10). So whether Americans are overtaxed or undertaxed lies in the eye of the beholder.

V. **ECONOMICS ON THE INTERNET** -- Need information on government expenditures and taxes? This section provides addresses for accessing this data.

■ ANSWERS TO CHAPTER QUESTIONS

1. **Explain three ways crowding out may occur.**

Crowding out may occur because individuals substitute government goods for private goods, because the interest rate increases and investment falls, or because saving increases to offset higher future taxes. For example, consider an increase in government spending on public education that increases the budget deficit. Crowding out may result because individuals buy less private education; because financing the deficit pushes interest rates upward and investment falls; or because taxpayers anticipate higher future taxes and increase current saving (and decrease current consumption).

2. Why is crowding out an important issue in the debate over the use of discretionary fiscal policy?

Those who advocate the use of discretionary fiscal policy believe it is capable of affecting the aggregate demand curve and therefore Real GDP. Crowding out calls the effectiveness of discretionary fiscal policy into question. For example, if an increase in government purchases causes private expenditures to fall by the same amount, then there is complete crowding out and the aggregate demand curve does not shift. Thus there is no change in Real GDP.

3. Some economists argue for the use of discretionary fiscal policy to solve economic problems; some argue against its use. What are some of the arguments on both sides?

We shall direct our answer to demand-side discretionary fiscal policy only. Those in favor often argue that the economy is not always self-regulating and that sometimes it needs a push to move it in the right direction. Discretionary fiscal policy is that push. They also argue that discretionary fiscal policy has worked. Those against often argue that the economy is self-regulating, that the existence of lags can turn a potentially effective fiscal policy measure into the "wrong medicine at the wrong time," and that the existence of crowding out places a question mark over the effectiveness of fiscal policy.

4. Assume MPC = .80 and that taxes are cut by $4 billion and government purchases are increased by $7 billion. By what dollar amount will Keynesian economists predict Real GDP will increase?

We know that
$$\Delta Q = m \times \Delta G \quad \text{and} \quad m = 1/(1 - MPC);$$
so,
$$\Delta Q = (1/1 - MPC) \times \Delta G = (1/1 - .80) \times (+ \$7\text{billion}) = 5 \times (+ \$7 \text{ billion}) = + \$35 \text{ billion}$$

We also know that
$$\Delta Q = - MPC \ (m) \times \Delta T;$$
so,
$$\Delta Q = - MPC(m) \times \Delta T = - .80(5) \times (- \$4 \text{ billion}) = - 4 \times (- \$4 \text{ billion}) = + \$16 \text{ billion}.$$

And, $35 billion   (the increase in Q due to the increase in G)
      + $16 billion   (the increase in Q due to the decrease in T)
      = $51 billion.

5. The debate over using government spending and taxing powers to stabilize the economy involves more than technical economic issues. Do you agree or disagree? Explain your answer.

We agree. Two technical issues that divide economists have to do with crowding out (Is there crowding out or not?) and the existence and importance of lags (Are there lags? To what degree do they diminish the effectiveness of fiscal policy? Are there ways to get around them?). Besides disagreeing on technical points, economists may disagree as to the right and wrong of running budget deficits on moral grounds, the long-run political consequences of permitting government to run continuous annual deficits, and much more. Simply put, economic debates are not always strictly limited to technical economic issues.

6. The Laffer curve, which shows (among other things) that a tax rate reduction can increase tax revenues, became very popular and was widely cited a couple of years before, during, and for a few years after the presidential election of 1980. Why do you think this happened?

Candidate Reagan, and later President Reagan, felt that the federal income tax was too high, and was hampering private spending initiatives. As a result, he wanted to push for tax cuts. The emergence of the Laffer curve as a (arguably) sound theoretical argument to support tax cuts, by suggesting that tax cuts may actually increase tax revenues, was seized by the Reagan camp and carried through the primaries, the presidential campaign, and on to Capitol Hill in 1981.

7. Is crowding out equally likely under all economic conditions? Explain your answer.

No. The closer the economy is to its production possibilities frontier (i.e., full employment) and/or the steeper the SRAS curve, the greater the likelihood of significant crowding out. The condition of the financial market is also important. The tighter the supply of money and/or loanable funds, the greater the likelihood of reduced private borrowing in the case of a budget deficit.

8. Tax cuts will likely impact aggregate demand and aggregate supply. Does it matter which is affected more? Explain in terms of the AD-AS framework.

Yes. If AD and SRAS both increase, real output will increase. However, the effect on the price level depends upon the relative magnitudes of the changes in AD and SRAS. If AD increases by more than SRAS, then the price level will rise. If SRAS increases by more than AD, then the price level will fall. And, if AD and SRAS increase proportionally, then the price level should remain constant.

9. Explain how a growing federal budget deficit may lead to a growing trade deficit.

Generally speaking, the trade deficit is the amount by which the value of imports exceeds the value of exports. As discussed in the chapter, deficit spending increases domestic real interest rates, causing the value of the dollar to appreciate, as foreign investors seek to take advantage of relatively higher interest rates in the U.S. As the value of the dollar rises, U.S.-made goods become relatively more expensive than foreign-made goods, causing foreign consumers to buy fewer U.S.-made goods -- decreasing the value of exports -- and causing U.S. consumers to buy more foreign-made goods -- increasing the value of imports. Thus, as the value of imports rises and the value of exports falls, the trade deficit increases. And, as long as deficit spending persists, one should expect the "trade gap" to persist as well.

10. What does complete crowding out imply about the value of the multiplier? Explain your answer.

In order for crowding out to be complete, the value of the multiplier must be 0 -- otherwise, there would be some net increase in Real GDP brought about by the increase in autonomous expenditures, despite the reduction in domestic investment and/or consumption in response to a higher real interest rate.

11. Assume MPC = .75 and that taxes are raised by $5 billion and government purchases are decreased by $12 billion. By what dollar amount will Keynesian economists predict real GDP will decrease?

Using the same methodology as in Question #4 above,

$$\Delta Q = (1/1 - MPC) \times \Delta G = (1/1 - .75) \times (- \$12 \text{billion}) = 4 \times (- \$12 \text{ billion}) = - \$48 \text{ billion}$$

and,

$$\Delta Q = - MPC(m) \times \Delta T = - .75(4) \times (+ \$5 \text{ billion}) = - 3 \times (+ \$5 \text{ billion}) = - \$15 \text{ billion}.$$

So,   - $48 billion   (the decrease in Q due to the decrease in G)
       - $15 billion   (the decrease in Q due to the increase in T)
    = - $63 billion.

■ LECTURE SUPPLEMENTS

Gene Epstein, "Despite Supply-Side Theory, Slimmer Tax Rates Don't Necessarily Fatten Uncle Sam's Wallet," _Barron's_, August 21, 1995, p. 29.

This article will allow your students to get a more current view of Laffer's supply curve which examines the relationship between taxes and work effort. Even though the article claims "we're all supply-siders" now, it shows that there are still many different positions on that side. Whereas it is certainly true that at a 0% income tax and a 100% income tax, the government would collect the same amount of revenue--zero--the shape of the curve in between those two points remains in doubt.

The article refers to a recent study, "The Taxation of Two-Earner Families," by the National Bureau of Economic Research President Martin Feldstein and NBER economist Daniel Feenberg. It focuses on the potential for extra work from the non-working spouse in a family with two adults. The question is, "Will higher tax rates keep the non-working spouse, usually a female, from going into the labor force?" The authors conclude that if there were a targeted tax break directed at non-working spouses, this would increase their labor participation.

Laffer claims that net tax revenues would increase. Their work shows the opposite, and the article would be useful for students at this point because it breaks down the costs and benefits, both to the government and consumers. The tax cut would cost the government $7.9 billion directly, though they would collect an extra $2.7 billion in social security and income taxes. Non-working spouses would gain $7.4 billion in income, but their work would cost them $3.6 billion in child care and other expenses. Individuals would gain a net $3.8 billion, and the government would lose a net $5.2 billion, contra Laffer.

Paul Krugman, "Long-Term Riches, Short-Term Pain," *New York Times,* **September 25, 1994, Business Section, p. 9.**

This opinion piece discusses the trade-offs countries face in imposing stringent fiscal policies on their economies. The short-term pain refers to the cutbacks in spending and the increases in taxes which countries must impose to get their fiscal house back in order, but as Paul Krugman points out, these changes do allow the country to begin growing again, and if these changes can place the country on the path of long-term economic growth, then the long-term benefits will more than justify the short-term costs. You might combine this opinion piece with the article below to give both a theoretical and empirical view of fiscal policy in action.

Matt Moffett, "Taking a Huge Risk, Argentina Intentionally Deflates Its Economy," *Wall Street Journal,* **March 21, 1995, p. A1.**

This article will provide your students with an example of fiscal policy in action. Argentina had one of the highest levels of per capita income in the world 75 years ago, but now it has been surpassed by many other countries. In recent years it has suffered from some of the highest inflation rates in the world. This history has made Argentina fervently dedicated to divorcing themselves from their past and creating an economy which has price stability, no matter what the costs. This dedication is exemplified by the slogan "Death before devaluation," which is quoted in the first paragraph.

Argentina has maintained its currency at one Argentinean peso to the U.S. dollar between 1992 and 1995, and the government had no desire to break this link for the fear that any devaluation would once again send the economy down the path to hyperinflation. The problem is that after the Mexican peso crisis, foreign inflows into Argentina dried up, and the only way Argentina could maintain its pegged currency rate was to deliberately deflate its economy to raise productivity and badly needed export earnings. The government also increased taxes and tariffs while cutting government expenditures. To put downward pressure on wages, the government trimmed official salaries exceeding $2,000 a month and extracted a pledge from the country's most powerful industrialists to cut executive salaries by around 20%. This deflation has been costly: unemployment is approaching 20%.

These are not easy choices and decisions to make. Although this is an extreme case of fiscal policy in action, it is a good one. Get your students to ask themselves whether they think the government's measures are too extreme. Make sure they see the role of the past in influencing current policy. Germany's aversion to inflation comes from their experiences in the 1920s. Will Argentina's inflation leave a similar legacy?

Martin Feldstein, "Behavioral Responses to Tax Rates: Evidence from the Tax Reform Act of 1986," *American Economic Review,* **May 1995, pp. 170-174.**

This article provides a quick summary of the lessons which economists have learned from the monumental tax changes which occurred during the 1980s. The Tax Reform Act of 1986 provided an ideal economic experiment in which ideas about how individuals respond to changes in their tax rates. His conclusions?

First, men showed a relatively small supply response to the tax changes; women showed a larger response. Changes in marginal tax rates had a large impact on the labor supply of married women. Second, tax changes affect the way people are compensated. The reduction in tax rates meant that people were more willing to take taxed income compensation, as opposed to nontaxed fringe benefits, than had been true before the tax reforms. The tax changes increased taxable income substantially more than aggregate hours, especially among taxpayers in high tax brackets. Third, capital gains realizations were found to be highly sensitive to tax rate changes.

Do individuals respond to marginal tax changes? The evidence says they do, and shows more clearly exactly how they respond to these changes.

CHAPTER 9

Money and Banking

What is *money*? Where does it come from? What purposes does it serve? To what extent can we control the amount and disposition of money? The answers to these questions lay a very significant part of the foundation of the macroeconomy. Money is essential in promoting the level of exchange and savings/investment essential to maintaining and expanding a $6 trillion economy. This chapter takes up the questions of what money is and is not, where it comes from, what gives money its value, and how banks and the banking system can influence and control the supply and disposition of money. Chapter 10 will continue this discussion, turning to the institution that oversees the U.S. banking system and the supply of money in the U.S. economy: the *Federal Reserve System* (the Fed).

■ CHAPTER OBJECTIVES

Upon completing this chapter, your students should be able to:

- define *money*, compare and contrast it to common (mis-)conceptions of what money is;

- discuss the three functions of money;

- trace the origins and evolution of money and banking;

- identify *M1* and *M2* and define the various components of each;

- understand the concept and reasons for *fractional reserve banking*; and,

- describe the process by which the banking system "creates" and "destroys" money, and the assumptions that underlie *multiplier* theory.

■ KEY TERMS

- money
- barter
- medium of exchange
- transaction costs
- unit of account
- store of value

- liquid asset
- overnight repurchase agreements
- overnight Eurodollar deposits
- fractional reserve banking
- Federal Reserve System (the Fed)
- reserves

- M1
- currency
- Federal Reserve Notes
- checkable deposits
- M2
- time deposits
- savings deposits
- double coincidence of wants

- required-reserve ratio
- required reserves
- excess reserves
- T-account
- simple deposit multiplier
- cash leakage
- money market accounts

■ CHAPTER OUTLINE

I. **THE NATURE AND ORIGINS OF MONEY**

   A. **Money: A Definition** -- While often confused with other things -- such as *income*, *wealth*, and *credit* -- **money** is *any good that is widely accepted in exchange for goods and services, as well as the payment of debts*.

   B. **Three Functions of Money** -- Perhaps the best way to define money is to look at the functions it serves.

      1. **Money as a Medium of Exchange** -- If there were no money, goods would have to be exchanged through the process of **barter** -- that is, goods would be traded for goods in transactions arranged on the basis of mutual need. For example, if I made shoes and want to "purchase" some bread, I would have to find a baker who needed shoes, and then arrange to trade him shoes for bread -- that is, there must be a *double coincidence of wants*. Money eliminates the need for such arrangements and the (often prohibitive) **transaction costs** that accompany arranging such trades. In a money economy, money, rather than goods, is the *medium of exchange* via which transactions are made.

      2. **Money as a Unit of Account** -- In a money economy, all goods, services, and debts are valued in terms of money. As such, money is the **unit of account** -- the common standard by which value is determined.

      3. **Money as a Store of Value** -- The *store of value* function refers to money's ability to retain its value over time. Since all transactions are made in money, and all values are based on money, money should also retain its value as money.

   C. **From a Barter to a Money Economy: The Origins of Money** -- Money was not "invented" by some clever government clerk or "ordained" by a ruler. The first forms of money simply developed out of the barter process. Even though barter involved trading goods for goods, some goods -- those that were commonly needed -- were more readily accepted than others. Over time, as people began more and more to accept one or more particular item(s) in trade -- even if they had no particular use for them, but felt they could always trade these goods for what they did need -- widely-accepted *media of exchange* sprang up. Soon after, people began to fix values of their wares in terms of this (these) particular item(s), thus establishing a reliable *unit of account*. Then it was only a matter of time until economies moved to goods like gold and silver which did not perish, and which would *retain their value* over time.

D. **What Gives Money its Value?** -- Under a system in which money was made of or "backed" by gold and/or silver, the value of money was determined by the value of its commodity base. In today's world, there is no gold backing the U.S. dollar. Rather, its value is established by its *general acceptability* in exchange for goods and services.

E. **Salty Money** -- Salt is an example of one of the many commodities which have been used as money. Because salt was traded extensively in hot-weather societies, it eventually became a medium of exchange in many African communities. If you want more examples of unusual media of exchange, see Paul Einzig's book *Primitive Money*. The example from this book (which always gets the students' attention) is the use of dead rats as a form of money on Easter Island.

II. **DEFINING THE MONEY SUPPLY** -- Just because we (may or may not) know what money is, that does not mean that we know exactly how the theory translates into the "real world." Here we discuss the two most frequently used empirical definitions of money: *M1* and *M2*.

A. **M1** -- consists of *currency outside banks* plus *demand deposits and other checkable deposits* plus *traveler's checks*. [See Exhibit 9-1]

   1. **Currency Held Outside Banks** -- includes *coins* minted by the U.S. Treasury and *paper money* which is the legal tender of the U.S. government, about 99% of which are *Federal Reserve Notes* issued by the Federal Reserve district banks.

   2. **Checkable Deposits** -- funds on which checks can be written.

   3. **Traveler's Checks** -- issued in specific denominations, these are treated as cash. So

      M1 = currency held outside banks + checkable deposits + traveler's checks

B. **M2** -- a broader definition of the money supply, it includes all of the components of *M1* plus *small-denomination time deposits* plus *savings deposits* plus *money market accounts* plus *overnight repurchase agreements* plus *overnight Eurodollar deposits*.

   1. **Time Deposits** -- interest-earning deposits with a specified maturity, which are subject to penalty for early withdrawal. Small-denomination time deposits have a value of less than $100,000.

   2. **Savings Deposits** -- interest-earning deposits with no specific maturity or maximum value, but which may require advanced written notice of withdrawal.

   3. **Money Market Accounts** -- accounts that take savings and invest them in short-term financial instruments, pay higher-than-savings-account interest, and offer limited check writing privileges.

4. **Overnight Repurchase Agreements** -- agreements by a financial institution to sell short-term securities to its customers, accompanied by an agreement to repurchase the securities within 24 hours.

5. **Overnight Eurodollar Deposits** -- dollar-denominated deposits held in financial institutions outside the U.S. Again, as was the case with repurchase agreements, only "overnight" (24-hour) Eurodollar deposits are counted in M2.

C. **Where Do Credit Cards Fit In?** -- Credit cards are commonly referred to as *"plastic money."* In fact, credit cards are not money, they are devices by which money is lent -- money that must be paid back. Thus, if we counted the value of credit card balances, as well as the value of the money that must be used to pay those balances off, we would be guilty of double counting.

III. HOW BANKING DEVELOPED

A. **The Early Bankers** -- In days of yore, most money was in the form of gold coins, which were heavy and difficult to transport. Seeing an entrepreneurial opportunity, goldsmiths began to offer gold storage services, in addition to their coining and melting services. In return for a customer's gold, the smith would issue a *warehouse receipt*, which became a form of money accepted in lieu of the gold itself. The growing acceptance of receipts, and the infrequency with which they were ever actually "cashed in" for the gold they represented, led smiths to believe that they could begin lending out part of their customers' gold and/or printing receipts in excess of actual gold holdings. In so doing, the system of *fractional reserve banking*, whereby banks create money by holding only a portion of their deposits on reserve, was born.

B. **The Federal Reserve System** -- The Federal Reserve System is the central bank for the United States whose chief function is to control the nation's money supply.

IV. THE MONEY CREATION PROCESS

A. **The Bank's Reserves and More** -- Just as individuals have despoits at banks, banks have deposits at the Fed.

1. **Bank Reserves** -- Total *bank reserves* equal the amount of cash in the bank's vault *plus* the value of funds held on account at the Federal Reserve. Neither vault cash or money held on account at the Fed earn interest.

2. **Required Reserves and Excess Reserves** -- Bank reserves may be separated into two categories: *required reserves* and *excess reserves*. **Required reserves** are the amount of reserves a bank must hold against deposits, as mandated by the Fed's *required-reserve ratio*. **Excess reserves** are any reserves held above and beyond the required amount.

3. **Lending Excess Reserves** -- Banks may lend their excess reserves either to their customers or to other banks in order to earn interest on the loan.

B. The Banking System and the Money Expansion Process -- Individual banks are prohibited from printing their own money. Nevertheless, *banks may create money by creating checkable deposits, which are a part of the money supply.* In order to see this, let's work through the process step-by-step.

STEP ONE: Suppose the Fed prints $1,000 and decides to deposit it into Bank A.

STEP TWO: Bank A sets aside the portion of that $1,000 that is required reserves. For this example, assume that the required reserve ratio is 10%. So, $100 is set aside, and the remaining $900 becomes excess reserves.

STEP THREE: Bank A decides to lend that $900 to Jenny, who then deposits that $900 in her account. At this point, the money supply has increased. The $1000 the Fed printed remains in the system, and we can now add Jenny's $900 to this.

STEP FOUR: Jenny's Bank B sets aside 10% of her $900 -- that is, $90 -- as required reserves. The remaining $810 becomes excess reserves.

STEP FIVE: Jenny's Bank B now has $810 which may be lent -- an action that will increase the money supply again. Exhibit 9-2 traces out the multiplier process to its end.

1. **How Far Does it Go?** -- The process continues until no new excess reserves can be created. The maximum amount of new money that may be created from any new money can be derived using the formula:

   Maximum change in checkable deposits = $1/r$ **x** ΔR,

   where r = the required-reserve ratio; and, ΔR = the change in total reserves resulting from the initial injection of funds.

2. **The Simple Deposit Multiplier** -- The expression ($1/r$) in the formula above is known as the *simple deposit multiplier*.

C. Why Maximum? Answer: No Cash Leakages and Zero Excess Reserves -- The deposit multiplier formula above can only tell us the change in money supply if we accept a couple of underlying assumptions: first, all funds are deposited into bank checking accounts -- that is, there is no **cash leakage** (no cash held out before depositing) and there are no non-checkable deposits; and, second, banks do not voluntarily hold excess reserves.

D. Who Created What? -- To summarize the money expansion process, there were two major players: the Fed and the Banking system. The Fed directly created $1000 which made it possible for banks to create $9000 in checkable deposits. In order to find out how much money the banking system can create out of any given amount of funds is:

Maximum change in checkable deposits (brought about by the banking system) = $1/r$ **x** ΔER,

where r = the required-reserve ratio; and, ΔER = the change in excess reserves of the first bank to receive the initial injection of funds.

E. **It Works in Reverse: The "Money Destruction" Process** -- The process described above works equally well in reverse. In this case, the Fed removes $1,000 from the banking system, creating a shortage of reserves. In order to remedy that shortage, banks reduce lending and/or sell assets (e.g., government securities), thus reducing the money supply. This process is illustrated in Exhibit 9-3.

F. **We Change Our Example** -- The Fed isn't the only actor in the economy who can get the money expansion ball rolling. If Jack had been hiding $1000 in a shoe box, and decided to take it out and deposit the money in the bank, he would add money to the banking system which could be lent out to other depositors. The money expansion process would now evolve in the same process as when the Fed printed $1000.

G. **Transferring Funds with a Push of a Button** -- Processing checks is expensive, so whenever possible, banks prefer to use the electronic funds transfer system (EFTS). This system is used whenever a debit card is used to pay for a purchase. No cash or checks are used, but payment is made nonetheless.

H. **Islamic Banking** -- In Islamic countries, banking faces a difficult problem: since the Koran forbids paying or receiving interest to another Muslim, borrowing and lending can be difficult. Islamic banks get around these restrictions in two ways. If a Muslim wants to borrow money for a house, the bank buys the house and leases the house to them. If you want to save money, the bank can't pay other Muslims interest, but they can invest the money for them and pay a return.

V. **ECONOMICS ON THE INTERNET** -- Data on the money supply and banks are highlighted in this chapter. Addresses for the Federal Reserve Bank of Chicago, the Federal Reserve Bank of Boston, and the Federal Deposit Insurance Corporation are provided.

■ ANSWERS TO CHAPTER QUESTIONS

1. **Suppose that $10,000 in new dollar bills (never seen before) falls magically from the sky into the hands of Joanna Ferris. What are the minimum increase and the maximum increase in the money supply that may result? Assume the required-reserve ratio is 10 percent.**

The minimum is $10,000. Joanna could simply keep the cash thus increasing currency in the hands of the nonbanking public by $10,000. Since currency is part of M1, the money supply increases by $10,000. The maximum is $100,000. To illustrate, suppose Joanna deposits the full $10,000 into her checking account at Bank A. This act increases the reserves of the banking system. If we assume no cash leakage, along with zero excess reserves, the maximum increase in checkable deposits (money) is $100,000. This is obtained by multiplying the simple deposit multiplier ($1/r = 1/.10 = 10$) *times* the change in reserves ($10,000). The $100,000 is composed of Joanna's original $10,000 and $90,000 in checking accounts created when new loans were extended to borrowers across the country.

2. Suppose Joanna Ferris receives $10,000 from her friend Ethel and deposits the money into a checking account. Ethel gave Joanna the money by writing a check on her checking account. Would the maximum increase in the money supply still be what you found it to be in question 1 where Joanna received the money from the sky? Explain your answer.

No, it would not be $100,000. In fact, there would be no increase in the money supply. The $10,000 Joanna received from Ethel was already part of the money supply. True, if Joanna receives the $10,000 and deposits it into her account at Bank A, the reserves of Bank A increase. But the reserves of Ethel's bank (Bank B) decrease by the same amount when it honors Ethel's check. Therefore there are no new reserves in the banking system. Thus no new demand deposits can be created by the banking system.

3. Suppose that instead of Joanna getting $10,000 from the sky, or a check from a friend, she gets it from her mother who had buried it in a can in her backyard. In this case, would the maximum increase in the money supply be what you found it to be in question 1? Explain your answer.

No, it would be $90,000. To illustrate, if Joanna takes the $10,000, formerly in her mother's can in the backyard, and deposits it into her checking account, the composition of the money supply changes (less currency, more deposits), and the reserves of her bank increase. And since the $10,000 was not originally a part of reserves, this represents an increase in reserves for the entire banking system. Once the $10,000 is deposited in the bank, reserves rise by $10,000 while required reserves rise by $1,000. This leaves the bank of deposit with $9,000 in excess reserves. The maximum change in the money supply is given by the formula:

Maximum change in checkable deposits (brought about by the banking system) $= 1/r \times \Delta ER$.

The initial deposit changes the composition of the money supply, but not its size.

4. What is the important point to be learned from the answers to questions 1, 2, and 3?

The maximum increase in the money supply based on an initial deposit in a bank (Joanna's deposit in Bank A) depends upon *where the money comes from:* the sky, currency holdings, or another checking account.

5. Does inflation, which is an increase in the price level, affect the three functions of money? If so, how?

Inflation should not affect either the *medium of exchange* or *unit of account* functions of money, unless it is so extreme that people refuse to accept money and insist on barter. However, it is possible that persistent inflation will erode the *store of value* function of money. As prices continue to rise and the real purchasing power of money falls, people who view value in real terms, and not nominal terms, will see money as a poor store of value -- though a better alternative may not be readily apparent.

6. **Some economists have proposed that the Fed move to a 100 percent required-reserve ratio. This would make the simple deposit multiplier 1 (1/r = 1/1.00 = 1). Do you think banks would argue for or against the move? Explain your answer.**

Clearly against. If the required-reserve ratio were 100%, banks would have no excess reserves with which to generate loans or purchase financial assets. Therefore, they would be unable to earn any interest from the deposits on which they must pay interest. In such a world, all banks would lose money and then fail.

7. **Money makes exchange easier. Would twice the money supply make exchange twice as easy? Would half the money supply make exchange one-half as easy?**

The answer is dependent upon the current relationship between the supply of money and the demand for money for transactions. As long as there is enough money to fund all desired trans-actions, then doubling the money supply will have no noticeable effect on exchange. If there is a shortage of money for transactions purposes, then expanding the money supply will increase exchange. However, whether doubling the money supply "doubles" the ease of transactions seems impossible to answer, but highly unlikely.

Reducing the money supply will not noticeably affect exchange if the new, smaller money supply is still sufficient to cover transactions. If, however, the new money supply creates a shortage of money to fund transactions, then exchange will be hampered. Again, though, exactly what "one-half as easy" means is unclear -- much like, "a 43% increase in quality."

8. **Explain why gold backing is not necessary to give paper money value.**

As long as people are willing to accept money in exchange for goods and services and in payment for debts, there is no need for any commodity, gold or otherwise, to "back" the money supply.

9. **Describe the money supply expansion process.**

See Section IV.B. of the outline for a detailed description of the money supply expansion process.

10. **Describe the money supply contraction process.**

The money creation process works equally well in reverse. Assuming a 10% required-reserve ratio, suppose that the Fed removes $1,000 from his checking account. This creates a shortage of reserves, as Bank A must take $1,000 out of its vault cash to pay him. In order to remedy the shortage, Bank A reduces its loans by $900 -- the amount by which reserves fell, since the other $100 was only on reserve to cover the Fed's $1,000 in the first place. Individuals and businesses counting on those $900 in loans must withdraw money from their bank accounts to make up the difference, thus further reducing the reserves of the banking system. And so on. The process continues until $9,000 worth of money is "destroyed." Recall,

Maximum change in checkable deposits (brought about by the banking system) = $1/r \times \Delta ER$.

In this case. $\Delta ER = -\$900$ and r = 10%. So, the change in checkable deposits = (1/.10) **x** (- $900) = (10) **x** (- $900) = - $9,000.

11. Suppose *r* = 10 percent and the Fed creates $20,000 in new money that ends up deposited in someone's checking account in a bank. What is the maximum change in checkable deposits (or the money supply) as a result.

As always, we rely on our formula for determining the change in the money supply. The formula is

Maximum change in checkable deposits (brought about by the banking system) = 1/r **x** ΔER .

In this case, $\Delta ER = -\$20,000$ and r = 10%. So, ΔDD = (1/.10) x $20,000 = $200,000.

12. Does a cash leakage affect the change in checkable deposits? Explain your answer.

Yes, a cash leakage does affect the change in checkable deposits. The essence of the money expansion process is that when a single bank creates new money by lending it out, that money is then spent purchasing goods, and the money is deposited in another bank which will continue the money expansion process. If at any point in the process, someone takes the money and hides it in their mattress, they stop the money expansion process. Any cash leakage will reduce the ultimate change in checkable deposits.

■ LECTURE SUPPLEMENTS

"The Future of Money," *Business Week*, **June 12, 1995, pp. 68-78**

This is an excellent article which covers the future of electronic money and discusses the evolution of money from early money (sea shells and gold) to bank money (checks and currencies) to its future incarnation in the form of electronic cash (E-cash). Although many people agree that some form of E-cash to be used for making payments over the Internet and other electronic means is inevitable, what form E-cash eventually takes remains uncertain.

Not only should students find this article interesting, but you can use the problem of what form electronic cash should take on to remind them of the functions of money. Money acts as a medium of exchange, a unit of account, and a store of value. The problem is to devise a means of payment which meets these requirements, and as the article points out, whoever can solve this problem will be as rich as Croesus. This is one reason Bill Gates is so attracted to the problem. Although the Justice Department prevented Bill Gates from buying Intuit, he is currently working with Visa to create a form of E-cash for his Microsoft network. Will he solve it, or will someone else?

Will Cybercash replace greenbacks? Will your money be carried on a credit-card-size piece of plastic in the future? Will the heavyweight championship of 1998 be paid for with E-cash? What will back the E-cash to insure its value? How can counterfeiting of E-cash be thwarted? How soon will greenbacks go the way of Confederate currency?

Rather than give you the answers to these questions, you and your students will have to read the article and debate the issues yourself. By the way, could you lend me a few bytes until Tuesday?

Leonard I. Nakamura, "Small Borrowers and the Survival of the Small Bank," *Federal Reserve Bank of Philadelphia Business Review*, November/December 1994, pp. 3-15.

This article is useful not only because it focuses on banks and their role in the economy, which is the subject of this chapter, but it also allows you to look at the trade-offs between bank size and efficiency. There are thousands of banks in the United States, some with hundreds of billions of dollars in assets, but 97% of banks have less than $1 billion in assets, and these banks represent only 33% of banks' total assets. Why are some banks successful as big banks, and others are successful as small banks? Or are smaller banks doomed to be absorbed by larger banks which can benefit from economies of scale? This question provides an excellent opportunity for students to apply the economic tools they have developed.

Large banks have several advantages over smaller banks. Big banks have more diversified portfolios, they make larger loans, they benefit from economies of scale in check processing and automation, they offer wider branch networks, and they can acquire capital more easily in public markets. Do smaller banks have a comparative advantage to offset these absolute disadvantages?

The answer is yes. In particular, smaller banks are closer to their customers and may be able to make better choices about lending to small businesses than large banks. Because small banks have fewer layers of management, they may be able to process credit information more efficiently than large banks. But as the article points out, small banks are less diversified, and thus, riskier than large banks. Depositors would be less willing to keep their money in a small bank if there were no FDIC insurance for small banks.

Review this article and get your students to think about the trade-offs that exist between big and small banks. The article does an excellent job of pointing out these trade-offs. Of course, each of the Federal Reserve Banks publish reviews which provide useful source material on money and banking. These reviews can be used as an on-going source of articles with which you can stimulate class-room discussion.

James North, "Is Nationwide Banking Making Some States Haves at the Expense of the Have-Nots?" *Barron's*, August 1, 1994, p. 40.

This article can be used as an introduction to the important changes which will be taking place in the nation's banking system in the coming years. The McFadden Act of 1925 disallowed interstate banking, but this restriction will be eliminated over the next few years as a result of the new banking law which was passed in 1994. Opposition to the repeal of the McFadden Act has come from banks and states which felt they would be adversely affected by the legal change.

Once banks are allowed to operate on an interstate basis, a period of consolidation will ensue in which banks which want to be national banks, such as Nationsbank, will buy out banks in different states in order to establish their interstate banking system. Through holding companies, however, banks are already making their presence felt across state lines.

The question the article raises is whether banks which move across state lines will lend disproportionately in their "home" states because they understand those capital markets better than the states they move into. The fear is that states such as Florida, Arizona, Nevada, Washington and Maine which have seen a large number of banks taken over by out of state banks will be used as sources of funds, rather than as lending targets.

Kenneth H. Thomas studied Great Western of California which had moved into Florida in the early 1990s. Although its Florida banks had $9.2 billion in deposits, Great Western loaned only $2 billion in Florida. In short, Great Western was using Florida's assets to fund loans in California. Great Western officials disagreed with Thomas's analysis. Thomas favors greater disclosure by banks of their lending practices to ensure that money is loaned out to communities which deposit the money. If local depositors are afraid their funds will be used for loans in distant states, they may choose local, smaller banks over megabanks.

CHAPTER 10

The Federal Reserve System

Chapter 9 introduced us to money, its role in the economy, and the degree to which the banking system could "create" money and control the supply of money. Most of the responsibility for creating and controlling money rests upon the broad shoulders of the *Federal Reserve System*, or *"The Fed"* for short, the *central bank* of the United States. Chapter 10 examines the structure and purpose of the Fed, and then turns to a detailed study of the tools with which the Fed controls the supply of money: *open market operations*, the *required-reserve ratio*, and the *discount rate*.

■ CHAPTER OBJECTIVES

Upon completing this chapter, your students should be able to:

- outline the structure of the Federal Reserve System and identify the major functions of the Federal Reserve System;

- define the *monetary base* and describe how it relates to the money supply;

- derive the *money multiplier* and contrast it to the simple deposit multiplier (Chapter 9); and,

- discuss the three major tools of monetary policy and demonstrate how they can be used to control the money supply.

■ KEY TERMS

- Board of Governors
- Federal Open Market Committee (FOMC)
- open market operations
- U.S. Treasury Securities
- monetary base
- money multiplier
- reserve requirement
- federal funds market
- federal funds rate
- discount rate

■ CHAPTER OUTLINE

I. THE STRUCTURE OF THE FEDERAL RESERVE SYSTEM

A. **The Structure of the Fed** -- The Federal Reserve System was created by the Federal Reserve Act of 1913. Its principal components are the *Board of Governors* and the *Federal Open Market Committee* (in Washington, D.C.), the 12 *Federal Reserve District Banks*. The boundaries of the twelve Federal Reserve Districts are shown in Exhibit 10-1.

1. **Board of Governors** -- The **Board of Governors** controls and coordinates the activities of the Federal Reserve System. The seven governors are presidentially-appointed and Senate-confirmed to staggered 14 year (non-renewable) terms. The president designates one member of the Board as the chairman for a four-year, renewable term.

2. **Federal Open Market Committee (FOMC)** -- The major policy-making group within the Fed, the **FOMC** is made-up of the seven governors plus five presidents of Federal Reserve District Banks (the president of the New York Fed has a permanent seat, the other four places rotate among the remaining 11 district banks). The authority to conduct **open market operations** -- *the buying and selling of government securities for purposes of manipulating the money supply* -- rests with the FOMC, and it is the responsibility of the New York Fed to carry out FOMC orders.

3. **Federal Reserve District Banks** -- In order to assist the Board of Governors in overseeing the banking system and controlling the money supply, the System was divided into 12 geographic districts, and each district is overseen by a *Federal Reserve District Bank*, or simply *Federal Reserve bank*.

B. **Functions of the Federal Reserve System** -- The Fed has eight major functions:

1. **Control the Money Supply** -- This will be explained in detail later in the chapter.

2. **Supply the Economy with Paper Money** -- The Federal Reserve banks have *Federal Reserve Notes* on hand to meet the needs of banks and the public.

3. **Provide Check-Clearing Services** -- When someone writes a check that is deposited in some bank other than the one it was written on, some arrangement must be made to transfer funds between the two banks. Rather than handle each transaction separately, most banks use a *clearinghouse* operation, which keeps track of each bank's claims against each other bank, determines who owes who what at the end of the day, and makes the necessary transfers. The Fed provides such services. This process is summarized in Exhibit 10-2.

4. **Hold Depository Institutions' Reserves** -- All depository institutions must keep a certain portion of their funds "on reserve," either as vault cash or on account at the Fed. These accounts are maintained by the Federal Reserve banks.

5. **Supervise Member Banks** -- The Fed conducts periodic examinations and audits of certain member banks (a task it shares with the *Comptroller of the Currency*).

6. **Serve as the Government's Banker** -- The federal government collects and spends hundreds of billions of dollars annually in the forms of taxes, transfers, purchases of goods and services, payroll, and interest and principal payments on debt. The Fed is the primary holder of U.S. government deposit accounts.

7. **Serve as "Lender of Last Resort"** -- When individuals need a loan, they go to their local bank. But where does their local bank go when *it* needs a loan? -- to the Fed, of course. The Fed acts as a *"lender of last resort,"* providing funds to banks suffering liquidity problems.

8. **Serve as Fiscal Agent for the Treasury** -- The U.S. Treasury often auctions **Treasury securities** to help pay the cost of running the government and all of its policies. The Fed aids the Treasury in conducting the weekly auctions. Remember, the U.S. Treasury manages the financial affairs of the government, collecting taxes and making payments; the Fed's job is to oversee the monetary system for the country as a whole.

C. **What Goes On at An FOMC Meeting?** -- The *Economics in Our Times* feature gives students some insight into what happens in an FOMC meeting by going over the notes from the November 1994 meeting. If you would like to do this for your class, get a recent copy of the *Federal Reserve Bulletin* which publishes the minutes of the meetings. Have your students read over the minutes and let them decide whether they think the Fed made the right decisions.

II. THE MONETARY BASE AND THE MONEY MULTIPLIER

A. **The Monetary Base** -- The *monetary base (high-powered money)* is comprised of *bank reserves* plus *currency held outside banks*. That is,

Monetary base (B) = bank reserves (R) + currency outside held banks (C);

or, simply, **B = R + C**.

The monetary base is the medium through which the Fed influences the money supply. The Fed uses the tools of monetary policy to "create" or "destroy" money by changing the value of either bank reserves or currency held by the nonbank public.

B. **From the Simple Deposit Multiplier to the Money Multiplier** -- In Chapter 9 we introduced the *simple deposit multiplier*, which told us the maximum amount of demand deposits (money) the banking system was capable of creating from a given injection of excess reserves, *assuming that there was no cash leakage and that no banks voluntarily held excess reserves*. But, in the real world, cash leakage and excess reserves are a fact of life; therefore, the simple deposit multiplier tends to overstate the actual change in the money supply that the banking system can generate from a given amount of excess reserves. In order to account for these "leakages," we use the money multiplier, which measures the actual change in the money supply for every dollar change in the monetary base. That is,

Money multiplier = money supply/monetary base

Rearranging the terms in this equation, you should be able to see that

Money supply = money multiplier x monetary base

III. FED TOOLS FOR CONTROLLING THE MONEY SUPPLY

A. **Open Market Operations** -- Anytime the Fed buys or sells anything, it affects the monetary base and, thus, the money supply. The main "thing" the Fed buys and sells is U.S. government securities, using *open market operations*.

   1. **Open Market Purchases** -- When the Fed purchases a government security from the nonbank public or from a bank, it does so with money that did not "exist" prior to the transaction. Thus, when the Fed makes the purchase bank reserves will rise -- either directly, in the case of the Fed purchasing from a bank; or, indirectly, when the individual seller deposits his/her Fed check in his/her bank account.

   2. **Open Market Sales** -- When the Fed sells a government security from the nonbank public or from a bank, it takes funds that were previously in the monetary base out of the monetary base -- either by taking funds from the public in the form of currency; from the public's demand deposits, therefore reducing bank reserves; or, directly reducing bank reserves.

B. **The Required-Reserve Ratio** -- The Fed can also influence the money supply by changing the required-reserve ratio. Recall that banks must hold a specified percentage of all deposits on reserve, thus limiting the amount by which banks may expand the money supply. If the Fed increases the reserve ratio, the deposit and money multipliers will be smaller, thereby further limiting the amount by which banks may expand the money supply. If the Fed decreases the reserve ratio, the deposit and money multipliers will be larger, thereby enabling banks to expand the money supply by a greater amount.

C. **The Discount Rate** -- Banks not only provide loans to their customers, they also borrow funds when needed. Why might a bank need to borrow funds? Perhaps the bank has a good loan candidate, but lacks the funds to make the loan. Or, the bank may be experiencing a reserve deficiency. In either case, the bank has a choice to make:

   1. **Borrowing in the Federal Funds Market** -- One of the two places where the bank could turn is the *federal funds market*, where it borrows excess reserves from another bank. The rate of interest it pays on such a loan is called the *federal funds rate*.

   2. **Borrowing from the Fed** -- The other choice is to borrow from the Fed, using the *discount window*. The rate of interest paid for bank loans from the Fed is called the discount rate.

D. **The Spread between the Discount Rate and the Federal Funds Rate** -- The decision on where to borrow depends upon a number of factors, most important of which is choosing the lower interest rate. However, even if the discount rate is lower, the bank may still choose to borrow in the federal funds market. Why? First, the Fed may restrict the amount of funds available. Second, the bank may not feel the Fed will "approve" of its reasons for borrowing, and knows that it will face significant bureaucratic problems. As a result, the bank may make its decision based upon the *"spread"* between the rates. If the discount rate is only slightly lower than the federal funds rate, the bank will likely choose federal funds. However, if he spread is significant, the bank may decide the interest saved is worth the administrative hassles.

1. **What Can the Fed Do?** -- So, what makes the discount rate a "tool" of monetary policy. First, the Fed may wish to control the actual rate, raising it to discourage borrowing and lowering it to encourage borrowing. And, secondly, the Fed may try to control the "spread" -- increasing the spread to encourage bank borrowing, and decreasing the spread to discourage borrowing.

2. **Effects on the Money Supply** -- Why does it matter? When a bank borrows from the Fed, bank reserves increase, thus increasing the monetary base and the money supply. When a bank borrows from another bank, all that happens is a transfer of bank reserves, which has no effect on the monetary base or the money supply.

E. **Central Banks Are Not All Alike** -- As the *Global Economy* feature points out, although all central banks have the job of overseeing the monetary policy of the nation in which they exist, they differ in the degree of independence which they have from political influence. For example, the Bundesbank in Germany is very independent, especially compared to the Bank of England. Economists have done research and found that independence matters. Countries which have independent central banks tend to also have lower inflation rates, *ceteris paribus*.

IV. **ECONOMICS ON THE INTERNET** -- Some addresses which discuss the role of the Federal Reserve in the economy are provided. Also included is information on using the University of Michigan Gopher to get data on the reserves of depository institutions.

■ ANSWERS TO CHAPTER QUESTIONS

1. **Identify the major responsibilities of the Federal Reserve System.**

The Federal Reserve System is responsible for conducting the nation's monetary policy. Their major responsibilities include (1) controlling the money supply, (2) supplying the economy with paper money (Federal Reserve Notes), (3) provide check-clearing services, (4) hold depository institutions' reserves, (5) supervise member banks, (6) serve as the government's banker, (7) serve as a lender of last resort, and (8) serve as a fiscal agent for the treasury.

2. **Is it possible for the monetary base to increase without an increase in reserves? If so, explain how.**

Yes, it is possible for the monetary base to increase without an increase in reserves. Monetary base = reserves + currency held outsidebanks. If the currency component rises, and there is no corresponding decline in reserves, the monetary base rises.

3. **Explain how an open market purchase increases the money supply.**

Suppose the Fed buys government securities from a commercial bank. At the end of the transaction, the Fed has more government securities than before and the commercial bank has fewer. What the commercial bank does have, however, is a higher balance in its account at the Fed. Since deposits at the Fed are part of reserves (reserves = deposits at the Fed + vault cash), then reserves in the banking system have risen. Since the United States has a fractional reserve banking system, only a fraction of the increased amount of reserves has to be placed in a required-reserve category. The remainder, or the positive excess reserves, can be used to extend more loans, create more demand deposits, and increase the money supply.

4. **Suppose the Fed raises the required-reserve ratio. This is normally thought to reduce the money supply. However, commercial banks find themselves with a reserve deficiency after the required-reserve ratio is increased and are likely to react by requesting a loan from the Fed. Does this action prevent the money supply from contracting as predicted by theory?**

It prevents the money supply from contracting as much and as fast as it would have contracted if the banks had not gone to the Fed for loans. However, this is only a short-run phenomenon. Once the banks repay the Fed loans (probably within the next two to four weeks), reserves will leave the banking system, and the money supply will decline as predicted. The loans the Fed makes to banks create a lag between the increase in the required-reserve ratio and the full contractionary effect on bank reserves and the money supply.

5. **Suppose Bank A borrows reserves from Bank B. Now that Bank A has more reserves than previously, will the money supply increase?**

No, it won't because there are no new reserves in the banking system. What has happened is that Bank A has more reserves and Bank B has fewer reserves, but the banking system as a whole has the same volume of reserves.

6. **If the simple deposit multiplier turned out to be equal to the money multiplier (which isn't likely), what would this imply?**

Easy. It would mean that cash leakages equaled zero and banks did not voluntarily hold any excess reserves.

7. **Two towns are located in two different Federal Reserve Districts. One is a tourist town, the other is not. In which town would you expect to find more Federal Reserve Notes issued by Federal Reserve District Banks outside the district in which the town is located? Explain why.**

The tourist town should have a higher percentage of Federal Reserve Notes issued by other District Banks, since many of the tourists will be coming from outside of the town's Federal Reserve District.

8. Suppose you read in the newspaper that all last week the Fed conducted open market purchases, and that on Tuesday of last week it lowered the discount rate. What would you say the Fed was up to?

If the Fed was conducting a policy in which it persistently bought securities and lowered the discount rate, it is obviously trying to boost the money supply by increasing the monetary base. A more discerning eye will also notice that, while taking expansionary measures with both the discount rate and open market operations, the Fed did not reduce the reserve requirement. This would suggest that the Fed is comfortable with the size of the money multiplier, and does not want the banking system to be any more or less able to "multiply" the effects of the other policy changes.

9. Suppose the Fed increases the monetary base by $350 million. Does it matter whether the $350 million is all in reserves, or all in currency, as to how much the money supply will expand? Explain your answer.

Yes. If the increase is in reserves, then banks have $350 million with which to "play." Whereas, if the increase is even partially in currency, banks cannot multiply currency; so, it is either untouchable (if it remains currency), or a portion of it will be sacrificed to required reserves, should the public decide to deposits that currency. Either way, if any of the increase is in the form of currency, the final amount of new money -- after the multiplier effect -- will be less than if the whole increase in the base was an increase in bank reserves.

10. Some people have referred to the Fed as a "legal counterfeiter." Explain why you think such terminology either is or is not a misrepresentation of the Fed's role.

I suppose this one is a judgment call, but I hope few, if any, students will agree that the Fed is a "legal counterfeiter." Unlike counterfeiters, the Fed is technically offering something of value to the party accepting a Federal Reserve Note: the full faith and credit of the United States government. One technical difference, or significant legal consequence were the Fed ever on trial, is that it, unlike a counterfeiter, does not print paper money -- that task is left to the Bureau of Engraving and Printing. Furthermore, one could make the functional argument that much of what the Fed does these days has little or nothing to do with paper money -- the vast majority of its transactions involve computerized accounts, not cash. I could go on, but . . .

11. Fill in the blanks (indicated by A, B, C, D, E, F).

Money Supply ($ billions)	Monetary Base ($ billions)	Money Multiplier
715	A	4.2
B	209	3.1
802	241	C
692	D	2.5
E	321	2.6
796	255	F

A. $170.24 billion.
B. $647.9 billion.
C. 3.33.
D. $276.8 billion
E. $834.6 billion.
F. 3.12.

■ LECTURE SUPPLEMENTS

"Symposium: The Fed Hikes Rates Again," *Challenge*, **January-February 1995, pp. 5-8.**

This is a good round-table symposium on the Federal Reserve interest rate hikes of November 15, 1994. It presents opposing views of whether the Federal Reserve was right to raise interest rates in November 1994. Most of the opinions are critical of the Fed.

The one person who comes out favoring the Fed's actions is David M. Jones in his piece, "A 'Soft Landing'." He says that the Fed's actions are designed to keep the economy from overheating and then falling into a recession. The goal is to keep the economy from reaching an inflationary gap which would then be followed by a recessionary gap when firms cut back. By using discretionary monetary policy, Jones believes that the Fed has engineered a "soft landing" in which the Fed slows down, without falling into a recession, before once again beginning a cycle of economic growth.

The other participants are critical of the Fed, generally believing that the Fed was unjustified by the economic evidence to raise interest rates, and that their policies may push the economy into a recession which otherwise would not have occurred, or they could unnecessarily slow down the rate of growth. The titles of their pieces, Jeff Faux's "A National Embarrassment", Jerry Jasinowski's "A Fundamental Misreading of the Economy", and Rudy Oswald's "The Mad Run-up of Interest Rates" quickly summarize their points of view. Use these articles as a starting point to debate how the Fed should interpret the economic variables they rely upon to determine its policies, and what is the impact on the economy of their actions.

Lawrence B. Lindsey, "The Limits of Monetary Policy," *The Public Interest*, **Fall 1993, pp. 28-39.**

This article was written to caution those who seek a more active monetary policy, trying to lay down what Lindsey's experience shows the Fed is capable and incapable of doing in attempting to influence the economy through monetary policy. He provides three primary lessons:

1. Excess money, not excess demand, causes sustained inflation.
2. The trade-off from excessive money creation is temporarily lower unemployment in return for permanently higher inflation.
3. Inflation is far more costly than once believed.

Lindsey's belief is that monetary policy has a single clear objective: to maintain inflation at a level low enough that it does not affect economic decisionmaking. He goes on to discuss the limits on monetary policy on solving microeconomic problems, on macroeconomic activism, and on international policy. The greater market freedom of the 1990s constrains policymakers options, but does not prevent them from being good stewards of their currency.

Stanley Fischer, "Central-Bank Independence Revisited," *American Economic Review,* **May 1995, pp. 201-206**

This article summarizes current views on central bank independence. As Fisher points out, most of the evidence supports the proposition that independent central banks provide their countries better protection from inflation than countries in which politicians interfere with the central bank's actions.

There are two theoretical approaches to why independent central banks control inflation better. The first uses a social welfare function in which central banks try to control inflation in order to develop a reputation for fighting inflation. Since central bankers attach more social costs to deviations from a steady inflation rate, they will be more dedicated to preserving low, stable inflation rates. The principal-agent approach looks at the central bank as an agent whose responsibility is to fulfill the contract of low inflation imposed upon it by the government, New Zealand providing a good example of this approach.

One conclusion of the research is that the government should set the inflation target which the central bank has to achieve, but the central bank should be free to use the instruments necessary to achieve that target. As Fisher puts it, central banks should have instrument independence, but not goal independence. The best target is an inflation target, rather than a price-level target or a nominal GDP target, both for reasons of measurement and the ease with which instruments can be direct at achieving these targets.

Fischer concludes by saying that good monetary policies encourage good fiscal policies, and that central banks can be too independent. A central bank which controls inflation despite the impact on Real GDP is not acting in the best interests of the country. He concludes that some central bank accountability is needed.

CHAPTER 11

Money and the Economy

In chapters 9 and 10 we learned about the monetary system in the United States, both how money is created and how the Federal Reserve conducts its monetary policy. Now that we have established these foundations, we want to find out how changes in the money supply affect the economy. In particular, we want to study in more detail the relationship between the money supply and inflation, analyzing the process that links monetary increases to inflation and determining how strong this causal link is. The appendix gives a more complete version of the monetarist model of the economy.

■ CHAPTER OBJECTIVES

Upon completing this chapter, your students should be able to:

- define *inflation*;

- distinguish between *temporary inflation* and *continued (or sustained) inflation*;

- identify some of the major causes of inflation;

- describe the effects of inflation;

- explain the difference between *adaptive expectations* and *rational expectations*, and explain how these different assumptions affects economists' view of inflation.

- understand the relationship between inflation and international competitiveness; and,

- understand the relationship between inflation and nominal and real interest rates.

- know why monetarists place such a heavy emphasis on money's role in the economy, and explain the relationship between money supply and money and how their interaction affects the economy.

■ KEY TERMS

- velocity
- equation of exchange
- simple quantity theory of money
- inflation
- one-shot inflation
- continued inflation
- nominal interest rate
- real interest rate

- ex ante real interest rate
- ex post real interest rate
- adaptive expectations
- rational expectations
- liquidity effect
- income effect
- expectations effect

■ CHAPTER OUTLINE

I. **MONEY AND THE PRICE LEVEL** -- The MV-PQ model addresses the relationship between money and nominal GDP, between total spending and total sales revenues. While the MV-PQ framework is essential to *monetarist* economic thought and the *quantity theories of money*, it is important to distinguish between the tool and its uses.

A. **The Equation of Exchange** -- The basic statement within the MV-PQ framework, the **equation of exchange** simply states

$$M \times V \equiv P \times Q,$$

where M = the money supply (usually though of as M1), V = the *velocity* of money (defined below), P = the price level, and Q = real output, or Real GDP.

1. **What is "Velocity?"** -- **Velocity** is *the number of times the average dollar is spent to buy final goods and services in a given year*. We measure velocity by dividing nominal GDP by the money supply, that is

$$V \equiv GDP/M.$$

2. **Interpreting the Equation of Exchange** -- The equation of exchange tells us a number of things. In addition to its literal reading, it also tells us that

$$M \times V \equiv (nominal) \ GDP,$$

since P x Q ≡ (nominal) GDP; and, it also tells us that

$$total \ spending \ (M \times V) \equiv total \ sales \ revenues \ (P \times Q).$$

B. **From the Equation of Exchange to the Simple Quantity Theory of Money** -- *velocity (V) and real output (Q) are effectively constant in the short run; and, therefore, any change in the money supply (M) must cause a proportional change in the price level (P) and nominal GDP.* The **simple quantity theory of money** predicts that changes in the money supply will bring about *strictly proportional* changes in the price level as illustrated in Exhibit 11-1. For real-world examples of the relationship between money and inflation, see *The Global Economy* feature on "Money and Inflation." The examples in Exhibit 11-2 shows the strong relationship between monetary growth and inflation.

    C.   **The Simple Quantity Theory of Money in an AD-AS Framework**

        1.   **The AD Curve of the Simple Quantity Theory of Money** -- Remember that in the simple quantity theory of money, MV stands for total expenditures. This is also the sum of the expenditures of the four sectors of the economy, or

$$MV = TE = C + I + G + (EX - IM)$$

An increase in the money supply will increase aggregate demand. Exhibit 11-3a shows the shape of the AD curve.

        2.   **The AS Curve in the Simple Quantity Theory of Money** -- In the simple quantity theory of money, the level of Real GDP is assumed to be constant in the short run. This is shown in Exhibit 11-3b.

        3.   **AD and AS in the Simple Quantity Theory of Money** -- Exhibit 11-3c shows what happens when the money supply increases and velocity remains constant. This would shift AD_1 to AD_2, and push the price level up from P_1 to P_2. Similarly, a decrease in the money supply would shift AD_1 to AD_3, and push the price level down from P_1 to P_3.

II.   **MONETARISM** -- Monetarists believe there is a strong relationship between changes in the money supply and inflation. They do not believe that velocity is constant, but they do believe it behaves in a predictable way.

    A. **Velocity and Money Demand** -- To show how monetarists view the economy, let's start with the equation of exchange

$$MVP \equiv PQ$$

and then substitute the money supply for "money,"

$$M^s \times V \equiv PQ$$

The money market is in equilibrium when *the **quantity supplied of money (M^s)** equals the **quantity demand of money (M^d)***; that is,

$$M^s = M^d .$$

Now we can rewrite the equation of exchange by substituting money demand for money supply, and by dividing both sides of the equation of exchange by the velocity (V).

$$M^d \equiv (1/V) \times PQ \text{ or } M^d \equiv (1/V) \times GDP.$$

    B. **Thinking of 1/ *V* as a Fraction** -- If velocity is 3, then 1/ V equals 1/3. If we let *k* represent 1/ V, then we can rewrite the last equations as

$$M^d \equiv k \times PQ \text{ or } M^d \equiv k \times GDP$$

This simplifies our equations, but it still doesn't answer the basic question, what can cause velocity to change?

1. **Interest Rate** -- The cost of holding money is the interest rate that could have been earned on that money. *If interest rates increase, individuals desire to hold a smaller fraction of their incomes as money, thus k decreases (and V increases). If interest rates fall, individuals will desire to hold larger money balances as a percentage of their incomes, thus k increases (and V decreases).*

2. **Expected Rate of Inflation** -- When individuals expect an increase in the inflation rate, they desire to hold a smaller fraction of their income as money balances, since inflation dilutes the purchasing power of money. Thus, *if inflation is expected to rise, k falls and V increases. If inflation is expected to fall, k will rise and V falls.*

3. **The Frequency with Which Employees are Paid** -- Economists argue that *the more frequently an employee is paid, the less money (on average) the employee will hold, and the smaller k (larger V) will be.* The reverse is also true. These three factors are summarized in Exhibit 11-4.

C. **Monetarism in the AD-AS Framework** -- Exhibit 11-5 explains some of the highlights of monetarism, showing the effects of changes in the money supply and velocity. There are four cases.

1. **The Money Supply Increases and Velocity Is Constant** -- In panel 11-5a, aggregate demand shifts to the right causing an increase in Real GDP and an inflationary gap. Wages rise, shifting the SRAS curve leftward. In the short run, *Real GDP rises and unemployment falls* (moving from point 1 to point 2), but in the long run, *Real GDP and unemployment are unchanged, though the price level has increased* (point 3).

2. **The Money Supply Falls and Velocity Is Constant** -- In panel 11-5b, aggregate demand shifts to the left causing a decrease in Real GDP and a recessionary gap. Wages fall, shifting the SRAS curve rightward. In the short run, *Real GDP falls and unemployment rises* (moving from point 1 to point 2), but in the long run, *Real GDP and unemployment are unchanged, though the price level has decreased* (point 3).

3. **The Money Supply Is Constant and Velocity Increases** -- An increase in velocity, as shown in panel 11-5c will cause the AD curve to shift to the right, causing an increase in Real GDP and an inflationary gap. Wages rise, shifting the SRAS curve leftward. In the short run, *Real GDP rises and unemployment falls* (moving from point 1 to point 2), but in the long run, *Real GDP and unemployment are unchanged, though the price level has increased* (point 3).

4. **The Money Supply Is Constant and Velocity Decreases** -- A decrease in velocity, as shown in panel 11-5d will cause the AD curve to shift to the left, causing a decrease in Real GDP and a recessionary gap. Wages fall, shifting the SRAS curve rightward. In the short run, *Real GDP falls and unemployment rises* (moving from

point 1 to point 2), but in the long run, *Real GDP and unemployment are unchanged, though the price level has decreased* (point 3).

III. **Inflation** -- Economists like to differentiate between a one-shot inflation and continued inflation.

    A. **One-Shot Inflation** -- This occurs when there is a single increase in the price level, e.g., (CPI) without any subsequent increases. One-shot inflation can originate on either the supply or the demand side.

        1. **One-Shot Inflation: Demand-Side Induced** -- This is shown in Exhibit 11-6. Some factor causes AD to shift to the right in panel (a), creating an inflationary gap and lowering unemployment below the natural unemployment rate. In the next round of wage negotiations, workers demand and receive higher wages, shifting the SRAS curve leftward, as in panel (b). The economy is back in equilibrium, and there is no reason for the price level to increase from this level.

        2. **One-Shot Inflation: Supply-Side Induced** -- This is shown in Exhibit 11-7. Some factor causes SRAS to shift leftward in panel (a), creating a recessionary gap and unemployment greater than the natural unemployment rate. Because jobs are scarce, in the next wage round, workers receive lower wages, shifting the SRAS curve rightward, as in panel (b). Net result: we're right back where we started with the same price level, but in the interim there had been inflation.

    B. **Confusing Demand-Induced and Supply-Induced One-Shot Inflation** -- It is difficult to tell whether an increase in the price level has its origins in a change in aggregate demand or aggregate supply. It is easy to mistake an increase in wage rates for an increase in the money supply.

    C. **Continued Inflation** -- Unlike temporary inflation, continued inflation is caused exclusively by demand-side factors. It occurs when, like the Energizer bunny, price increases keep going, and going, and going.

        1. **From One-Shot Inflation to Continued Inflation** -- The only thing that can turn temporary inflation into sustained inflation is *continued increases in aggregate demand.* As Exhibit 11-8b demonstrates, a decrease in AS will raise prices, but the natural tendency of the market will be to return to the original price level; whereas, as AD increases, the price level continues to rise, causing sustained inflation.

        2. **What Causes Continued Increases in Aggregate Demand** -- While increases in any of the autonomous components of total expenditures will shift the AD curve to the right, *the only factor which can change continually in such a way as to cause continued increases in the price level is the money supply.* Some people also blame rising government purchases as a possible culprit. But there are two problems with this argument. First, there is a limit, both economic (100% of GDP) and political on how much government purchases can increase, so at some point the inflation would stop. Second, an increase in government purchases might be offset by decreases in consumption, reducing the inflationary impact.

D. **Tickets to the Letterman Show Are Free, So How Can There Be "Ticket Inflation"?** -- As this *Economics And the Media* feature shows, monetary inflation isn't the only type of inflation that people run into. Although tickets to the Letterman show have no monetary cost, they do have a temporal cost--standing in line. If you have to stand in line longer than in the past, the result is "ticket inflation."

IV. **THE EFFECTS OF INFLATION** -- In examining the effects of inflation, it is important to note that inflation may be either anticipated or unanticipated; and, if anticipated, it may be either anticipated correctly or incorrectly. To a large extent, the degree to which inflation causes any of the harms below depends upon how poorly anticipated it is, if at all.

A. **Inflation and People Who Hold Money** -- With inflation, the purchasing power of money declines. As a result, people who hold their assets in a liquid form experience an erosion of their purchasing power during periods of inflation.

B. **Inflation and Savers** -- Inflation may also erode the value of money set aside in savings. In an attempt to offset inflation's effects, interest rates are adjusted for the expected rate of inflation, so that the actual interest rate paid (the **nominal interest rate**) is equal to the *real interest rate* plus the *expected inflation rate*. That is,

$$\text{Nominal interest rate} = \text{real interest rate} + \text{expected inflation rate.}$$

Of course, simply because interest rates attempt to adjust for expected inflation does not necessarily mean that savers won't lose purchasing power. That will depend upon how well the market does at anticipating the inflation rate.

C. **Inflation and Lenders and Borrowers** -- Does inflation help borrowers at the expense of lenders, or vice versa? It all depends upon how well anticipated the inflation is. If there is unanticipated inflation, borrowers will gain purchasing power at the expense of lenders, since they will be paying back the loan with money that is worth less than the money they borrowed; if inflation is less than anticipated, then lenders gain at the expense of borrowers.

D. **Inflation and Social Tension** -- To the extent that people seek "scapegoats" to blame for their losses during a period of inflation, social tensions may increase.

E. **Inflation and Past Decisions** -- Inflation often turns past decisions into "mistakes," by changing the underlying conditions that were presumed when the decision was made.

F. **Inflation and Uncertainty** -- Inflation creates uncertainty. This uncertainty may well discourage people from entering into otherwise beneficial long-term agreements, causing mutually advantageous exchanges to be foregone. Such a result is inefficient.

G. **Inflation and Hedging Against Inflation** -- Individuals in an inflation-prone economy will tend to seek those investments that offer the best "hedge" (i.e., protection) against inflation, rather than those investments with the most productive potential. Resources are expended in the search for "inflation-proof" investments, and resource expansion is foregone by choosing a defensive position over an aggressive one.

H. Inflation and International Competitiveness -- When prices rise in the United States faster than they do in other countries, American-made goods become relatively more expensive to both U.S. and foreign consumers, while foreign-made goods become relatively cheaper to both groups. In such a situation, we would expect domestic purchasers to buy more foreign goods and foreign purchasers to buy fewer American-made goods. The net result: U.S. competitiveness in the international economy is hampered.

V. EXPECTATIONS, NOMINAL INTEREST RATES, AND INFLATION -- How are inflationary expectations formed; and, how do nominal interest rates respond to changes in the real interest rate and in inflationary expectations brought about by changes in the money supply?

A. The Expected Inflation Rate: How is it Formed? -- There are two key theories of inflationary expectations-formation: *adaptive expectations* and *rational expectations*.

  1. Adaptive Expectations -- holds that *individuals form their inflationary expectations based upon (recent) past experience, and that expectations change slowly and over a length of time*. Such a process of forming and reforming expectations opens the door to substantial short-term differences between expected and actual inflation.

  2. Rational Expectations -- holds that *individuals form their inflationary expectations on the basis of past experience as well as their predictions about the effects of present and future policy actions*. The catch-phrase often used to describe rational expectations is that they are formed using "all available information." By their nature, rational expectations adjust more rapidly to missed predictions than do adaptive expectations. The fundamental difference between adaptive and rational expectations-formation can be summed up as: "reactive" (adaptive) vs. "proactive" (rational).

B. Increases in the Money Supply and Changes in the Nominal Interest Rate -- A change in the money supply will affect the nominal interest rate in two ways: first, it will change the real interest rate; and, second, it will change the expected inflation rate.

  1. How the Money Supply Affects the Real Interest Rate

    a. The Liquidity Effect -- A change in the money supply affects the supply of loanable funds -- specifically, an increase in the money supply increases the supply of loanable funds. This, in turn, lowers the real interest rate -- the price of loanable funds. When the real interest rate falls, so does the nominal rate. This *decrease in real and nominal interest rates due to an increase in the supply of loanable funds* is the **liquidity effect** of an increase in the money supply.

    b. The Income Effect -- Increases in the money supply also lead to an increase in aggregate demand and to an increase in nominal GDP. Most economists believe that increases in national income will increase the demand for loanable funds, putting upward pressure on real and nominal interest rates. This *increase in real and nominal interest rates due to an increase in nominal GDP* is the **income effect** of an increase in the money supply.

2. **How the Money Supply Affects the Expected Inflation Rate** -- To the extent that continued increases in the money supply cause continued inflation, and that inflationary expectations (adaptive or rational) are at least partly determined by past inflationary experience, there is a link between the expected inflation rate and the money supply. We would expect expected inflation to be a positive function of changes in the money supply -- as increases in the money supply increase inflation and, thus, expected inflation. The *increase in the nominal interest rates brought about by an increase in the expected inflation rate* is the **expectations effect** of an increase in the money supply.

C. **Timing of the Adjustment** -- Exhibit 11-9 "maps" the timing of adjustments in the nominal interest rate to changes in the money supply, highlighting each of the effects discussed above.

VI. **APPENDIX B: A MORE COMPLETE MONETARIST MODEL** -- This appendix shows how changes in the money supply affect the economy in the monetarist model by looking at money supply and money demand.

A. **An Increase in the Money Supply** -- If the Fed increases the money supply, the initial effect is a disequilibrium at point 2 in Exhibit 11B-3. Individuals are holding *"too much" money*. Though people might think they could never have too much money, in economics this is a relative concept. Individuals hold too much money relative to other goods, so they spend the money. This increases aggregate demand, and thus GDP. The economy moves *along* the money demand curve until it reaches the new equilibrium at point 3.

B. **A Decrease in the Money Supply** -- This is the reverse of an increase in the money supply and is illustrated in Exhibit 11B-4. As a result of a decrease in the money supply, individuals hold too little money relative to goods and are in a disequilibrium at point 2. Individuals increase their money balances, and decrease their spending. The economy moves along the money demand curve until it reaches the new equilibrium at point 3.

C. **A Change in GDP Without a Change in the Money Supply** -- A decrease in the demand for money (a decrease in k) will cause the money demand line to rotate downward as illustrated in Exhibit 11B-5. Now $M^s > M^d$ and individuals are holding too much money. Individuals spend money, demand for goods increases, and GDP increases as illustrated.

D. **Three States of the Economy in Monetarism** -- Just as the economy was classified into three different states in the AD-AS model (recessionary gap, inflationary gap, and long-run equilibrium), there are three different states in the monetarist view of the economy. These three states are

1. **Too much money ($M^s > M^d$), in which case spending increases and GDP rises;**

2. **Too little money ($M^s < M^d$), in which case spending decreases and GDP falls; and,**

3. **The right amount of money ($M^s = M^d$), in which case spending and GDP do not change.**

E. **The Big Question: How Stable are k and V?** -- If k (and, therefore, V) does not change, it means that the **demand for money** -- *how much money people want to hold as a percentage of their income* -- is stable. This does not mean, however, that the quantity demanded of money is stable. That will change with the level of GDP. But just how stable are k and V? The monetarists hold that *k and V are both highly stable and predictable*. As a result, any change in the money supply will have a significant (and predictable) impact on nominal GDP. [See Exhibit 11B-7]

F. **Keynesian and Monetarist Theory Contrasted** -- Whereas Keynesians focus on the spending components of total expenditures, Monetarists focus on the money supply and money demand. Keynesians study the expenditure multiplier and its stability, while monetarists study velocity and its stability. For Keynesians, the link between changes in the money supply and GDP works indirectly through expenditures, but monetarists believe the link is direct through changes in money holdings.

G. **Association Is Not Causation: The Lesson Again** -- Although monetarists have shown a clear link between changes in the money supply and changes in GDP, association does not imply causation. Keynesians argue that the causation runs from changes in spending to changes in GDP to changes in the money supply, not from changes in the money supply to changes in GDP as the monetarists assert. To prove their point, Monetarists cite historical examples in which changes in the money supply clearly occurred before changes in GDP, such as in 1936-1937. The debate continues.

VI. **ECONOMICS ON THE INTERNET** -- Sources for money supply, interest rate, and federal funds data are provided. Also, the address for DowVision which provides the full text of the *Wall Street Journal* is given.

■ ANSWERS TO CHAPTER QUESTIONS

1. What are the assumptions and predictions of the simple quantity theory of money? Does the simple quantity theory of money predict well?

The assumptions of the simple quantity theory of money are that velocity and output are constant. If these two assumptions hold true, then there is a direct link between changes in the money supply, and changes in prices. Over a long period of time (ten years), there is a strong relationship between changes in the money supply and changes in prices; however, in the short run the relationship can be weak because of changes in output or velocity which might occur.

2. In the simple quantity theory of money, the AS curve is vertical. Explain why.

One of the assumptions of the simple quantity theory of money is that output is fixed, which means that the AS curve is vertical. Without this assumption, there would not be a direct link between changes in the money supply and changes in prices.

3. In the simple quantity theory of money, what will lead to an increase in aggregate demand? In monetarism, what will lead to an increase in aggregate demand?

In the simple quantity theory of money (since velocity and output are assumed to be constant), a rise in the money supply will lead to an increase in aggregate demand. In monetarism, an increase in the money supply or in velocity will lead to an increase in aggregate demand.

4. **Explain how each of the following will affect velocity: (a) a decrease in the interest rate; (b) an increase in the frequency with which employees receive paychecks; and (c) a decrease in the expected inflation rate.**

(a) A decrease in interest rates would decrease velocity because the opportunity cost of holding money would decrease.

(b) An increase in the frequency of when employees receive paychecks would increase velocity because employees wouldn't have to hold as much money between paychecks.

(c) A decrease in the expected inflation rate would cause individuals to be willing to hold more money because the opportunity cost of holding money would fall. This change would decrease velocity.

5. **How will each of the changes in question 4 affect the price level and Real GDP in both the short run and the long run, assuming that the economy is in long-run equilibrium before each of the changes takes place? Explain your answer.**

Assuming the money supply remains constant, the effects of changes in velocity are illustrated in Exhibit 11-5. For an increase in velocity, as in 4(b), the first-round effect would be to shift the AD curve to the right, creating an inflationary gap in which the price level and Real GDP increase in the short run. The second-round effect would be higher wages in response to the low unemployment rate, shifting the SRAS curve to the left. The net effect in the long run, would be an increase in the price level, but no change in Real GDP. For a decrease in velocity, as in 4(a) and 4(c), the first-round effect would be to shift the AD curve to the left, creating a recessionary gap in which the price level and Real GDP decrease in the short run. The higher unemployment rate would lead to lower wages, shifting the SRAS curve to the right. The net effect in the long run would be a lower price level, but no change in Real GDP.

6. **"A loaf of bread, a computer, and automobile tires have gone up in price; therefore, we are experiencing inflation." Do you agree or disagree with this statement? Explain your answer.**

Given the information, we would disagree. Simply because the prices of three goods have increased, it does not follow that there is inflation, which is an increase in the price level. It could be that three prices have increased, and three (other) prices have decreased. The price level is not necessarily higher because three prices are higher.

7. **What is the difference in the long run between a one-shot increase in aggregate demand and a one-shot decrease in short-run aggregate supply?**

The difference is seen in terms of the price level. If aggregate demand increases, the short-run price level increases. In the long-run, the price level is higher than it was in the short run. This is illustrated in Exhibit 11-1. If aggregate supply decreases, the short-run price level increases. But in the long run, the price level is lower than it was in the short run. It has returned to its original level. This is illustrated in Exhibit 11-2.

8. "One-shot inflation may be a demand-side (of the economy) or supply-side phenomenon, but continued inflation is likely to be a demand-side phenomenon." Do you agree or disagree with this statement? Explain your answer.

Agree. The reason is that it is easier to produce continuous increases in aggregate demand which increase the price level than for there to be continuous supply shocks to the economy. If the Federal Reserve increased the money supply, this would cause an increase in aggregate demand and a one-shot increase in inflation to a higher price level. In order to cause continued inflation, the Federal Reserve would have to increase the money supply every year, which it is capable of doing. On the other hand, a supply shock (such as a crop failure) would have to occur. This would shift the SRAS curve to the left causing an increase in the supply level. For inflation to continue, there would have to be crop failures every year without a reallocation of resources to farming to offset the decrease in supply. This is unlikely to occur.

9. Explain how demand-induced one-shot inflation may appear as supply-induced one-shot inflation.

Suppose the money supply increases, boosting aggregate demand and raising the prices that consumer-laborers must pay for goods and services, while the short-run aggregate supply curve remains unchanged. Faced with these higher prices, the consumer-laborers will demand higher wages from their employers, shifting the SRAS leftward, *ceteris paribus*, and raising the price level. From the producers' perspective, the inflation was caused by higher wage demands.

10. In recent years, economists have argued over what the true value of the real interest rate is at any one time and over time. Given that the nominal interest rate = real interest rate + expected inflation rate, it follows that the real interest rate = nominal interest rate - expected inflation rate. Therefore isn't computing the real interest rate quite easy? Why is there so much disagreement on the true value of the real interest rate?

Theoretically, it is easy to compute the real interest rate. As we said, it is equal to the nominal interest rate *minus* the expected inflation rate. The problem is that it is difficult, if not impossible, to observe the expected inflation rate. Consider a nominal interest rate of 15 percent. We know that this 15 percent nominal interest rate is composed of the real interest rate and the expected inflation rate. But there are numerous combinations of real interest rates and expected inflation rates that will give us a 15 percent nominal interest rate. We could have a 10 percent real interest rate and a 5 percent expected inflation rate, or a 9 percent real interest rate and a 6 percent expected inflation rate, or a 4 percent real interest rate and an 11 percent expected inflation rate, and so on. Some economists believe the real interest rate is relatively stable over time, so changes in the nominal interest rate are due to changes in the expected inflation rate; but other economists do not agree with this, at least not to the same degree.

11. How does unanticipated inflation affect people who hold money? How does it affect borrowers? Explain your answers.

Unanticipated inflation hurts people who hold money because it reduces the purchasing power of the money they hold. Borrowers benefit from inflation because the real value of their loans declines, and they are able to pay back the loans in inflated dollars.

12. How might the Fed influence the international competitiveness of the United States?

As we discussed in Chapter 10, the Federal Reserve System has several tools at its disposal which may be used to influence the domestic macroeconomy and, in turn, the international competitiveness of the United States. The discussion in this chapter focuses upon the role that inflation has on competitiveness -- to wit, the higher domestic inflation is relative to inflation in competing economies, the more likely domestic purchasers are to look outside the United States for goods and services, and the less likely foreign purchasers are to look to the United States. Thus, to the extent that the Fed can affect inflation -- through the use of open market operations, the discount rate, and/or the reserve requirement -- it can have a marked influence on the international competitiveness of the U.S. economy.

13. What is the difference between adaptive and rational expectations?

Under adaptive expectations, people learn from the past over time. If prices go up, they will demand an increase in wages equal to the inflation rate in the last period to compensate them for the loss in purchasing power. Under rational expectations, individuals not only try to adjust to past inflation rates, but predict what future inflation rates will be and make their demands based upon their rational expectations of what will happen in their future, rather than just adaptively adjusting to changes which have occurred in the past. Someone using adaptive expectations would say, "Prices rose by 5% last year, so I'm going to demand a 5% wage increase." Someone using rational expectations would say, "Prices rose by 5% last year and will probably rise by 8% next year, so I'm going to demand an 8% wage increase."

14. Explain how the money supply can affect both the real interest rate and the expected inflation rate.

Changes in the money supply affect the real interest rate through the liquidity effect and the income effect. An increase in the money supply increases the supply of loanable funds and lowers the real interest rate via the liquidity effect. An increase in the money supply increases the demand for goods which also causes an increased demand for loanable funds which in turn raises interest rates. When people have experienced inflation in the past as a result of increases in the money supply, then new changes in the money supply will create expectations of future inflation which can become self-fulfilling.

15. Suppose the money supply increased 30 days ago. Whether the nominal interest rate is higher, lower, or the same today as it was 30 days ago depends upon what? Explain your answer.

Whether the nominal interest rate is higher, lower, or the same after 30 days depends upon whether the expenditure effect outweighs the liquidity and income effects yet. If expectations are formed rationally, consumers will realize that the increase in the money supply will soon cause inflation which will raise the nominal interest rate. Prices will immediately adjust to the change in expectations. On the other hand, if expectations are formed adaptively, they will respond to past changes in prices, not future changes. In this case, the increased liquidity will lower nominal interest rates, and it may take more than 30 days for the expenditure effect to outweigh the liquidity and income effects.

■ ANSWERS TO APPENDIX QUESTIONS

1. What are different ways of saying the demand for money is stable?

One can say: (1) k is stable; (2) V is stable; (3) The percentage of their incomes that individuals hold in the form of money balances is stable -- that is, the ratio M^d/PQ is stable.

2. Calculate M^d at each of the following different levels of k and PQ: (a) k = 1/4; PQ = $350 billion; (b) k = 1/5; PQ = $700 billion; (c) k = 1/10; PQ = $1,000 billion; (d) k = 1/3; PQ = $1,250 billion; (e) k = 1/8; PQ = $2,000 billion.

a. M^d = 1/4 ($350 billion) = $87.5 billion
b. M^d = 1/5 ($700 billion) = $140 billion
c. M^d = 1/10 ($1,000 billion) = $100 billion
d. M^d = 1/3 ($1,250 billion) = $416.7 billion
e. M^d = 1/8 ($2,000 billion) = $250 billion

3. Suppose M^d is $300 billion at a GDP level of $900 billion in year 1, and $400 billion at a GDP level of $1,000 in year 2. Is the demand for money the same in both years? Explain your answer.

Generally speaking, the demand for money refers to individuals holding money. Specifically, it refers to the percentage of their incomes they hold in money form. Viewed in this way, it is a ratio--specifically, M^d/PQ. In year 1, this ratio is $300/$900 or 1/3. In year 2, the ratio is $400/$1,000 or 2/5. We know that 2/5 is greater than 1/3, thus the demand for money in year 1 is greater than the demand for money in year 2. Another way of stating this, is to say that k is higher in year 2 than in year 1 (thus the money demand line in year 2 lies above the money demand line in year 1).

4. If individuals collectively are holding too much money, how can they ever hold the optimum or right amount of money, since no one is ever going to burn money or throw it away?

Individuals need not burn money or throw it away in order to go from a position where they are holding too much money to where they are holding the optimum amount of money. If individuals are holding too much money, they simply trade it for goods and services, thus increasing prices and/or output. This in turn leads to a higher nominal national income, and individuals desire to hold more money at higher nominal national income than at a lower nominal national income.

5. Suppose M^s = $300, M^d = $250, and GDP = $1,200 (all numbers in billions). From this, we know that M^s/GDP > M^d/GDP. We also know that we are in monetary disequilibrium. If the _k_ in M^d = k X GDP is the same at the new monetary equilibrium point as it is at present, by how much must GDP increase?

By $240 (to $1,440). The object is to get the two ratios to equal. At present,

$$M^s/GDP_1 = 300/1200 = .25 \text{ while } M^d/GDP_1 = 250/1200 = .208.$$

In order to make things equal, we add $240 and get

$$M^s/GDP_2 = 300/1440 = .208 = 300/1440 = M^d/GDP_2.$$

6. What would be the directional change in GDP, given the following changes: (a) a decrease in the interest rate; (b) an increase in the expected rate of inflation; (c) an increase in money supply; (d) a decrease in money demand.

a. A decrease in interest rates would increase money demand, shifting AD to the left, and *decreasing* nominal national income.
b. An increase in the expected rate of inflation would decrease money demand, shifting AD to the right, and *increasing* nominal national income.
c. An increase in the money supply shifts AD to the right and *increases* nominal national income.
d. A decrease in money demand shifts AD to the right and *increases* nominal national income.

7. Suppose you are explaining to a friend who has had no training in economics that there are times when individuals find themselves holding too much money. Your friend says that that would never happen to her. She says that she has never held too much money, but rather that she has always held too little money. As she says this, she hands a ten-dollar bill to the cashier in the grocery store. What might you say that would help your friend understand that individuals can and do sometimes find that they are holding too much money?

Think of holding money as opposed to spending money. Holding 'too much' money means that, as you have just done, you prefer goods to money given your current cash holdings. Holding 'too little' money, on the other hand, would mean that you would rather hold cash than spend it."

8. In this chapter, we learned that PQ, or GDP does not change unless either M or V changes (recall that MV = PQ). This implies that before a fiscal policy measure can affect GDP, it must affect V. Do you think a change in government spending or taxes would affect V directly or indirectly through a change in some variable that directly affects V? If indirectly, what variable do you suggest?

The stronger case can be made for an indirect effect on V. In the case of changes in government spending, the most likely effect on V will come via the effect of government borrowing (increased or decreased) on interest rates, though expectations of inflation may also be affected by the fiscal policy move, and affect V in turn. In the case of taxes, V would also be indirectly affected via inflationary expectations; however, in this instance, there may also be a direct effect on k -- and, by necessity, an opposite effect on V.

132

■ LECTURE SUPPLEMENTS

"Death by Deflation," *The Economist*, **June 17, 1995, p. 80.**

Although most countries have suffered inflation during the twentieth century, Japan is currently facing the problem of deflation. This article allows you to explore the costs of deflation. Just as inflation creates economic costs, so does deflation. The deflation has been a general decrease in prices: land, equities, even goods and services. Official measures of both the wholesale price index and the consumer price index both show lower prices, even though these indices have an inflationary bias.

Why the deflation? Primarily, it is the strength of the yen. What problems can deflation cause? The expectation of lower prices can cause consumers to delay purchases creating recession. Lower prices make debtors' real burden increase in size. Falling prices increase real interest rates, making it more difficult for the government to use monetary policy to get the economy going again.

Will Japan's deflation lead to a 1930s' type depression? Probably not. Economists better understand how to avoid the type of depression that occurred in the 1930s. The greatest risk is that a financial collapse occurs due to banks' bad debts. As long as this does not occur, the probability of a depression is low.

Matt Moffett and Jonathan Friedland, "Taking a Huge Risk, Argentina Intentionally Deflates Its Economy," *Wall Street Journal,* **March 21, 1995, p. A1, column 1.**

Unlike Japan, Argentina is not actually deflating, but it is making an attempt to stop inflation rather than have deflation. Argentina has had one of the longest bouts of inflation of any country in the world. Successfully stopping inflation would be a monumental change for an economy which has lived with persistent, high inflation for decades. If there were an Inflation Anonymous twelve-step program, Argentina would have to attend twice a day. Nevertheless, Argentina is making a valiant effort to stop inflation. This and another article on page A11 in this *Wall Street Journal* look at Argentina's efforts.

Using the motto "Death before devaluation", Jaime Campos led the battle against inflation. The battle against inflation, and the inevitable devaluation which it leads to, was treated as a war. Argentina set its peso at an exchange rate of one peso to the U.S. dollar, and so far it has maintained that exchange rate and has battled the menace of inflation. The pegging of the peso to the dollar initially spurred foreign investors' confidence in Argentina and brought capital in for investment.

When the Mexican peso crisis occurred, however, the capital flow dried up. Argentina was found guilty by association. Now deflation has set in. Real estate prices are falling as are the prices of some consumer durables. To insure that inflation doesn't occur, the government is even trimming officials' salaries, both in the private and in the public sector. Use this article so students can understand the effects of stopping inflation.

Steve Stecklow, "Colleges Inflate SATs and Graduation Rates in Popular Guidebooks," **Wall Street Journal" April 5, 1995, page A1, column 1.**

Students should find this article interesting, especially if they are freshmen who have just spent a year comparing colleges to find out which college best suits their needs. The article is also useful to remind students that inflation does not occur only in the economic sector, but it is a general phenomenon which can occur in any area of life.

To what extent the way colleges play with the truth is outright lying and what part is marketing is a matter of debate, but the article shows how some colleges adjust their figures to put themselves in a more favorable light. The reason? Schools not in the top rankings find it difficult to get students.

For example, Northeastern University in Boston excludes both international students and remedial students, who together represent 20 percent of the freshman class, in order to calculate the school's average SAT scores. By doing so, they raised their school's SAT average by 50 points. Schools argue that many of the lower-scoring students were admitted under special circumstances, and so, they should not be included in the calculation of average SAT scores.

As in the economic sector, when demand goes up, inflation occurs. When demand for schools to have high SAT scores for their students occurs, inflation is inevitable.

CHAPTER 12

Monetary Policy

Chapter 8 discussed fiscal policy, the first of two general types of policy that may be used to address macroeconomic problems. In this chapter, we consider the second: *monetary policy* -- changes in the money supply, or in the rate of growth of the money supply, to achieve particular macroeconomic goals. Chapter 12 begins with a discussion of the *money demand curve*, and how it interacts with the supply of money to create equilibrium (disequilibrium) in the money market. The chapter then turns to the effectiveness of monetary policy in affecting interest rates, investment, real output, and the price level. The chapter concludes with a look at the *activist-nonactivist* debate, and two key proposals for conducting *nonactivist monetary policy*.

■ CHAPTER OBJECTIVES

Upon completing this chapter, your students should be able to:

- compare and contrast the Keynesian *transmission mechanism* (for changes in the money supply) to the monetarist and new classical transmission mechanisms;

- describe the relationship between interest rates and bond prices;

- discuss the main points of the *activist-nonactivist* debate;

- define *monetary rule*, explain how one might work, and discuss the arguments for and against rule-based monetary policy; and,

- explain the workings of a *gold standard*.

■ KEY TERMS

- monetary policy
- demand for money (balances)
- transmission mechanism
- liquidity trap
- expansionary monetary policy
- contractionary monetary policy

- activists
- fine-tuning
- nonactivists
- monetary rule
- gold standard

135

■ CHAPTER OUTLINE

I. **THE MONEY MARKET**

   A. **The Demand for Money Balances** -- In Chapter 3, we introduced the concepts of supply and demand, placing price on the vertical axis and quantity on the horizontal axis. Here we see the **demand curve for money balances**, which *illustrates the inverse relationship between the quantity demanded of money and the interest rate*, which is the opportunity cost, or "price," of holding money (as opposed to some other asset). [See Exhibit 12-1a]

   B. **The Supply of Money** -- Exhibit 12-1b shows the money supply curve as a vertical line, suggesting that the quantity of money is fixed at a level largely determined by the Fed.

   C. **Equilibrium in the Money Market** -- Equilibrium in the money market exists when the *quantity demanded of money equals the quantity supplied*. Graphically, equilibrium is represented by the intersection of the demand curve of money and the supply curve of money. *At any interest rate above the equilibrium rate, there is an* **excess supply of money**. *At any interest rate below the equilibrium rate, there is an* **excess demand for money**. [See Exhibit 12-2]

II. **TRANSMISSION MECHANISMS** -- To what degree do changes in the money market affect the product market? And, how do changes in the money market get "transmitted" to the product market? Here we look at three different **transmission mechanisms** -- *the routes, or channels, by which changes in the money market affect the product market.*

   A. **The Keynesian Transmission Mechanism** -- The Keynesian link between the money market and product market is indirect and fairly complicated.

   1. **How Does it Work?** -- Exhibit 12-3 traces the effects of an increase in the money supply, step-by-step. In summary, *an increase in the money supply creates an excess supply of money, decreasing the interest rate* (panel a); *as the interest rate falls, investment spending increases* (panel b), *which, in turn, shifts the AD curve to the right, increasing Real GDP* (panel c). The process works the same for a decrease in the money supply.

   2. **The Keynesian Mechanism May Get Blocked**

      a. **Interest-Insensitive Investment** -- As we discussed before, Keynes did not agree with the classical notion that investment was always responsive to changes in the interest rate. Exhibit 12-4a presents the extreme cases of investment demand that is completely interest-insensitive. *To the extent that investment does not respond to changes in the interest rate, a change in interest rates, brought about by a change in the money supply, will have little or no effect on total planned expenditures, aggregate demand, and Real GDP.*

      b. **The Liquidity Trap** -- Keynesian economists have argued that, under certain circumstances, the money demand curve can become horizontal at very low interest rates. This so-called **liquidity trap** -- *the horizontal section of the demand curve for money* -- creates yet another potential problem for the Keynesian transmission mechanism. As Exhibit 12-4b shows, *if we are "in" a liquidity trap, a change in the supply of money has no effect on the interest rate, nor is an excess supply of money generated. As a result, there will be no overflow into the loanable funds market, meaning that the effects of the change in money supply are isolated to the money market.*

136

3. **The Effectiveness of Monetary Policy** -- Due to the potential problems of interest-insensitive investment and the liquidity trap, Keynesian economists see expansionary monetary policy as being less effective than expansionary fiscal policy. But the problem is asymmetric. That is, since they do not consider interest-insensitive investment and the liquidity trap to be pertinent to contractionary monetary policy, Keynesians feel that contractionary monetary policy is more effective at decreasing Real GDP than expansionary monetary policy is at increasing Real GDP.

4. **Bond Prices and Interest Rates** -- There is an inverse relationship between bond prices and the interest rate. If interest rates go up from 8% to 10%, and you own a bond which pays 6%, you won't be able to sell the bond at its face value of $1000 because investors can now buy a bond which pays 10% for $1000. The only way you can sell the bond is to lower the price from $1000 to $800 so it will yield a 10% return. Since the simple Keynesian model assumes two alternative uses for an individual's financial resources: hold it as money or buy bonds; the liquidity trap can be seen as an expression of individuals' beliefs that bond prices are too high. If you expect interest rates to rise, don't buy bonds, but wait until the price drops.

B. **The Monetarist Transmission Mechanism** -- The monetarist transmission mechanism is much more direct and much less complicated. Specifically, an increase in the money supply creates an excess supply of money. Individuals respond to this excess by spending it on all manner of goods and services, thus AD shifts to the right as a direct result of the increase in the money supply -- the loanable funds market is bypassed. [See Exhibit 12-5]

III. **MONETARY POLICY AND THE PROBLEM OF INFLATIONARY AND RECESSIONARY GAPS** -- Exhibits 12-6 and 12-7 show how AD may be manipulated, through the use of expansionary and contractionary monetary policy, to deal with the problems of inflationary and recessionary gaps. In Exhibit 12-6, the economy is in a recessionary gap. **Expansionary monetary policy** through an appropriate increase in the money supply will shift the AD curve rightward, moving the economy back to long-run equilibrium. In Exhibit 12-7, the economy is in an inflationary gap. An appropriate decrease in the money supply will shift the AD curve leftward moving the economy back to long-run equilibrium. Most Keynesians feel that *the market economy is more likely to act on its own to address an inflationary gap than it is to address a recessionary gap.* As a result, Keynesians are more likely to advocate expansionary monetary policy to eliminate a stubborn recessionary gap than **contractionary monetary policy** to eliminate an inflationary gap. [Exhibit 12-8]

IV. **MONETARY POLICY AND THE ACTIVIST-NONACTIVIST DEBATE** -- In Chapter 8, we discussed perceived problems with discretionary fiscal policy -- specifically, "crowding out" and time lags. We also presented the counter-arguments that suggested that discretionary fiscal policy is both workable and beneficial. This discretionary vs. non-discretionary, or activist-nonactivist, debate carries over into monetary policy issues as well.

A. **Activists vs. Nonactivists** -- **Activists** argue that discretionary monetary and fiscal policy should be deliberately used to address macroeconomic problems. **Nonactivists** argue against the deliberate use of discretionary fiscal and monetary policies.

B. **The Case for Activist Monetary Policy** -- The case for activist monetary policy rests on three major claims:

137

1. **The Economy Adjusts Too Slowly** -- The economy does not always reach full-employment equilibrium quickly enough, by itself, to avoid serious losses in real output and high unemployment.

2. **Activist Monetary Policy Works** -- Previous experience with nonactivist monetary policy has been disappointing, whereas activist policy has worked very well on several occasions.

3. **Increased Flexibility** -- Activist monetary policy is more flexible than rule-based, nonactivist monetary policy. To the extent that policy should address the particular conditions at the time, the increased flexibility afforded by activist policy is preferable.

C. **The Case for Nonactivist Monetary Policy** -- The case for nonactivist monetary policy (against activist monetary policy) rests on three major claims:

1. **Wage-Price Flexibility Allows Quick Adjustment** -- Wage-price flexibility allows the economy to achieve full-employment equilibrium at a reasonable speed.

2. **Activist Monetary Policy May Not Work** -- Economists who believe individuals form their expectations rationally argue that anticipated monetary policy will be ineffective at changing Real GDP or unemployment. [See Exhibit 12-9]

3. **Activist Policies are Likely to be Destabilizing** -- Due to the effect of time lags, activist policy is more likely to be destabilizing than stabilizing -- that is, activist policy may make matters worse, rather than better. [See Exhibit 12-10]

4. **Christmas, the Fed, and the *Wall Street Journal*** -- This *Economics And the Media* feature is a good example of the mating dance which the Fed and bond traders do with one another, as they constantly try to interpret and influence the other's actions. In this case, a normal pre-holiday liquidity injection before Thanksgiving 1993 was wrongly interpreted as a signal that the Fed wanted to lower interest rates. The Fed's dilemma was to convince bond traders that this was not their intention without causing the bond market to overreact in the other direction. Eventually, the Fed and the bond traders got things right.

V. **NONACTIVIST MONETARY PROPOSALS**

A. **A Monetary Rule** -- Most nonactivist favor the use of a **monetary rule**, whereby the growth rate of the money supply is *predetermined*. Specifically, *the annual growth rate of the money supply should equal the average annual growth rate of Real GDP.*

1. **The Monetary Rule Over Time** -- Some years will see Real GDP grow less than its natural rate, thereby making money supply grow "too fast" and cause inflation, while other years Real GDP growth will be greater than average, causing money supply to go "too slowly," and reducing the price level. Over the long haul, monetary rule advocates argue, the price level will be more stable than with discretionary policy.

2. **Criticisms of the Monetary Rule** -- The problems with this rule, say critics, are: (1) it assumes that velocity is constant, which it clearly is not; and, (2) it assumes that we can correctly define and measure the money supply, both of which are arguable.

3. **A "Variable Growth" Rule** -- Largely in response to the criticism that velocity is not constant, some monetary rule advocates prefer a rule such that the annual growth rate of the

money supply equal the annual growth rate of Real GDP minus the growth rate of velocity. This way, they say, the money supply can adjust to changes in both real output and velocity.

B. **A Gold Standard** -- A more politically-charged alternative is to return the U.S. economy to some type of **gold standard**, *where the value of paper money is partially or totally determined by the market value of gold, and where the government guarantees that it can redeem its paper money in gold*, according to the percentage of "backing" it establishes.

1. **The Mechanics of a Gold Standard** -- Running a gold standard requires two steps. First, the government "pegs" the price of gold at some dollar amount, thus setting the official price of gold. Then, the government agrees to buy and sell gold so as to keep the official price of gold equal to its market price. When the government buys gold, it increases the supply of money in circulation; when the government sells gold, it takes money out of circulation. [See Exhibit 12-11]

2. **The Case for a Gold Standard** -- Proponents of the gold standard argue that, as long as the government keeps the official price of gold equal to the market price, the general price level will remain constant.

3. **Criticisms of the Gold Standard** -- Critics argue that the gold standard is no guarantee against inflation. If the supply of gold were to increase unexpectedly, the market price would fall below the official price, forcing the government to buy gold, and putting upward pressure on the money supply and the price level. Furthermore, critics argue that, if the price level does not fall in proportion to a decrease in the gold-backed money supply, Real GDP will fall and unemployment will rise.

4. **Does the Fed Occasionally Look to Gold? Or, How Can Monetary Policy Be too Expansionary if the CPI Is Constant?** -- According to Wayne Angell, a former governor of the Federal Reserve, gold is the single best predictor of future inflation, a fact Alan Greenspan has alluded to during his testimony before Congress. If the CPI is stable, but the price of gold is rising, some would interpret this as meaning that the CPI could begin rising soon. Whether the Fed should have a *gold-price target* is debatable, but the Fed does monitor the price of gold in formulating its policies.

VI. **ECONOMICS ON THE INTERNET** -- The source for U.S. Treasury Auction results is given, as well as sources for discount rate data and exchange rate data.

■ ANSWERS TO CHAPTER QUESTIONS

1. **Consider the following: Two researchers, A and B, are trying to determine whether eating fatty foods leads to heart attacks. Researchers A and B proceed differently. Researcher A builds a model where fatty foods *may* first affect X in one's body, and if X is affected, then Y may be affected, and if Y is affected, then Z may be affected. Finally, if Z is affected, the heart is affected, and the individual has an increased probability of suffering a heart attack. Researcher B doesn't proceed in this step-by-step fashion. She conducts an experiment to see if people who eat many fatty foods have a higher, lower, or equal incidence of heart attacks as people who eat few fatty foods. Which researcher's methods have more in common with the research methodology implicit in the Keynesian transmission mechanism? Which researcher's methods have more in common with the research methodology implicit in the monetarist transmission mechanism? Explain your answer.**

Researcher A's methods remind us of the Keynesian transmission mechanism where there is an indirect link between the money market and the goods and services market. Researcher A appears to see an indirect link between fatty foods and heart attacks. Before the heart attack result, X, Y, and Z have to be affected. Researcher B's methods remind us of the monetarist transmission mechanism where there is a direct link between the money market and the goods and services market. Researcher B looks at the intake of fatty foods and heart attacks and little else. We raised this question to demonstrate to you that when it comes to different approaches to finding the truth, there are "Keynesians" and "monetarists" in fields other than economics, although they are not called by those names.

2. If bond prices fall, will individuals want to hold more or less money? Explain your answer.

They will want to hold less money. As bond prices fall, interest rates rise. As interest rates rise, the opportunity cost of holding money increases, and individuals will want to hold less money.

3. It has been suggested that nonactivists are not concerned with the level of real output and employment, since most (if not all) nonactivist monetary proposals set as their immediate objective the stabilization of the price level. Discuss.

This is a false charge since most nonactivists believe that a stable price level will lead to the desirable ends. For example, many nonactivist-monetarists argue that if the price level is stabilized, the expected inflation rate will be zero and nominal interest rates will be lower and more stable. Additionally, they claim that the economic mistakes individuals naturally make when their expected inflation rate is unequal to the actual inflation rate will decrease in size and number due to the convergence of the two rates.

4. Suppose the combination of more accurate data and better forecasting techniques made it easy for the Fed to predict a recession 10 to 16 months in advance. Would this strengthen the case for activism or nonactivism? Explain your answer.

It would strengthen the case for activism. For example, one of the reasons nonactivists argue against activist monetary policy is that by the time the Fed realizes the economic problem at hand, takes action, and the policy begins to bear consequences, it is too late. The Fed policy might have been the right medicine for an earlier time, but turns out to be the wrong medicine by the time it takes hold. If it were possible to predict events *accurately* far in advance, this wouldn't be such a problem. For example, if the total lag in monetary policy is 13.3 months, and it is possible for the Fed to predict accurately, say, a recession 13.3 months in advance, then there would be less chance of its policy measures turning out to be the wrong medicine at the wrong time. The Fed would be better able to time the right medicine to hit at the right time.

5. Suppose it were proved that there is no liquidity trap and that investment is not interest insensitive. Would this be enough to disprove the Keynesian claim that expansionary monetary policy is not always effective at changing Real GDP? Why or why not?

It would not be enough to disprove the Keynesian claim. It is possible that something other than the liquidity trap and interest-insensitive investment spending could break the link between the money market and the goods and services market. However, it would be enough to say the Keynesians were wrong in what they believed could break the link.

6. **Both the activists and nonactivists make good points for their respective positions. Do you think there is anything an activist could say to a nonactivist to convince him or her to accept the activist position, and vice versa? If so, what is it? If not, why not?**

This one is probably right up there with world peace and harmony. The activists cling to the basic proposition that the market economy is not inherently self-stabilizing and that, therefore, government and/or the monetary authority has (have) a legitimate role to play in making discretionary policy moves aimed at fighting unemployment and inflation. They see activist policy as a superior alternative to rule-based policy. And, they favor the added flexibility that discretionary policy affords, allowing policymakers to adapt to changing conditions.

On the other hand, nonactivists consider activist policy to be unreliable at best, and reckless and dangerous at worst. The problems of crowding out (with fiscal policy) and time lags (with both fiscal and monetary policy), along with other factors, suggest that discretionary policy is doomed to be either ineffective or, worse, to have effects contrary to its intentions. Such a likelihood, given the nonactivist belief in the inherent stability of the market system, is enough to drive a good man to make a rule.

7. **In the discussion of supply and demand in Chapter 3, we noted that if two goods are substitutes, the price of one and the demand for the other are directly related. For example, if Pepsi-Cola and Coca-Cola are substitutes, an increase in the price of Pepsi-Cola will increase the demand for Coca-Cola. Suppose that bonds and stocks are substitutes. We know that interest rates and bond prices are inversely related. What do you predict is the relationship between stock prices and interest rates? Explain your answer.**

Given that stocks and bonds are substitutes, that the price of one good and the demand for its substitute are inversely related, and that interest rates and bond prices are inversely related, we would expect interest rates and stock prices to be inversely related as well. We know that an increase in bond prices will increase the demand for stock. Assuming that the quantity supplied of stock is not fixed, but rather will increase as stock prices rise; then an increase in the demand for stock should increase the price of stock. So, an increase in bond prices leads to an increase in stock prices. Now, since interest rates are inversely related to bond prices, and bond prices and stock prices move together, we should find that interest rates and stock prices are inversely related, q.e.d.

8. **Argue the case for and against a gold standard.**

Proponents of the gold standard argue that, as long as the government keeps the official price of gold equal to the market price, the general price level will remain constant. Critics argue that the gold standard is no guarantee against inflation. If the supply of gold were to increase unexpectedly, the market price would fall below the official price, forcing the government to buy gold, and putting upward pressure on the money supply and the price level. Furthermore, critics argue that, if the price level does not fall in proportion to a decrease in the gold-backed money supply, Real GDP will fall and unemployment will rise.

9. **Conduct the following exercise. Pick any week of the year. Quickly read through all the issues of the *Wall Street Journal* for that week, and write down the number of articles in which the word *Fed* is used, along with a brief summary of each article. Usually, the article will have to do with monetary policy. Many articles will also present opinions as to what the Fed has done, is doing, and will do. The chief economist at a major firm may say that he thinks the Fed is positioning itself to ease up on money supply growth in the upcoming months. An economic**

forecaster at a major bank may say she thinks the newest member of the Board of Governors will be persuasive in arguing for a slight tightening of the money supply because of his reputation as a fierce opponent of inflation.

What is the point of this exercise? First, the large number of articles in which the Fed is mentioned will show you how important the Fed and monetary policy are to the economics, political, banking, and business communities. Second, the quotations from people (supposedly) in the know will show you how much guessing and difference of opinion surrounds Fed monetary policy. Third, the factors cited as influencing Fed actions will give you a rough idea of how individuals think the Fed determines monetary policy.

After you conduct this exercise, sit down and reflect on the following questions:

a. Is the Fed implementing an activist monetary policy?

b. How does the Fed go about deciding whether it should increase or decrease the rate of growth of the money supply?

c. Would there be as many articles in the *Wall Street Journal* on monetary policy if there were a monetary rule or gold standard? If not, why not?

d. Would I be better off or worse off if I could accurately predict monetary policy? What monetary institutions are necessary for the accurate prediction of monetary policy?

e. Is the secrecy and guessing that surrounds Fed monetary policy a small price to pay for what the Fed has done to stabilize the economy, or is it a high price to pay for what the Fed has done to destabilize the economy?

If answers to these questions are not easily forthcoming, do not be concerned. As long as you can either ask or recognize questions relevant to monetary policy and possess some knowledge as to what the answers may be, you are ready to join the interesting and continuing debate on monetary policy. That is an important accomplishment.

Need we say more?

■ LECTURE SUPPLEMENTS

Jerry J. Jasinowski, "The Case Against Further Monetary Tightening," *Challenge*, January-February 1995, pp. 9-14, and Dimitri B. Papadimitriou and L. Randall Wray, "The Fed: Wrong Turn in Risky Traffic," *Challenge*, January-February 1995, pp. 15-21.

The articles which were suggested in Chapter 10 were brief reviews of the Fed's actions. These are longer articles which deal in length with the Fed and its monetary policies. These two articles can be good sources of debate and will enlighten students about the real world variables that the Fed and critics look at to determine whether the Fed should tighten or loosen monetary policy.

As you will see from these two articles, theory and practice are two different matters. It is easy to state that the Fed should keep the economy from sliding into a recession and control inflationary tendencies within the economy. The problem is determining whether the economy is booming or beginning to slide into a recession and determining the proper response.

In the real world, there are almost always contradictory signals. The government may revise GDP figures upward while housing starts are slowing. Purchasing managers may increase their orders while consumer confidence is weakening. And even the Fed's response can seem contradictory. During 1994 at the same time that the Fed was raising short-term interest rates dramatically, it was being rather liberal with the money supply. Use these two articles to make students realize that the most difficult part of monetary policy is determining what the condition of the economy is in, whether the Fed should respond, and what kind of response is needed.

"The Bond Market's Crystal Ball," *The Economist*, **May 27, 1995, p. 72.**

This article can be used to remind students that markets are one way of measuring individuals' expectations about government policy. Market participants who can correctly predict the course of future monetary policy can profit handsomely from their investments. If the Fed decides to lower interest rates, anyone who is long Treasury bonds will profit from the Fed's actions. This fact can be seen in the Fed's decision to lower interest rates in June 1995, reversing the pattern of 1994. Long-term interest rates had been declining for most of the year prior to the interest-rate cut signaling the market's belief that the Fed would not continue to raise interest rates anymore.

As the article points out, some countries (Australia, Canada, Sweden and Britain) issue both inflation-indexed bonds and nominal interest bonds. Both the coupon and the redemption payment are revalued in line with inflation for the inflation-indexed bonds. By comparing the yields on the nominal and the inflation-indexed bonds, you can determine the market's inflationary expectations. Comparing the difference in the bonds' yields provides a better indication of future inflation than the consumer price index because it looks to the future, not the past. This information can be used by the central bank to determine what the market's expectations about the economy are and what their response should be.

Ask your students what other measures the Fed could use to anticipate future inflationary movements. Examples would be commodity price indices and the predictions of economic policymakers.

"Rattling the Piggy Bank," *The Economist*, **May 6, 1995, p. 78.**

This article can be used to remind students of the relationship between interest rates and economic growth. As the author relates, the world has faced a secular decline in savings rates over the past twenty years, with most of the decline coming in the industrial countries where the savings rate has fallen from 25 percent to 20 percent.

This is important because studies show that there is a strong relationship between domestic savings and domestic investment. More savings mean lower interest rates, higher investment, and higher rates of growth. Real long-term interest rates have increased from 0.5 percent in the 1970s to 5 percent since 1981, reflecting the lack of savings available relative to the demand (part of the increase in demand has come from government budget deficits). The IMF estimates that each one percentage point rise in the world ratio of government debt to GDP adds 14 basis points to real long-term interest rates

The article also relates that 14 of the 20 fastest growing countries had savings rates of more than 25 percent of GDP while 14 of the 20 slowest growing countries had savings rates below 15 percent of GDP. Whether higher growth calls higher savings or vice versa is unclear. The article concludes that lower budget deficits would free up capital and lower real interest rates generating higher rates of growth in the future.

CHAPTER 13

Expectations Theory and the Economy

Chapter 11 discussed the importance of inflationary expectations in determining who might be harmed by inflation, and to what extent. It also introduced two prominent theories of how inflationary expectations are formed: adaptive expectations and rational expectations. This chapter continues that discussion, focusing on the development and modification of the Phillips curve, the controversy surrounding it, and the views of various schools of thought toward what the Phillips curve can and cannot tell us.

■ CHAPTER OBJECTIVES

Upon completing this chapter, your students should be able to:

- describe the process by which the optimal length of job search can be determined;

- explain the relationship between the length of search and the unemployment rate;

- understand how job search theory fits into the AD-AS framework;

- understand the concept of the *Phillips curve*, in both its original and Samuelson-Solow forms, and the consequences of the Phillips curve for economic *fine-tuning*;

- differentiate between a *short-run Phillips curve* and a (the) *long-run Phillips curve*;

- explain the Friedman natural rate theory and the role of expectations play in the working of the Phillips curve;

- define *stagflation* and explain how it does or does not fit into the Phillips curve framework;

- describe and distinguish between the *new classical ratex* model and the *new Keynesian ratex* model; and,

- trace the development of modern macroeconomic theory, with regard to questions of inflation, unemployment, and inflationary expectations, using Phillips curve analysis.

■ KEY TERMS

- reservation wage
- Phillips Curve
- stagflation

- Friedman natural rate theory
- ratex
- policy ineffectiveness proposition (PIP)

■ CHAPTER OUTLINE

I. **THE ECONOMIC THEORY OF JOB SEARCH** -- How long does an unemployed person search for a job? Or, perhaps more to the point, how long *should* an unemployed person search for a job; and, what factors will affect that search?

A. **The Rational Search for Jobs** -- All of these people are looking for work, the question is: How and how long do they look?

1. **The Wage Offer Curve** -- Most job searchers do not accept the first job they are offered, on the assumption that something better might be available. Up to a point, we assume that the more time someone spends looking, the better offers they will find. This relationship is represented by the *wage offer curve*, Exhibit 13-1a.

2. **The Reservation Wage Curve** -- Individuals searching for jobs realize that the search is costly to them. The main cost is wages foregone while the search is being carried out. For this reason, each searcher has in mind a minimum wage/salary offer that will be sufficient to stop the job search and accept the offer. This minimum wage is called the **reservation wage**. As time passes, we assume that people become somewhat more desperate to find a job, and therefore their reservation wage falls. The *reservation wage curve*, Exhibit 13-1b, demonstrates the negative relationship between duration of job search and a person's reservation wage.

3. **The Optimal Search Time** -- As Exhibit 13-2 shows, the optimal search time is the point where the reservation wage curve meets the wage offer curve; or, in words, *a searcher should take the first job offer that meets his/her reservation wage at the time of the offer.*

B. **Optimal Search Time and the Unemployment Rate** -- *An increase in optimal search time will increase the unemployment rate, ceteris paribus.* Exhibit 13-3 demonstrates this idea.

C. **Inflation Expectations and Optimal Search Time** -- A worker's inflation expectations affect how long he or she searches for a job. If job searchers have "too high" ("too low") an expected inflation rate, wage offers will seem to have less purchasing power (more purchasing power) than they actually have and therefore affect their perception of the wages they are being offered. Consequently, this affects the wage offer curve and the optimal search time. See Exhibit 13-4.

D. **Job Hunting on the Information Superhighway** -- This *Economics In Our Times* feature shows how individuals and firms are using the information superhighway and computers to search for jobs and to hire people. Compuserve, Prodigy, and America On-Line all provide help wanted listings. There are also electronic data bases which list companies hiring in your area of expertise. Finally, some firms are using computer interviews to screen applicants for jobs before the applicants are allowed to talk with a real person.

II. PHILLIPS CURVE ANALYSIS

A. **1958: The Phillips Curve** -- British economist A. W. Phillips first developed the relationship between increases in money wages -- **wage inflation** -- and the level of unemployment, in the British economy.

B. **An Inverse Relationship** -- The original **Phillips curve** depicted an *inverse relationship between wage inflation and unemployment rates*, and further implied that a trade-off existed, such that higher wage inflation meant lower unemployment, and lower wage inflation meant higher unemployment. [See Exhibit 13-5]

C. **The Theoretical Explanation for the Phillips Curve** -- When AD is increasing, businesses expand production and hire more labor. As the unemployment rate falls, wages rise. Thus, unemployment and wages are inversely related.

D. **1960: Samuelson and Solow: The Phillips Curve Is Americanized** -- American economists Paul Samuelson and Robert Solow tested Phillips' results on the American economy, using *price inflation*, rather than wage inflation. Using data from 1939 to 1959, they found a marked inverse relationship between price inflation and unemployment. [See Exhibit 13-6] As a result of the findings of Phillips and Samuelson-Solow, economists drew two conclusions:

1. **Stagflation is Unlikely** -- The simultaneous occurrence of high inflation and high unemployment, better known as **stagflation**, was not consistent with the inverse relationship between inflation and unemployment.

2. **Policy Makers May "Choose" Between Inflation-Unemployment Combinations** -- The Phillips curve offers a menu of choices that seemingly allowed policy makers to *"fine-tune"* the economy, moving it away from undesirable conditions.

III. THE CONTROVERSY BEGINS: Are There Really Two Phillips Curves?

A. **The 1970s and 1980s: Things Aren't Always As We Thought** -- In the 1970s and early 1980s, economists began to question many of the conclusions about the Phillips curve. As Exhibit 13-7 shows, the period from 1970-1987 does not "fit" the Phillips curve mold, as did the 1960s. Specifically, two items stand out.

1. **Stagflation is a Possibility** -- For one, the combination of high unemployment and high inflation in 1975, 1981, and 1982, suggest that stagflation has occurred.

2. **A Long-Run Phillips Curve?** -- Secondly, the unemployment and inflation rates have moved in cycles which appear to gravitate around a 6 percent unemployment rate -- suggesting that the unemployment rate may move toward some natural level over time.

B. **Flashback to 1967: Friedman and the Natural Rate Hypothesis** -- This second point smacks of something that Milton Friedman first suggested in 1967: that there are *two* Phillips curves -- one for the short-run, and one for the long-run. Further, Friedman said, *"There is always a temporary trade-off between inflation and unemployment; there is no permanent trade-off."*

1. **The Short-Run Phillips Curve** -- The **short-run Phillips curve** *shows all possible combinations of inflation and unemployment given a fixed set of inflationary expectations.*

During the short-run, when inflationary expectations are fixed, it is possible to increase (decrease) AD, in order to decrease unemployment (decrease inflation). [See Exhibit 13-8]

2. **From One Short-Run Phillips Curve to Another** -- Over time, inflationary expectations adjust to account for changes in the actual rate of inflation. When that happens, the short-term gains that were created by manipulating the short-run Phillips curve are neutralized. This adjustment is represented as a shift to a new short-run Phillips curve -- higher than the former, if inflation increases; lower than the former, if inflation decreases.

3. **The Long-Run Phillips Curve** -- Given a sufficient length of time, people fully adjust their inflationary expectations, such that no sustainable trade-off exists between inflation and unemployment. The **long-run Phillips curve** connects all of the corrected inflationary expectations, and is *represented by a vertical line at the natural rate of unemployment.*

4. **The Friedman Natural Rate Hypothesis** -- Friedman hypothesized that, *in the long run, the economy returns to the natural rate of unemployment,* and that lower unemployment cannot be permanently sustained, even at the cost of higher inflation. The only reason why the economy was able to move away from the natural unemployment rate is that workers were "fooled" (in the short-run) into thinking the expected inflation rate was lower than it was. Workers thought they were getting a *real wage increase,* so they increased their production; however, they only received a *nominal wage increase.* Their expectations were wrong. [See Exhibit 13-9]

IV. RATIONAL EXPECTATIONS AND NEW CLASSICAL MACROECONOMICS

A. **1973: Rational Expectations and the New Classical Theory** -- In the early 1970s, a few economists, most notably Robert Lucas, began to question even a short-run trade-off between inflation and unemployment. Lucas and others pointed out that Friedman's natural rate hypothesis was based upon adaptive expectations, and that was the source of the short-run trade-off. Rational expectations theory, or **"ratex"** for short, argues that *individuals form their inflationary expectations based upon all available information; and, therefore, that people actually anticipate policy actions.*

B. **Do People Anticipate Policy?** -- Although most individuals may not even know what the Fed is, individuals on Wall Street who actively trade financial instruments are constantly trying to anticipate policy changes at the Fed. As the saying goes, "buy the rumor and sell the news." Anticipating policy occurs outside Wall Street as well. Unions try to predict the inflation rate, exporters try to predict changes in the value of the dollar, and so on. Everyone tries to anticipate that portion of the market which is important to them.

C. **New Classical Theory: The Effects of Unanticipated and Anticipated Policy** -- New classical theory makes two major assumptions: (1) expectations are formed rationally; (2) wages and prices are flexible.

1. **Unanticipated Policy** -- Consider Exhibit 13-10a. Unexpectedly, the Fed begins to buy government securities, increasing the money supply. As a result AD also increases (to AD_2). Since the policy was unanticipated, even rational actors are caught by surprise, so the actual price level is likely to change before the expected price level does. As a result, the economy may briefly enjoy lower unemployment; at the expense of higher-than-expected inflation. As expectations adjust, however, the economy will move back to the LRAS, eliminating the short-lived reduction in unemployment.

147

2. **Anticipated Policy** -- If individuals correctly anticipate policy actions, then the economy will move directly from one point on the LRAS to another, as shown in Exhibit 13-10b. There is not a short-run trade-off between inflation and unemployment. In fact, there is not even a short-run Phillips curve, *per se* -- the short-run and long-run Phillips curves are one and the same. By example, if students begin anticipating that their teacher will arrive late each day, then the students will arrive late as well.

D. **Policy Ineffectiveness Proposition** -- The **policy ineffectiveness proposition** (PIP) of new classical economics holds that if (1) the expansionary policy change is correctly anticipated, (2) individuals form their expectations rationally, and (3) wages and prices are flexible, then neither expansionary fiscal policy nor expansionary monetary policy will be able to increase Real GDP and lower the unemployment rate in the short run. If the policy ineffectiveness proposition holds, then attempts by the government to fine-tune the economy will not be effective.

E. **Rational Expectations and Incorrectly Anticipated Policy Actions** -- If the public anticipates a particular policy move, but mis-estimates its effects, it is actually possible for an increase in AD to lower Real GDP and raise unemployment. [See Exhibit 13-11] Remember, when discussing rational expectations, different outcomes result in the short-run depending on whether policy is (1) anticipated correctly, (2) unanticipated, (3) anticipated incorrectly in one direction, or (4) anticipated incorrectly in the other direction.

V. **NEW KEYNESIANS AND RATIONAL EXPECTATIONS** -- Implicit in the new classical ratex theory is the assumption of fully flexible wages and prices, but in reality, long-run labor contracts often prevent wages and prices from fully adjusting to changes in the anticipated price level. In response to this, a few New Keynesian economists have assumed that *inflationary expectations are formed rationally, but drops the assumption of fully flexible wages and prices.* Exhibit 13-12 illustrates the effects of anticipated policy in this adaptation of the rational expectations model by New Keynesians. Under these assumptions, the economy does not fully adjust to an anticipated increase in aggregate demand. Instead of the economy moving back to the original Real GDP of Q_N at point 2, the economy only moves back to Real GDP level Q_A at point 2'. Inflexible wages and prices prevented the economy from fully adjusting.

VI. **Looking at Things from the Supply Side: Real Business Cycle Theorists** -- This group of economists believes that changes on the supply side of the economy can lead to changes in Real GDP and unemployment.

A. **The Real Business Cycle** -- Real business cycle theorists argue that a decrease in Real GDP can be brought about by a major supply-side change that *reduces the capacity of the economy to produce.* This is illustrated in Exhibit 13-13. An adverse supply shock would cause a leftward shift in the long-run aggregate supply curve. Real GDP, employment and real wages decline, causing consumption to fall. The decrease in demand causes firms to become less optimistic, so they reduce their bank borrowing, reducing the money supply, and thus aggregate demand. Hence, changes in the money supply may be an *effect* of a contraction in Real GDP, and not its *cause.* In detail, the process works like this:

1. **An adverse supply shock reduces the economy's ability to produce.**

2. **The LRAS curve shifts leftward.**

3. As a result, Real GDP declines and the price level rises.

4. The number of persons employed falls, as do real wages, owing to a decrease in the demand for labor, which lowers money wages, and a higher price level.

5. Incomes decline.

6. Consumption and investment decline.

7. The volume of outstanding loans declines.

8. The money supply falls.

9. The AD curve shifts leftward.

B. **The Middle East, the LRAS Curve, College Graduates, and You** -- Had Saddam Hussein succeeded in capturing Kuwait's and Saudi Arabia's oil supplies and withheld them from the west, a real supply shock would have occurred. Real GDP would have fallen, hiring by firms would have fallen, and college graduates would have found it more difficult to get jobs. The lesson? What happens thousands of miles away can affect your economic situation.

VII. ECONOMICS ON THE INTERNET -- This section shows how you can access unemployment and inflation data from the University of Michigan Gopher to study their relationship.

■ ANSWERS TO CHAPTER QUESTIONS

1. **Optimal search time will change if either the wage offer curve shifts, the reservation wage curve shifts, or both curves shift. Name three factors that can change each curve. In each case, specify the directional change in the curve and the effect on optimal search time. Give reasons for the factors you choose and the directional changes you specify.**

(1) An increase in AD will shift the wage offer curve to the left (upward) as output and labor demand rises to meet the rising AD, this will reduce optimal search time and the unemployment rate. (2) Over time, an increase in labor demand will shift the reservation wage curve to the right, as workers adjust their wage demands to new market conditions. This will also increase the duration of job search and the unemployment rate. (3) The availability of unemployment benefits shifts the reservation wage curve to the right, as job searchers have some source of income during job search, thus reducing the cost of extending the search. As a result, optimal duration of job search gets longer, and the unemployment rate is raised.

2. **What is a major difference between adaptive and rational expectations? Give an example to illustrate.**

With adaptive expectations, it does not matter whether a policy is anticipated or unanticipated -- the effects are the same. With rational expectations, it does matter whether a policy is anticipated or unanticipated -- the effects are different. This is a major difference between the two types of expectations theory. Adaptive expectations theory implicitly assumes that individuals wait to see what happens, and then act. For example, suppose individuals know that aggregate demand will increase. Adaptive

149

expectations theory holds that individuals will wait until AD increases to see how higher AD affects the price level; and then they will revise their anticipated price level. On the other hand, rational expectations theory assumes that individuals look to the future, make an educated guess as to what is going to happen, and then act accordingly .

For example, rational expectations theory holds that if individuals anticipate that aggregate demand will increase, they will not wait to revise their inflation expectations until it has increased and the price level has risen. Simply put, adaptive expectations holds that the future will only be acted upon when it has become the present or the past; rational expectations holds that the future will be acted upon (or rather what individuals think the future will be, will be acted upon) before it has become the present or the past.

3.   It has been said that the policy ineffectiveness proposition (connected with new classical theory) does not eliminate policy makers' ability to reduce unemployment through aggregate demand-increasing policies, since they can always increase aggregate demand by more than the public expects. What might be the weak point in this argument?

The argument is implicitly based on the assumption that policy makers have an accurate idea of how much the public expects aggregate demand will increase. This would be nearly impossible to know. That is, if a policy maker says that the public *thinks* aggregate demand will only be increased by X amount, one might reasonably question how much faith he or she should put in such a statement. Additionally, one must ask how a policy maker can possibly know what the public is thinking.

4.   Why does the new classical ratex theory have the word "classical" associated with it? Also, why has it been said that the classical theory failed where the new classical ratex theory succeeds, as the former could not explain the business cycle (loosely "the ups and downs of the economy"), but the latter can?

The new classical ratex theory has the word "classical" associated with it because when policy is (correctly) anticipated, both the new classical ratex and the classical theories predict that Real GDP remains at its natural level. For the most part, the classical theory could not explain the business cycle because it implicitly assumed that the effects of unanticipated policy and anticipated policy were the same. The new classical ratex theory does not make this assumption. In the new classical ratex theory, movements away from Natural Real GDP and the natural rate of unemployment are the result of unanticipated policy or less than correctly anticipated policy.

5.   Suppose there were a permanent downward-sloping Phillips curve that offered a menu of choices of different combinations of inflation and unemployment rates to policy makers. How do you think society would go about deciding which point on the Phillips curve it wanted to occupy?

The decision would have to be made on the basis of some normative judgment about the relative importance of low unemployment vs. low inflation, taking into account public perceptions about the maximum acceptable levels of each.

6.   Suppose a short-run trade-off between inflation and unemployment currently exists. How would you expect this trade-off to be affected by a change in technology that permits the wider dispersion of economic policy news? Explain your answer.

A wider dispersion of economic news should have two effects. First, it may affect people's attitudes about the acceptability of high inflation and/or unemployment. As such, it may change the slope of the short-run Phillips curve. Secondly, individuals should be able to form and adjust their inflationary expectations better and more rapidly, thus creating a world closer to the ratex model(s) than the simple Phillips curve.

7.   New Keynesian theory holds that wages are not completely flexible because of such things as long-term labor contracts. New classical economists often respond that experience teaches labor leaders to develop and bargain for contracts that allow for wage adjustments. Do you think the new classical economists have a good point? Why?

Yes and no. Certainly, many labor contracts include cost-of-living-adjustments (or COLAs), which automatically adjust wages to changes in the price level. However, most such devices only increase wages if prices rise; they do not decrease wages if prices fall. This seems to be the sticking point between the new classical and nonclassical ratex models, just as it was a major sticking point between classical economics and Keynes -- as long as wages and prices do not adjust freely, both upward and downward, then there is a clear argument for the nonclassical view.

8.   What evidence can you point to that suggests individuals form their expectations adaptively? What evidence can you point to that suggests individuals form their expectations rationally?

Using fairly simple examples, people tend to make many day-to-day purchasing decisions -- such as what to buy at the grocery, whether or not to go out to dinner, etc. -- on the basis of how today's price compares to recent memory. While individuals may be aware of major market conditions, such as a widespread drought or a major boycott, they do not spend much time researching the market conditions of the avocado industry when preparing to go to the grocery store. On the other hand, individuals seek to gather a great amount of information and advice on stock market purchases/sales, housing decisions, and the like, suggesting that they are trying to form their price expectations, and make their purchasing decisions, as rationally as possible.

9.   Explain both the short-run and long-run movements of the Friedman natural rate theory if expectations are formed adaptively.

If people form their expectations adaptively, then short-run changes in AD brought about by fiscal or monetary policy will cause a movement along a short-run Phillips curve, like PC_1 in Exhibit 13-8. This enables the government (or the Fed) to "manipulate" the inflation and unemployment rates until people adapt their inflationary expectations. Over time, the natural rate hypothesis holds that people will continue to modify their expectations such that the government (or the Fed) cannot sustain its "manipulation," causing the economy to tend toward full employment.

10. Explain both the short-run and long-run movements of the natural rate theory if expectations are formed rationally and policy is unanticipated.

See Exhibit 13-10a and accompanying discussion.

11. "Even if some people do not form their expectations rationally, this does not necessarily mean that new classical theory is of no value." Discuss.

Obviously. To the extent that anyone forms their expectations rationally, that can have an impact on the viability of expansionary or contractionary economic policy. The more economic actors who do so (or even endeavor to do so), the more important it is to understand the theory and implications of rational expectations-formation.

12. Illustrate graphically what would happen if (1) individuals form their expectations rationally, (2) prices and wages are flexible, and (3) individuals underestimate the decrease in aggregate demand.

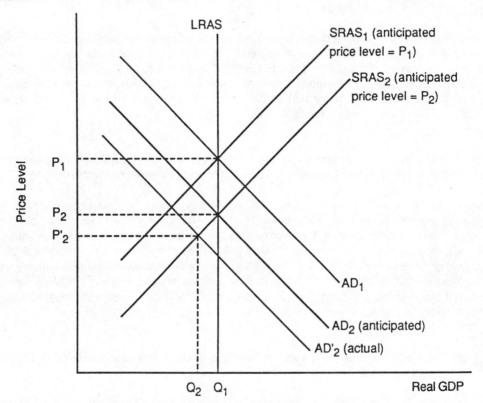

Conceptually, this is very similar to the process illustrated and described in Exhibit 13-11. Here, we start at (Q_1,P_1). Public anticipation of an increase in AD from AD_1 to AD_2 triggers a rightward shift of the SRAS curve to $SRAS_2$, as wage demands and input price expectations rise in anticipation of a drop in the price level to P_2. Thus, if all goes as expected, the economy will re-equilibrate at (Q_1,P_2). However, if AD rises more than expected -- here, to AD'_2 (to be consistent with the taxonomy in Exhibit 13-11) -- then the new equilibrium level of Real GDP will be less than Q_1, the natural (full employment) level. Indeed, as can be seen by examining the intersection of AD'_2 and $SRAS_2$, the new equilibrium in (Q_2,P'_2). Thus, both the price level and Real GDP will be lower than if the decrease in AD had been as anticipated.

13. In the real business cycle theory, why can't the change in the money supply prompted by a series of events catalyzed by an adverse supply shock be considered the "cause" of the business cycle?

152

In real business cycle theory, decreases in consumption which result from supply shocks cause firms to cut back on their expansion plans and reduce their borrowing from banks. This, in turn, reduces the money supply and shifts the AD curve leftward. Notice that the reduction in the money supply results from the supply shock, and not vice versa. Without the supply shock, there would have been no reduction in the money supply, and no shift in the AD curve. For the money supply to "cause" the business cycle, it would have to be the first economic factor which changed, not the last.

■ LECTURE SUPPLEMENTS

John Lipman, "How a Red Hot Script That Made a Fortune Never Became a Movie," *Wall Street Journal*, June 13, 1995, p. A1, column 1.

Since this chapter is about expectations, you might use this article to show that expectations shape business decisions, not just discussions among economists. Before movies are made, there is a script, and a good script can make a young Hollywood writer a fortune. Hollywood executives have to evaluate how successful a script will be when made into a film and then bid on the film based upon their expectations. If they fail to buy a film which turns into a blockbuster, their hesitation could create an opportunity cost of millions of dollars in forgone profits.

This article relates the story of "The Ticking Man." Two unemployed Hollywood writers sold the screenplay for this film to Hollywood for $1.2 million, and despite four rewrites and more than $1 million in extra costs, the film has yet to be made and still sits on the shelves. The problems lay in packaging the film about a nuclear bomb which becomes sentient and starts thinking and behaving like a human being. The studio had to get the right person for the film, which appeared to be Bruce Willis, but he was involved in another film at the time. This and other problems kept the film from being given the green light and it remains on hold.

Obviously, when the studio paid $1.2 million for the script, they had expectations of huge profits, not of having a script which collected dust. Yet their expectations proved wrong, and costly. I hope this shows your students the importance of expectations, and that you don't have your students drop their economics course to write movie scripts.

Gene Epstein, "An Economist Preaches the Gospel of 4% Unemployment and Says It Wouldn't Trigger Higher Inflation," *Barron's*, July 24, 1995, p. 19.

Robert Eisner argues that the non-accelerating inflation rate of unemployment (NAIRU) is lower than most economists think. Whereas the Congressional Budget Office currently estimates NAIRU to be around 6 percent, Eisner thinks it could be closer to 4 percent. The reason? Unemployment has remained below 6 percent for months without generating any signs of inflationary pressures.

How to decrease unemployment? Eisner recommends providing tax incentives which encourage firms to hire more individuals, and to pay for training programs in the form of subsidies to private industry. Eisner feels that too much attention is paid to the budget deficit and not enough to programs designed to reduce unemployment. He also disputes the fact that government spending crowds out the private sector. Read the article and judge for yourself.

Steve Hanke and Sir Alan Walters, "Greenspan Bonds," *Forbes*, September 12, 1994, p. 149.

Can you build expectations into the economy? Yes. The two authors suggest that the United States Treasury begin offering inflation-indexed bonds. The chairman of the Federal Reserve, Alan Greenspan, has called on the U.S. Treasury to begin issuing indexed debt. Investors would benefit from indexed bonds because they would no longer have to worry about the impact of inflation on their wealth. Inflation would not transfer wealth from debtors to creditors as is true with non-indexed bonds. The bonds would also force the government to be more realistic about its own debt costs. With indexed bonds, the government would be unable to reduce its debt burden through inflation.

Until now, bondholder, not the government, have borne the risk of inflation. Perhaps if inflation created a cost for the government rather than a benefit, the government would be less likely to pursue inflationary policies.

CHAPTER 14

Economic Growth: Resources, Technology, and Ideas

Chapters 5 through 8 developed the aggregate supply-aggregate demand model to study fluctuations in Real GDP around the natural rate. Both the production possibilities curve and the long-run aggregate supply curve were assumed to be fixed. But experience shows that these curves are not fixed. In the long run, the standard of living depends more upon creating economic growth and shifting out the production possibilities curve and long-run aggregate supply curve than minimizing fluctuations around these curves. Chapter 14 looks at how *economic growth* can occur. What can cause a rightward shift in the production possibilities curve, or the long-run aggregate supply curve? After reading this chapter, you and your students should have a better answer to this question.

■ CHAPTER OBJECTIVES

Upon completing this chapter, your students should be able to:

- distinguish between real economic growth and per-capita Real GDP economic growth;

- understand how economic growth influences the price level;

- know the five factors which are related to economic growth, and explain how each of these factors contributes to economic growth;

- explain how demand-side and supply-side policies can be used to achieve economic growth; and,

- know what industrial policy is, how it can be used to promote economic growth, and what its shortcomings might be.

■ KEY TERMS

- (absolute) real economic growth
- per-capita real economic growth
- industrial policy

■ CHAPTER OUTLINE

I. **A FEW BASICS ABOUT ECONOMIC GROWTH**

   A. **What Is Economic Growth?** -- *Economic growth* refers to either real economic growth or to per-capita real economic growth. **Absolute real economic growth** is an increase in Real GDP from one period to the next. [Exhibit 14-1] **Per-capita real economic growth** is an increase in per-capita Real GDP from one period to the next where

   Per-capita Real GDP = Real GDP/ Population

   B. **Do Economic Growth Rates Matter?** -- Absolutely! Just look at these examples. An economy which grows at 4 percent per year will take 18 years to double its Real GDP (using the *Rule of 72*), but an economy which grows at 3 percent per year will take 24 years to double its Real GDP. If Country A has three times the Real GDP of Country B, but Country A grows at 3 percent and Country B grows at 6 percent, in only 15 years their Real GDP will be the same.

   C. **Two Types of Economic Growth** -- Economic growth can occur from an inefficient level of production or from an efficient level of production.

      1. **Economic Growth from an Inefficient Level of Production** -- This is illustrated in Exhibit 14-2a. The economy is in a recessionary gap and operating below its production possibilities frontier (PPF). Expansionary fiscal or monetary policy could push the economy from point A (below the PPF) to point B (on the PPF) and bring the economy back to an efficient level of production.

      2. **Economic Growth from an Efficient Level of Production** -- As shown in Exhibit 14-3, this occurs when either the PPF shifts to the right, as in Exhibit 14-3a, or the long-run aggregate supply (LRAS) curve shifts to the right as in Exhibit 14-3b. This is what economists are referring to when they talk about *economic growth*.

      3. **Economic Growth and the Price Level** -- How the price level changes when there is a rightward shift in the LRAS curve depends on the position of the aggregate demand curve. The price level can fall (AD_1), remain unchanged (AD_2), or rise (AD_3), as illustrated in Exhibit 14-3b.

II. **WHAT CAUSES ECONOMIC GROWTH?** -- There are five principal sources of economic growth.

   A. **Natural Resources** -- Natural resources are neither a necessary nor a sufficient source of economic growth. Some countries with natural resources have failed to grow (Zaire), while other countries with few natural resources have seen rapid rates of growth (Singapore and Hong Kong). *Natural resources may enhance economic growth, but they are not a requirement for economic growth.*

   B. **Labor** -- Increases in both the size of the labor force and in labor productivity can increase Real GDP, but *only an increase in labor productivity can increase per-capita Real GDP.* The best ways to increase labor productivity are to increase education and training of workers, and to carry out capital investment.

156

C. **Capital** -- Capital investment can increase labor productivity, but the resources for capital investment come from current reductions in consumption and increases in savings. As Exhibit 14-4 shows, *countries with higher investment rates tend to have higher per-capita Real GDP growth.*

D. **Technological Advances** -- Technological advances make current production methods more efficient, increasing Real GDP. In order to get a technological advance, firms must carry out research and development. As the *Economics in Our Times* feature, "California's Silicon Valley and Boston's Route 128" shows, technological change requires more than just money. It also requires a synergistic environment in which people with similar interests can collaborate to produce new ways of doing things. The university research centers around Boston and San Francisco provided this environment and the computer revolution.

E. **Property Rights Structure** -- **Property rights** refers to *the range of laws, rules, and regulations that define rights over use and transfer of resources.*

F. **Policies to Promote Economic Growth** -- Government policies attempt to shift either aggregate demand (*demand-side policies*), or the PPF and LRAS curves (*supply-side policies*). Two examples of supply-side policies are

   1. **Tax Policy** -- Lowering taxes on income and money placed in savings accounts would increase individuals' willingness to work and their desire to save money. These changes could increase per-capita Real GDP through capital goods growth and higher labor.

   2. **Regulatory Policy** -- Regulations are costly. Firms must spend time filling out paper work to show that they have complied with these regulations, and they must spend money on equipment which reduces pollution and other hazards. If the costs of these regulations exceed their benefits, then society would be better off without these regulations.

G. **What about Industrial Policy?** -- **Industrial policy** refers to a deliberate government policy of aiding industries which are most likely to be successful in the world marketplace. Proponents of industrial policy say that the United States must help growth industries because other countries aid their potential winners, and this help gives them an edge over American firms. Critics maintain that politics, rather than economics, may be the determining factor in which industries are aided; the government may not be better at choosing successful industries than the market; and that in providing protection to industries, the government may hamper economic growth. Less free trade hurts consumers.

H. **Two Worries over Future Economic Growth** -- Some worry about the impact of economic growth on the quality of life and the availability of resources.

   1. **Quality of Life** -- Although per-capita income has increased, so has pollution, crowding in cities, drug use, the number of single mothers, and so on. Supporters of growth rejoin that growth has also reduced poverty, and that better enforcement of property rights could reduce the "ills" of economic growth.

2. **Future Availability of Resources** -- Has economic growth occurred only because we have depleted the earth's resources? Will these resources run out at some point in the future, ending growth? Julian Simon retorts that there is not an inverse relationship between population growth and per-capita income growth, and we are not running out of natural resources. If natural resources become scarce, their price will rise forcing society to make more efficient use of those resources.

I. **Economic Growth and Democracy** -- Do democratic governments have higher rates of growth than nondemocratic governments? Does economic growth encourage democracy. Two of the *Economics in Our Times* features debate these questions. "Economic Growth and Democracy" reprints an article by Gary Becker in which he claims democracies have higher rates of growth than non-democracies. "Free Markets, Controlled Press: Or, Who Is Afraid of a Satellite Dish?" looks at the East Asian tigers who have had high rates of Real GDP growth in political environments which have not been open and democratic by western standards. Singapore, Malaysia and China limit freedom of speech and impose restrictions on satellite dishes.

III. NEW GROWTH THEORY

A. **What Was Wrong With the Old Theory? Or, What's New with New Growth Theory?** -- *New growth theory* came into existence because *neoclassical growth theory* failed to answer some important questions, and the two differ in some important ways.

1. **Technology** -- Neoclassical growth theory treated technology as being *exogenous*, as something that fell from the sky and could not be explained as part of the process of economic growth. The new growth theory treats technology as *endogenous* to the economic system, and emphasizes that the amount of resources society devotes to research affects the amount of technological change which occurs.

2. **Discovery, Ideas and Institutions** -- In the new growth theory, the process of discovering new ways of doing things and testing ideas are a central part of economic growth. If this is so, society will benefit from setting up institutions devoted to discovering new inventions and testing new ideas.

B. **Expanding Our Horizons** -- Paul Romer, who has been central to the new growth theory, says that economic growth occurs whenever people rearrange resources in ways that make them more valuable. The only way to find out which chemical compounds make more effective drugs is by testing different chemical combinations over and over again. How to improve the discovery process remains a matter of debate, but it is clear that countries which institutionalize the discovery process in profitable ways will have the highest rates of growth in the 21st century.

IV. **ECONOMICS ON THE INTERNET** -- This section shows how to access information from the University of Michigan and the University of California at Berkeley for data on economic growth. Information on downloading FTP files is also provided.

■ ANSWERS TO CHAPTER QUESTIONS

1. Why might per-capita real economic growth be a more useful measurement than (absolute) real economic growth?

Real economic growth measures changes in the output of a country, but does not measure the improvement in the average standard of living for people living in that country. For example, if Real GDP increased by 5 percent, and population also increased by 5 percent, on average individuals living in that country would see no change in their standard of living. Per-capita real economic growth measures improvements in the standard of living in a country whereas (absolute) real economic growth measures increases in output without taking into consideration changes in the population.

2. Country X is currently growing at 2 percent a year. How many years will the Real GDP of country X take to double?

The Rule of 72 can be used to find out how long it would take for the Real GDP to double. Divide 72 by the rate of growth (2 percent) and you get the number of years it takes for Real GDP to double at a 2 percent rate of growth--36 years.

3. Diagrammatically represent each of the following: (1) economic growth from an inefficient level of production, (2) economic growth from an efficient level of production.

Economic growth from an inefficient level of production is shown in Exhibit 14-2a by moving from point A to point B on the production possibilities frontier, and from point A' to point B' in Exhibit 14-2b. Economic growth from an efficient level of production is represented by a movement from point B on PPF_1 to point C on PPF_2 in Exhibit 14-3a, and by the shift of the LRAS curve from $LRAS_1$ to $LRAS_2$ in Exhibit 14-3b.

4. Diagrammatically represent each of the following: (1) economic growth with a stable price level; (2) economic growth with a rising price level; and (3) economic growth with a falling price level.

These changes are illustrated in Exhibit 14-3b. Economic growth is represented by the shift in the LRAS curve. Whether the price level rises or declines depends upon the AD curve. Economic growth with a stable price level is represented by point C" at the intersection of $LRAS_2$ and AD_2. Economic growth with a rising price level is represented by point C"' at the intersection of $LRAS_2$ and AD_3, and economic growth with a falling price level is represented by point C' at the intersection of $LRAS_2$ and AD_1.

5. What does it mean to say "natural resources are neither a sufficient nor a necessary factor for growth?"

Saying that natural resources are not a sufficient factor for growth means that nations which have natural resources will not necessarily achieve economic growth. A country such as Zaire would be a good example of this. Saying that natural resources are not a necessary factor for growth means that nations which do not have an endowment of natural resources can still achieve high rates of economic growth. Hong Kong and Singapore could be used as examples for this case. In short, although natural resources may promote economic growth, they are not necessary for economic growth, and not all countries which have natural resources will grow.

6.   How do we compute (average) labor productivity?

Average labor productivity equals total output divided by total labor hours. For example if $6 trillion of output is produced in 200 billion labor hours, then average labor productivity is $30 per hour.

7.   Is it possible to have more workers working, producing higher Real GDP at the same time that labor productivity is declining? Explain your answer.

If the increase in the number of workers exceeded the decline in labor productivity, then Real GDP would be higher; however, per-capita Real GDP would not be greater. Only an increase in labor productivity will tend to lead to an increase in per-capita Real GDP.

8.   How does an increased saving rate relate to increased labor productivity?

If the savings rate increases, more funds are available for investment. If these funds are used to introduce more capital which workers can use to increase their productivity, then an increase in the savings rate can lead to increased labor productivity.

9.   "Economic growth doesn't simply depend on having more natural resources, more or higher-quality labor, more capital, and so on; it depends on people's incentives to put these resources together to produce goods and services." Do you agree or disagree? Explain your answer.

I agree. The presence of more natural resources, more labor and more capital will not in and of itself generate economic growth. Individuals must have the incentives which allow them to profit from their efforts to combine these resources in a more efficient manner. If individuals faced marginal tax rates of 90%, they could not benefit from their productive activities and would likely choose leisure over labor. Similarly, well-defined property rights are important if economic growth is going to occur. If you found a new, more efficient way of making mousetraps, but anyone could imitate your invention and generate profits for themselves rather than you, you would not have the incentive to come up with your invention. Incentives are important.

10. It is possible to promote economic growth from either the demand side or the supply side. Do you agree or disagree? Explain your answer.

I agree; however, demand-side and supply-side policies are used to achieve different types of growth. Demand-side policies are associated with generating economic growth from an inefficient level of production, moving the economy from some point below the PPF to a point on the PPF. Monetary and fiscal policy could be used here to promote growth. Supply-side policies are associated with generating economic growth from an efficient level of production, shifting the PPF out to a higher level of output, and shifting the LRAS curve to the right. Examples of supply-side policies would be lowering marginal income taxes to encourage an increase in labor input, or reducing government regulation to lower firms' cost of producing goods.

11. What is new about new growth theory?

Neoclassical growth theory emphasized two factors: labor and capital. Technology was treated as an exogenous variable. In new growth theory, technology is treated as being endogenous. Improvements in technology depend on the amount of resources devoted to research and development, not to exogenous changes over which society has no control. The new growth theory also focuses on the process of discovery and ideas which generate new technology.

12. How does discovering and implementing new ideas cause economic growth?

New ideas introduce new, more productive ways of doing things. In the computer industry, there is constant change. Individuals are constantly discovering new ways of producing computer hardware and software that increases economic efficiency. When they implement these ideas, labor productivity increases, generating economic growth. Companies which create environments which are conducive to discovering and implementing new ideas are ones which can generate economic change and economic growth.

■ LECTURE SUPPLEMENTS

Gene Epstein, "How an Economist Tries to Beat Uncle Sam At the Game of Gauging GDP Growth," *Barron's*, October 24, 1994, p. 43.

This article is interesting because it shows how forecasters predict what GDP growth is before those figures are released by the government. You will often hear predictions of future GDP growth from different analysts, but they rarely explain how they come up with these predictions. This article lets you in on their secrets.

Lacy Hunt, of HSBC Securities, regularly predicts the U.S. Bureau of Economic Analysis' (BEA) GDP estimates prior to their announcement. Hunt estimates GDP from the expenditure side, by measuring consumption, investment, government purchases and net exports. The article reveals what Ms. Hunt uses to put together numbers for each of these components of expenditures, as well as the complications which exist in calculating GDP. For example, are apples a final good or an intermediate good? If used to produce applesauce, an intermediate good.

As anyone who follows the GDP revisions knows, GDP estimates can change substantially between the first estimate and the final revision. The reason is that the BEA doesn't receive all of the data until months after the quarter ends, so it must guess at some of the numbers. This means that Ms. Hunt must guess what guesstimates the BEA will make on the data they don't have. For example, retail sales can be used to estimate total consumption, but retail sales exclude such important items as medical services, payments for housing, telephone bills, and transportation. Read the article and see how an economist does her work.

Gary Becker, "Why So Many Mice Are Roaring," *Business Week,* **November 7, 1994, p. 20.**

Does the size of the country affect the rate of economic growth? Can small countries grow faster than large countries? Becker answers in the affirmative to these questions. He says that countries, like firms, can find their economic niches and concentrate on those areas where they have a comparative advantage to generate economic growth. He uses Hong Kong, Singapore, Monaco and Mauritius as examples of countries which have benefited from being small.

He also says that from an economic point of view, political dissolution can be beneficial. he points to the breakup of Czechoslovakia into the Czech Republic and Slovakia, each of which has different economic structures. Would Quebec be economically better off as a separate country rather than as part of Canada? If it generated more international trade, Becker would argue that it would.

There are costs to being small, however, namely the fixed costs of having a government. And the fallacy of composition may apply here. Some countries may benefit from being small, but a world in which there were 5000 countries might be chaotic. Still, the article provides some interesting food for thought.

"How Does Your Economy Grow?" *The Economist*, **September 30, 1995, p. 96.**

This article tries to answer the question, Is it possible to foster economic growth? Research has shown that economies which grow quickly have a number of traits in common with one another, but can these traits be imitated?

According to Gregory Mankiw, neoclassical growth models can teach policymakers everything they need to know about how to foster growth. The key is capital accumulation. As incomes begin to rise, so do savings rates, and at some point, savings become sufficient to replace depreciating capital.

Why does Mankiw rely on the neoclassical model? He asserts that all countries have equal access to technological ideas, so learning about technological change cannot help to explain differences in countries' growth rates. Mankiw also estimates that two-thirds of all labor income derives from investments in human capital, and four-fifths of a nation's total income is created by human and physical capital, not raw labor.

Paul Romer and other new growth theorists would disagree, arguing that human capital alone cannot explain the differences in growth rates, and technological change is important. Romer would argue that technology is not universally applicable to all countries. The article concludes that both sides ignore some important factors, such as the extent to which a country embraces free trade and free enterprise. In short, if countries want to promote growth, they have to give up their desire to control it.

CHAPTER 15

International Impacts on the Economy

Previous chapters on the macroeconomy looked at changes in aggregate demand and changes in aggregate supply, Real GDP, and the price level. However, these chapters ignored the impact of international factors on the economy. Chapter 15 focuses on international factors and how they impact the economy. In particular, this chapter looks at the impact of exchanges rates, foreign income, and other factors which can influence domestic aggregate demand and domestic aggregate supply. The chapter then shows how these changes in domestic aggregate demand and domestic aggregate supply affect the U.S. price level, Real GDP, and the unemployment rate.

■ CHAPTER OBJECTIVES

Upon completing this chapter, your students should be able to:

- understand how changes in net exports affect domestic aggregate demand, and know how changes in foreign Real GDP, exchange rates and relative price levels influence net exports;

- know how a change in foreign input prices impacts the U.S. SRAS curve, and what can cause changes in foreign input prices;

- determine how a change in the exchange rate will affect the AD curve and the SRAS curve;

- explain how a change in real interest rates will affect the AD curve and the SRAS curve;

- understand the relationship between the budget and trade deficits as well as ways that the trade deficit can be reduced; and,

- show whether expansionary or contractionary monetary and fiscal policies will be more effective in a closed economy or in an open economy.

■ KEY TERMS

- J-curve
- closed economy

- open economy

■ CHAPTER OUTLINE

I. **International Factors and Aggregate Demand**

    A. **Net Exports** -- *Net exports* are the difference between exports (EX) and imports (IM). If net exports rise, the AD curve shifts to the right, and if net exports fall, the AD curve shifts to the left. But this begs the question, what causes net exports to change? Three factors are important here.

        1. **Foreign Real GDP (or Foreign Real National Income)** -- If Japan's Real GDP rises, the Japanese buy more goods. Some of their purchases will include American goods. As U.S. net exports rise, the AD curve shifts to the right. A contraction in Japan would generate the opposite result.

        2. **Exchange Rate** -- If a country's currency *appreciates*, it takes less of that country's currency to buy another country's currency. On the other hand, if a country's currency *depreciates*, it takes more of that country's currency to buy another country's currency. If the dollar appreciates, American goods become more expensive to Japanese consumers, and Japanese goods become less expensive to American consumers. Americans would import more Japanese goods, and the Japanese would purchase fewer American exports. As a result, net exports would decline, and the AD curve would shift to the left, lowering U.S. Real GDP and raising the U.S. unemployment rate. The opposite would occur if the dollar depreciated.

        3. **Relative Price Levels** -- Under fixed exchange rates, if American goods increase in price more than Japanese goods increase in price, then relatively speaking, American goods have become more expensive. In response to this, Americans would import more Japanese goods, and the Japanese would purchase fewer American exports. As a result, net exports would decline, and the AD curve would shift to the left, lowering U.S. Real GDP and raising the U.S. unemployment rate. The opposite would occur if Japanese goods increased in price more than American goods did. Exhibit 15-1 summarizes these three changes.

    B. **Japan and the University of California at Irvine Bookstore** -- Although many U.S. goods are bought indirectly from the U.S. through Japanese retailers, now Japanese consumers can buy directly from the United States through the Internet. The University of California at Irvine Bookstore has an Internet site which allows Japanese university professors, and others, to order books electronically from the University of California at Irvine. Selling American goods to other countries is not always as easy as this. As *The Global Economy* feature "Doing Business with China" shows, in China personal connections, or *guanxi*, are important in generating business. For this reason, many politicians who have had dealings with Chinese officials now use their connections to help American firms sell their products to Chinese companies. The costs of doing business are often referred to as *transaction costs* by economists.

    C. **The J-Curve** -- The *J-curve* shows how net exports change over time in response to an appreciation or depreciation in the exchange rate (see Exhibit 15-2). Although the exchange rate immediately changes, it will take time for the actual quantities of goods which are imported and exported to change. If the currency depreciates, and *initially* the quantity of imported goods remains unchanged. However, in time, Americans will respond to the higher price of Japanese goods by lowering the quantity of Japanese goods which are imported into the United States. As this change occurs, import spending will decrease. You must differentiate between what *initially* happens to import spending as a result of a depreciation, and what *ultimately* happens.

II. INTERNATIONAL FACTORS AND AGGREGATE SUPPLY

A. **Foreign Input Prices** -- A rise in the price of foreign inputs leads to a leftward shift in the U.S. SRAS curve, and a fall in the price of foreign inputs leads to a rightward shift in the U.S. SRAS curve. Two factors could cause a rise in the price of foreign inputs. [See Exhibit 15-3]

   1. **Supply and Demand in the Input Market** -- Changes in supply and demand could change the price of the good in the input market affecting the price U.S. producers have to pay. An increase in input prices in Japan would shift the SRAS curve to the left.

   2. **Exchange Rate** -- If the Japanese yen depreciated, and Japanese input prices remained the same, Japanese inputs would be cheaper to U.S. producers. The SRAS curve would shift to the right. *While a change in the exchange rate can affect both the AD and the SRAS curves, a change in the price of foreign inputs affects only the SRAS curve.*

B. **The Exchange Rate and AD and SRAS** -- When the exchange rate changes, both AD and SRAS are affected. The overall effect on Real GDP depends on how much the AD curve shifts relative to the shift in the SRAS curve.

   1. **Dollar Depreciation** -- If the dollar depreciates, as illustrated in Exhibit 15-4, the price level will rise. Whether Real GDP expands, contracts or remains constant depends upon the relative shifts of the AD and SRAS curves. If the AD curve shifts rightward by more than the SRAS curve shifts leftward, Real GDP rises (see Exhibit 15-4a). If the AD curve shifts rightward by less than the SRAS curve shifts leftward, Real GDP falls (see Exhibit 15-4b), and if the AD curve shifts rightward by the same amount that the SRAS curve shifts leftward, Real GDP does not change (see Exhibit 15-4c).

   2. **Dollar Appreciation** -- In this case, the AD curve shifts leftward and the SRAS curve rightward. The price level would fall, but whether Real GDP responded in an expansionary, contractionary or constant manner would depend upon the relative shifts of the two curves.

C. **What Role Do Interest Rates Play?** -- As in the case of prices, it is the *relative* changes in interest rates which are important here. Higher real interest rates in the United States will attract foreign capital. This increases the demand for the dollar which appreciates. The dollar appreciation will shift the AD curve leftward and the SRAS curve rightward. Although the effect on Real GDP depends upon the relative shifts of the two curves, economists believe that in this case, the AD curve typically tends to shift leftward by more than the SRAS curve shifts rightward, so Real GDP will fall. [See Exhibit 15-5a] The opposite case is illustrated in Exhibit 15-5b. Higher Japanese interest rates attracts capital in Japan causing the yen to appreciate, and typically, an increase in Real GDP.

D. The Budget Deficit: International Effects and Domestic Feedbacks -- What is the relationship between the budget deficit and the trade deficit? There are two effects. On the one hand, a rising budget deficit affects the domestic economy directly and *pushes Real GDP upward*. On the other hand, the increased deficit raises U.S. interest rates, attracting capital, causing the dollar to appreciate, and *pushing Real GDP downward*. Which of these two effects is stronger? The result depends upon whether the economy is an open economy or a closed economy. *In a closed economy, the international feedback effects that reduce Real GDP are absent*, so the budget deficit will push Real GDP upward. In a closed economy, Real GDP would end up at Q_2 as illustrated in Exhibit 15-6a, and in an open economy where international feedback effects play a role, Real GDP would end up at a lower level, Q_3.

E. What About Contractionary Fiscal Policy? -- What would happen if the government cut spending? The cut in government spending reduces the budget deficit but it also reduces aggregate demand, pushing Real GDP downward. Reduced borrowing by the government lowers U.S. interest rates causing capital outflows and a dollar depreciation, a sequence which would push Real GDP upward through a rightward shift in the AD curve that is greater than the leftward shift in the SRAS curve. Again, the ultimate result will depend upon how much the AD and SRAS curves move relative to one another. Regardless of the strength of these shifts, we can conclude that *contractionary fiscal policy lowers Real GDP more in a closed economy than in an open economy*. In a closed economy, as illustrated in Exhibit 15-6b, Real GDP falls from Q_1 to Q_2. In an open economy, where international feedback effects play a role, Real GDP would end up at a relatively higher level, such as Q_3.

F. The Budget and Trade Deficits -- Is there a relationship between the "twin deficits"? Here's how the budget deficit can, and sometimes does, affect the trade deficit. We have two different ways of expressing GDP, one way in terms of income, and the other way in terms of expenditures. By setting expenditures equal to income, we have

$$C + I + G + (EX - IM) = C + S + T.$$

Rearranging the terms to focus on macroeconomic and international effects we get:

$$G - T = (S - I) - (EX - IM).$$

Since (G - T) is the budget deficit, and (IM - EX) is the trade deficit, then

$$\text{Budget deficit} = (S - I) + \text{trade deficit}.$$

This says that *the budget deficit equals the amount of saving over investment plus the trade deficit*. If the budget deficit rises, and the difference between *S* and *I* remains constant, then the trade deficit rises. So one way to reduce the trade deficit is to reduce the budget deficit.

G. How Might the Trade Deficit Be Reduced?

1. **Reduce the budget deficit** -- A smaller budget deficit reduces the government's borrowing needs. This puts downward pressure on interest rates, a depreciating dollar, and over time, a smaller trade deficit.

2. **Promote rapid economic growth in the trading partners of the United States** -- As foreign Real GDP rises, U.S. exports will increase, reducing the trade deficit.

3. **Raise saving and/or reduce investment** -- Higher savings or reduced investment would increase the difference between S and I, and the trade deficit could fall. If the United States borrowed excessively to finance the budget deficit and the trade deficit, at some point foreigners might demand higher interest rates. Higher interest rates could reduce demand, causing an economic recession, which would ultimately lower the trade deficit; however, this "recession solution" is a painful one.

4. **Protectionism** -- The U.S. government could put tariffs on foreign goods imported into the United States to reduce imports; however, foreign countries might retaliate by doing the same thing.

H. **Where Does Monetary Policy Fit In?**

1. **Expansionary Monetary Policy** -- Expansionary monetary policy causes interest rates to fall in the short run, shifting the AD curve rightward and raising Real GDP. This effect is shown in Exhibit 15-7 as an increase from Q_1 to Q_2. In a closed economy, the story stops here, but in an open economy, lower interest rates cause an outflow of funds from the United States, a depreciation in the dollar, and increased net exports. In Exhibit 15-7a, this is shown by a rightward shift in the AD curve. (The depreciated dollar causes a leftward shift in the SRAS curve.) This change causes Real GDP to rise from Q_2 to Q_3. *Expansionary monetary policy raises Real GDP more in an open economy than in a closed economy.* This is just the opposite of expansionary fiscal policy.

2. **Contractionary Monetary Policy** -- Contractionary monetary policy would shift AD leftward and lower Real GDP, decreasing it from Q_1 to Q_2 in Exhibit 15-7b. Interest rates rise producing an inflow of funds into the Untied States, an appreciation in the dollar, and decreased net exports. The fall in net exports would shift the AD curve leftward, and the depreciated dollar would shift the SRAS curve rightward. Real GDP would fall from Q_2 to Q_3.

III. **ECONOMICS ON THE INTERNET** -- Need information on the General Agreement on Tariffs and Trade (GATT) or the North American Free Trade Agreement (NAFTA)? This section provides information on how to access this data using the Sam Houston State University Gopher and the University of Michigan Gopher.

■ **ANSWERS TO CHAPTER QUESTIONS**

1. **Assume a two-country world where the two countries are the United States and Japan. Note the impact on U.S. Real GDP of each of the following:**
a. A fall in the real interest rate in the United States relative to the real interest rate in Japan.
b. An economic expansion in Japan.

a. Lower real interest rates in the United States will send capital out of the United States. This decreases the demand for the dollar which depreciates. The dollar depreciation will shift the AD curve rightward and the SRAS curve leftward. Although the effect on Real GDP depends upon the relative shifts of the two curves, economists believe that in this case, the AD curve typically tends to shift rightward by more than the SRAS curve shifts leftward, so Real GDP will rise.

b. An economic expansion in Japan will increase the demand for U.S. exports. As U.S. net exports rise, the AD curve shifts to the right, and Real GDP will increase.

2. Suppose country A undertakes a policy mix of contractionary fiscal policy and expansionary monetary policy. What would you predict would happen to real interest rates, the value of country A's currency, and net exports? Explain your answer.

Contractionary fiscal policy reduces the government's need to borrow funds placing downward pressure on interest rates. Similarly, expansionary monetary policy also places downward pressure on interest rates. Both contractionary fiscal policy and expansionary monetary policy would place downward pressure on interest rates. Lower interest rates would decrease demand for country A's currency causing it to depreciate. As the currency depreciated, demand for country A's goods would increase causing net exports to rise. Net exports would also rise because the contractionary fiscal policy would reduce country A's demand for imports.

3. If prices in the United States rise relative to prices in Japan, and the exchange rate is fixed, what is likely to happen to the net exports of each country? To the AD curve in each country? To Real GDP in each country? Explain your answers.

Under fixed exchange rates, if American goods increase in price more than Japanese goods increase in price, then relatively speaking, American goods have become more expensive. In response to this, Americans would import more Japanese goods, and the Japanese would purchase fewer American exports. As a result, net exports would decline, and the AD curve would shift to the left, lowering U.S. Real GDP. The opposite would occur in Japan. Americans would buy more Japanese goods causing net exports to increase, the AD curve to shift to the right, and increasing Japanese Real GDP.

4. Explain the relationship of saving to both the budget deficit and the trade deficits.

If a country runs a budget deficit, or a trade deficit, these deficits must be funded. Let's say the government runs a budget deficit. If there is insufficient savings within that country to fund the deficit, then the country must borrow the money from abroad. They will do this, in part, by offering higher interest rates to those who will lend the government money to cover its deficit. Remember the formula:

$$\text{Budget Deficit} = (S - I) + \text{Trade Deficit}$$

If net savings (S - I) are sufficiently high, the government can run a budget deficit without being forced to run a trade deficit, but if net savings are small or negative, then a budget deficit implies a trade deficit.

5. If you were an economic adviser to the president of the United States, and the country was running a large trade deficit, what policy or policies would you suggest for reducing it? Why would you recommend these particular policies?

There are four ways which a country can reduce its trade deficit: reduce the budget deficit, promote economic growth in the trading partners of the United States, raise savings and/or reduce investment, and pursue protectionist policies. Although higher growth among the United States' trading partners would generate economic growth, the United States' ability to promote growth is limited and the impact on foreign exports would probably be relatively small. Protectionist policies might produce retaliatory measures from our trading partners, reducing demand for U.S. exports. Reducing investment could lower Real GDP. This leaves two choices: lower the budget deficit, and/or raise the level of saving in the United States. The budget deficit could be lowered by raising taxes or cutting spending. Savings could be increased by providing tax breaks to people who saved money, for example, allowing deductions from income taxes for money placed into IRAs, not taxing interest which is earned, or repealing the capital gains tax.

6. Suppose that currently the United States runs a trade deficit with Japan and that Japan runs a trade surplus with the United States. If Japan stimulates its economy, and at the same time the United States reduces its budget deficit, how will the trade position between the two countries change?

If Japan stimulates its economy, this will increase the demand for American goods reducing Japan's net exports. If the United States reduces its budget deficit, this will lower domestic interest rates causing the dollar to depreciate which in turn will increase the demand for U.S. exports. The United States' trade deficit with Japan would shrink, and Japan's trade surplus with the United States would also shrink.

7. Why might import spending rise in a country soon after a depreciation in its currency? Is import spending likely to fall over time? Explain your answer.

A depreciated currency makes imports more expensive and people will cut back on buying imported goods – but they will probably cut back very little in the short run. If the percentage cutback in the physical quantity of imported goods is less than the percentage increase in price, then overall spending on imports will rise. In time, though, the percentage cutback in the physical quantity of imported goods is likely to be greater than the percentage increase in price, and overall spending on imports will decline.

8. A change in foreign input prices will affect both the AD curve and the SRAS curve. Do you agree or disagree? Explain your answer. (Hint: Does it matter *how* foreign input prices change?)

It depends. If foreign input prices change because of changes in demand and supply within that country, then the AD curve will not be affected by the change in foreign input prices. Only the SRAS curve will be affected. However, if foreign input prices change as a result of an appreciation or depreciation in the value of the currency, then the change in foreign input prices which the appreciation/depreciation generates will shift the SRAS curve, and the appreciation/ depreciation will shift the AD curve.

9. Explain why expansionary monetary policy is more likely to increase Real GDP in an open economy than in a closed economy.

In an open economy, expansionary monetary policy causes interest rates to fall in the short run, shifting the AD curve rightward and raising Real GDP. In a closed economy, the story stops here. In an open economy, lower interest rates causes an outflow of funds from the United States, a depreciation in the dollar, and increased net exports. The increase in net exports causes a rightward shift in the AD curve which increases Real GDP even more.

10. Explain why contractionary fiscal policy is more likely to decrease Real GDP in a closed economy than in an open economy.

The reduction in government spending reduces the budget deficit but it also reduces aggregate demand, pushing Real GDP downward. In a closed economy, the story would stop here, but in an open economy there are international feedback effects which must be considered. Reduced borrowing by the government lowers U.S. interest rates causing capital outflows and a dollar depreciation, a sequence which would push Real GDP upward through a rightward shift in the AD curve that is greater than the leftward shift in the SRAS curve. Again, the ultimate result will depend upon how much the AD and SRAS curves move relative to one another. Regardless of the strength of these shifts, we can conclude that contractionary fiscal policy lowers Real GDP more in a closed economy than in an open economy.

■ LECTURE SUPPLEMENTS

"Capital Punishment," *The Economist*, **February 4, 1995, p. 72.**

No, this article doesn't favor the death penalty for economists. Instead, it discusses the impact of capital controls on the macroeconomy. In the wake of the peso crisis of December 1994, this article explored the consequences of controlling capital flows in developing countries in order to limit the impact of the international economy on the domestic economy.

Should capital controls be reduced prior to economic reforms, or after they have been put in place? Chile, for example, requires that foreigners who invest in the Santiago stock market keep their money in the country for at least one year to reduce short-term capital flow disruptions. The reason for this is that Chile has tried to maintain a competitive real exchange rate in order to foster exports. If there are large capital flows into the country, this drives up the value of the currency, reducing Chile's ability to export. Capital inflows have been large enough that Chile has had to allow its real exchange rate to rise, despite initial attempts to sterilize capital inflows.

The World Bank found that a competitive real exchange rate, as opposed to a stable one, is better achieved by keeping fiscal policy tight and interest rates low. Though capital controls may provide some stability, they also interfere with the allocation of global financial resources. And as the article points out, fiscal policy and monetary policy must be married to international economic policy so that all three are coordinated to achieve the country's economic goals.

"Argentina's Currency Strengths," *The Economist*, **January 14, 1995, p. 68.**

Also published in the wake of the peso crisis, this article compares the policies of Mexico and Argentina to see what went wrong with Mexico, and why Argentina succeeded in its policies. In both countries, a stable nominal exchange rate was central to the countries' economic programs. As capital flowed into the countries, their currencies appreciated, increasing the real exchange rate, and reducing their competitiveness.

As the article shows, it wasn't economic factors alone which forced Mexico to devalue. Mexico faced a crisis of confidence which compounded the economic problems the country was facing. When Mexico's foreign reserves began to dry up, investors abandoned the peso, correctly perceiving that devaluation became inevitable because Mexico would no longer be able to defend the currency.

Both countries pegged their currency to the dollar, but Argentina used a currency-board mechanism to peg their currency to the dollar making the two fully convertible into one another. To make this system work, the central bank must keep its foreign currency reserves as large as the monetary base. Nevertheless, if there were a crisis of confidence, Argentina would face a problem similar to the one banks face when there is a run on the bank. So far, the Argentinean approach has worked. Use this article to get your students thinking about which policies are successful in providing exchange rate stability to a country.

Paul Craig Roberts, "Russia Should Bet the Bank on the Ruble," *Business Week*, **July 31, 1995, p. 20.**

In this article, Roberts discusses the benefits that a stable ruble would provide to Russia, as well as the steps Yeltsin's economic team has taken to stabilize the Russian economy. After the breakup of the Soviet Union, Russia, as well as many of the other members of the Confederation of Independent States, ran the printing presses to pay for government purchases. The resulting inflation created as many problems as they solved. The ruble has collapsed to almost 5000 to the dollar, a far cry from the official exchange rate of about one-to-one which prevailed twenty years ago. As Roberts points out, exchange rate stability can improve economic stability and provide political stability as well.

CHAPTER 16

Taxes, Deficits, and Debt

Up until now we have talked about fiscal policy primarily in terms of how changes in fiscal policy will affect the economy, inflation, unemployment, and so forth. In this chapter, we look at the facts, discussing in detail, taxes, deficits and the debt. First, the chapter analyzes the different types of taxes which individuals must pay in order that we can understand the sources of government revenue. Next, the chapter looks at the government deficit and debt. By separating the debt into its structural and cyclical components, we can separate the portion of the deficit which comes from the business cycle and the portion which is inherent to the budgeting process. The presence of the deficit and debt raises several important questions. Who bears the burden of the debt? Are budget deficits inflationary? Do budget deficits increase the trade deficit? And finally, how can we reduce the deficit? The chapter provides some preliminary answers to these questions

■ CHAPTER OBJECTIVES

Upon completing this chapter, your students should be able to:

- know the different types of taxes which individuals pay, and be able to differentiate between progressive, regressive, and proportional taxes;

- define and clearly distinguish between the *budget deficit* and the *national debt*;

- discuss the issue of national debt ownership and its consequences;

- explain whether current generations or future generations bear the burden of the government's debt, and why;

- understand the relationship between budget deficits and inflation, and the relationship between budget deficits and trade deficits; and,

- identify and present the key arguments for and against the *balanced budget amendment*, as well as the *line-item veto*, a *consumption tax*, a *value-added tax* (VAT), and increased *privatization* of government operations.

■ KEY TERMS

- budget deficit
- national debt

172

■ CHAPTER OUTLINE

I. **TAXES**

A. **What are the Major Federal Taxes?** -- Exhibit 16-1 illustrates the major sources of taxes for the federal government.

1. **Personal Income Taxes** -- This is the tax someone pays on his or her *taxable income*. In 1994, this represented 43.18 percent of all federal government receipts.

2. **Corporate Income Tax** -- This is the income tax corporations pay on their profits. This represented 11.16 percent of all federal government receipts in 1994.

3. **Social Security Tax** -- This is the payroll tax and is a tax generated from employment. In 1994, this tax represented over 36.9 percent of all federal government receipts.

B. **The Income Tax Structure** -- An income tax can be *progressive, proportional*, or *regressive*. Under a *progressive income tax*, individuals pay a higher proportion of their income in taxes as their income increases. Under a *regressive income tax*, individuals may pay a lower tax rate as their income increases. A *proportional income tax* is also known as a *flat tax*. Under a proportional tax, individuals face the same marginal tax rate at every level of income. With a proportional income tax, a person pays the same tax rate no matter what his or her income. Exhibit 16-2 reviews the three income tax structures.

C. **What Are the Major Federal Government Spending Programs?** -- The federal government spent $1,460.9 billion in 1994. Here's how.

1. **National Defense** -- These expenditures are for the military. In 1994 this totaled $281.6 billion.

2. **Income Security** -- This refers to government programs which provide assistance to the poor and disabled as well as federal pensioners. In 1994 these programs cost $214 billion.

3. **Health** -- These are government expenditures on health excluding Medicare, and these expenditures came to $107.1 billion.

4. **Medicare** -- This program provides hospital and medical care to Social Security beneficiaries. It totaled $144.7 billion.

5. **Social Security** -- This program provides Social Security payments to retirees and cost $319.6 billion in 1994.

6. **Net Interest on the National Debt** -- The federal government paid $203 billion in 1994 to service its debt.

II. **Deficits and the National Debt**

A. **The Difference between the Deficit and the Debt** -- A **budget deficit** occurs within a single year when government expenditures outstrip tax receipts. The **national debt** is the accumulated deficits of the federal government and represents the obligations the government owes to its creditors. In 1994, the *gross national debt* was $4,643.7 billion with 26 percent held by agencies of the U.S. government and 74 percent held by the public. The *net national debt* is that portion of the gross national debt which is held by the public, and in 1994 this totaled $3,432.2 billion. Exhibit 16-4 provides evidence on the government budget deficit for fiscal years 1988 through 1996 and Exhibit 16-5 measures the government debt in terms of GDP.

B. **What is the Difference between the Cyclical and Structural Deficit?** -- The *cyclical deficit* refers to that portion of the budget deficit which results from a downturn in economic activity; the *structural deficit* refers to that portion of the budget deficit which would exit if the economy were operating at full employment, and

Total budget deficit = structural deficit + cyclical deficit.

During an economic downturn, the government will receive lower corporate and personal income taxes, and will have to provide more transfer payments. These two factors will increase the size of the deficit.

C. **Is the Budget Deficit Bigger or Smaller Than Reported?** -- The Social Security system runs a surplus which reduces the overall deficit of the government. Robert Eisner differentiates between the *real budget deficit* and the *nominal budget deficit* where the

Real Budget Deficit = Nominal Budget Deficit - (National Debt x Inflation Rate).

The purpose of this measure is to deduct from the actual budget deficit the reduction in the real budget deficit which occurs from higher inflation because *inflation reduces the value of the debt*. Inflation redistributes income from creditors to debtors, and since the government is a debtor, it benefits from inflation.

III. **Who Bears the Burden of the Debt?** -- Who actually "pays" for deficit spending and for the accumulated IOUs represented by the national debt?

A. **The Current Generation Bears the Burden of the Debt** -- One school of thought says that the current generation bears the *burden* of the debt. Because more resources are devoted to making goods for the government, less resources are available for private consumption and investment. This sacrifice of private goods for more public spending is seen as the true "cost" of government borrowing. If the debt is entirely held by Americans, then the debt recirculates payments between American *taxpayers* and American *bondholders*. Since about 14 percent of the national debt is held by foreigners, future generations do not entirely escape the burden of the debt. On the other hand, the current budget deficit may reduce the amount of capital that future generations have to work with.

B. **The Future Generation Bears the Burden of the Debt** -- The alternative view is that future generations bear the true burden of the debt. According to this line of reasoning, the current generation makes voluntary transfers of current private spending for additional future spending -- that is, they finance the deficit and the debt by buying government bonds, which then act like a savings account, storing purchasing power until the bonds mature. However, the future generations that must pay off these bonds on maturity gain no increase in purchasing power, nor have they made a voluntary decision to repay (whereas the current generation *did* make a voluntary decision to lend). Instead, the future generations transfer their purchasing power to bondholders in return for past spending. Bondholders do not gain anything, and taxpayers lose something, so on net the next generation loses.

IV. **Budget Deficits, Trade Deficits, and Inflation**

A. **Do Budget Deficits Cause Inflation?** -- Exhibit 16-6 shows how a budget deficit could create a one-shot increase in inflation. The increase in government spending shifts the AD curve out from AD_1 to AD_2 which in turn raises the price level from P_1 to P_2. Notice that the price increase depends upon the shape of the SRAS curve. If the SRAS curve had been horizontal, as illustrated in Exhibit 16-7, no increase in the price level would have occurred. The story gets more complex when monetary policy is introduced. Assume that the government pays for its increased spending by borrowing money. This raises the interest rate, and assume also that the Fed increases the money supply to offset the higher interest rates. The Fed's action will shift the AD curve to the right, increasing the price level. In this case, the price level rises, not because of expansionary fiscal policy but because of expansionary monetary policy.

B. **The Budget Deficit and the Trade Deficit: Any Connection?** -- Yes, there is. Here's why.

1. As the budget deficit grows larger, the U.S. Treasury has to borrow more funds.

2. Higher U.S. interest rates cause an inflow of foreign capital.

3. Demand for the dollar increases, and the dollar appreciates.

4. The appreciation of the dollar makes American goods more expensive to foreigners, and it makes foreign goods cheaper to Americans.

5. U.S. residents buy more foreign goods, and foreigners buy fewer American goods.

6. These two changes increase the trade deficit. [See Exhibit 16-9]

C. **When it Comes to Economics, Do National Borders Really Mean Much Any More?** -- If the government provides benefits to one group of individuals, such as farmers, and borrows the money to pay for these benefits, interest rates will rise and the dollar will appreciate. This can reduce the demand for American exports. Farmers may directly benefit from the subsidies, but exporters may indirectly be hurt by these benefits. Individuals may see the results, but not understand the causes.

D. **Real Deficits and Debt** -- Some economists believe that much of the talk about debts and deficits is misleading. To the extent that inflation reduces the "pay back" value of the national debt, some economists argue that the national debt should be adjusted annually for inflation, and any reduction in the value of the national debt should be subtracted from the budget deficit to get the *real budget deficit*. For instance, if we look at the real value of the national debt -- that is, if we adjust for inflation -- the 3,900% nominal increase between 1940 and 1986 becomes a 385% (real) increase.

E. **Implicit Obligations and the Implicit Debt** -- Many federal programs, most notably Social Security, imply an obligation on the part of the federal government to make monetary payments at some future date. Some economists believe that the estimated value of these *implied obligations* should be included in calculations of the national debt, since they must be paid out of future tax revenues and/or borrowing.

V. TO BALANCE OR NOT TO BALANCE THE BUDGET? THAT IS THE QUESTION

A. Should the Federal Budget Be Balanced? -- Budget deficits increase the government's debt and tend to cause federal spending as a percentage of GDP to grow over time. Deficits have to be paid for by either raising taxes or borrowing money. Critics of budget deficits argue that budget deficits are "dishonest" because they hide the costs of budget deficits in the form of borrowing which can generate higher interest rates. Deficits make people think they get something for nothing when they don't. Other economists argue that it is more important to balance the economy than the budget, and if the economy is in a recession, the cost of the recession can exceed the cost of the budget deficit. On March 2, 1995, the Senate failed to pass a balanced budget amendment by one vote after the House of Representatives had passed a similar amendment. See the *Economics In Our Times* feature, "Two Economists Give Testimony on the Balanced Budget Amendment" for different views on whether the government should pass a balanced budget amendment.

B. Other Proposals to Deal With the Deficit

1. **The Presidential Line-Item Veto** -- Current law restricts the president to accepting or rejecting the proposed federal budget *in toto* -- that is, "all or nothing." The presidential line-item veto would allow the president to decide on the merits of proposed spending program by program; thus, better enabling him/her to "hold the line" on the budget. The main drawback to such a proposal is that it might unduly skew the balance of powers established in the Constitution in favor of the Executive. Nevertheless, on March 23, 1995, the U.S. Senate passed a line-item veto bill which must now be reconciled with the House version before the president can sign the final bill into law.

2. **National Consumption Tax** -- A percentage tax on consumption spending has been proposed as either an alternative to the current income tax, or as an additional tax. Those who support the consumption tax see it as encouraging saving and providing a preferable tax base to total income. In addition, if the consumption tax is used in addition to existing taxes, it would obviously go a long way toward reducing the deficit.

3. **The Value-Added Tax** -- A value-added tax is, essentially, a multi-stage sales tax collected from firms at each stage in the production and distribution process, rather than from consumers at the point of purchase. The idea is to tax the price of the good each producer sells less the cost of purchasing material inputs from other firms. Proponents of the VAT argue that it is more easily collected than the income tax, and that it also offers a preferable tax base. Critics say that the VAT is a "hidden" tax, since consumers never actually see what they are paying. As a result, it can be raised more easily, leading to a greater tax burden.

4. **Privatization** -- Some economists maintain that many of the functions currently served by government would be better and more efficiently provided by the private sector. As a result of eliminating these programs, the budget deficit would almost, as a matter of course, have to fall.

VI. ECONOMICS ON THE INTERNET -- A Usenet newsgroup on taxes and sources for accessing data on the government's budget are provided.

■ ANSWERS TO CHAPTER QUESTIONS

1. How do proportional, progressive, and regressive income tax structures differ?

Under a progressive income tax, individuals pay a higher proportion of their income in taxes as their income increases. Under a regressive income tax, individuals pay a lower tax rate as their incomes increase. A proportional income tax is also known as a flat tax in which the individuals' tax rate remains constant as income changes. Exhibit 16-2 reviews the three income tax structures.

2. Is it true that under a proportional tax structure a person who earns a higher income will pay more taxes than a person who earns a lower income? Explain your answer.

Yes, it is true. Under a proportional tax structure, the absolute level of taxes someone pays increases, but taxes as a proportion of income remains the same. For example, if the income tax rate were 20 percent, someone earning $20,000 would pay $4,000 in taxes, and someone earning $50,000 would pay $10,000 in taxes. The person earning $50,000 pays more in taxes, but as a proportion of income, pays the same amount as the person earning $20,000.

3. Why is it important to separate the structural deficit from the cyclical deficit?

Only by focusing on the structural deficit do we get a correct reading of fiscal policy. For example, with a structural deficit of $50 billion, it is clear that fiscal policy is intended to be expansionary, but not as expansionary as a simple reading of the total budget deficit (which contains the cyclical and structural deficits) might be

4. "The budget deficit is larger than is usually reported." Do you agree or disagree? Explain your answer.

Deficits are not always what they seem to be. The Social Security Administration runs a surplus which, if excluded, would make the deficit larger than it actually is. On the other hand, inflation eats away at the size of the real budget deficit because inflation reduces the real size of the government's outstanding debt. A 3 percent annual inflation rate would reduce the real value of the government's $5 trillion debt by $150 billion in any given year.

5. The national debt in year 1 is $1,500 billion, the national debt in year 2 is $1,575. The price level in year 2 is 20 percent higher than it was in year 1. What is the nominal deficit and the real deficit?

The nominal deficit is $75 billion. There is no real deficit but instead a surplus of $225 billion. To get this number, first multiply the percentage increase in the price level times the previous year's national debt ($1,500 billion **x** .20 = $300 billion) and then subtract this amount from the nominal (official) deficit. The "inflation tax" has conveniently turned a deficit into a surplus.

6. "The national debt is a fraction of the GDP. The Jensens' private debt is equal to their family income. It follows that the national debt is less of a problem than the Jensens' private debt. Since

you rarely hear anyone getting upset about the Jensens' private debt, there is even less reason to get upset about the national debt. All this talk about the seriousness of the national debt is simply empty talk." Discuss.

These facts bring up the importance of being able to bear the burden of debt. If the Jensens' debt is equal to their income, and the average interest rate on their debt is 10 percent, they must set aside 10 percent of their income each year to keep their debt from growing. The same is true of the United States government. It must collect a certain level of taxes each year in order to pay off the debt and keep the debt/GDP ratio from rising. If the deficit grows faster than the economy, then the debt burden will grow.

The concern for the federal debt is twofold. First, if the debt grows faster than GDP, the burden of the interest payments will grow over time. Second, the more money which the government spends on interest, the less the amount of money which is available for other expenditures, and the higher taxes are in the United States. "Getting upset" here implies a fear of bankruptcy, but bankruptcy is not the primary problem. A higher government debt leads to higher interest costs and higher taxes, and many people believe that these effects are something to get upset about. Also, the government debt absorbs savings which could be used for private investment which, in turn, can affect economic efficiency.

7. Economists are quick to point out that economics and politics are often at war with each other over deficits and debt. What do you think this means?

Certain economic issues that relate to the deficit may or may not be ignored, depending upon the politics of the deficit. For example, an economist may argue that, given the current state of the economy (let's say inflation is raging), the deficit should be reduced. Specifically, he or she advocates either an increase in taxes, a reduction in federal spending, or some of both. These are certainly not easy political actions. Few politicians like to go to their constituents and say, "We want to cut your spending benefits; we want to raise your taxes." When economics disagrees with politics, many economists predict that economics will be the loser.

8. "A liberal president would not use the presidential line-item veto to restrain government spending, but a conservative president would." Discuss.

More likely, both a liberal and a conservative president would use the presidential line-item veto. In either case, however, we could not be sure that a president, liberal or conservative, who used the line-item veto would be using it to hold down federal spending. The president might simply dislike a particular spending program that had been passed by Congress (and really care next-to-nothing about the total amount of federal spending). No matter what the motivation, though, the line-item veto would have the effect of restraining federal spending. Less would be spent with it than without it since every time it is used, no matter the reason, the result is less spending than would have existed without it -- assuming the veto is not overridden by the Congress.

9. Are you in favor of the balanced budget amendment? Why? To what degree does your answer depend on your view of the stabilizing effects of fiscal policy?

The answer to the first question depends on one's opinion. The arguments for and against a balanced budget amendment are laid out in detail in this *Instructor's Manual*, so we won't repeat them here. Obviously, the more important one believes discretionary fiscal policy to be, the harder it is to support the balanced budget amendment.

10. In the 52 years between 1944 and 1995, the United States has witnessed a budget deficit in 40 years and a budget surplus in 12 years. Some people have concluded that recent U.S. fiscal history shows a bias towards running budget deficits. Offer some explanations for this deficit bias.

The spread of income-support programs in the 1960s, coupled with rapid increases in consumer prices (and, thus, the prices of those goods which were being "targeted" by income supports) are certainly part of the problem. In addition, there has been a considerable buildup of military goods and services, despite the lack of an active war since the early 1970s. Finally, as deficits persist, the national debt grows, requiring increased interest payments, which are part of the budget. Thus, in order to maintain the same level of government service while increasing debt interest payments, the government must either raise taxes (a political "no-no") or run a deficit.

11. Under what conditions, if any, does a budget deficit cause inflation.

If the SRAS curve is horizontal or there is complete crowding out, then the increase in AD generated by the budget deficit will not be inflationary. If the SRAS is upward-sloping, or if crowding out is incomplete or zero, then a budget deficit is inflationary (in the sense of one-shot inflation). If the government pays for its deficit by "printing money" through open market purchases, this adds to the money supply which can cause inflation through the increase in aggregate demand which the increase in the money supply generates.

■ LECTURE SUPPLEMENTS

James K. Galbraith and William Darity, Jr., "A Guide to the Deficit," *Challenge*, July-August 1995, pp. 5-12.

If you want to provide your students with more information about the government budget deficit, this is an excellent place to start. They argue that it is more important how governments spend money than whether the budget is balanced. In large part, the authors rely upon the arguments of Robert Eisner that deficits can prove beneficial, and are not always harmful.

First, they discuss the difference between nominal and real deficits. This topic is covered in the text, but the article goes into more detail in discussing the two types of deficits. Second, they point out that the best measure of the size of the debt is as a percentage of GDP, not its absolute level. Third, they discuss the structural and cyclical deficits, discussing several myths about structural deficits, including the view that the structural deficit should always be balanced.

Fourth, the concept of sustainable deficits is introduced. Budgets are unsustainable when the real burden of interest that must be paid on the existing debt is greater than the budget surplus excluding interest payments. Fifth, they discuss several objectives, or goals, for the deficit, in particular, what type of balanced budget (annually? over the business cycle?) the government should aim for. Finally, they discuss some basic principles concerning the government budget deficit.

I think you will find this article a useful supplement to the material covered in this chapter.

Gene Epstein, "When It Comes to Taxes and a Balanced Budget, The GOP Has Promised a Lot More Than It Can Deliver," *Barron's*, February 20, 1995, p. 43.

The GOP's Contract with America promised to both lower taxes and balance the budget. The impossible dream? According to the Congressional Budget Office (CBO), to balance the budget by the year 2002, the government cannot simply cut the budget in the year 2002 and leave it at that. Instead, the government would have to cut programs over a period of years which would lead to a balanced budget by the year 2002. This would mean cutting the deficit by $1.2 trillion over the coming years with the last $322 billion in savings coming in 2002.

Many portions of the budget, such as Social Security, interest payments on the government debt, national defense, will be difficult to cut. Of course, the problem doesn't lie with Congress alone. Ask most Americans if they want to balance the budget, and they will say yes. Ask them if they want to cut Social Security, and they will say no. But cutting the deficit without cutting Medicare and Medicaid is almost impossible. Even eliminating agricultural subsides won't help much. These total only $10 billion.

Use this article to show students that calling for a balanced budget is one thing. Making the cuts necessary to balance the budget is quite another matter.

Gene Epstein, "If the Ratio of Federal Debt to GDP Keeps Rising, Coming Generations Face a Very Rough Tomorrow," *Barron's*, March 20, 1995, p. 37.

Could the federal government default on its debt. Although the government's debt has increased dramatically as a percentage of GDP since 1980, it still remains below the levels of debt reached in the aftermath of World War II in the United States. Moreover, compared to countries such as Belgium and Ireland, where the government deficit is currently greater than GDP, the United States' deficit remains low.

The article discusses the history of the debt/GDP ratio. Historically, the debt/GDP ratio increases during wartime, and declines during peacetime. However, since 1975, the debt/GDP ratio has been rising as a percentage of GDP. A possible consequence of the higher debt/GDP ratio is crowding out of the private sector by the government producing higher interest rates and a lower capital stock in the future.

Using an article by Laurence Ball and N. Gregory Mankiw, Epstein points out that the name of the game is to keep the debt/GDP ratio from rising, not necessarily to balance the budget every year. In fact, 1994 was the first time in 15 years in which the primary budget (ignoring interest payments) was balanced, allowing the debt/GDP ratio to decline. One problem is that in recent years the nominal average interest rate on the debt has been higher than the nominal economic growth rate. This makes it more difficult to reduce the debt/GDP ratio.

Finally, Ball and Mankiw point out that it is important to get the debt under control now. When the baby boomers begin to retire beginning around the year 2020, there will be an explosion in government deficits. At that point, the deficit problem could become overwhelming.

CHAPTER 17

The Logic of Consumer Choice

This chapter discusses the basic theory of consumer choice from two angles. First, in the chapter itself, we look at utility theory: what *utility* is, how individuals set about maximizing utility, how decisions between goods can best be made, and how all of that relates to consumer demand and the downward-sloping demand curve developed back in Chapter 3. Then, in Appendix C, we address the same questions using *indifference curve* analysis. In the course of this chapter, we see such important concepts as *diminishing marginal utility*, the *diamond-water paradox*, *consumer equilibrium*, the *income* and *substitution effects* of a price change, and the consumer's *budget constraint*, and the effect it has on his/her purchasing decisions.

■ CHAPTER OBJECTIVES

Upon completing this chapter and Appendix C, your students should be able to:

- define *total* and *marginal utility*, and explain the law of *diminishing marginal utility*;

- state and resolve the *diamond-water paradox* using utility theory;

- calculate marginal utility-per-dollar (relative marginal utility), given the necessary information, and determine the optimal combination of two or more goods a given consumer should purchase to achieve *consumer equilibrium*;

- understand the relationship between consumer equilibrium and the law of demand;

- describe the *income* and *substitution effects* of a price change;

- identify the various combinations of two goods that a consumer might buy, on the basis of her/his *budget constraint*;

- find the optimum purchase combination for an individual using the budget constraint and *indifference curve* analysis; and,

- derive an individual's (downward-sloping) demand curve for a particular good by using an *indifference map* and different budget constraints.

■ KEY TERMS

- diamond-water paradox
- utility
- util
- consumer equilibrium
- real income
- substitution effect
- budget constraint
- indifference set
- indifference curve

- total utility
- marginal utility
- law of diminishing marginal utility
- interpersonal utility comparison
- income effect
- consumers' surplus
- marginal rate of substitution
- indifference curve map
- transitivity

■ CHAPTER OUTLINE

I. **UTILITY THEORY** -- Adam Smith wondered why something as necessary to life as water had a lower price than diamonds, something with no "survival value" at all. This **diamond-water paradox** pointed to the fact that goods have two types of values. The first, *value in use*, is what we will call *utility*. The second, *value in exchange*, is best represented by price. The purpose of this section is to explain both ideas, and to reconcile them. In so doing, we will offer a solution to the diamond-water paradox.

   A. **Utility, Total and Marginal** -- To say that a good gives you **utility**, or *value in use*, is to say that it satisfies some want or desire, or that it gives you satisfaction. Utility can be measured in two ways: by using an artificial construct, called a **util**; or, by using dollar values. Any good that you consume offers utility -- otherwise, you would not consume it.

      1. **Total Utility** -- the total amount of satisfaction, or "use value," you receive from consuming a particular quantity of a good. *Total utility* (TU) is the sum of the utility gained from consuming each unit of a good.

      2. **Marginal Utility** -- the additional utility gained from consuming an additional unit of a good. *Marginal utility* (MU) is the change in total utility brought about by additional consumption. That is,

$$MU = \Delta TU / \Delta Q.$$

   B. **Law of Diminishing Marginal Utility** -- Marginal utility seems to behave in a particular way. For the most part, the more units of a goods we consume during a period of time, the less additional satisfaction we get from the additional units. This observation can be stated as the **law of diminishing marginal utility**: *for a given period of time, the marginal utility gained from consuming equal successive units of a good will decline as the amount consumed increases.* Individuals will choose to consume the goods which provide them with the greatest satisfaction first. After that, they will choose goods which provide them with relatively less satisfaction. [See Exhibit 17-1]

   C. **Utility and the One-Hundredth Game of Chess** -- The law of diminishing marginal utility does not seem to hold in all cases. That is, for some goods marginal utility does not begin to fall immediately after consuming the first unit. Rather, it seems to rise, then fall. As a result, many people prefer to use the terminology "principle of diminishing utility," rather than "law of diminishing utility." As individuals get better at playing chess, they may enjoy the one-hundredth game much more than they enjoyed the first game, but there will be some point where additional games of chess do not bring as much pleasure. At the very least, perhaps we should restate the law to say: for a given period of time, the marginal utility gained from consuming equal successive units of a good will *eventually* decline as the amount consumed increases. For an application of diminishing marginal utility, see the *Economics in Our Times* feature, "Do You Know Why You Sometimes Get Bored?" The Global Economy feature "Coffee and Tea in Vancouver" discusses why fads are fads. Although coffee has become increasingly popular in the past few years, helping Starbucks to expand at a very rapid pace, and even causing some McDonald's to provide cappuccino, there is evidence that the coffee fad may be fading.

D. **The Millionaire and the Pauper: What the Law Says and Doesn't Say** -- Regardless of which form we take it in, the law of diminishing marginal utility tells us that, at some point, successive units of a good consumed by the same individual will become less "valuable" to that individual. But what about the value of those units to someone else? We must be careful not to fall into the trap of making **interpersonal utility comparisons**, assuming that we know someone else's preferences on the basis of knowing our own. So, for example, we cannot tell whether an additional dollar of income is worth more to a poor man or a rich man, because we don't know those individuals' preferences with any degree of accuracy.

E. **The Solution to the Water-Diamond Paradox** -- Goods have both total utility and marginal utility. Water, something necessary for life, has a high degree of total utility. However, since it is in plentiful supply, and we consume it in large quantities, the marginal utility afforded by one more glass is fairly low (unless, of course, you just got back from jogging). On the other hand, diamonds, which have no real life-sustaining qualities, have a fairly low total utility. However, since they are available in very limited supply, and we consume them in small quantities (except, perhaps, for Zsa Zsa Gabor and a few others), one more diamond would likely have a high marginal utility. The solution to the diamond-water paradox comes from the fact that *prices, **value in exchange**, are most often determined by marginal utility, rather than total utility.*

F. **Is Gambling Worth It?** -- For those persons who derive no pleasure from gambling itself, but only gamble to win, the answer is no. The reason is that losing a dollar bet in a fair game (in which the value of the expected gain equals the wager made), causes most people to lose more utility than winning a dollar would cause a gain in utility.

II. **CONSUMER EQUILIBRIUM AND DEMAND**

A. **Equating Marginal Utilities per Dollar** -- How can consumers relate the marginal utility offered by additional units of different goods? For example, how can I compare the additional utility I might gain from eating an apple to the additional utility I might gain from eating an orange? The way to make such comparisons is to look at the MU gained *per dollar of purchase price*, otherwise known as the ***relative marginal utility*** of the good.

1. **Choosing Between Goods** -- If the MU of good A, relative to its price, is greater than the MU of good B, relative to its price, we should buy more of A and less of B. If we don't, then we are failing to maximize our total utility, given our income. For example, if we are buying 10 oranges and 10 apples, each of which costs $1, but the

last orange yields 30 utils of satisfaction, whereas the last apple only yields 20 utils, we could do better. If MU $_{oranges}$ / P $_{oranges}$ > MU $_{apples}$ / P $_{apples}$, then we should buy one less apple and one more orange. In doing so, we will increase our total utility. If this does not make MU $_{oranges}$ / P $_{oranges}$ = MU $_{apples}$ / P $_{apples}$, then we should further *redirect* our spending until the two ratios are equal (or, at least, as close to equal as we can get them).

2. **Consumer Equilibrium** -- Using that logic, we reach a point where we have divided our income between its available uses so that we cannot improve our total utility by buying more of one thing and giving up one of something else. That combination of goods where our income is used in such a way that we cannot improve our situation by redirecting our purchases is called **consumer equilibrium**, and is represented mathematically by the statement:

$$MU_A/P_A = MU_B/P_B = MU_C/P_C = \ldots = MU_Z/P_Z$$

where the letters A-Z represent all the goods a person buys.

B. **Consumer Equilibrium and the Law of Demand** -- Suppose that our consumer buys 11 oranges and 9 apples, so that MU $_{oranges}$ / P $_{oranges}$ = MU $_{apples}$ / P $_{apples}$. What happens if the price of oranges falls? Then we are back to the problem we started with, where MU $_{oranges}$ / P $_{oranges}$ > MU $_{apples}$ / P $_{apples}$. In order to return to equilibrium, our consumer will buy more oranges. We notice a pattern arising. As the price of a good falls, the relative marginal utility of that good rises, so we buy more of it. This is the same inverse relationship that we expressed in Chapter 3 between the (own) price of a good and the quantity demanded of it. Now we have a plausible theoretical argument: *As a good's (own) price falls, consumers buy more of it, in order to regain consumer equilibrium between the relative MU of that good and all other goods they buy; therefore, there is an inverse relationship between a good's (own) price and the quantity of it that people buy.* Exhibit 17-2 works another example demonstrating this principle more thoroughly.

C. **Are Rats Rational?** -- Human beings are not the only ones who understand the concept of downward-sloping demand curves. In experiments, researchers have shown that when the opportunity costs of liquids which rats are allowed to consume change, they will begin to consume more of the "cheaper" good.

D. **Should the Government Provide the Necessities of Life for Free?** -- People cannot survive without food and water, and possibly some other goods (medical care and education, for example). Should the government provide these goods for free? If the cost of a good is zero, then according to marginal utility theory, individuals would consume these goods until the marginal utility of consuming those goods was zero. If these necessities were free, some people might go to the doctor or college not for their utility, but simply to have something to do because the cost would be zero, and the opportunity cost of alternative goods would be relatively high.

E. **Income and Substitution Effects of a Price Change** -- What exactly happens when the price of a good drops? Two things: first, the *relative price* of the good *falls*; and, second, consumers' ***real income***, or purchasing power, *rises*.

1. **The Substitution Effect** -- When a good's (own) price falls relative to the prices of other goods, people tend to buy more of it. *That portion of the change in quantity*

demanded for a good that is attributable to a change in its relative price is referred to as the **substitution effect** *of the price change.*

2. **The Income Effect** -- A person's real income, or purchasing power, rises if he or she can purchase more goods and services, given a fixed level of dollar income. When the price of a good falls, purchasers of that good have to devote less of their income to buying that good; therefore, they find themselves with more purchasing power left over to spend on other goods, or more units of the good in question. As long as the good in question is normal, consumers should buy more of it when their real income rises. *That portion of the change in quantity demanded of a good that is attributable to a change in real income, brought about by a change in the good's (own) price, is called the* **income effect** *of the price change.* [See Exhibit 17-3]

F. **Consumers' Surplus** -- *the difference between the actual price buyers pay for a good and the maximum price they are willing and able to pay for it.* It is a dollar measure of the benefit gained by being able to purchase a unit of a good for less than one is willing to pay for it. [See Exhibit 17-4a]

G. **Using Consumers' Surplus** -- Exhibit 17-4b provides an application of consumers' surplus, showing how government regulations or monopolists can reduce consumers' welfare. Firms can increase their profits if they are able to capture more of consumers' surplus and convert it into producers' surplus. This is illustrated in the *Economics in Our Times* feature, "It Looks and Sounds Like a Deal, But Is It?" Bob would pay $40 for his second pair of trousers. If the store charged the same price for each pair of trousers, it would receive $60 for two pair (see Exhibit 17-5b). But what if the store knew about consumers' surplus, and charged a higher price for the first pair ($40), and sold the second pair at a lower price ($20)? Bob clearly would not benefit from this "bargain" because it would transfer a portion of his consumers' surplus to the store, as is illustrated in Exhibit 17-5c.

III. **ECONOMICS ON THE INTERNET** -- Sources for data on prices, income, consumption, and saving are provided.

IV. **APPENDIX C: BUDGET CONSTRAINT AND INDIFFERENCE CURVE ANALYSIS**

A. **The Budget Constraint** -- In our discussion of consumer equilibrium, we said that a consumer should always try to maximize his/her utility, given available income. In developing the first part of indifference analysis, we focus on the question of available income. The income that an individual has to spend on any two goods is his/her *budget* for those goods. The individual's **budget constraint** *shows all possible combinations of those two goods that may be purchased given a certain amount of money and the prices of the two goods.* Exhibit 17C-1 illustrates the budget constraint for a hypothetical consumer, O'Brien, based upon his available income and the prices of two goods: X and Y. The budget constraint tells us more than just the various combinations of X and Y that O'Brien can buy with his income. The *slope* of the budget constraint tells us the relative prices of goods X and Y. That is, the slope of the budget constraint = P_X / P_Y.

B. **What Will Change the Budget Constraint?** -- A change in any of three factors -- the individual's budget, the price of good X (P_X), or the price of good Y (P_Y) -- will shift the budget constraint. Specifically, *if the price of one good rises (falls) relative to the other, the budget constraint will rotate to reflect the new, lower (higher) maximum available quantity of that good.* [See Exhibit 17C-2a] *If the consumer's budget changes, the budget constraint will shift -- outward, if budget increases; inward, if budget decreases --* as is shown in Exhibit 17C-2b.

C. **Indifference Curves** -- A consumer may, of course, choose any combination ("bundle") of goods that is within her/his budget; but, how does a consumer identify which bundle is best, given her/his preferences and budget?

1. **Constructing an Indifference Curve** -- The first step we must take is to determine those bundles that a consumer views as equally satisfying; or, put another way, that a consumer is *indifferent* between (because they are equally satisfying). The listing of all the different bundles of two goods that generate the same total utility for our consumer is called an **indifference set**. *The graphical representation of all the different bundles of two goods which have the same total utility for that individual is called an **indifference curve**.* [See Exhibit 17C-3]

2. **Characteristics of Indifference Curves** -- Indifference curves have certain characteristics that are based upon an assumption of rational consumer behavior.

   a. **Indifference Curves are Downward Sloping** (from left to right) -- The assumption that consumers always prefer more of a (normal) good to less requires that indifference curves slope downward from left to right.

   b. **Indifference Curves are Convex to the Origin** -- The slope of an indifference curve diminishes (becomes flatter) as we move down and to the right along a given indifference curve. This is consistent with the notion of diminishing marginal utility. As we increase our consumption of one good, the MU of that good decreases; as a result, the more of one good a consumer has, the more of it he/she is willing to give up to get another unit of the good he/she has less of.

   An important peripheral point here is that the *absolute value of the slope of the indifference curve* represents the **marginal rate of substitution (MRS)** between the two goods X and Y at that point on the indifference curve. Furthermore, the MRS *represents the ratio of the MU of the good on the horizontal axis to the MU of the good on the vertical axis.* That is,

$$MU_{\text{good on horizontal axis}} / MU_{\text{good on vertical axis}}$$

   Put another way, *the MRS is the amount of one good an individual is willing to give up to obtain an additional unit of another good and maintain equal total utility.* The absolute value of the slope of the indifference curve equals the marginal rate of substitution which equals $MU_{\text{good on horizontal axis}} / MU_{\text{good on vertical axis}}$.

   c. **Indifference Curves Farther from the Origin are Preferable Because They Represent Larger Bundles of Goods** -- An **indifference curve map** plots several indifference curves on the same diagram. [See Exhibit 17C-5]. As we move away from the origin, each successive indifference curve represents a higher level of total utility, and is, therefore, preferable to any curve closer to the origin.

d. **Indifference Curves Do Not Cross** -- Individuals preferences are transitive -- that is, if I prefer A to B and B to C, I must prefer A to C. Since individuals have transitive preferences, then no two indifference curves may cross. Otherwise, we could say, "I am indifferent between A and B and between A and C, but I prefer C to B," or some other nonsense. [See Exhibit 17C-6].

D. **The Indifference Map and the Budget Constraint Come Together** -- Exhibit 17C-7 combines the indifference map with the individual's budget constraint in order to determine the optimal (equilibrium) bundle of goods X and Y. Given the discussion to this point, we know that a rational individual will try to reach a bundle on the highest (farthest from the origin) indifference curve possible. This point will be where the budget constraint is *tangent to* the highest attainable indifference curve. At that point, the slope of the indifference curve will equal the slope of the budget constraint, and consumer equilibrium will have been achieved. That is,

slope of budget constraint = slope of indifference curve.

Put another way, consumer equilibrium occurs when,

$$P_X / P_Y = MU_X / MU_Y,$$

or when

$$MU_X / P_X = MU_Y / P_Y.$$

E. **From Indifference Curves to the Demand Curve** -- Finally, Exhibit 17C-8 shows how we can use the indifference map and different budget constraints to derive a demand curve for either product X or Y (or both, as long as they are done individually). We vary the price of X, thus causing the budget constraint to rotate. In so doing, we get different optimal quantities of X. All that is left is to graph these optimal quantities of X with the prices of X that correspond to them, as seen in Exhibit 17C-8b.

■ ANSWERS TO CHAPTER QUESTIONS

1. If we take $1 away from a rich person and give it to a poor person, the rich person loses less utility than the poor person gains. Comment.

This statement may or may not be true. We do not know how much utility the rich person loses, nor how much utility the poor person gains.

2. Is it possible to get so much of a good that it turns into a bad? If so, give an example.

It is possible to get so much of a good that it turns into a bad. For example, consider hamburgers. The first hamburger a person eats usually tastes good and does a lot to satisfy his hunger. The second one tastes good too, but not as good as the first, and does less to satisfy his hunger (since it has already largely been satisfied). The third hamburger doesn't taste anywhere as good as the first or second. The fourth hamburger makes the person feel somewhat nauseous. The fifth hamburger makes the person sick. A hamburger, which was once a good that gave a person utility, is now a bad, giving a person disutility.

3. If a person consumes fewer units of a good, will the marginal utility of the good increase as total utility decreases? Why?

Yes, it will, as long as the marginal utility of the units of the good no longer consumed was not negative. To illustrate, suppose the situation is as shown in Exhibit 17-1a. If the consumer consumes 5 units of good X, total utility is 40 utils and marginal utility is 6 utils. If she consumes one less unit of good X, or 4 units, total utility drops to 34 utils but marginal utility rises to 7 utils.

4. If the marginal utility of good A is 4 utils and its price is $2, and the marginal utility of good B is 6 utils and its price is $1, is the individual consumer maximizing (total) utility if she spends a total of $3 buying one unit of each good? If not, how can more utility be obtained?

The individual consumer is not maximizing utility. She is receiving 2 utils per dollar spent on good A and 6 utils per dollar spent on good B. She can increase her utility by purchasing more of good B (the good for which she receives more utility per dollar) and less of good A (the good for which she receives less utility per dollar).

5. Individuals who buy second homes usually spend less for them than they do for their first homes. Why is this the case?

The marginal utility, in terms of additional comfort, protection, etc., of the second home is not as great as the that of the first. Therefore, since the marginal utility is less, so is the price that consumers are willing to pay.

6. Think up five everyday examples where you or someone else makes an interpersonal utility comparison.

Of course, these will be personalized, but here are a few examples. Bob and Linda want to do different things on Sunday afternoon. Linda wants to go to the museum, while Bob wants to take a nap. Linda thinks to herself: I'm sure that I'd enjoy going to the museum more than Bob would getting two hours of sleep. . .

Dave and Buster are at the Pizza Hut, where they are rapidly approaching the end of a very enjoyable large pepperoni pizza. As Buster finishes his piece, he notices that there is only one slice left. Rationalizing that he will enjoy it more, since he's only eaten five slices, while Dave is currently working on his sixth, Buster eats it.

On the freeway, Gladys forces Marietta to move to the next lane so Gladys can get by, all the while assuming that her (Gladys') time and comfort is more valuable than Marietta's.

Jimmy Fong is spending his afternoons mowing lawns, trying to save money towards purchasing his first car. One day he approaches a new neighbor, inquiring about cutting their lawn. "Sure," says Mrs. Wills, "we'll be glad to pay you $10 to cut and edge our lawn." Jimmy stops to think for a minute. "Well, I guess that's okay," he says; "but the Petersons pay me $15 for the same size lawn."

Like most couples, Ken and Debbie use teenagers for baby-sitters, and pay them a fairly small amount per hour, based upon the assumption that a teenager's time is worth less than an adult's.

7. Is there a logical link between the law of demand and the assumption that individuals seek to maximize utility? (Hint: Think of how the condition for consumer equilibrium can be used to express the inverse relationship between price and quantity demanded.)

Sure. Individuals, seeking to maximize the utility they receive from the goods they purchase as well as the money they have to spend, will only buy more of a good if the price of that good reflects their diminishing marginal utility.

8. List five sets of two goods (each set is composed of two goods; for example, diamonds and water is one set) where the good with the greater value in use has a lower value in exchange than the good with the lower value in use.

A book and a movie ticket. A loaf of bread and a custom T-shirt. One week's worth of house payments and one week's vacation in Acapulco. A Yugo and a $10,000 diamond and emerald necklace (my friends have expensive tastes). A week's groceries and a Nagel print.

9. Do you think people with high IQs are in consumer equilibrium (equate marginal utilities per dollar) more often than people with low IQs? Why?

Purely a thought question. . . No pun intended!

■ ANSWERS TO APPENDIX QUESTIONS

1. Diagram the following budget constraints:
   a.   income = $4,000; P_X = $50; P_Y = $100
   b.   income = $3,000; P_X = $25; P_Y = $200
   c.   income = $2,000; P_X = $40; P_Y = $150

With good X on the horizontal axis and good Y on the vertical axis, (a) is a straight line running from 80X, 0Y to 0X, 40Y; (b) is a straight line running from 120X, 0Y to 0X, 15Y; and, (c) is a straight line running from 50X, 0Y to 0X, 13.33Y.

2. Explain why indifference curves are (a) downward sloping, (b) convex to the origin, and (c) do not cross.

I don't think I can usefully elaborate on the explanation offered in Appendix C.

3. Explain why consumer equilibrium is equivalent using marginal utility and indifference curve analysis.

Consumer equilibrium is consumer equilibrium -- that is, that single combination of all goods purchased by a given consumer such that the marginal utility per dollar of the last dollar spent on each good is equal. Marginal utility and indifference curve analysis are just two ways of "measuring" equilibrium -- sort of like inches and centimeters, or Fahrenheit and centigrade.

4. Derive a demand curve using indifference curve analysis.

See Exhibit 17C-8 and the accompanying discussion.

■ LECTURE SUPPLEMENTS

"It's Official: Some Ads Work," *The Economist*, **April 1, 1995, p. 52.**

There has always been debate over the role of advertisements in consumer choice. Do advertisements provide useful information, or are they designed to manipulate consumers' choices? For an executive, there is another question, "Will these advertisements pay for themselves and increase sales, or am I just throwing money away?" If an executive knew which advertisements were effective and which were not, he/she could greatly reduce their advertising costs.

This article provides a partial answer to this question. The conclusion? About half of ads work in the sense that they do influence people to change their spending habit, and about half the ads have no effect at all. The effect was strong in only 30 percent of the cases, and had a long-term effect in only 46 percent of campaigns. John Philip Jones' study also noted that blitz campaigns in which advertisements are repeated suffer diminishing marginal returns. So some ads do work. The problem is knowing which ones will work beforehand.

"Human Rights," *The Economist*, **June 3, 1995, pp. 58-59, and Bob Ortega, "Conduct Codes Garner Goodwill for Retailers, But Violations Go On,"** *The Wall Street Journal*, **June 29, 1995, p. A1, column 1.**

These articles might be used as an interesting source of debate. The question these articles raise is how retailers do or should respond to consumer demands that firms treat employees working in developing countries better and do not mistreat animals used for testing and other purposes. If firms change their source of production, but doing so increases their costs, will consumers be willing to pay higher prices for the goods they consume?

As an example, Levi's sub-contracts the production of some of its jeans in southeast Asia. What should the firm do if some of the sub-contractors use child labor or virtual slave labor? Levi responded by firing some of its sub-contractors. The risk firms run is that if it turns out a twelve-year-old boy dies while providing virtual slave labor (as happened recently in India), consumers may boycott the firm's products. So it is in the firm's economic interest to behave ethically. And as the article points out, if child labor is used to produce a good, it is usually the middleman who pockets these extra profits, not the retailing firm in the United States.

On the other hand, what happens to these children if they lose their job. One member of Oxfarm found that in Bangladesh some children had turned to prostitution or more dangerous jobs such as welding when they became unemployed. So which is the lesser evil? And besides, it is difficult for firms to keep track of the activities of every single sub-contractor.   Nevertheless, the article shows that doing what is ethically right can have an economic reward for firms.

"CBS Tests Out its Pilots at a Las Vegas Lab," *Wall Street Journal*, **February 15, 1995, p. B1.**

Hollywood is always interested in consumer choice and taste because trying to keep one step ahead of consumer tastes is their job. How does Hollywood know which new movies and TV shows will be successful? New TV shows cost millions of dollars to start up. A poor choice and a lot of money goes down the drain quickly. A right choice, and the producers can become multimillionaires.

This article describes one way that CBS finds out what people want to see. They get people in Las Vegas to come in and watch pilots for their new season and find out what their response is. By doing this they can try and separate potential winners from losers, reducing losses. Each show is screened by several hundred people. If successful, the producers move on. If unsuccessful, the producers try to redo the show and try again.

Ask your students if they can think of other ways of determining consumer tastes. Too often Hollywood waits until something is successful and then copies it until everyone is sick of it. This may not seem very scientific, but Hollywood is still looking for alternatives.

CHAPTER 18

Elasticity

Chapter 17 provided a sound theoretical explanation for the inverse relationship between quantity demanded and the price of a good. Part I of this chapter addresses an equally important question: By *how much* will the quantity demanded of a good change as the price of that good rises or falls? The approach used to answer this question is to calculate the *price elasticity of demand* for the good in question. Part II then looks at where the price elasticity of demand comes from, and how it relates to and is reflected in the demand curve. The last part of the chapter then turns to other measures of elasticity: *cross elasticity of demand*, *income elasticity of demand*, and *price elasticity of supply*; and, concludes with a discussion of how the price elasticities of demand and supply affect how the burden of a tax is shared between consumers and producers.

■ CHAPTER OBJECTIVES

Upon completing this chapter, your students should be able to:

- define elasticity and understand the role of *elasticity* analysis in economics;

- calculate the *price elasticity of demand* for a good, interpret it, and explain how the price elasticity of demand relates to *total expenditures (total revenue);*

- identify the key determinants of the price elasticity of demand and describe how each will affect the observed elasticity;

- understand why a straight line doesn't necessarily have the same elasticity over its entire length;

- calculate the *cross elasticity of demand* between two goods, interpret it, and explain how cross elasticity can be used to determine whether two goods are *substitutes*, *complements*, or unrelated;

- calculate the *income elasticity of demand* for a good, interpret it, and explain how the income elasticity of demand can be used to determine whether a good in question is *normal* or *inferior*;

- calculate the *price elasticity of supply* for a good, interpret it, and describe the relationship between the price elasticity of supply and the shape of the short-run and long-run supply curves; and,

192

• use the price elasticities of demand and supply to determine who will bear the burden of a proposed tax (increase).

■ KEY TERMS

- price elasticity of demand
- elastic demand
- inelastic demand
- unit elastic demand
- perfectly elastic demand
- perfectly inelastic demand
- total revenue
- cross elasticity of demand

- income elasticity of demand
- normal good
- inferior good
- income elastic
- income inelastic
- income unit elastic
- price elasticity of demand

■ CHAPTER OUTLINE

I. **ELASTICITY: PART 1** -- Chapters 3 and 17 gave us the downward sloping demand curve, beginning with the law of demand, then explaining it in terms of utility analysis and the relationship between marginal utility and price. What is left is to discover by how much quantity demanded changes when price changes, and to do this we use **elasticity** analysis, which *estimates the response of one variable* -- in this case, the quantity demanded of a good -- *to changes in some other variable* -- in this case, the price of that good.

   A. **Price Elasticity of Demand** -- The **price elasticity of demand (E_d)** *measures the responsiveness of quantity demanded of a product to a change in the price of that product.* Specifically,

   $$E_d = \frac{\text{percentage change in quantity demanded}}{\text{percentage change in price}} = \frac{\% \Delta Q_d}{\% \Delta P}$$

   1. **Point Elasticity and Arc Elasticity** -- When calculating the price elasticity of demand -- or, in fact, most any measure of elasticity -- we may choose between two methods: *point elasticity* and *arc elasticity*.

      a. **Point Elasticity** -- *measures the change between two observed points based upon the value at one of those points.* For instance, when measuring price elasticity of demand between two points A and B, we would calculate:

      $$E_d = \left| \frac{\frac{\Delta Q_d}{Q_d}}{\frac{\Delta P}{P}} \right| = \left| \frac{\frac{Q_B - Q_A}{Q_A}}{\frac{P_B - P_A}{P_A}} \right|$$

193

The problem that we run into is : Which point is point "A" -- that is, where do we start? This becomes very important the larger the change we're looking at, as the *elasticity coefficient* will vary considerably depending on which point we use as our "base."

b. **Arc Elasticity** -- The best way to avoid deciding which endpoint should be our "base" is to *take the elasticity value at the midpoint of the arc between the two points* -- that is, calculate the **arc elasticity**. The midpoint formula is stated:

$$E_d = \left| \frac{\dfrac{\Delta Q_d}{(Q_{d1} + Q_{d2})/2}}{\dfrac{\Delta P}{(P_1 + P_2)/2}} \right| = \left| \frac{\dfrac{Q_{d2} - Q_{d1}}{(Q_{d1} + Q_{d2})/2}}{\dfrac{P_2 - P_1}{(P_1 + P_2)/2}} \right|$$

where P_1 represents the first price, P_2 the second price, and Q_{d1} and Q_{d2} are the respective quantities demanded.

2. **Perfectly Elastic and Perfectly Inelastic Demand** -- The price elasticity of demand can yield five basic results -- the numerator may be greater than the denominator, the denominator may be greater than the numerator, the numerator and denominator may be equal, the numerator may be zero, or the denominator may be zero. Each of these results has a specific name and implies specific results for E_d. Exhibits 18-1 and 18-2 summarize these possibilities and demonstrate them graphically in terms of a demand curve.

a. **Elastic Demand (E_d > 1)** -- *If the percentage change in quantity demanded is greater than the percentage change in price,* demand is said to be **price elastic**, and a change in price will cause a larger opposite change in quantity.

b. **Inelastic Demand (E_d < 1)** -- *If the percentage change in price is greater than the percentage change in quantity*, demand is said to be **price inelastic**, and a change in price will cause a smaller opposite change in quantity.

c. **Unit Elastic Demand (E_d = 1)** -- *If the percentage change in quantity equals the percentage change in price,* demand is said to be **unit elastic**, and a change in price will cause a proportional change in quantity.

d. **Perfectly Elastic Demand (E_d = ∞)** -- If quantity demanded changes dramatically in response to a change in price -- indeed, in the purist sense, *if quantity demanded drops to zero in light of a price increase* -- demand is said to be **perfectly elastic.**

e. **Perfectly Inelastic Demand (E_d = 0)** -- *If quantity demanded is completely unresponsive to a change in price*, demand is said to be **perfectly inelastic**.

194

B. **Price Elasticity of Demand and Total Revenue (Total Expenditures)** -- What effect will a change in price have on the total revenue (P **x** Q) of firms? The answer is that it all depends on the price elasticity of demand. The importance of elasticity is addressed in the *Economics and the Media* feature, "What Does Michael Jordan Have to Do with Price Elasticity of Demand?" If Michael Jordan can convince kids that there is *no* substitute for Nike shoes, demand may become inelastic, allowing Nike to charge a higher price for their shoes and increase total revenue. Exhibit 18-3 provides a review of the material in this section.

1. **If Demand is Elastic** -- If demand is elastic, the percentage change in quantity demanded is greater than the percentage change in price; therefore, *if price is increased, total expenditures fall as do producers' total revenue, if price falls, total revenue rises.*

2. **If Demand is Inelastic** -- If demand is inelastic, the percentage change in quantity demanded is less than the percentage change in price; therefore, *if price is increased, total revenues rise; and if price falls, total revenues fall.*

3. **If Demand is Unit Elastic** -- If demand is unit elastic, then a change in price is met with a proportional opposite change in quantity demanded; therefore, *if price rises or falls, quantity demanded falls or rises (respectively) such that total revenues remain unchanged.*

C. **When Is a Half-Packed Auditorium Better Than a Packed One?** -- If you could sell 10,000 tickets for $25, you would have more revenue than if you sold 20,000 tickets for $10. Of course, you could only do this if 10,000 people would be willing to pay $25. On the other hand, you would be even better off if you could charge 10,000 people $25 for the good seats, and the remaining 10,000 people $10 for the not-so-good seats. The goal is to maximize total revenue. Another application of elasticity is provided in the *Economics In Our Times* feature, "If Cars Get More Miles Per Gallon, Will There Be More or Less Car Pollution?" Improved fuel efficiency might cause people to drive more as the cost per mile traveled fell. If people drove more, the result of fuel efficiency might be greater pollution, not less.

II. ELASTICITY: PART 2

A. **Price Elasticity of Demand Along a Demand Curve** -- The price elasticity of demand for a straight-line, downward-sloping demand curve varies from highly elastic to highly inelastic. Take a look at Exhibit 18-4. At the upper end of the curve, where quantity demanded is low and prices are high, a 1-unit change in Q_D is much larger, in terms of percent, than the corresponding change in P. At the lower end of the curve, where Q_D is high and P is low, a one-unit change in Q_D is much smaller, in terms of percent, than the corresponding change in P. To summarize, as we move down the demand curve from higher to lower prices (top-left to bottom-right), the price elasticity of demand goes from elastic to unit elastic to inelastic.

B. **Determinants of Price Elasticity of Demand** -- There are three major determinants of the price elasticity of demand: (1) the number of substitute goods available; (2) the percentage of one's budget spent on the good in question; and, (3) the amount of time that has passed since the price change.

1. **Number of Substitutes** -- The more broadly defined the good, the fewer the substitutes; the more narrowly defined the good, the greater the substitutes. *The more substitutes that are available for a good, the higher its price elasticity of demand; the fewer substitutes, the lower the price elasticity of demand.* So, for example, there are more substitutes for Chevrolets than for cars (as a group); therefore, the price elasticity of demand is greater for Chevrolets than for cars (as a group).

2. **Percentage of One's Budget Spent on the Good** -- Buyers are (and thus quantity demanded is) more responsive to price the larger the percentage of their budget that is devoted to the purchase of the good. That is, people are more concerned about the price of automobiles than of oranges. In short, *the greater the percentage of one's budget that goes to purchase a good, the higher the price elasticity of demand; the smaller the percentage of one's budget that goes to purchase a good, the lower the price elasticity of demand.*

3. **Time** -- As time passes, buyers have greater opportunities to respond to a price change. Time allows for people to seek out substitute goods, alter their behavior, and so on. We conclude, *the more time that passes (after a price change), the higher the price elasticity of demand for the good; the shorter the time span, the lower the price elasticity of demand.* That is, price elasticity is higher in the long run than in the short run.

III. **OTHER ELASTICITY CONCEPTS** -- In this section we present three other measures of elasticity: *cross elasticity of demand, income elasticity of demand,* and *price elasticity of supply.* We conclude with a look at how the price elasticities of demand and supply affect who bears the burden of a tax.

A. **Cross Elasticity of Demand** -- measures the responsiveness of the quantity demanded of one good to a change in the price of another good. **Cross elasticity of demand (E_C)** is defined as

$$E_c = \frac{\text{percentage change in quantity demanded of good X}}{\text{percentage change in price of good Y}} = \frac{\dfrac{Q_{X2} - Q_{X1}}{(Q_{X1} + Q_{X2})/2}}{\dfrac{P_{Y2} - P_{Y1}}{(P_{Y1} + P_{Y2})/2}}.$$

We use cross elasticity to determine whether two goods are substitutes, complements, or unrelated. *If $E_C > 0$, the two goods (X and Y) are substitutes; if $E_C < 0$, the two goods are complements; and, if $E_C = 0$, the two goods are unrelated.*

B. **Income Elasticity of Demand** -- measures the responsiveness of the quantity demanded of a good to a change in income. **Income elasticity of demand (E_Y)** is defined as

196

$$E_Y = \frac{\text{percentage change in quantity demanded of good X}}{\text{percentage change in income}} = \frac{\frac{Q_{X2}-Q_{X1}}{(Q_{X1}+Q_{X2})/2}}{\frac{Y_2-Y_1}{(Y_1+Y_2)/2}}.$$

We use income elasticity to distinguish between normal and inferior goods. *If $E_Y > 0$, X is a normal good; if $E_Y < 0$, X is an inferior good.* We also look at the *degree* of income elasticity. *If $|E_Y| > 1$, demand is* **income elastic***; if $|E_Y| < 1$, demand in* **income inelastic***; and if $|E_Y| = 1$, demand is* **income unit elastic***.*

C. **Price Elasticity of Supply** -- measures the responsiveness of quantity supplied of a good to a change in the price of that good. **Price elasticity of supply (E_s)** is defined as

$$E_S = \frac{\text{percentage change in quantity supplied of good X}}{\text{percentage change in price of good X}} = \left| \frac{\frac{Q_{S2}-Q_{S1}}{(Q_{S1}+Q_{S2})/2}}{\frac{P_2-P_1}{(P_1+P_2)/2}} \right|.$$

As with demand, we classify supply as *elastic, inelastic, unit elastic, perfectly elastic,* and *perfectly inelastic.* If $E_S > 1$, supply is **elastic**; if $E_S < 1$, supply is **inelastic**; and, if $E_S = 1$, supply is **unit elastic**. Any of these three conditions can occur on a "normal" upward sloping supply curve. Two "special" conditions are also possible: if $E_S = \infty$, supply is **perfectly elastic**, meaning that the supply curve (or at least the portion we're observing) is horizontal; and, if $E_S = 0$, supply is **perfectly inelastic**, meaning that the supply curve (or at least the portion of it we're observing) is vertical. [See Exhibit 18-5]

D. **Price Elasticity of Supply and Time** -- Time plays a role with the price elasticity of supply, just as it does with the price elasticity of demand. *Over time, as producers are able to adjust their behavior and production patterns, supply becomes more price elastic than it is in the short run.*

E. **Who Pays the Tax: Elasticity Matters** -- Suppose the government levies a tax on the production of good Z. Who pays that tax: producers, consumers, some of each? To find out, we look at the price elasticities of demand and supply. Look at Exhibit 18-7. Here the government has levied a $1 tax on VCR tapes, shifting the supply curve to the left by $1 per tape. In this instance, the burden of the tax is shared fairly equally between consumers (who must pay $ 0.50 more per tape) and producers (whose after-tax revenues fall by $0.50 per tape). But this is not always the case. To show the possibilities, we look at four extreme examples.

1. **Perfectly Inelastic Demand** -- In Exhibit 18-8a, demand is perfectly inelastic. Under these conditions, demand is completely unresponsive to price changes; therefore, producers will raise price by $1 per unit, making *consumers pay the full tax.*

197

2. **Perfectly Elastic Demand** -- In Exhibit 18-8b, demand is perfectly elastic. Under these conditions, demand is perfectly responsive to a price change, such that a 1¢ price increase will eliminate demand. Here producers are unable to "pass on" any of the tax to consumers in the form of increased prices; therefore, *producers must pay the full tax.*

3. **Perfectly Elastic Supply** -- In Exhibit 18-8c, supply is perfectly elastic. In this instance, production will disappear if producers are asked to bear any part of the tax burden; therefore, *consumers pay the full tax.*

4. **Perfectly Inelastic Supply** -- In Exhibit 18-8d, supply is perfectly inelastic. Here consumers are more responsive to price changes than producers; therefore, *producers will bear the burden of the tax.*

While these are extreme examples, they are instructional, since every other possibility is bounded by these four extremes. As a rule, *if $E_S > E_D$, consumers will bear more of the burden of the tax than producers; if $E_S < E_D$, producers will bear more of the burden of the tax than consumers; and, if $E_S = E_D$, the burden will be evenly distributed between producers and consumers.*

F. **Degree of Elasticity and Tax Revenue** -- Suppose that the government's goal is to maximize tax revenues. Exhibit 18-9 shows that the government can do this by following a simple rule: *tax revenues are maximized by placing the tax on the producer who faces the more inelastic (less elastic) demand curve.*

IV. **ECONOMICS ON THE INTERNET** -- This section repeats some of the sources for information on prices, consumption, income and income growth.

■ ANSWERS TO CHAPTER QUESTIONS

1. **Explain how a seller can determine whether the demand for his or her good is inelastic, elastic, or unit elastic between two prices.**

The seller can raise the price and see what happens to total revenue. If total revenue rises, demand is inelastic (between the two prices). If total revenue falls, demand is elastic. If total revenue remains constant, demand is unit elastic.

2. **Suppose the current price of gasoline at the pump is $1 per gallon and that one million gallons are sold per month. A politician proposes to add a 10-cent tax to the price of a gallon of gasoline. She says the tax will generate $100,000 tax revenues per month (one million gallons x 10 cents = $100,000). What assumption is she making?**

She assumes that the demand for gasoline at the pump (between a price of $1 and $1.10 a gallon) is perfectly inelastic. In other words, a higher price for gasoline does not change the quantity demanded of gasoline at all. This is not likely to be the case. We conclude that the tax revenues will not be as high as the politician thinks it will be.

3. A college in the South raises its annual tuition from $2,000 to $2,500, and its student enrollment falls from 4,877 to 4,705. Compute the price elasticity of demand. Is demand elastic or inelastic?

Using the formula for E_d, we find

$$E_d = \left| \frac{\frac{\Delta Q_d}{(Q_{d1}+Q_{d2})/2}}{\frac{\Delta P}{(P_1+P_2)/2}} \right| = \frac{\frac{172}{(4876+4705)/2}}{\frac{500}{(2000+2500)/2}} = \frac{\frac{172}{4791}}{\frac{500}{2250}} = .1615.$$

Therefore, demand is inelastic, since $E_d < 1$.

4. Suppose a straight-line, downward-sloping demand curve shifts rightward. Is the price elasticity of demand higher, lower, or the same between any two prices on the new (higher) demand curve than on the old (lower) demand curve?

It is lower. As the exhibit below shows, when a straight-one, downward-sloping demand curve shifts rightward (leftward), price elasticity of demand falls (rises). Between the prices of $7 and $9 on D_1, price elasticity of demand is 1.33. Between the same prices on D_2, price elasticity of demand is .73.

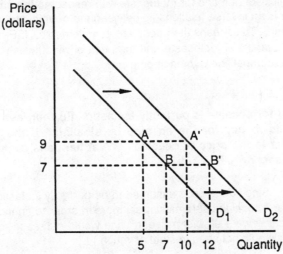

5. Suppose Austin, Texas is hit by a tornado that destroys 25 percent of the housing in the area. Would you expect the total expenditure on housing after the tornado to be higher than, less than, or equal to what it was before the tornado?

It depends. The tornado shifts the supply curve of housing leftward, which raises the price of housing. The question now is: What is the percentage change in quantity demanded compared to the percentage change in price? If the percentage change in quantity demanded is greater than

199

the percentage change in price, total expenditure after the tornado (TE $_{at}$) is less than total expenditure before the tornado (TE $_{bt}$). If the percentage change in quantity demanded is less than the percentage change in price, TE $_{at}$ > TE $_{bt}$.   And if the percentage change in quantity demanded is equal to the percentage change in price, TE $_{at}$ = TE $_{bt}$.

The tornado causes the supply curve of housing to shift leftward. Whether total expenditure after the tornado is greater than, less than, or equal to the total expenditure before the tornado depends upon the price elasticity of demand between points A and B.

6. Which of the following goods has the higher price elasticity of demand: (a) airline travel in the short run or airline travel in the long run; (b) television sets or Sony television sets; (c) cars or Toyotas; (d) telephones or AT&T telephones; (e) popcorn or Orville Redenbacher popcorn?

a. Airline travel in the long run.
b. Sony television sets.
c. Toyotas.
d. AT&T telephones.
e. Orville Redenbacher popcorn.

7. How might you determine whether toothpaste and mouthwash manufacturers are in competition with each other?

Determine the cross elasticity of demand for toothpaste with respect to the price of mouthwash. If E_C < 0, this means there is an inverse relationship between the quantity demanded of toothpaste and the price of mouthwash. This means the goods are complements. If E_C > 0, there is a direct relationship between the quantity of toothpaste and the price of mouthwash. The two goods are substitutes and thus are in competition with each other.

8. Assume the demand for cocaine is perfectly inelastic. Further, assume that the users of cocaine get the funds to pay for the cocaine by stealing. If the supply of cocaine decreases, what happens to the price of cocaine? What happens to the amount of crime committed by cocaine users?

The price of cocaine rises. Since demand is assumed to be perfectly inelastic, total expenditures on cocaine rise. This means cocaine users must steal more in order to finance their habit. (Note that if the demand for cocaine were elastic, a rise in price would decrease total expenditures on cocaine and cocaine users would not need to steal as much.)

9. Suppose you learned that the price elasticity of demand for wheat is 0.7 between the current price for wheat and a price $2 higher per bushel. Do you think farmers collectively would try to reduce the supply of wheat and drive the price up $2 higher per bushel? Why? Assuming that they would try to reduce supply, what problems might they have in actually doing so?

It would appear to be in the farmers' collective best interest to raise price by up to $2 per bushel, since to do so will increase the value of consumer's total expenditures on wheat by more than the revenues lost due to selling less wheat. However, whether or not such a program worked would depend upon a couple of factors. First, the availability of wheat from abroad may limit the farmers' ability to raise price by restricting domestic output. Secondly, if the price elasticity of supply is high enough, then many farmers may feel it in their personal best interest to "cheat" and increase their production as prices begin to rise (due to the general production cutbacks).

10. It has been said that if government wishes to tax certain goods, it should tax goods that have inelastic rather than elastic demand. What is the rationale for this?

Of course, it depends on the government's motives for taxing those particular items. As long as the government is taxing them for revenue purposes, and not to discourage their consumption, then taxing price inelastic goods makes sense. If demand is inelastic, the tax will not significantly reduce the quantity demanded; therefore, producers will not be appreciably harmed, and the government will earn more tax revenues than if the demand was elastic and people bought less. On the other hand, if the government is taxing the item in question primarily to discourage its use -- say, for example, cigarettes -- then a more elastic demand curve would be preferable, so that the government could, literally, price consumers out of the market for that undesirable good.

11. In 1947, the U.S. Justice Department brought a suit against the DuPont Company (which at the time sold 75 percent of all the cellophane in the United States) for monopolizing the production and sale of cellophane. In court, the DuPont Company tried to show that cellophane was only one of several goods in the market in which it was sold. It argued that its market was not the cellophane market but the "flexible packaging materials" market, which included (besides cellophane) waxed paper, aluminum foil, and so forth. DuPont pointed out that it had only 20 percent of all sales in this more broadly defined market. Using this information, discuss how the concept of cross elasticity of demand would help establish whether DuPont should have been viewed as a firm in the cellophane market or as a firm in the "flexible packaging materials" market.

Simple. Look at the cross-elasticity of demand (E_C) between cellophane and the other products that DuPont alleges serve as suitable substitutes. If $E_C > 0$, then the two goods in question are substitutes for one another, and DuPont has a valid case. If $E_C \leq 0$, then the goods are either unrelated or complements, in which case the case against DuPont would be wrapped up. Get it?

■ LECTURE SUPPLEMENTS

Alex Freedman, "Phone Firms Wrestle for Prisoners Business in Hot Growth Market," *The Wall Street Journal*, **February 15, 1995, p. A1, column 6.**

What would a prisoner's supply curve of time look like? Very inelastic. Time is not an item which prisoners have in short supply. So a prisoner's demand for activities which help time pass should be almost inelastic. And what happens when inelastic demand meets inelastic supply? An opportunity to raise prices very easily.

Phone companies understand this and do their most to tap into the lucrative phone market for prisoners. Prisoners must make collect calls, and calls tend to be longer than average phone calls. The result? A single phone can gross up to $15,000 a year, five times more than a pay phone on a street corner. This is one case where someone, competing phone companies, is trying to get **in** prison and stay there. Crime may not pay, but prisoners do.

There are more than one million inmates, and who can ignore a market like that. Moreover, it is a growing market, and prisoners are not bothered during dinner time being asked by cold callers to switch from AT&T to MCI or vice versa. They take what they can get. As one person put it, this is the only growth market in the collect-call business. Use this article to show students how elasticities create markets.

J. Andrew Hoerner, "Economists Discuss Sin Taxes, Work Incentives, Environmental Cleanup," *Tax Notes*, May 30, 1994, 63 (9), pp. 1088-1089.

This article would be good source material for showing how economists use elasticity as a means of determining which goods to tax. Taxes are often imposed on goods which produce negative externalities, while subsidies are provided for goods which produce positive externalities. If a good produces a negative externality and demand for that good is elastic, the tax will cause a larger decrease in the demand of that good than if the demand is inelastic. This is why "sin" taxes exist. Demand for these goods, such as tobacco and alcohol, is inelastic. Taxes can be imposed upon them without a large change in demand. Gasoline produces pollution, and demand for it is inelastic, hence the effectiveness of a tax on gasoline. Use this article to remind students of the relationship between elasticity and taxes.

Gary S. Becker, "Warning: A Health Tax May Be Hazardous to Health Financing," *Business Week*, August 15, 1994, p. 18.

Should the government raise taxes on cigarettes to help defray rising health-care costs? The article discusses research by Michael Grossman, Kevin Murphy and Gary Becker which found that although imposing cigarette taxes would not initially cause a large decrease in the demand for cigarettes, after one year, a 10% increase in price cut smoking by about 4 percent and by 8 percent after three years. They found the firm could maximize its revenue, i.e. raise the tax to the point where demand was unit elastic, by having a tax of 95 cents a pack which would bring in $6 billion in revenue. These numbers differed from Congressional studies which predicted that a higher tax could be imposed which would bring in more revenue.

Canada has had a high tax on cigarettes ($2.69 a pack) and this led to cigarette smuggling from the United States. Since poor people smoke more than middle- and upper-income individuals, the tax would be regressive. Here is an example of how elasticity is used to measure the impact of changes in government policies.

CHAPTER 19

The Firm

Chapter 19 turns our attention from individual decisionmaking to the second key set of factors in the demand-supply equation: suppliers. Chapters 19 and 20 discuss the nature of the firm and how rational producers make their decisions as to what to supply and at what price. Before we can move to the "meat" of supplier decisionmaking, though, we need a better grasp on exactly who suppliers are and how they function. To this end, Chapter 19 introduces us to the firm, starting with the theory of the firm as a productive "team," and then moving into some factual and legal insights as to the various types of businesses and the pros and cons of various business organizations. The chapter concludes with a look at the balance sheet of the typical firm, and a discussion of how firms raise outside funds to support their activities.

■ CHAPTER OBJECTIVES

Upon completing this chapter, your students should be able to:

- distinguish between *market coordination* and *managerial coordination*;

- understand the theory of the firm as a cooperative "team" and the role of management in *monitoring* team activity;

- identify the three types of business organizations and discuss the advantages and disadvantages of each, with particular regard to liability, rewards, control, and sustainability;

- draw up a simple balance sheet listing the basic *assets* and *liabilities* of a firm and demonstrate how a firm's *net worth* is calculated from this information;

- describe the two main financial instruments used to raise funds for a corporation; and,

- discuss the objective(s) of a firm, and how its "for-profit"-vs.-*nonprofit* status affects that (those) objective(s).

■ KEY TERMS

- business firm
- market coordination
- managerial coordination
- shirking
- monitor
- residual claimant
- corporation
- limited liability
- separation of ownership from control (or management)
- liabilities
- net worth (equity or capital stock)
- bond

- proprietorship
- unlimited liability
- partnership
- limited partnership
- face value (par value)
- coupon rate
- dividends
- assets
- balance sheet
- (shares of) stock
- nonprofit firms
- inside information

■ CHAPTER OUTLINE

I. **WHY FIRMS EXIST** -- A **business firm** is an entity that employs factors of production and produces goods and services to be sold to consumers, other firms, and/or the government. We work for firms, we buy things from firms; but, why do they exist?

   A. The Market and the Firm: Invisible Hand versus Visible Hand -- The economy is made up of millions of individuals, each doing their own things. How do those individuals come together to make economic transactions and to produce things?

      1. Market Coordination -- One answer is *market coordination* -- Adam Smith's "invisible hand." The market guides individuals into the activities at which they are most efficient, and enables them to express their preferences for goods, instructing producers as to what is wanted and what is not.

      2. Managerial Coordination -- In a firm, the decisions of what to produce and how is made by management. *Managerial coordination* guides and coordinates individuals' actions in a chosen productive endeavor.

   B. The Alchian and Demsetz Answer -- Why do people subject themselves to managerial control? Economists Armen Alchian and Harold Demsetz suggest that *firms are formed when the benefits that can be gained from working as a team are greater than the sum of the benefits that could be gained by acting individually.*

      1. Shirking in a Team -- Team production also has disadvantages, the most significant of which is the problem of **shirking** -- *putting forth less than the agreed-to effort.* Shirking is significant because the individual gains all of the benefits of shirking, while the consequences are spread across the entire team.

      2. The Monitor (Manager): Taking Care of Shirking -- The **monitor** (manager) plays an important role in the firm. He/she is the person who *reduces the amount of shirking by rewarding productive workers and punishing shirkers.* In so doing, the monitor can preserve the benefits of team production while reducing, if not eliminating, the costs of shirking.

But this raises another question: *Who monitors the monitor?* One possibility is to make the monitor a **residual claimant** – a person who shares in the profits of the firm. If the monitor shirks, then the monitor will suffer lost profits.

3. **Can Above-Market Wages Cause People to Shirk Less?** -- Some firms may pay above-market wages to discourage shirking and encourage employees to monitor themselves. The argument is that workers will not want to lose a job which pays them an above-market wage, and they will reduce shirking to ensure this. Monitoring costs fall more than wages go up. This is known as the *efficiency wage theory*.

4. **Markets: Outside and Inside the Firm** -- We can see why it's efficient to have monitors, but that still doesn't answer the question of why workers would submit to such a relationship. Individuals join a firm because they expect to be made better off. Shirking by other members of the team reduces the benefits to non-shirking workers. Monitors reduce the amount of shirking, thereby increasing the benefits gained from teamwork. Thus, employees submit to the monitor's commands because they realize that only a well-monitored team will yield the benefits they desire.

C. **The Objective of the Firm** -- What is the objective of the firm? Most economists will answer: profit maximization. However, not all economists agree. Some argue that firms try to maximize sales. Others argue that managers try to maximize their own power and rewards, rather than the firm's profits. Much of this is a result of the **separation of ownership from control** -- *most businesses are owned and run by two different sets of people.* Still, most economists feel that profit maximization is the driving force for most firms over time.

II. **DIFFERENT TYPES OF BUSINESS FIRMS** -- Business firms are organized in one of three basic ways: *(sole) proprietorships*, *partnerships*, and *corporations*.

A. **Proprietorships** -- *a form of business that is owned by one individual who makes all the business decisions, receives the entire profits, and is legally responsible for the debts of the firm.* As Exhibit 19-1 shows, sole proprietorship make up the vast majority of business firms in the United States.

1. **Advantages of Proprietorships** -- Sole proprietorships offer three distinct advantages: (1) *they are easy to form and easy to dissolve*, allowing for quick entry into and exit from a market; (2) *all decision-making power rests with the sole proprietor*, eliminating the need for group decisionmaking; and, (3) *since the profit of the proprietorship is the owner's income, it is taxed only once.*

2. **Disadvantages of Proprietorships** -- There are three major disadvantages of sole proprietorships: (1) *the sole proprietor faces **unlimited liability*** -- that is, the owner is responsible for all the debts of the proprietorship, and his/her personal property can be attached to settle those debts; (2) *proprietorships often end with the death of their founder*, creating a problem of sustainability; and, (3) due to their size, liability problems, and lack of sustainability, *proprietorships have a limited ability to raise funds for business expansion.*

B. **Partnerships** -- *a form of business that is owned by two or more co-owners, called partners, who share any profits the business earns and who are legally responsible for any debts incurred by the firm.* Partnerships may be thought of as proprietorships with more than one owner, since they share many of the same advantages and disadvantages.

1. **Advantages of Partnerships** -- Partnerships offer four advantages: (1) a partnership is *easy to organize*; (2) *partnerships work particularly well where team production involves skills that are difficult to monitor*; (3) partnerships *allow for the benefits of specialization*; and, (4) as with sole proprietorships, *the profit of the partnership is the partners' income, and only personal income taxes apply to it.*

2. **Disadvantages of Partnerships** -- Partnerships have three disadvantages: (1) *the partners have unlimited liability*, creating a particular problem when the debts for which you are liable are not your own; (2) *decisionmaking can be complicated and frustrating*; and, (3) *the loss of a partner, for whatever reason, can cause the partnership to be dissolved or restructured.* To deal with the problem of unlimited liability, most states allow the formation of **limited partnerships**, which allow the limited partners to limit their liability to the amount they have invested in the firm.

C. **Corporations** -- *a legal entity that can conduct business in its own name in the same way an individual does. Ownership of the corporation rests with stockholders who have limited liability in the debts of the corporation.* As Exhibit 19-1 shows, while only 18.3 percent of all U.S. firms are corporations, they account for almost 90 percent of all business revenues. Exhibit 19-2 shows where many of the world's 500 largest industrial corporations are located.

1. **Advantages of Corporations** -- Corporations offer three distinct advantages over partnerships and sole proprietorships: (1) *the owners of the corporation (the stockholders) are not personally liable for the debts of the corporation* -- that is, they have **limited liability**, which *assures that the stockholders can never lose more than the money they've invested in the corporation's stock*; (2) *corporations continue to exist if one or more owners sell their shares or die*; and, (3) due to their size, limited liability, and sustainability, *corporations are usually able to raise large sums of capital for investment purposes.*

2. **Disadvantages of Corporations** -- Corporations suffer from two distinct disadvantages: (1) *corporate profits are subject to* **double taxation** -- *that is, they are taxed when the corporation earns them, then they are taxed again when they are distributed as* **dividends** *to the shareholders and become subject to the personal income tax*; and, (2) *the separation of ownership from control* can create disagreement between stockholders and management if their priorities are not the same.

Exhibit 19-3 summarizes the advantages and disadvantages of corporations, proprietorships, and partnerships.

D. **The Conflict between What Business Leaders Say and What They (Sometimes) Do** -- As this *Economics In Our Times* feature points out, corporate executives appear to be hypocritical. On the one hand, they praise free enterprise and say that government should reduce its role in the economy. On the other hand, they go to the government for their piece of the corporate welfare pie. Although the economy would be better off if the government ended corporate welfare, it could still be rational for corporations to seek out some corporate welfare as long as some businesses receive support. Hypocrisy or rationality? You decide.

E. **Japanese Proprietorships and American Corporations** -- Proprietorships receive approximately 50 percent of retail sales in Japan as opposed to 6 percent in the United States. This makes it much more difficult for U.S. corporations to break into the Japanese market because of the cost of setting up distribution agreements with so many small proprietorships, and puts the U.S. at a disadvantage, relative to Japan, in exporting goods.

III. **The Balance Sheet of the Firm** -- All business firms have a **balance sheet**, *which presents a picture of the financial status of the firm*, and which accounts for all the *assets* and *liabilities* of the firm.

A. **Assets** -- The left-hand side of the balance sheet lists the values of the firm's **assets** -- *anything of value to which the firm has legal claim.*

B. **Liabilities and Net Worth** -- The right-hand side of the balance sheet lists the values of the firm's **liabilities** -- *the debts of the firm* -- as well as the **net worth (equity or capital stock)** of the firm, which is *the value of the firm to its owners.*

IV. **Financing Corporate Activity** -- Corporations have several options for raising financial capital. While corporations (as well as partnerships and proprietorships) often borrow from banks and other lending institutions, they have two other avenues that are unique: they can sell *bonds* (sometime referred to as *issuing debt*) and shares of *stock*.

A. **Stocks and Bonds**

1. **Bonds** -- promises to pay for the use of someone else's money. More specifically, *a debt obligation that promises to pay a certain sum of money* -- the **face value (par value)** -- *at maturity and also to make periodic fixed interest payments, at the stated* **coupon rate** *of interest, until maturity.* **Junk bonds** are bonds which have a high degree of risk, but which offer a higher expected return to compensate for the risk.

2. **Stock** -- *a claim on the assets of the corporation that gives the purchaser a share of ownership of that corporation.* Whereas the buyer of a bond is lending funds to the corporation, the buyer of stock is putting up his/her money for a share of ownership, and the right to share in the profits (and losses) of the corporation.

B. **The Monkey and the Economist** -- This *Economics In Our Times* feature can be used to introduce your students to the concept of efficient markets. If two stocks, Ford and IBM, both sell for $100, then neither stock is a better buy than the other because their prices reflect all current information available to the investing public about those companies. Only if someone has **inside information**, which is not publicly available, or if they *can better evaluate given information* than other analysts can they outperform a market average such as the Standard and Poor's 500 Index.

C. **Nonprofit Firms** -- Not all firms are business firms. Put another way, not all firms are out to make a profit. Nonprofit firms are firms with no residual claimants. Any revenues that are earned in excess of costs must be plowed back into the operation of the firm; or, perhaps, handed over to the state, in the case of public nonprofit institutions (like the police force, for instance).

1. **Incentives in Nonprofit Firms** -- It has been argued that the lack of profit, and residual claimants to reap that profit, *eliminates the incentive to monitor shirking* in nonprofit organizations. Furthermore, since any excess revenues must be "re-invested" in the firm, rather than distributed among the owners, the top administrators of nonprofit organizations are expected to use those "excess" funds to improve the quality of life *within* the organization.

2. **Types of Nonprofit Firms** -- Nonprofit firms can be either private or public. A charitable organization, such as the United Way, as well as churches, private colleges, etc., are examples of *private nonprofit firms*. Tax-supported state universities, police forces, and public schools, are examples of *public nonprofit firms*.

3. **Funding and Control of Nonprofit Firms** -- Private nonprofit firms are funded by contributions from private citizens. As such, their activities are somewhat controlled by the need to attract funds, and the ability of contributors to withhold funds to protest bad policies and/or shirking. Public nonprofit firms are supported by taxpayers, who have very little to say about the uses of their taxes, and who have little recourse if they disagree with the policies or methods of public nonprofit firms.

4. **Public Nonprofit Firms and Taxes** -- Private nonprofit firms use contributions as a source of funding for the firm's operations. If the quality of a nonprofit's services declines, contributors might reduce their contributions until their services improve. These contributions are tax deductible. Whereas contributors voluntarily give money to their favorite nonprofit corporation, taxpayers who, in essence, "pay" for others' tax breaks have no say in how these tax benefits are allocated.

V. **ECONOMICS ON THE INTERNET** -- Sources for information on the most important stock indices is provided as well as the Yahoo WWW page for accessing information on specific corporations.

■ ANSWERS TO CHAPTER QUESTIONS

1. **Explain the difference between managerial coordination and market coordination.**

Market coordination is impersonal: individuals are guided to do X instead of Y by impersonal forces, such as changes in price. Managerial coordination is personal: someone (a manager or monitor) tells someone else what to do.

2. **Is the managerial coordination that goes on inside a business firm independent of market forces? Explain your answer.**

No it is not, as the following examples illustrate. A manager might direct employees to make 100 units of good X instead of 50 units of A and 50 units of B, but we assume (reasonably so) that the manager of a profit-seeking business firm does not issue this directive independent of what she thinks can be sold in the marketplace. Similarly the manager of a McDonald's might direct employees to make more fish sandwiches and fewer hamburgers for the lunch crowd if he has reason to believe that the lunch crowd wants to buy more fish sandwiches and fewer hamburgers.

3. Explain why even conscientious workers will shirk more when the cost of shirking falls.

As long as shirking provides utility to a person (Do longer coffee breaks provide utility? Does working at less than full capacity provide utility? Does working a little less hard and daydreaming a little more provide utility?), then a fall in the cost of shirking will cause even a hard and conscientious worker to shirk more. This is based on the idea that individuals are utility maximizers who will not turn their backs on a way to obtain more utility. Saying even hard and conscientious workers will shirk more when the cost of shirking falls is not saying that such persons are bad, immoral, or deserving of reprimand. It simply acknowledges the fact that utility-maximizing individuals respond to a change in costs relative to benefits.

4. What does the phrase "separation of ownership from control" refer to?

It refers to the owners of the firm not being the persons who control the firm or manage it on a daily basis. The connotation here is that where ownership is separated from control, the managers (or controllers) of the firm will sacrifice meeting the objectives of the owners of the firm to meeting their own objectives.

5. Discuss the different types of liability (limited versus unlimited) that proprietorships, partnerships, and corporations face.

In a proprietorship the owner faces unlimited liability. This means that the personal assets of the owner can be used to pay off the debts of the proprietorship. In a partnership the owners face unlimited liability, too. In a corporation the owners face limited liability. The personal assets of the owners cannot be used to pay off the debts of the corporation.

6. The chapter implied that business firms might operate differently than nonprofit firms. What might make this so?

Business firms are seeking to maximize something (profits to residual claimants) that nonprofit firms are not seeking to maximize. In short, the two types of firms have different objectives.

7. Profit sharing is more often found in partnerships, where the number of owners is small, than in corporations where the number of owners tends to be relatively large. Could there be an economic reason for this? If so, what could it be?

Sure. By sharing profits, each partner is made a residual claimant to the business' revenue performance. As a result, each partner has a stronger incentive not to shirk, and to monitor the other partners' activities to prevent them from shirking, as well. In a corporation, the number of employees involved would likely "water down" the monetary and psychological significance of profit sharing. Plus, few individual employees in a corporation feel their role is significant enough to make an appreciable difference in the firm's performance; therefore, profit sharing would not be a strong incentive for harder work, or a stronger disincentive against shirking.

8. Your economics class can be viewed as a team. You come together with other individuals to learn economics. There is a hierarchical scheme in the classroom. Your instructor is the monitor, and he or she instructs you as to what to read and when the tests will be given, and then grades your performance. Consider what would happen if, instead of this system, you were not graded. Would you shirk more or less? Explain your answer. In which setting would you expect to learn more economics? Why? Can you relate any of your answers to the performance of an employee in a firm? If so, explain how.

The majority of students would probably shirk more under a non-graded system than under a graded system. This is not true for everyone, as some schools and colleges pride themselves in proving; however, it probably is true on the average. Just as an employer without the ability to fire and give raises; without an effective means of monitoring, the instructor cannot control shirking or reward effort. As a result, no one has an incentive to work hard -- other than those in the class, foremost to learn the subject, who will put forth a good effort regardless of the grading scheme. Thus, the average student will probably learn less economics, having put forth less effort.

9. What differences, if any, do you think there might be between the behavior of the president of your college or university, as chief administrator of a nonprofit firm, and the behavior of the president of a business firm, as chief administrator of a business firm?

To the extent that a nonprofit institution has no incentives to make revenues greater than its operating costs (plus debt servicing), the university president and his advisors would probably tend to pursue policies based more on their educational and "service" values, rather than on the basis of the "bottom line."

◼ LECTURE SUPPLEMENTS

Joseph Pereira, "Toy Sellers Wish That Pocahontas Were a Lion," *Wall Street Journal*, July 24, 1995, p. B1.

Entertainment companies provide an excellent example of the advantages of economies of scale and managerial coordination. The number of spin-offs which come from a single film is simply amazing as any "blockbuster" movie can show. For example, the movie for the Mighty Morphin Power Rangers took in around $40 million, but the related toys generated more than $300 million in sales in 1995 and $225 million in 1994.

If Mighty Morphin Power Rangers is an example of a TV show and a movie generating toy sales, then the advantage of "Pocahontas" is that it generates toy sales on its own, close to $100 million in fact. So what's wrong with "Pocahontas?" It appeals primarily to girls, rather than to both boys and girls as "The Lion King" did.

Of course, this is what a firm is all about. The firm should reduce transaction costs, gain from economies of scale, and create "internalities" for itself. Maximizing the profits of the products which the firm produces, and Hollywood provides no better example.

Kyle Pope, "Charged With Libel, Pair of Activists Puts McDonald's on the Grill," *The Wall Street Journal*, July 18, 1995, p. A1, column 1; and "Big Mac's Folly," *The Economist*, July 1, 1995, p. 59.

Whatever you or your students think of this case, it should certainly generate interest and discussion. The article details the case of Dave Morris and Helen Steel, two out-of-work, vegetarian activists, who handed out a six-page document to customers of McDonald's accusing the company of destroying rain forests, causing health problems, and abusing workers. The result has been the most expensive libel trial in British history.

McDonald's charged both with libel and sued them, putting the company's lawyers to work on the case. But instead of prevailing, the case has turned into an embarrassment for McDonald's. The reason? The trial at that point had lasted over a year as a McLibel Support Group has sprung up to help pay for the costs of defending themselves against the libel suit. One reason the trial has become such a long, drawn out affair is a difference in the definition of libel. In the United States, a company suing for libel must show that what was printed was false. But in England, the defendants have the more difficult burden of proving that what they said was true. So instead of stopping the two critics, the case has provided them with a forum to advertise their ideas.

Ask your students if they think the case is a valid one or whether the whole case is a waste of taxpayers' money. What lessons can be learned about how firms should respond to cases like this?

Don Clark, "A Big Bet Made Intel What It Is Today, Now It Wagers Again," *The Wall Street Journal*, June 7, 1995, p. A1, column 6.

In 1995, Intel was becoming the most profitable company in the world. How did it reach this position, and what must it do to maintain its lead in the semiconductor industry? This article addresses these questions by looking at the company that Andrew Grove and Craig Barret built.

As the article shows, producing a new chip is no fly-by-night decision. It cost Intel $100 million to develop the 386 chip, $1 billion to develop the 486 chip, and $5 billion to develop the Pentium chip. Now it is working on the successor to the Pentium, a sixth-generation chip dubbed the Pentium Pro.

This was a "bet-the-company" decision because if Intel did not accurately appraise the demand for the Pentium chip, the $5 billion development costs were not ones which could be quickly recovered. Of course, the project succeeded, but this example should show the risks that firms must take in order to maintain their leadership in the market and make profits. There is more to profitability than setting marginal revenue equal to marginal cost. As a result of their efforts, Intel has a 75 percent market share, and therefore anyone who has worked on an IBM-compatible has probably used an Intel chip. Use Intel as an example to explore how firms compete in the real world.

211

CHAPTER 20

Production and Costs

Having taken a look at the nature of the firm, the rationale for producing cooperatively, the various types of business organizations, and (briefly) some of the financial concerns of business firms, we now turn to the mechanics of supply. The decision of how much to produce and at what price to sell it are functions of three variables: *costs, revenues,* and *market structure.* Chapters 21-23 will discuss market structure and the revenue conditions facing firms under each of the different market structures. This chapter looks at costs. All production involves costs. In fact, all economic activity (as we discussed in the introductory chapters of this text) involves costs. Chapter 20 looks at a variety of important cost concepts, and relates them to the decisions of the producing firm in both the short run and the long run. In the process, the student is introduced to *total cost, average cost,* and *marginal cost, fixed cost* and *variable cost,* and the various combinations of these concepts that are vital to cost analysis, as well as *economies* (and *diseconomies*) *of scale.*

■ CHAPTER OBJECTIVES

Upon completing this chapter, your students should be able to:

- understand the concept of *implicit costs,* and how they relate to opportunity costs;

- define economic *profit, accounting profit,* and normal profit, and discuss how these concepts are related and how they affect (or don't) economic decisions;

- describe the relationship between production and costs, in both the short run and the long run;

- distinguish between *fixed* and *variable inputs,* and *fixed* and *variable costs;*

- define the *short run* and the *long run,* in economic terminology, and describe how they relate to the various cost concepts;

- explain the relationship between *total, average,* and *marginal costs;*

- derive the *average total cost (ATC), average variable cost (AVC), average fixed cost (AFC),* and *marginal cost (MC)* curves;

- state the *law of diminishing marginal returns* and explain its relationship to marginal cost;

- discuss the concept of *economies of scale* and *minimum efficient scale*; and,

- identify the various factors that will shift the marginal, variable, and total cost curve.

■ KEY TERMS

- explicit costs
- implicit costs
- accounting profit
- economic profit
- normal profit
- sunk cost
- production function
- fixed inputs
- variable inputs
- fixed costs (FC)
- variable costs (VC)
- total cost (TC)
- short run

- long run
- average fixed cost (AFC)
- average variable cost (AVC)
- average total cost (ATC)
- marginal cost (MC)
- law of diminishing marginal returns
- marginal physical product (MPP)
- average-marginal rule
- long-run average total cost (LRATC)
- economies of scale
- constant returns to scale
- diseconomies of scale
- minimum efficient scale

■ CHAPTER OUTLINE

I. **ALL ABOUT COSTS**

A. **Explicit and Implicit Costs** -- All economic decisions entail opportunity costs -- something given up when one action is taken rather than another. Those costs may be either *explicit* or *implicit*.

1. **Explicit Costs** -- *costs incurred when an actual monetary payment is made.* For instance, the explicit cost of a gallon of milk is $1.89.

2. **Implicit Costs** -- represent *the value of resources used in the production or acquisition of a good for which no monetary payment is made.* For example, the implicit cost to the dairy farmer is the money he could have earned had he chosen another pursuit; the implicit cost to the purchaser of the milk is the utility she could have gained by using that $1.89 to buy other goods.

B. **Accounting Profit and Economic Profit** -- The "profitability" of a firm depends upon which measure of profit we use: *accounting profit* or *economic profit*.

1. **Accounting Profit** -- the difference between total revenues and explicit costs. That is,

accounting profit = total revenue - total (explicit) costs.

Accounting profit is what most people think of when they hear (or say) the word "profit." [See Exhibit 20-1a] There is another measure of profit that has more value in economic analysis:

2. **Economic Profit** -- *the difference between total revenue and total opportunity cost,* including both implicit and explicit costs. That is,

economic profit = total revenue - (explicit costs + implicit costs).

Economic profit is usually lower (and never higher) than accounting profit, because economic profit includes implicit costs.

A firm that just covers its operating costs plus its implicit costs (often thought of as the cost of capital/ownership) is making *zero economic profit.* In economics, a firm that is making zero economic profit is said to be making **normal profit.** Any profit greater than normal profit (i.e., if the firm is making positive economic profit) is considered to be "excess" profit. [See Exhibit 20-1b]

C. **Zero Economic Profit Is Not as Bad as It Sounds** -- *Economic profit is the difference between total revenue and total opportunity costs,* including both explicit and implicit costs, whereas accounting profit is the difference between total revenue and only explicit costs. A firm which earns zero economic profits is said to be making a **normal profit.** Zero economic profit simply means that the owner is "doing as well as could have been done," not that the owner has failed to generate profits for the firm.

D. **Sunk Costs** -- *a cost incurred in the past that cannot be changed by current decisions and cannot be recovered.* In contrast to fixed costs, which we will discuss in a minute, sunk costs are completely "lost." With fixed costs (land, equipment, etc.), there is at least the possibility of resale in order to recover some of the cost; but, with sunk cost, there is not even that chance.

E. **"I Have to Get a Job as an Accountant, I've Invested Four Years in Accounting"** -- If you understand the concept of sunk costs, you would disagree with this statement. The four years of college are a sunk costs which cannot be recovered. If a better job opportunity than an accounting position comes along, you should take that job regardless of what your degree was in. Individuals should "let bygones be bygones" and not allow sunk costs to act as a constraint on their economic decisionmaking.

II. **PRODUCTION AND COSTS IN THE SHORT RUN** -- Production involves costs and takes time to complete. That is to say, there is an important link between production, costs, and time. This section looks at production and costs in the short run. The next section looks at production and costs in the long run.

A. **Fixed and Variable Inputs: Fixed and Variable Costs** -- Let's look at the linkages between inputs and costs in the short run.

1. **Fixed and Variable Inputs** -- A **fixed input** is *an input whose quantity cannot be changed as output changes in the short run.* A **variable input**, on the other hand, is *an input whose quantity can be changed as output changes in the short run.*

214

2. **Fixed and Variable Costs** -- The costs associated with a fixed input are called **fixed costs (FC)**. These are *costs that do not change as output changes*. Such things as insurance premiums and rent would be fixed costs (in the short run). The costs of variable inputs are called **variable costs (VC)**. These costs *will change as output changes to the extent that more (less) variable inputs are used as output increases (decreases)*. For example, if McMahon and McGee hire additional production workers to increase output, they will have to pay additional wage costs.

3. **Total Cost** -- If we add fixed costs to variable costs, we get *total cost*, such that

$$\text{total cost (TC)} = \text{fixed costs (FC)} + \text{variable costs (VC)}.$$

B. **Periods of Production: Short Run and Long Run** -- The **short run** is a period in which *some* inputs are fixed. The **long run** is a period in which *all* inputs can be varied. Exhibit 20-2 reviews periods of production, inputs, and costs connected with the production process.

C. **Computing and Graphing Total, Average and Marginal Cost Curves** -- Exhibit 20-3 computes and graphs the cost functions discussed below.

1. **Average Costs** -- Fixed, variable, and total costs can all be turned into average magnitudes by dividing each by the firm's output (Q). In other words,

$$\text{average fixed cost (AFC)} = \text{total fixed costs / quantity} = TFC/Q;$$

$$\text{average variable cost (AVC)} = \text{total variable costs / quantity} = TVC/Q; \text{ and,}$$

$$\text{average total cost, or unit cost, (ATC)} = \text{total cost / quantity} = TC/Q.$$

2. **Marginal Cost** -- *the change in total cost that results from a change in output.* Alternately, we could say that MC is the *change in (total) variable costs* that results from a change in output, since only variable costs will respond to a change in output and will, in turn, cause total cost to change. Another way of putting it is that MC is the additional cost of producing an additional unit of output. Simply put,

$$\text{marginal cost (MC)} = \text{change in total cost / change in quantity} = \Delta TC / \Delta Q.$$

D. **The Law of Diminishing Marginal Returns** -- In order to understand the shape of the MC, AVC, and ATC curves, we must first discuss *the law of diminishing marginal returns*. This law was first noted by David Ricardo who noticed that *as ever larger amounts of a variable input are combined with fixed inputs, eventually, the marginal physical product of the variable input declines*. This is illustrated in columns 1-3 in Exhibit 20-4.
    Marginal Physical Product (MPP) is the change in output that results from changing the variable input by one unit, holding all other inputs fixed. With respect to labor, this would mean that the marginal physical product of labor would be defined as

$$MPP_L = \text{change in output / change in labor input} = \Delta Q / \Delta L.$$

E. **Average productivity** -- is the output divided by the inputs, usually labor, or

$$AP = Q / L.$$

The average physical productivity of labor is what is meant by *labor productivity*.

F. **The Law of Diminishing Marginal Returns and Marginal Cost** -- As Exhibit 20-5 illustrates, marginal cost and marginal physical product are related. There is an important relationship which should be noted here: *as the marginal physical product of labor increases, marginal cost decreases; and as the marginal physical product of labor decreases, marginal cost increases.* Specifically, assuming only one variable input, *as MPP rises, MC decreases; as MPP falls, MC increases.*

G. **The Average-Marginal Rule** -- What do the ATC and AVC curves look like in relation to the MC curve? The **average-marginal rule** tells us when the marginal magnitude is above the average magnitude, the average magnitude rises; and, when the marginal magnitude is below the average magnitude, the average magnitude falls. In other words, as Exhibit 20-6 shows, *when MC > AVC (ATC) the AVC (ATC) curve rises; when MC < AVC (ATC) the AVC (ATC) curve falls.* Additionally, we can infer from these relationships that *the MC curve must intersect the AVC and ATC curves at their respective minimum points.* The average-marginal rule does not apply to the AFC curve, since marginal costs do not affect fixed costs. In this case, the AFC curve will decrease continuously as output rises.

III. **PRODUCTION AND COSTS IN THE LONG RUN** -- As noted before, the distinction between the short run and the long run is that there are no fixed inputs and, therefore, no fixed costs in the long run. As a result, all costs are variable costs; so, we simply refer to *long-run total cost* and *long-run average total cost.*

A. **The Long-Run Average Total Cost Curve** -- The short-run ATC curve presented in Exhibit 20-6 assumed a fixed plant size; and, each possible plant size has a short-run ATC curve associated with it. The **long-run average total cost (LRATC) curve** for a given firm combines the short-run ATC curves which represent all possible plant sizes, such that the LRATC curve *shows the lowest average cost at which the firm can produce any given level of output.* Put another way, *the LRATC curve touches each short-run ATC curve at its lowest point.* [See Exhibit 20-7]

B. **Economies of Scale, Diseconomies of Scale, and Constant Returns to Scale** -- As output increase, the LRATC curve tends to slope downward up to a point, then become flat, then begin to slope upward. This fact is very important when we try to find a firm's optimal long-run output level.

    1. **Economies of Scale** -- The downward sloping portion of the LRATC curve indicates that *average (unit) costs are falling as we increase output* -- this is a clear indication of **economies of scale**. Here a one percent increase in input usage results in a greater-than-one percent increase in output. Economies of scale usually occur as a result of increased specialization and proficiency, and as increases in output make more efficient mass production techniques affordable.

    2. **Constant Returns to Scale** -- The flat portion of the LRATC curve is the region of **constant returns to scale,** where *unit costs remain the same as we increase output.* Here a one percent increase input usage results in a one percent increase in output.

The *lowest level of output that results in constant returns to scale* is called the **minimum efficient scale** (for example, point A in Exhibit 20-7b).

3. **Diseconomies of Scale** -- The upward sloping portion of the LRATC curve indicates that *unit costs are rising as we increase output.* Here **diseconomies of scale** exist, meaning that a one percent increase in input usage results in a less-than-one percent increase in output. Diseconomies of scale usually arise when a firm gets so large that it causes communication, coordination, and monitoring problems.

C. **Why Economies of Scale?** -- Economies of scale exist for two main reasons: growing firms offer greater opportunities for employees to specialize, and growing firms can take advantage of highly efficient mass production techniques.

D. **Why Diseconomies of Scale?** -- Diseconomies of scale occur because a firm's size produces coordination, communication and monitoring problems. Knowing that this problem exists, firms will reorganize, divide operations, hire new managers, and take other measures to reverse the diseconomies of scale.

E. **Minimum Efficient Scale and Number of Firms in an Industry** -- Exhibit 20-8 provides evidence on the minimum efficient scale for six industries. As can be seen, the minimum efficient scale varies from one industry to another.

IV. **SHIFTS IN COST CURVES** -- What factors will cause the short-run and long-run total cost and marginal cost curves to shift? How ?

A. **Taxes** -- Taxes on the production of a good will increase the per-unit costs of production, shifting the MC, AVC, and ATC curves upward.

B. **Input Prices** -- A rise or fall in input prices brings about a corresponding change in the firm's MC, AVC, and ATC curves, shifting them upward if input prices rise, and downward if input prices fall. *The Global Economy* feature on Mexican *maquiladoras* can be used to illustrate the impact of exchange rates on firms' input costs.

C. **Technology** -- Technological advances can affect costs in two ways. First, they may improve the production process, so that less inputs have to be used to produce a unit of the good. Secondly, they may lower input prices. In either case, technological advances lower variable costs; and, consequently, shift the MC, AVC, and ATC curves downward.

V. **ECONOMICS ON THE INTERNET** -- This section looks at how to access production data through the Sam Houston University Gopher.

■ ANSWERS TO CHAPTER QUESTIONS

1. **Illustrate the average-marginal rule in a noncost setting.**

The average rating per TV show for a television network is 24. The network introduces a new TV show that has a rating of 28. The new show -- the marginal show -- pulls up the average rating. If the new show had had a rating of 20, it would have pulled down the average rating.

2. "People who earn big salaries are less likely to go into business for themselves than people who earn small salaries, because their implicit costs are higher." Do you agree or disagree? Explain your answer.

Agree, given the important proviso "all other things are equal." Higher implicit costs for people who earn big salaries mean lower economic profits and thus less reason to go into business. Do not confuse what is being said here. The commonly-held belief is that people who earn big salaries will go into business for themselves more often than people who earn small salaries because they are more likely to have the start-up costs for a business (Who can go into business without a penny to his name?). We do not doubt that the more financially capable one is, the more likely he can go into business if he decides to. What we are saying is that given the proviso of all other things are equal, people who earn big salaries have less reason to go into business. Their implicit costs are higher and economic profits lower than people who earn small salaries.

3. A quick glance at Exhibit 20-6(c) shows that the average variable cost curve and the average total cost curve get closer to each other as output increases. What explains this?

Average total cost is equal to average variable cost and average fixed cost. As output increases, average fixed cost decreases (AFC = TC/Q); therefore, as output increases most of what makes up ATC is AVC. It follow that the ATC curve and AVC curve would get closer to each other as output increases.

4. When would total costs equal fixed costs?

When there are no variable costs, which is another way of saying when output is zero.

5. Is studying for an economics exam subject to the law of diminishing marginal returns? If so, what is the fixed input? What is the variable input?

Yes. The fixed input is time until the exam. The variable inputs are time spent studying, attention, and retention.

6. Some individuals decry the decline of the small family farm and its replacement with the huge corporate megafarm. Discuss the possibility that this is a consequence of economics of scale.

If the minimum efficient scale for agricultural production is sufficiently high, small, family farms simply cannot produce enough to be competitive with large, corporate farms. To the extent that the replacement of family farms with corporate farms is in response to issues of scale economies, then, economically speaking, it is a good (read "efficient") thing.

7. We know that there is a link between productivity and costs. For example, recall the link between the marginal physical product of the variable input and marginal cost. With this in mind, what link might there be between productivity and prices?

If costs are inversely related to productivity, then price should be as well; assuming that price and cost are positively related and fairly close to one another.

8. Some people's everyday behavior suggests that they do not hold sunk costs irrelevant to present decisions. Give some examples.

Rather than putting $1,000 down toward the purchase of a new car, Jim and Jeanette spend $1,000 on repairs to their 1979 Eldorado, figuring "We've already spent so much on this car . . ." Rather than going out to a movie, Clarice stays home and watches a video on her VCR. "Well," she thinks aloud, "I guess I'd better get my money's worth out of this thing."

9. Explain why a firm might want to produce its good even after diminishing marginal returns have set in and marginal cost is on the rise.

As long as price is greater than marginal cost, a firm will increase its total profits by increasing its production. So, even after MC begins to rise (as diminishing returns set in), producers will likely continue to produce until MC = the price of the good.

10. Fill in the appropriate number in each lettered space.

(1) Quantity of Output	(2) Total Fixed Cost	(3) Average Fixed Cost	(4) Total Variable Cost	(5) Average Variable Cost	(6) Total Cost	(7) Average Total Cost	(8) Marginal Cost
0	$ 200	A	$ 0		V		
1	200	B	30	L	W	GG	QQ
2	200	C	50	M	X	HH	RR
3	200	D	60	N	Y	II	SS
4	200	E	65	O	Z	JJ	TT
5	200	F	75	P	AA	KK	UU
6	200	G	95	Q	BB	LL	VV
7	200	H	125	R	CC	MM	WW
8	200	I	165	S	DD	NN	XX
9	200	J	215	T	EE	OO	YY
10	200	K	275	U	FF	PP	ZZ

The answers are:

(1) Quantity of Output	(2) Total Fixed Cost	(3) Average Fixed Cost	(4) Total Variable Cost	(5) Average Variable Cost	(6) Total Cost	(7) Average Total Cost	(8) Marginal Cost
0	$ 200	_	$ 0		$ 200		
1	200	200	30	30	230	230	30
2	200	100	50	25	250	125	20
3	200	66.7	60	20	260	86.67	10
4	200	50	65	16.25	265	66.25	5
5	200	40	75	15	275	55	10
6	200	33.3	95	15.84	295	49.67	20
7	200	28.6	125	17.86	325	46.43	30
8	200	25	165	20.62	365	45.63	40
9	200	22.2	215	23.89	415	46.11	50
10	200	20	275	27.5	475	47.5	60

■ LECTURE SUPPLEMENTS

"Unseemly Couplings," *The Economist*, **May 13, 1995, pp. 66, 69.**

This article will provide your students with a good insight into the role of costs in the production of pharmaceutical products. The problem is that the biotechnology industry is rich in ideas, and the pharmaceutical industry has a lot of cash which comes from the patents they have on existing goods. How can the two get together to benefit one another?

There are two choices. First, pharmaceutical companies can use biotech firms as research laboratories, keeping them independent, but providing capital to the biotech firms to help them do their research and then sharing in the profits once the product is discovered. The idea here is to keep the companies small because laboratories tend to suffer from diseconomies of scale. The larger they get the more internal conflict they generate. This is what Ciba did when it took a major interest in Chiron which is developing beta interferon to treat multiple sclerosis.

Second, pharmaceutical companies can buy the companies outright in order to have complete control over the production and distribution of the drug. The article points out that American companies tend to favor partnerships whereas European countries are more likely to favor direct control and ownership. The key here is whether partnership or ownership will increase or decrease economies of scale. Although the result may be more obvious in a factory, the role of economies of scale are less tangible in research and development. Use this article to generate discussion of this issue.

Rhonda L. Rundle, "How One Company Controls Health Costs: Office Nurses," *The Wall Street Journal*, **August 4, 1995, p. B1, column 3.**

Since this chapter is about costs, a look at how firms make an effort to reduce costs would be appropriate. The article looks at how International Rectifier Corp., a semiconductor company, found a way to reduce health-care costs without scrimping on quality or choice. The firm's solution was to hire two nurses whose jobs were to monitor costly cases, review bills and counsel employees on how to become smarter health-care consumers.

What is important here is that the nurses interact with the firm's employees and get involved in individual cases. Instead of monitoring costs remotely using computers in an office in another state, the nurses keep direct tabs on what is going on. International Rectifier uses a fee-for-service system in which it pays 80 percent of healthcare costs if the employee uses their own physician, and 90 percent if the employee uses a company-approved physician. The nurses review bills and advise employees on treatments which are beneficial. The primary problem the nurses have is convincing both employer and employees that they are acting in both parties' interest.

This article should provide a useful application to the theory in the chapter on costs.

Fred R. Bleakley, "High-School Seniors Mind Their Business and Even Profit by It," *The Wall Street Journal*, **June 20, 1995, p. A1, column 4.**

This article should prove useful by showing students what happens when other students try to apply the lessons learned in economics to the real world. The article discusses the activities of Junior Achievement students at Edsel Ford High School in Dearborn, Michigan in putting their economic knowledge in practice, trying to import and export goods from other students in Spain.

The students found that business contains a lot of trial and error. For example, one idea they had was to export playing cards to Spain, only to discover that they don't uses Aces in Spain. So an alternative was needed. The solution? Giant sexy beach towels.

The purpose of this and other articles is not only to show the difficulties which exist in controlling costs and making profits in the real world, but also to emphasize that the principles learned in this chapter DO apply in the real world. The realities of business may distract or sidetrack people from the basic economic ideas which are learned here, but the applications are omnipresent.

CHAPTER 21

Perfect Competition

In macroeconomics we talk about aggregate supply, suggesting that all producers find themselves in similar situations, face similar choices, and will make similar rational decisions. In Chapter 20, we talked about the relationship between costs and production. Again, we treated all producers as essentially the same. Now we begin to delve into the situations, choices, and rational decisions that firms face. Chapters 21-23 are about **market structure** -- the particular environment in which a firm operates -- and how it affects a firm's pricing and output decisions. In this chapter, we look at the theory of *perfect competition*, optimal short-run behavior for a perfectly competitive firm, optimal long-run behavior of the perfectly competitive market, and the relationship between perfect competition, *resource allocative efficiency*, and *productive efficiency*.

■ CHAPTER OBJECTIVES

Upon completing this chapter, your students should be able to:

- state the assumptions of the theory of *perfect competition*;

- define *price taker*, and explain its significance to the short-run behavior of perfectly competitive firms;

- determine whether a perfectly competitive firm should produce in the short run or shut down, given information about a firm's cost and revenue situation;

- find the *profit-maximizing* level of output, and explain why this is the best level of output for the firm in the short run;

- describe how the perfectly competitive market adjusts to profits and losses over time;

- identify the conditions that characterize *long-run competitive equilibrium*; and,

- relate perfect competition to *resource allocative efficiency* and *productive efficiency*.

■ KEY TERMS

- market structure
- perfect competition
- productive efficiency
- price taker
- marginal revenue (MR)
- profit-maximization rule
- short-run (firm) supply curve

- short-run industry (market) supply curve
- long-run competitive equilibrium
- constant-cost industry
- long-run (industry) supply curve
- increasing-cost industry
- decreasing-cost industry
- resource allocative efficiency

■ CHAPTER OUTLINE

I. THE THEORY OF PERFECT COMPETITION

A. **Basic Assumptions** -- The theory of *perfect competition* rests on four basic assumptions:

1. **There Are Many Sellers and Buyers, None of Which Is Large In Relation to Total Sales or Purchases** -- There are many sellers and many buyers, none of which is large in relation to total sales or purchases, such that *no single seller or buyer has any power to significantly influence market price.*

2. **Each Firm Produces and Sells a Homogeneous Product** -- Each supplying firm produces a **homogeneous product** -- that is, *a product that is indistinguishable from the product of any other firm in the industry.*

3. **Buyers and Sellers Have All Relevant Information About Prices, Product Quality, Sources of Supply, and So Forth.**

4. **Firms Have Easy Entry and Exit** -- New firms can enter the market easily (i.e., there are no prohibitive start-up costs or regulations) and existing firms can exit the market easily.

B. **A Perfectly Competitive Firm Is A Price Taker** -- Since the perfectly competitive firm has no market power, offers a product that is indistinguishable from its competition, is subject to new competitors, and does its business in a market where all buyers and sellers are well informed, a perfectly competitive firms is said to be a *price taker*. A **price taker** is *a seller that cannot control the price of the product it sells, but must rely on the market to set the price at which its output will be sold.*

C. **The Demand Curve for a Perfectly Competitive Firm Is Horizontal** -- Because of the nature of the perfectly competitive market, while the industry as a whole faces a downward-sloping market demand curve (as is shown in Exhibit 21-1a), each individual firm faces a demand curve that is *horizontal* at the market price (as is shown in Exhibit 21-1b). The reason? Since the firm is a price taker, it may sell all of the output it is capable of producing at or below the market price; but, will not be able to sell *anything* at a price higher than the market price.

D. **The Marginal Revenue Curve of the Perfectly Competitive Firm Is the Same as Its Demand Curve** -- Remember that total revenue equals price times quantity. The *change in total revenue as output increases* is called **marginal revenue (MR)**. That is,

$$\text{marginal revenue} = \Delta\text{total revenue} / \Delta\text{quantity;}$$

or,

$$MR = \Delta TR / \Delta Q.$$

For a perfectly competitive firm, *price equals marginal revenue*, since price will not change as output changes. Since P = MR, it follows that *the marginal revenue curve for the perfectly competitive firm is the same as the firm's demand curve*. [See Exhibit 21-2]

E. **The Importance of "As If" in Economic Theories** -- For markets to behave in a perfectly competitive manner, the four assumptions given at the beginning of this chapter must hold true. If these assumptions do not hold, then those markets will still *approximate* the behavior of perfectly competitive markets, depending upon the degree to which those assumptions hold within that market.

II. **PERFECT COMPETITION IN THE SHORT RUN**

A. **What Level of Output Does the Profit-Maximizing Firm Produce?** -- Consider Exhibit 21-3. Any profit-seeking firm will continue to produce as long as MR > MC. Any profit-seeking firm will not continue to produce once MC > MR. There is one output level at which MR = MC, and at that output level, the firm is maximizing profits (minimizing losses).

The **profit-maximization rule** for the firm says, *produce the quantity at which MR = MC*. This rule holds true *no matter what market structure prevails*. Specifically for the perfectly competitive firm, the rule may be rewritten as

$$P = MC;$$

or, since P = MR, then

$$P = MR = MC.$$

B. **To Produce or Not to Produce: That Is The Question** -- The following three cases illustrate the use of the profit-maximizing rule and cost analysis by a perfectly competitive firm:

1. **Case 1: Price Is above Average Total Cost** -- Look at Exhibit 21-4a. If market price exceeds the firm's ATC at the level of output where MR = MC, then *the firm will maximize profits by producing at the quantity where MR = MC*.

2. **Case 2: Price Is below Average Variable Cost** -- Look at Exhibit 21-4b. If market price fails to "cover" even variable costs, *the firm would do better by shutting down than by continuing to produce*. If the firm shuts down, it only has to pay off fixed costs. If the firm continues to produce, it will lose not only its fixed cost, but part of its variable costs as well.

224

3. **Case 3: Price Is below Average Total Cost but above Average Variable Cost** -- Look at Exhibit 21-4c. If price is sufficient to "cover" variable costs, then the firm is better off producing than shutting down; since producing will provide it with the opportunity to cover part of its fixed costs. Here *the firm will minimize short-run losses by producing at the quantity where MR = MC*; however, over time, the firm will either need to alter its production costs or leave the market. Exhibit 21-5 reviews some of the material discussed in this section.

C. **The Perfectly Competitive Firm's Short-Run Supply Curve** -- Since the firm produces in the short run if P > AVC, and shuts down if P < AVC, it follows that *the firm's short-run supply curve is that portion of its marginal cost curve that lies above the AVC curve.* [See Exhibit 21-6]

D. **Job Security and Fixed Costs in the Short Run** -- Exhibit 21-7 can be used to illustrate an important point: *the greater the fixed cost-total cost ratio (TFC/TC), the more likely the firm will operate in the short run.* The reason is that greater the fixed-cost-total cost ratio, the farther total revenue can fall before the firm shutdowns. For this reason, some unions have negotiated a reduction in fringe benefits (which are a fixed cost) as a way of increasing job security.

E. **From Firm to Market (Industry) Supply Curve** -- Once we know each firm's short-run supply curves, *all we have to do to find the short-run market supply curve is horizontally sum the individual firm's supply curves*, in much the same manner as we derived the market demand curve in Chapter 3. [See Exhibit 21-8]

F. **Why Is the Market Supply Curve Upward Sloping** -- Because of the law of diminishing marginal returns, marginal cost curves are upward sloping, and because marginal cost curves are upward sloping, so are market supply curves.

III. **PERFECT COMPETITION IN THE LONG RUN**

A. **The Conditions of Long-Run Competitive Equilibrium** -- The following conditions characterize *long-run competitive equilibrium*:

1. **Economic Profit Is Zero: Price Is Equal to Short-run Average Total Cost (P = SRATC)** -- For long-run competitive equilibrium to exist, there must be no incentive for firms to enter or exit the market. This condition is brought about by *zero economic profit* (normal profit), which is a consequence of market price being equal to short-run average total cost (SRATC).

2. **Firms Are Producing the Quantity of Output at Which Price Is Equal to Marginal Cost (P = MC)** -- Firms naturally move toward the profit-maximizing level of output. At that level of output, MR = MC; and, as shown earlier, since P = MR, P = MC.

3. **No Firm Has an Incentive to Change Its Plant Size to Produce Its Current Output; That Is, SRATC = LRATC at the Quantity of Output at Which P = MC** -- Finally, no firm must have an incentive to change its plant size. That is, at the level of output where P = MC, short-run ATC must equal long-run ATC, indicating that the firm is producing at its optimal scale.

225

Looking at Exhibit 21-9, we may summarize the three points with the statement: *Long-run competitive equilibrium* exists when

$$P = MC = SRATC = LRATC.$$

At the long-run equilibrium, several incentive effects occur:

a. **There is no incentive for firms to enter or exit the industry.**

b. **There is no incentive for firms to produce more or less output.**

c. **There is no incentive for firms to change plant size.**

B. **Industry Adjustment to an Increase in Demand** -- Suppose we start at long-run competitive equilibrium. What happens if demand increases? Look at Exhibit 21-10. First, equilibrium price will rise, shifting the individual firms' demand curve upward. Second, existing firms will increase output, since P = MC now at a higher level of output (since P has increased). As a result, existing firms will enjoy additional profits in the short-run. Over time, new firms will enter the industry in search of economic profits. This will, in turn, shift the industry supply curve outward (rightward), lowering equilibrium price. Entry will continue until long-run competitive equilibrium (specifically, zero economic profit) is re-established. Where will the new long-run equilibrium price be? Higher than the old one? Lower than the old one? The same as the old one? The answer depends upon the industry.

1. **Constant-Cost Industry** -- *an industry in which average total costs do not change as (industry) output increases or decreases.* If market demand increases for a good produced by firms in a constant-cost industry, price will initially rise and then fall, eventually reaching its *original level.* [See Exhibit 21-11a]

2. **Increasing-Cost Industry** -- *an industry in which average total costs rise as output increases and fall as output decreases.* If market demand increases for a good produced by firms in an increasing-cost industry, price will initially rise and then fall, eventually settling at a price *above the original equilibrium price.* [See Exhibit 21-11b]

3. **Decreasing-Cost Industry** -- *an industry in which average total costs fall as output increases and rise as output decreases.* If the market demand increases for a good produced by firms in a decreasing-cost industry, price will initially rise and then fall, settling at a price *below the original equilibrium price.* [See Exhibit 21-11c]

C. **Entry Into the Industry and Price Declines** -- The price of computers, videocassette recorders, and other goods have fallen in price dramatically in the past. One reason for this is the entry of new firms into those industries. These firms' action shifted the industry supply curve outward causing the equilibrium price to decline. The *Economics And the Media* feature "Talk Shows in the Afternoon, or Go Ricki! Go Ricki!" applies this concept to the current plethora of afternoon talk shows.

D. **Industry Adjustment to a Decrease in Demand** -- Starting at long-run competitive equilibrium, suppose that market demand decreases. What happens? First, equilibrium price will fall, shifting the individual firms' demand curve downward. Second, existing firms will decrease output, since P = MC is now at a lower level of output (since P has

226

decreased). As a result, existing firms will suffer losses in the short-run. Over time, firms will exit the industry until losses "dry up." This will, in turn, shift the industry supply curve inward (leftward), raising equilibrium price. Exit will continue until long-run competitive equilibrium (specifically, zero economic profit) is re-established.

E. **Differences in Costs, Differences in Profits: Now You See It, Now You Don't** -- If one farmer's land is more productive than another farmer's land, he will be able to sell or rent his land for a higher price. The new owner will now have higher total costs, and the ATC curve will shift upward to reflect this fact. The profitability of the land has been incorporated in the price of the land. [See Exhibit 21-12]

F. **Profit and Discrimination** -- A firm in a perfectly competitive market which discriminates because of a worker's race, religion, or gender will see an increase in their total costs, making the firm less competitive. The more discrimination costs, the less there will be.

IV. TOPICS FOR ANALYSIS WITHIN THE THEORY OF PERFECT COMPETITION

A. **Do Higher Costs Mean Higher Prices?** -- To what extent are cost increases passed on to consumers? If the cost increase is experienced by just one firm (or even a handful), will not result in a higher price, because the market price is set based upon the cost conditions prevailing in the entire market. On the other hand, if there is a widespread cost increase, then the market supply curve will shift, and consumers will have to pay higher prices.

B. **Will Perfectly Competitive Firms Advertise?** -- The main point of advertising is to differentiate your product from that of your (nearest) competitors'. In a perfectly competitive market there are two problems. First, there are too many competitors to advertise "against." Second, everyone's product is the same; thus, there is no basis for product differentiation. The only advertising that is rational is advertising by the entire industry, aimed at pulling customers away from a competing industry.

C. **Supplier-Set Price Versus Market-Determined Price: Collusion or Competition?** -- If all the firms in an industry charge the same price, is this evidence of collusion? Not necessarily. It could be that all the firms are price takers.

V. RESOURCE ALLOCATIVE EFFICIENCY AND PRODUCTIVE EFFICIENCY

A. **Resource Allocative Efficiency** -- Resources are allocated efficiently when the value of the resources to demanders equals the opportunity cost of the resources. Since P represents the value of the resources to the demanders of the goods made from those resources, and MC represents the cost to suppliers of hiring (purchasing) resources to make their goods, then P = MC fulfills the condition for resource allocative efficiency.

B. **Productive Efficiency** -- A firm that produces its output at the lowest possible per unit cost (lowest ATC) is said to exhibit **productive efficiency**.

227

VI. ECONOMICS ON THE INTERNET -- Cost information can be accessed through the University of Michigan Gopher. This section shows you the paths to follow to reach this data.

■ ANSWERS TO CHAPTER QUESTIONS

1. True or false. The firm's entire marginal cost curve is its short-run supply curve. Explain your answer.

The statement is false. Only that portion of the firm's marginal cost curve that lies above the average variable cost curve is its supply curve.

2. True or false. In a perfectly competitive market, firms always operate at the lowest per-unit cost. Explain your answer.

False. A perfectly competitive firm will maximize profit (minimize losses) by producing that level of output where MR = MC. If the firm is breaking even, then P = MR = MC = SRATC. However, if P > SRATC or if P < SRATC, then P = MR = MC which does not equal SRATC. See Exhibit 21-4.

3. "Firm A, one firm in a competitive industry, faces higher costs of production. As a result, consumers end up paying higher prices." Discuss.

This is likely not the case, or certainly won't be so for long. If one firm has higher costs and, as a result, must charge a higher price than its competitors, the other perfectly competitive firms will drive the less efficient firm out of the market.

4. Suppose each firm in a perfectly competitive market structure is in long-run equilibrium. Then demand for the firms' product increases. Initially, price and economic profits rise. Soon afterward, the government decides to tax away most (but not all) of the economic profits, arguing that the firms in the industry did not earn them -- the profits were simply the result of an increase in demand. What effect, if any, would the tax have on market adjustment?

New firms will no longer have as great an incentive to enter the industry. Consequently, the industry supply curve will not increase by as much, and the new price will not be as low as it would have been had there been no tax.

5. Explain why one firm sometimes appears to be making higher profits than another, but in reality is not.

To illustrate, suppose Fanning and Clemente both operate a single proprietorship that produces pasta. They both have identical fixed costs. Fanning, however, is much better at making pasta than Clemente and, as a result, has lower average variable and average total costs. Given that Fanning and Clemente sell their pasta at the same price, Fanning appears to have higher profits than Clemente. We say "appears" because Fanning's implicit opportunity cost ought to be adjusted to reflect the higher pay he could receive (as compared to Clemente) if he were to work for someone else producing pasta. Once this is done, his variable costs will be the same as Clemente's, and he will not be making any economic profits. This does not say that Fanning will not be making more dollars than Clemente, only that these "more dollars" are not profits. They are a payment to Fanning's superior skill at making pasta. Without this superior skill, this payment would not exist.

6. For a perfectly competitive firm, profit maximization does not conflict with resource allocative efficiency. Do you agree or disagree? Explain your answer.

The statement is correct. Not only does profit maximization for the perfectly competitive firm not conflict with resource allocative efficiency, it assures it. If the firm maximizes profit, it will produce the quantity of output at which MR = MC. Since P = MR for the perfectly competitive firm, it follows that the firm assures resource allocative efficiency (P = MC) by maximizing profit (MR = MC).

7. The perfectly competitive firm does not increase its quantity of output without limit even though it can sell all it wants at the going price. Why not?

Regardless of the limitless demand, the perfectly competitive firm has to take its own cost curves into account. Therefore, it will only sell up to the quantity where P = MC, because to go beyond that point would cause the firm to lose money.

8. Suppose you read in a business magazine that computer firms are reaping high profits. With the theory of perfect competition in mind, what would you expect to happen over time to the following: computer prices, the profits of computer firms, the number of computers on the market, the number of computer firms?

Assuming that the computer industry is perfectly competitive (or, at least *acts as if it is*), we would expect the existence of economic profits to attract new entrants into the market. This would, in turn, shift the market supply curve righttward, increasing sales, decreasing prices, and slashing profits.

9. In your own words, explain resource allocative efficiency.

We want to put our resources to the most efficient use possible. Therefore, we want to make sure that they are creating marginal benefits at least equal to the marginal cost of obtaining them.

10. The term *price taker* can apply to buyers as well as sellers. A price-taking buyer is one who cannot influence price by changing the amount she buys. What goods do you buy for which you are a price taker? What goods do you buy for which you are not a price taker?

In most cases, the average consumer is a price taker. Large ticket items, such as houses and cars, may be the exception, since these purchases often involve bargaining over price and amenities.

11. Why study perfect competition if it does not exist in the real world?

While perfect competition may not exist in pristine form in the "real world," many markets approximate some or all of the underlying conditions for perfect competition -- many buyers and sellers with no market power, homogeneous product, perfect information, ease of entry and exit -- for example, commodities markets, such as corn, wheat, and barley, and stock markets. In addition, even lacking perfect information or perfectly homogeneous products, a market may approximate these conditions such that it behaves "as if" it were perfectly competitive.

12. Explain why a perfectly competitive firm will not produce in the short run if price is lower than average variable cost, but it will produce if price is below average total cost (but above average variable cost).

If price is lower than average variable cost, a perfectly competitive firm will be unable to pay its variable factors of production (labor, electricity, etc.) without losing money; whereas, if price is above average variable cost but below average total cost, only fixed costs will go "unpaid" -- and, presumably, they've been "paid" already, it is simply a matter of recouping them.

13. In long-run competitive equilibrium, P = MC = SRATC = LRATC. Since we know that P = MR, we can rewrite the condition as P = MR = MC = SRATC = LRATC. Now let's look at the condition as being made of four parts: (a) P = MR, (b) MR = MC, (c) P = SRATC, and (d) SRATC = LRATC. If we were to explain *why* MR = MC, we would say because the perfectly competitive firm attempts to maximize profits and this is how it does it. What is the *why* for (a), (c), and (d)?

a. P = MR because, given the perfectly competitive firm's horizontal demand curve, every unit sold yields the same price, so $\Delta TR/ \Delta Q$ is constant, just as price is constant.
c. P = SRATC because if that were not so the market would respond -- to wit, if P > SRATC, then one or more firms in the market would be making economic profit, and new firms would enter the market to absorb it; likewise, if P < SRATC, then one or more firms in the market would be experiencing losses, and if the condition persisted they would be forced out of the market by "leaner" competitors.
d. If SRATC = LRATC, then firms would have an incentive to change their plant size until they achieved minimum average total cost, and once they did that SRATC = LRATC.

14. Why is perfect competition used as a benchmark to judge other market structures?

Because it exhibits productive and allocative efficiency.

15. Suppose the government imposes a production tax on one perfectly competitive firm in the industry. For each unit the firm produces, it must pay $1 to the government. Will consumers in this market end up paying higher price because of the tax? Why?

No. Since there are many producers and all producers' products are interchangeable, if the firm's costs are such that it is unable to pay the additional tax without raising its prices above the market price, the firm will be driven out of the market by other producers who can charge the market price and still cover costs. See answer #3 above.

16. Given the following information, state whether the firm should shut down or continue to operate in the short run.
a. Q = 100; P = $10; AFC = $3; AVC = $4.
b. Q = 70; P = $5; AFC = $2; AVC = $7.
c. Q = 150; P = $7; AFC = $5; AVC = $6.

a. Continue to operate, P > AVC.
b. Shut down, P < AVC.
c. Continue to operate, P > AVC.

■ LECTURE SUPPLEMENTS

"Fizz Bang," *The Economist,* **July 1, 1995, p. 63**

The battle which between Coca-Cola and Cott Corporation which is recounted here is interesting because Cott Corp. is trying to turn a monopolistic competitive market into a perfectly competitive market. Coca-Cola has several times been chosen as having the most important franchise/brand name of any firm in the world. Cott Corporation has tried to undo this advantage by creating generic, own-label colas which are much cheaper than Coca-Cola.

Cott Corporation is run by Dave Nichol and his goal is to eliminate the "brand tax" which Coca-Cola imposes on consumers. This article will allow you to ask your students a very important question, what keeps markets (such as the market for soft drinks) from becoming competitive, and why do some markets become competitive and others do not.

The article shows that it is a combination of economics and marketing. There are economies of scale in advertising and reputation building. Distribution also plays a role, getting shelf space is very important. Despite the success that Cott Corp. has had, gaining almost one-third of the market in England, its profits remain small. The article should make clear that why some markets are perfectly competitive and others are not is not as obvious as it first may seem.

Gabriella Stern and Neal Templin, "Sold! Big Used-Car Auctions Meet Critical Needs of Detroit and Dealers," *The Wall Street Journal,* **June 27, 1995, p. A1, column 6.**

Because perfectly competitive firms cannot make profits in the long run, most firms try to create some monopoly power in order that they can provide profits to their owners. So examples of perfectly competitive markets are not as common as it would seem. Auction markets provide one example of a competitive market, and this article investigates the auction market for used cars.

Giant dealer-only auctions are an important part of the auto industry. Every year, fourteen million used vehicles are traded in for new cars, have their leases expire, are grabbed by the repo man, or for one reason or another, are returned to dealers who then must sell the cars to someone else. As one person put it, "Auctions are the best way to turn cash into cars and cars into cash." Used vehicles handled by U.S. auto auctions were worth $50 billion in 1994.

231

Late model cars provide a good mark-up, and as the article relates, many new car dealerships are expanding the "previously owned" portions of their auto lots. For example, a new Taurus costs about $19,000, but a two-year-old Taurus sells for $10,000 at the auction and will be resold for $12,000 on the lot. And since all cars are sold "as is", the lemon problem is one afflicting buyers of used cars who are dealers, just as the problem affects individual customers. The dealer who found the airbag in a car he had bought had been replaced with a sponge was not very happy. This article could be used to illuminate three topics: competition, auction markets, and lemons.

Stephanie Mehta, "Visions of Wealth and Independence Lead Professionals to Try Multilevel Marketing," *The Wall Street Journal*, June 23, 1995, p. B1, column 1.

Multilevel marketing is another example of a competitive market. The idea behind multilevel marketing is that individuals sell products to their friends, acquaintances, or anyone else they can find; however, they not only sell the product, but they also try to get them to become salesmen who will sell the products to their friends and acquaintances, *ad infinitum*. As you bring other individuals into the firm to sell the company's products, you get a cut of the profits which those individuals generate.

Multilevel marketing is a pyramid scheme which was successfully used by companies such as Amway and Mary Kay to market their products. Individuals are attracted to the firms because they have greater freedom as an independent contractor and if they bring a large number of people into the firm, they can make substantially more off of these individuals' sales than their own. LCI International has used this as a way of competing against MCI and AT&T for long-distance service. A trade group estimates there are over 3 million multilevel salespeople.

CHAPTER 22

Monopoly

Chapter 21 introduced students to the theory of perfect competition and the workings of the perfectly competitive market. Chapters 22 and 23 deal with markets that are not perfectly competitive. They are, in fact, often referred to as "structural market failures." This chapter focuses upon the theory of *monopoly* and optimal behavior for a monopolist. In so doing, we see the polar opposite to perfect competition. Here we have one firm with considerable market power which sets its own prices, can make a sustained economic profit, and has little concern over new competition -- all factors which are different from perfect competition. Chapter 22 begins with the theory of monopoly, paying particular attention to the issue of *barriers to entry*, then moves to optimal short-run and long-run pricing and output behavior for the monopolist, price discrimination, and, finally, the welfare costs of monopoly (as compared to perfect competition).

■ CHAPTER OBJECTIVES

Upon completing this chapter, your students should be able to:

- state the assumptions of the theory of *monopoly* and compare them to the assumptions of the theory of perfect competition (presented in Chapter 21);

- define *barriers to entry*, describe the various barriers to entry that protect monopolists, and explain how they affect the competition and potential competition monopolists face;

- distinguish between a price taker and a *price searcher*, and describe how the monopolist's role as a price searcher affects its short-run pricing and output decisions;

- identify the short-run profit-maximizing level of output and the corresponding price a (single-price) monopolist would charge for that output;

- describe the fundamental differences between short-run competitive and monopolistic behavior and results (in terms of price, output, and economic profits);

- argue for monopoly under certain conditions and against it under others, fully understanding why monopolies are sometimes "good" and sometimes "bad;"

- discuss the means by which monopoly profits may be reduced over time;

- define *price discrimination*, explain the rationale for it, and discuss the economic consequences of each of the types of price discrimination discussed in the chapter; and,

- explain the *welfare cost* of a monopoly (as compared to perfect competition), and why monopolies are considered to be "wasteful."

■ KEY TERMS

- monopoly
- public franchise
- natural monopoly
- price searcher
- economic or monopoly rent
- rent seeking
- welfare cost of monopoly

- welfare cost triangle
- X-inefficiency
- price discrimination
- perfect price discrimination
- second-degree price discrimination
- third-degree price discrimination
- arbitrage

■ CHAPTER OUTLINE

I. THE THEORY OF MONOPOLY

A. Basic Assumptions -- The theory of *monopoly* rests on three basic assumptions:

1. There is One Seller -- In a pure monopoly there is only one seller, meaning that the firm *is* the industry; and will, therefore, have significant influence over price.

2. The Single Seller Sells a Product for Which There Are No Close Substitutes -- The monopolist sells a product for which there are no close substitutes; thus, the monopolist faces little, if any, competition.

3. There Are Extremely High Barriers to Entry -- Government restrictions, high costs, and/or exclusive ownership of vital resources make it very hard (if not impossible) for new firms to enter the monopolized industry, further limiting the competition faced by monopolists.

B. Barriers to Entry -- Where do entry barriers come from?

1. Legal Barriers -- One major source of monopoly power is government. The government grants monopoly status to firms in three ways:

a. Public Franchise -- a right granted to a firm by government that permits the firm to be the *exclusive provider* of a particular good or service. What the government gives, the government can take away. See *The Global Economy* feature "Sweden and the Mail" for a discussion of the introduction of competition in Sweden in postal service.

b. **Patents** -- The U.S. government grants patents to inventors of products or processes for a period of 17 years. During the patent period, the patent-holder has the exclusive right to make and use the patented product or process. He/she may allow others to use it under license, but otherwise no one else may legally have access to it.

c. **Licenses** -- Entry into some industries and occupations requires a government-granted license, the quantity of which may be controlled to restrict entry.

2. **Economies of Scale** -- In some industries, start-up and/or distribution costs are so high that production doesn't become cost-effective until fairly high levels of output. This means that new entrants must enter on a large scale, if they hope to be competitive, and must be able to afford such an entry.

   If economies of scale are so pronounced in an industry that only one firm can be cost-effective, this firm is called a **natural monopoly**.

3. **Exclusive Ownership of a Necessary Resource** -- Existing firms may be protected from new entry by the exclusive or near-exclusive ownership of a resource needed to enter and produce in the industry. You should differentiate between firms such as Alcoa which for a time controlled almost all sources of bauxite in the United States, and firms such as DeBeers which is more of a *marketing cartel* than a monopolist.

C. **Barriers to Entry and the Legal Prohibition of Competition: Government Monopoly vs. Market Monopoly** -- Thus, monopolies may avoid competition through one of two routes: legal mandate and economic rationale. Monopolies that are legally protected from competition are referred to as **government monopolies**. Monopolies that are protected from competition due to economies of scale or the exclusive ownership of some vital resource are called **market monopolies**.

II. **MONOPOLY PRICING AND OUTPUT DECISIONS** -- Because of its unique status in its market, the monopolist has some ability to control the price of the product it sells -- as such, it is referred to as a **price searcher**. In contrast to a price taker, a price searcher can raise its price and still sell its product, although the number of units sold will fall as price rises.

A. **The Monopolist's Demand and Marginal Revenue Curves** -- Since the monopolist is the sole supplier in its market, the monopoly firm faces the (downward-sloping) market demand curve. If the monopolist wants to sell additional output, it must lower price in order to do so. If the monopolist wants to charge a higher price, it will do so at the expense of a reduction in quantity sold. [See Exhibit 22-1]

B. **The Monopolist's Demand and Marginal Revenue Curves Are Not the Same** -- Since lowering the price of additional units of the good will lower the price of all units sold (except in the case of the price-discriminating monopolist, who we will discuss later in this chapter), marginal revenue will fall more rapidly than price. As a result, the monopolist's marginal revenue (MR) curve will, after the first unit of output is sold, always lie *below* its demand curve. [See Exhibit 22-2]

C. **A Digression: The Revenue-Maximizing Price Is Usually Not the Profit Maximizing Price** -- The goal of the monopolist is to maximize profits, not to maximize revenues, and maximizing revenues is the same as maximizing profits *only when the firm has no variable costs.*

   D. **Monopoly Price and Output for a Profit-Maximizing Monopolist** -- Assuming the monopolist is a profit-maximizer, its optimal (short-run) level of output will be that quantity where MR = MC (the same as with the perfectly competitive firm), and it will charge the highest price per unit at which that quantity can be sold. In terms of Exhibit 22-4, the monopolist produces Q_1 where MR = MC, and sells Q_1 at the price on the demand curve that corresponds tot hat level of output. Notice that the monopolist charges a price greater than marginal cost (P > MC).

   Whether profits are earned will depend upon the relationship between P and ATC at Q_1 -- if P > ATC, the monopolist *will* earn economic profits; if P $\leq$ ATC, the monopolist will *not* earn economic profits. It is important to note, however, that even if the monopolist suffers a loss, it will be a smaller loss than would be suffered by a competitive industry under similar circumstances. [See Exhibit 22-5]

   E. **Differences Between Perfect Competition and Monopoly** -- There are two important differences between perfect competition and monopoly that deserve emphasis: (1) *For the perfectly competitive firm, P = MR; while, for the monopolist, P > MR*; and, (2) *For the perfectly competitive firm P = MC; while, for the monopolist, P > MC.*

   F. **In Perspective** -- Perfectly competitive and monopolistic firms also have many things in common. Both try to maximize profits; both are constrained by their demand curves; and both equate marginal revenue with marginal cost. There is one major difference between perfectly competitive and monopolistic firms, however. If the perfectly competitive firm tries to sell its product for a price other than the market price, it will sell nothing. This fact is not true for monopolies.

III. **MONOPOLY PROFITS IN THE LONG RUN** -- In perfect competition, economic profits are reduced to zero in the long run by the entry of new firms. Since monopolies are generally protected from new entry, what other factors might tend to reduce monopoly profits over time?

   A. **The Capitalization of Profits** -- Over time, a firm's owners will likely sell it. In the case of a monopoly, the sellers will likely take monopoly profits into account when setting the price for the company. As a result, the new owners will be faced with higher fixed and, therefore, average total costs than the former owners faced. As a result, ATC shifts up and eliminates much, if not all, of the economic profits. [See Exhibit 22-6]

   B. **The Politics of Monopoly: Monopoly Rent Seeking** -- If a monopoly earns positive economic profits, these monopoly profits are sometimes referred to as **economic rent** -- which is *any payment in excess of opportunity cost.* Market participants who expend resources trying to capture economic rents are engaging in **rent seeking**, and rent seeking will tend to decrease the actual (net) value of any economic rents earned, because the cost of rent seeking must be deducted from the rent earned.

IV. **THE CASE AGAINST MONOPOLY** -- Monopoly is often considered to be inefficient, when compared to perfect competition. Here we examine some of those arguments.

A. **The Welfare Costs of a Monopoly** -- Exhibit 22-7 shows a monopolist's demand, marginal revenue (MR), marginal cost (MC), and average total cost (ATC) curves. If the product were produced under perfectly competitive conditions, output would be Q_C and price would be P_C. Under monopoly conditions, output will be Q_M and price P_M. Notice that the monopolist produces a lower quantity of output and sells it at a higher price. *The net value (in terms of price) of the difference between Q_M and Q_C is called the* **welfare cost** *of the monopoly*. The actual value of the welfare costs is illustrated graphically by the triangle BCA, known as the **welfare cost triangle**.

B. **Rent Seeking is Socially Wasteful** -- Not only do monopoly profits represent a welfare cost to society, they also create an (inefficient) incentive to expend resources trying to compete for them. Rent seeking expends otherwise-productive resources in an effort to redistribute exiting value, rather than trying to create additional value.

C. **X-Inefficiency** -- Since the monopolist lacks substantial competition, it is not under any pressure to minimize costs. As a result, it is possible for the monopolist to produce at a level above the minimum ATC and still prosper. Economist Harvey Leibenstein referred to *monopolists operating at higher-than-minimum cost, and to the organizational slack that is directly tied to this*, as **X-inefficiency**.

D. **What is Price Discrimination?** -- So far we have assumed that the monopolist charges the same price for all units of the good sold. However, since the monopolist is the market, and the monopolist-as-market has some control over price, the monopolist may, under certain circumstances, *charge different customers different prices for the same product*. To do so is called **price discrimination**. Price discrimination comes in three varieties which a monopolist may mix and match as conditions permit:

1. **First-Degree (Perfect) Price Discrimination** -- *charging each customer the highest price he or she is willing and able to pay for an additional unit of the good* -- that is, charging precisely the price for each unit of output that is indicated on the market demand curve. The *Economics In Our Times* feature, "Does Your College Or University Practice Price Discrimination," provides an excellent example of first-degree price discrimination with which they can directly identify.

2. **Second-Degree Price Discrimination** -- *charging different prices based upon quantity purchased*, such that the first unit or group of units is sold at the highest price, the next unit or group at a lower price, and so on.

3. **Third-Degree Price Discrimination** -- *charging different prices to different segments of the market or the buying population*.

E. **Why Would the Monopolist Want to Price Discriminate?** -- Why would a monopolist discriminate? Price discrimination allows the monopolist to re-capture some of the *consumer surplus* it loses by charging all customers the same price, even though some are willing and able to pay more. In fact, *if the monopolist can successfully perfectly price discriminate, then P = MR for all units sold, significantly increasing marginal and total revenue*, and completely eliminating consumer surplus.

F. **Conditions of Price Discrimination** -- Given the revenue-enhancing benefits of price discrimination, why doesn't everybody do it? In order to price-discriminate, the following conditions must hold:

1. **The Seller Must Exercise Some Control Over Price; It Must Be a Price Searcher.**

2. **The Seller Must Be Able to Distinguish Between Customers and Determine Their Willingness to Pay.**

3. **It Must Be Impossible for One Buyer to Resell the Good to Others** -- The possibility of **arbitrage**, "buying low and selling high," must not exist.

G. **Moving to P = MC through Price Discrimination** -- Chapter 21 told us that the perfectly competitive firm exhibits *resource allocative efficiency* because it produced at the quantity where P = MC. The perfectly price discriminating monopolist also produces at a quantity where P = MC; whereas, the *single-price monopolist* produces at a quantity where P > MC, and therefore does not exhibit resource allocative efficiency. [See Exhibit 22-8]

H. **You Can Have the Comics, Just Give Me the Coupons Section** -- Coupons provide an example of price discrimination. Shoppers who value time are less likely to cut coupons than those who do not. This fact enables manufacturers and grocery stores to discriminate between those who have a lot of shopping time and those who have little shopping time.

I. **In Perspective**

1. **Rent Seeking** -- The purpose of rent-seeking behavior is to "buy" a monopoly position which provides them fewer constraints on their market behavior than the firm would face in a competitive market.

2. **Price Discrimination** -- Firms will also make an effort to introduce into the market the three conditions which enable price discrimination to be effective. Auto dealerships usually sell their autos for less than the sticker price. Salespeople can use their knowledge of the person's income to adjust the price of the car to the buyer's purchasing power.

V. **ECONOMICS ON THE INTERNET** -- Sources for three types of information are provided here: information on the corporations in particular industries, energy statistics, and a very exact value for pi.

■ ANSWERS TO CHAPTER QUESTIONS

1. The perfectly competitive firm exhibits resource allocative efficiency (P = MC) and the single-price monopolist does not. What is the reason for this difference?

The reason is that the perfectly competitive firm faces a horizontal demand curve and the monopolist faces a downward-sloping demand curve. As long as the demand curve is horizontal, price will equal marginal revenue. This means that if the firm produces the quantity of output at which MR equals MC, it naturally equates P and MC. When the demand curve is downward-sloping, price will be greater than marginal revenue. This means that if the firm produces the quantity of output at which MR equals MC, it cannot equate P and MC (since P and MR are not the same). In summary, the differences between a perfectly competitive firm and monopolist are the result of one facing a horizontal demand curve and the other facing a downward-sloping demand curve.

2.   Since the monopolist is a single seller of a product with no close substitutes, is it able to obtain any price for its good that it wants?

No, it isn't. The monopolist is constrained by the demand curve it faces. It can only obtain as high a price as the demand curve warrants. The price the monopolist *wants* might be (probably is) higher than the price that its demand curve allows it to charge.

3.   When a single-price monopolist maximizes profits, price is greater than marginal cost. This means that consumers would be willing to pay more for additional units of output than they cost to produce. Given this, why doesn't the monopolist produce more?

In order to sell additional units the monopolist has to lower price on all previous units, thus marginal revenue (MR) will be less than price. It is MR, not price, that the monopolist compares with marginal cost (MC). It will not produce those units for which MC > MR, even if for them P > MC.

4.   Is there a welfare cost triangle if the firm produces the quantity of output at which price equals marginal cost?

No, there isn't. There would be no welfare cost triangle in perfect competition, for example.

5.   It has been noted that rent seeking is individually rational, but socially wasteful. Explain.

Consider a monopolist whose profits (rents) are being sought after through the rent-seeking actions of persons A, B, and C. From the point of view of A, B, and C, it makes sense to go after the monopoly profits (rents); after all profit is profit. However, from a social perspective, rent seeking does not produce any more goods. It is simply a transfer activity, not a production activity; resources that could be used to produce goods are instead used to affect a transfer of profits from one entity to another. Resources that go into lobbying, knocking on the doors of members of Congress, taking politicians out to dinner, and so on could be used to build houses, television sets, or water slides for children.

6.   Occasionally, students accuse their instructors, rightly or wrongly, of practicing grade discrimination. What these students mean is that the instructor "charges" some students a higher price for a given grade than other students (by requiring some students to do more or better). Grade discrimination involves no money, price discrimination does. Discuss the similarities and differences between the two types of discrimination. Which do you prefer less, or perhaps, dislike more? Why?

239

If the instructor "charges" more to students who are capable of "paying" more -- in terms of effort, time, and performance -- then this would be similar to price discrimination which charges customers what they are willing to pay. The problem is that price discrimination focuses upon willingness to pay, while grade discrimination focuses on ability to pay (regardless of willingness). For this reason, most people would find price discrimination more "fair" than grade discrimination.

7. Make a list of real-world price discrimination practices. Do they meet the conditions posited for price discrimination?

Two examples with which most people should be familiar is the price discrimination between local and long-distance telephone calls and between daytime, evening, and night long-distance rates. The discrimination between local and long-distance rates is third-degree, as the phone companies (and the rate-setting commissions) view local and long-distance calling as distinct segments of the market. The setting of daytime, evening, and night long-distance rates involves all three types of price discrimination. To the extent that rates vary directly with perceived demand, there is an attempt at first-degree discrimination. Since rates tend to be highest for the first few minutes, and then lower (per minute) after that, there is second-degree discrimination as well. And, to the extent that business calls would be concentrated during the daytime, while most personal calls would take place in the evening and nighttime hours, higher long-distance rates during the day are an attempt at third-degree price discrimination.

Other "real-world" examples of price discrimination include: first-class, coach, and excursion fares on airplane tickets; variable tolls depending on the size and number of axles a vehicle has; student, employee, and senior citizen discounts; and, commercial vs. residential electricity rates. The student must be careful to only include those situations where prices vary but quality and quantity of the good or service does not. So, for example, different prices for different seats at a football game would not be true price discrimination; whereas, offering a discount to season ticket holders, students, or senior citizens would be.

8. For many years in California, car washes would advertise "Ladies Day." This was one day out of the week when a woman could have her car washed for a price lower than a man could have his car washed. It was argued that this was a form of sexual discrimination. The argument was accepted, and a California court ruled that there could no longer be a "Ladies Day." Do you think that this was a case of sexual discrimination or price discrimination? Explain your answer.

Both. Clearly, using gender as a litmus test for qualifying for some service is sexual discrimination. However, if the intent was to appeal to a particular segment of the market -- specifically, those who stay home during the day, and could, therefore, have their cars washed at "off-peak" hours -- then it would also be price discrimination.

9. Make a list of both market monopolies and government monopolies. Which list is longer? Why do you think this is so?

Almost all of the monopolies that might come to the students' minds are government monopolies, to the extent that the definition of government monopolies includes public franchises, as well as monopolies created by patents and licenses. The reason for this is that the government has, over most of the past eighty years, aggressively pursued and divested non-government monopolies such as Aluminum Corporation of America, Standard Oil, and AT&T.

10. Fast-food stores often charge higher prices for their products in high-crime areas than in low-crime areas. Is this an act of price discrimination? Why?

Not exactly. More likely it is an attempt at self-insurance. Since stock lost to crime raises the unit cost of products actually sold, the firm may choose to raise prices to cover those higher costs. Also, a high incidence of crime makes it harder and more expensive to hire employees, thus labor costs will rise, raising unit costs even higher. For this to be price discrimination would imply that the firm is trying to discourage purchases in high-crime areas. If that were the case, the firm could simply shut down is stores in high-crime areas, rather than run the risk of inciting additional crime by charging higher-than-normal prices.

11. Coupons are usually more common on small-ticket items than on big-ticket items. Explain why.

There is probably less distinction among potential purchasers of big-ticket items as to their willingness to spend time to save money than there is among potential purchasers of small-ticket items. To wit, most anyone would take an extra ten minutes to browse the "coupons" to save 10% off a $100,000 house, whereas many people will not spend those ten minutes browsing for a coupon to save 20% off a $1.00 loaf of bread.

12. Fill in the lettered spaces with the appropriate numbers.

Price	Quantity Demanded	Total Revenue	Marginal Revenue	Total Cost	Marginal Cost	Profit or Loss
$ 18	0	A		$ 10		Q
15	2	B	G	14	L	R
11	5	C	H	19	M	S
9	7	D	I	25	N	T
7	10	E	J	31	O	U
0	25	F	K	38	P	V

The answers are:

Price	Quantity Demanded	Total Revenue	Marginal Revenue	Total Cost	Marginal Cost	Profit or Loss
$ 18	0	$ 0	0	$ 10		- $10
15	2	30	15	14	2	+ 16
11	5	55	8.33	19	1.67	+ 36
9	7	63	4	25	2.5	+ 38
7	10	70	2.33	31	2	+ 39
0	25	0	0	38	0.47	- 38

■ LECTURE SUPPLEMENTS

"Europe's Great Mail Robbery," *The Economist*, **January 7, 1995, p. 49-51.**

This article looks at the monopolies which European governments have over postal delivery in European countries. Almost all countries provide their post offices with a monopoly and do not allow any competition. Originally, governments justified their mail monopolies so they could intercept seditious correspondence, but today the usual justification is that private services would not provide delivery to all customers (excluding individuals in distant rural areas, for example). The United States, which allows some competition from UPS and Federal Express, is free-market oriented by comparison with most European countries.

Nevertheless, private firms are pushing for the opportunity to compete, no matter how small the opening is. In fact, three countries (Sweden, Finland and New Zealand) have abolished their postal monopolies. The reason for wanting to liberalize European mails is that this would, it is felt, improve the quality of service and lower prices.

One example of how firms have circumvented the mail services in Europe is "remailing." Since different countries charge different prices for mail and provide different qualities of service, it might be better to post letters to Germany from Holland than from Britain. The article details how the European Postal Union got together to undo the efforts of remailers. Instead of improving the quality of their services, European post offices changed the rules to undermine the remailers. So next time your students complain about the postal service in the United States, tell them about Europe.

"A New Electronic Messiah," *The Economist*, **August 5, 1995, p. 62.**

Where do monopolies come from and how do they sustain their monopoly power? The example of Netscape provides an excellent example which your students should immediately identify with if they have ever used the World Wide Web. The article explains how Marc Andreessen from the University of Illinois discovered the potential that a browser for the Internet held in helping individuals access the Internet. To solve this problem, he created Netscape's Navigator to help surf the web. In one year, the Netscape Navigator went from less than 20 percent market share to over 80 percent. Netscape has become to the Internet what Microsoft was to software for IBM compatible PCs.

The debut of Netscape's stock on NASDAQ is as mythic as the product itself. The stock was originally going to be offered at $14 per share, but there was such high demand that Netscape doubled the price to $28 and then increased the number of shares which were made available. When Netscape first opened, it traded at $72, later declined to the $46, then moved up above $100 a share.

By the time Netscape's stock reached 100 later in 1995, Marc Andreessen had become a billionaire! Not bad for a company and product which didn't even exist two years before the initial public offering.

If you want a real-world example of how firms create semi-monopolies rather than the theoretical ones covered in the book, Netscape provides as good an example as any. Of course, no monopoly is permanent, especially if it is not protected by the government. Netscape faces competition from Spyglass, Microsoft and others. Regardless of the outcome, I think Netscape will open up discussion in your class.

Greg Steinmetz, "Customer-Service Era Is Reaching Germany Late, Hurting Business," *The Wall Street Journal*, **June 1, 1995, p. A1, column 1.**

This article looks at telecommunications companies in Europe, another monopoly which is less than responsive to consumer demands, as well as other European businesses which do not put the customer first.

European laws usually limit the hours that stores can stay open. For example, in Germany shops must close by 1:30 p.m. on Saturday and remain closed until Monday morning. I can remember when I was in Nuremberg. I went into the museum around 10 a.m. when the streets were bustling with shoppers. When I left at 2 p.m. I thought I had entered a ghost town. The results are high bills, antiquated technology, poor service and a rush to shop as soon as you leave work to buy goods before the stores close.

Students who have not traveled through Europe will be surprised at the rules and regulations which reign in Europe, and students who have traveled in Europe will be quickly reminded of their experiences. One justification for the short shopping hours is that it helps smaller businesses which could not compete against stores which hired employees at low wages to mind the store.

Do your students think this is an adequate justification? Would they like to see the same situation in the United States? See what your students think of the monopoly power which European governments provide some firms.

CHAPTER 23

Monopolistic Competition and Oligopoly

In addition to monopoly, the subject of Chapter 22, there are two other forms of "structural market failure" which we need to discuss. The first, *monopolistic competition*, deals with markets that are basically competitive but which have the extra twist of *product differentiation*, which makes each good slightly different from its substitutes. The second, *oligopoly*, often referred to as "monopoly of the few," occurs when a small number of firms control a large enough share of the market that, if they were to band together, they could act like a monopoly. Chapter 23 begins with the theory of monopolistic competition, then briefly explains short-run pricing and output behavior and the problem of excess capacity which plagues monopolistically competitive firms. The chapter then moves into the theory of oligopoly and looks at short-run oligopoly pricing and output decisions according to four different theories: the *"kinked" demand curve*, *price leadership*, *cartel*, and *game theory*. The chapter concludes with a brief look at the theory of *contestable markets* and its impact on our perceptions of non-competitive market structures.

■ CHAPTER OBJECTIVES

Upon completing this chapter, your students should be able to:

- define *monopolistic competition* and compare and contrast it to perfect competition;

- explain the *excess capacity theorem* and its relevance to monopolistic competition;

- state the basic assumptions of *oligopoly* theory and understand why there are more theories of oligopoly behavior than for any other market structure we have studied;

- discuss the *"kinked" demand curve*, *price leadership*, *cartel*, and *game theory* models of oligopoly behavior, with particular emphasis on both common themes and important distinctions between the three;

- identify and explain some of the key problems with forming and maintaining a cartel; and,

- describe the theory of *contestable markets* and explain how it challenges basic market structure theory.

■ KEY TERMS

- monopolistic competition
- excess capacity theorem
- oligopoly
- concentration ratio
- kinked demand curve theory

- price leadership theory
- cartel theory
- cartel
- game theory
- contestable markets

■ CHAPTER OUTLINE

I. THE THEORY OF MONOPOLISTIC COMPETITION

A. **Basic Assumptions** -- The theory of *monopolistic competition* is built on three basic assumptions:

1. **There Are Many Sellers and Buyers** -- Much like perfect competition, there are many sellers and many buyers; however, unlike perfect competition, monopolistically competitive firms have some control over price for the following reason.

2. **Each Firm (In the Industry) Produces and Sells a Slightly Differentiated Product** -- Differences among products may be due to brand names, packaging, location, advertising, service, etc. Product differentiation may be real or imagined -- that is, the perceived difference between products may or may not actually exist.

3. **There Is Easy Entry and Exit** -- Again, like a perfectly competitive market, new firms can enter the market easily and existing firms may exit the market easily, as well.

B. **You Already know More about Monopolistic Competition Than you Think: Answer These Questions And See** -- Given our knowledge of perfect competition and monopoly, understanding monopolistic competition is fairly simple. Answer these questions to find out.

1. **Does the Monopolistic Competitor Face a Horizontal or a Downward-sloping Demand Curve?** -- Downward sloping. Because each firm in the monopolistically competitive market sells a slightly differentiated product, each producer has some control over the price of its good. As such, *the monopolistically competitive firm faces a downward-sloping demand curve* and is a *price searcher*.

2. **Is the Demand Curve Facing the Monopolistic Competitive Firm More Elastic or Less Elastic than the Demand Curve Facing the Monopoly Seller?** -- More elastic. At the same time, easy entry into the market prevents the monopolistically competitive firm from exercising as much control over price as the monopolist. As a result, while downward-sloping, *the monopolistically competitive firm's demand curve tends to be more elastic than the monopolist's.*

3. **Is P = MR or Is P > MR?** -- P > MR. Since the monopolistically competitive firm faces a downward-sloping demand curve, its marginal revenue curve (like that of the

monopolist) must lie below the demand curve. Thus, instead of producing a quantity where P = MR (as in the case of perfect competition), the monopolistically competitive firm will produce a quantity where P > MR.

4. **Does the Monopolistic Competitor Exhibit Resource Allocative Efficiency?** -- No. Does the monopolistically competitive firm produce a quantity where P = MC, meaning that all resources are allocated efficiently? No. Since all firms profit-maximize by producing where MR = MC, and the monopolistically competitive firm sells at P > MR, then it must be true that P > MC at that quantity. [See Exhibit 23-1a]

5. **Will There Be Economic Profits in the Long Run?** -- No. Given that the monopolistically competitive firm has some control over price, it is quite possible that it will make economic profits in the short run. However, since there is easy entry into the market, the existence of economic profits will lure new firms into the market, raising costs and decreasing the demand for any single producer's product, until the economic profits are eliminated. [See Exhibit 23-1b]

C. **Excess Capacity: What Is It, and Is It "Good" or "Bad"?** -- *In equilibrium, a monopolistically competitive firm will produce an output smaller than the one that would minimize its (per unit) costs of production.* Take a look at Exhibit 23-2a. Notice that, when the monopolistically competitive firm is producing at the quantity where MR = MC (q_{MC1}) in the long run, ATC is not at its minimum.

The difference between actual output (q_{MC1}) and the quantity that minimizes average costs (q_{MC2}) is the amount of excess capacity. Now, compare this result to that of the perfectly competitive firm illustrated in Exhibit 23-2b.

D. **Many Monopolistic Competitors Would Rather Be Monopolists: Or, What's in a Designer Label?** -- Since monopolists make larger profits than firms in markets where there are several sellers, most firms try to create monopoly power for themselves. The purpose of advertising and "designer" labels is to convince consumers that their product is unique, creating monopoly power for that firm. See the *Economics In Our Times* feature, "Are There Too Many Gas Stations at the Corner" to stimulate further discussion on this topic.

II. OLIGOPOLY: ASSUMPTIONS AND REAL-WORLD BEHAVIOR

A. **Basic Assumptions** -- While we will discuss several different view of *oligopoly* behavior, there are three basic assumptions that are integral to all of them:

1. **There Are Few Sellers and Many Buyers** -- Oligopoly is characterized by a small number of firms controlling a large share of the market. Furthermore, these firms are considered to be **mutually interdependent** -- meaning that each one is aware that its actions will influence the other firms in the market and that the actions of those other firms will affect it.

2. **Firms Produce and Sell Either Homogeneous Or Differentiated Products** -- Firms in an oligopoly may sell either homogeneous or differentiated products. Regardless of that decision, limited competition gives the oligopolist limited control over price.

3. **There Are Significant Barriers to Entry** -- Like the monopolist, the oligopolist is generally protected by barriers to entry. In the case of oligopoly, economies of scale are likely to be the most important barrier, though legal barriers may exist and/or existing firms may control vital inputs.

B. **Oligopoly and the Real World** -- How do we find oligopolies? Economists use **concentration ratios** to *measure the percentage of sales, assets, output, employment, or some other factor, that is controlled by a particular number of firms in the industry.* For instance, a four-firm sales concentration ratio would compare the total value of the top four firms' sales to those of the industry. If the percentage is fairly high (usually over 50%), then we would say that the industry is "concentrated." As to whether or not it is a true oligopoly, that will depend upon how it behaves and on the presence of alternative suppliers, such as foreign competitors or substitute domestic goods.

III. **PRICE AND OUTPUT UNDER OLIGOPOLY: THREE THEORIES** -- When inter-dependence exists among firms, the significant question becomes how one firm reacts to the actions of one or more other firm(s) in the market.

A. **The "Kinked" Demand Curve Theory** -- The basic behavioral assumption in the **kinked demand curve theory** is that *if a single firms lowers its price, the other firms in the industry will move to match it; but, if a single firm raises price, the other firms in the industry will not necessarily follow suit.*

1. **The Kinked Demand Curve Theory** -- As a result, *each firm in the industry faces a demand curve that is "kinked" at the prevailing price, is fairly flat above that price --* indicating that its demand is highly elastic, should it choose to raise prices -- *and fairly steep below that price --* indicating that a reduction in price will not significantly enhance total revenues, since the other firms in the market will likely lower their prices, too. [See Exhibit 23-5]

2. **Price Rigidity and Oligopoly** -- Given these conditions, we would expect price to tend to remain at or near the kink; therefore, we say that price is rigid, or "sticky," at the prevailing market price. Furthermore, because of the nature of the oligopolist's marginal revenue curve (as illustrated in Exhibit 23-5), even noticeable changes in marginal cost may not result in a price change, as long as MC continues to intersect MR at the quantity where the demand curve is "kinked."

3. **Criticisms of the Kinked Demand Curve Theory** -- There are two basic shortcomings of this theory: first, it ignores where the prevailing ("kink") price came from; and, second, empirical evidence points out a number of suspected oligopolies whose behavior could not be explained by a kinked demand curve.

B. **The Price Leadership Theory** -- One possible answer to the question of where the "kink" price came from, as well as an explanation of oligopoly pricing and output that can stand on its own -- that is, with or without the kinked demand curve -- is the *price leadership theory.* The key behavioral assumption of the **price leadership theory** is that *one firm (the **dominant firm**) sets the market price, and all other firms in the industry (the **fringe firms**) take this price as given.* As is illustrated in Exhibit 23-6b, the dominant firms sets price so that it maximizes its own profits. The fringe firms then act as *price takers*, and equate that price to their own marginal costs. [See Exhibit 23-6a]

C. **Cartel Theory** -- In a **cartel**, *several firms band together in order to act as if they were a monopolist, so that they may capture the benefits that would accrue to a monopolist in that market.*

1. **Optimal Cartel Behavior** -- As a group, the cartel will reduce output and increase price (compared to what they would produce as individuals) in an effort to increase total profits, and will then distribute the profits among the cartel members according to some agreed upon system. As Exhibit 23-7 shows, cartel members earn monopoly profits that they otherwise would not, assuming that members act as agreed upon.

2. **Problems with Cartels** -- Unfortunately for the firms involved, there are several problems associated with forming and maintaining a cartel.

    a. **The Problem of Forming the Cartel** -- Forming a cartel poses two major problems. First, in many parts of the world, cartels are illegal. Second, even if the cartel is legal, they are expensive to set up (especially when the number of producers is fairly large), and many potential cartel members may resist the cost when they may benefit from the cartel as a "free rider."

    b. **The Problem of Formulating Cartel Policy** -- Once the cartel is formed, each member is likely to have its own priorities. Thus, making policy for the whole cartel is liable to be painstakingly complicated and frustrating.

    c. **The Problem of Entry into the Industry** -- Even if cartel members manage to agree upon policy and achieve monopoly profits, those high profits may attract new firms into the industry -- if profits are high enough, potential barriers to entry are easy to overlook. If cartel members cannot prevent entry, then their production targets will be upset by the presence of additional suppliers.

    d. **The Problem of Cheating** -- Once the cartel agreement has been made, there is an incentive for cartel members to cheat on the agreement and sell additional output. As Exhibit 23-8 shows, as long as the cartel price remains intact, the cheating firm may sell additional output at the cartel price and, thus, reap additional profits.

3. **An Enforcer of the Cartel Agreement** -- Although the government is in the business of breaking up cartels, it also helps create and maintain some cartels. Examples include farmers and the acreage allotment program, and in the past, airlines through the Civil Aeronautics Board, and railroads through the Interstate Commerce Commission. For a comparison between cartels and New Year's resolutions, see the *Economics In Our Times* feature, "How Is a New Year's Resolution Like a Cartel Agreement? or, Why Is It So Hard to Exercise Regularly?"

IV. **GAME THEORY AND OLIGOPOLY** -- **Game theory** is *a mathematical technique used to analyze the behavior of decision makers who try to reach an optimal position through the use of **strategic behavior**, being fully aware of their mutual interdependence with the other players in the game, and attempting to anticipate the decisions of those other players.*

248

A. **The Prisoner's Dilemma** -- Perhaps the most familiar model of game theory involves a situation in which *two players each have a choice between two actions, and are fully aware that the decision made by the other player will affect the outcome of their own choice*. This type of game is called a **prisoner's dilemma**. The text walks the student through a game involving two players, Bob and Nathan, who have been arrested and charged with committing a crime. Bob and Nathan must each decide whether or not to confess to the crime, knowing that the penalty they must pay for their decision will vary depending upon the decision that the other person makes. Exhibit 23-9 summarizes the various penalties that Bob and Nathan face depending upon their and their "opponents" decisions. As is usually the case, Bob and Nathan make decisions that guarantee that they will not suffer the worst possible penalty. But, as a result, they pay a higher price than if they had acted "cooperatively."

B. **Prisoner's Dilemma and Oligopolists** -- The point of this exercise is to get yet another look at oligopoly behavior. Exhibit 23-10 restates the dilemma in terms of potential profits to two firms depending upon each firm's decisions as to whether or not it should abide by a pricing agreement. As with Bob and Nathan, most economists feel that the two firms are more likely to act in order to avoid the worst result for themselves, rather than acting cooperatively; and, as a result, will earn much lower profits than they could have if they had cooperated.

C. **Constraints and Oligopolists: Are Some Constraints Good?** -- Not all restraints on economic behavior reduce economic efficiency. Economic actors will try to remove those constraints that make it harder to meet an objective, and to add those constraints that make it easier to meet an objective. Removing constraints that make it easier to meet an objective, such as forming a cartel, can increase economic efficiency.

V. **THE THEORY OF CONTESTABLE MARKETS: CHALLENGING ORTHODOXY** -- Over the past several years, the focus of market structure theory has shifted away from the number of firms in the industry to the issue of entry into and exit from an industry. In this light, economist William Baumol and others have developed the theory of *contestable markets*.

A. **What is a Contestable Market?** -- A **contestable market** is one in which the following three conditions are met: (1) there is extremely easy entry into the market and virtually costless exit from the market; (2) new firms entering the market can produce at the same (per unit) costs as existing firms; and, (3) firms exiting the market can easily dispose of their fixed assets by selling or using them elsewhere. One widely used example of a contestable market is any given domestic airline route. Suppose that only two airlines currently serve the Omaha to Denver route. While this might result in oligopoly behavior, a number of other air carriers could easily transfer planes from another route to the Omaha-Denver route if it became unusually profitable. Similarly, they could take those planes off of that route should it become less profitable.

B. **Conclusions of Contestable Market Theory** -- Even though the theory of contestable markets is still quite young, there are some basic conclusions that we can draw from it:

1. **Noncompetitive Behavior** -- Even if an industry is composed of a small number of firms, the presence of potential entrants may keep existing firms from behaving in a noncompetitive way.

2. **Economic Profits** -- By preventing noncompetitive behavior, the presence of potential entrants may cause economic profits to be zero, even in a highly concentrated industry where the product is in great demand.

3. **Contestability Endangers Inefficient Producers** -- Market concentration often allows producers to act inefficiently in an effort to maximize profits. If existing firms fail to produce at minimum ATC, new firms will likely enter, driving prices down, and forcing existing firms to either become efficient or leave the market.

4. **P = MC** -- Since the presence of potential entrants encourages firms to produce at the lowest possible ATC, then it follows that their P = MC; therefore, contestability encourages resource allocative efficiency.

VI. The Four Market Structures Reviewed -- The four different market structures--perfect competition, monopoly, monopolistic competition, and oligopoly--are compared in Exhibit 23-11.

VII. ECONOMICS ON THE INTERNET -- Sites which contain information on anticompetitive behavior, mergers, and the competitiveness of markets are provided.

■ ANSWERS TO CHAPTER QUESTIONS

1. What, if anything, do all firms in all four market structures have in common?

All firms, no matter what the market structure, produce the quantity of output at which marginal revenue equals marginal cost. For some of their similarities and differences, see Exhibit 23-11.

2. Why does the marginal revenue curve have the unusual look that it does in the kinked demand curve model?

The marginal revenue curve in the kinked demand curve model looks the way it does because of the shape of the demand curve in the model: namely, it is kinked with a steeper slope at prices below the kink and a less steep slope at prices above the kink. The marginal revenue curve has a gap in it (directly below the kink in the demand curve), reflecting the fact that if a firm reduces price below the kink, marginal revenue takes a sharp drop.

3. Would you expect cartel formation to be more likely in industries that comprise a few firms or many firms? Explain your answer.

Cartel formation will be more likely in industries comprised of a few firms because it is easier and less costly for a few firms to get together and form a cartel than it is for many firms to do so.

4. Does the theory of contestable markets shed any light on oligopoly pricing theories?

Yes, it does. It predicts that oligopolistic firms will price their products differently if the market they are in is contestable than if it is not.

5. There are 60 types or varieties of product X on the market. Is product X made in a monopolistically competitive market?

That is not necessarily the case. The 60 different types of product could be made by four firms. If this were the case, it would be an oligopolistic market.

6. Why does interdependence of firms play a major role in oligopoly, but not perfect competition or monopolistic competition?

The size of the firms in an oligopoly, relative to the market and to one another, is a marked departure from more competitive market structures. Similarly, the ability of the other firms in the market to "steal" customers away from a price raiser, or to match price decreases in order to preserve market share, makes anticipating your competitors' reactions much more important than in either perfect competition -- where no firm has enough market power to worry -- or monopolistic competition -- where product differentiation insulates the firm somewhat from competitors' actions.

7. Airline companies sometimes fly airplanes that are one-quarter full between cities. Some people point to this as evidence of economic waste. What do you think? Would it be better to have fewer airline companies and more full planes?

As long as the airlines are able to cover average total cost (ATC) flying at 1/4 capacity, a large number of smaller airlines is preferable to a smaller number of large airlines -- in terms of the price consumers will pay and resource allocative efficiency.

8. Concentration ratios have often been used to note the tightness of an oligopoly market. A high concentration ratio indicates a tight oligopoly, and a low concentration ratio indicates a loose oligopoly. Would you expect firms in tight markets to reap higher profits, on average, than firms in loose markets? Would it matter if the markets were contestable?

Yes. Yes. The "tighter" the oligopoly the greater the likelihood of *collusion* -- concerted action -- that will make the oligopoly more like a cartel, and allow it to charge monopoly prices and reap monopoly profits. The presence of potential entrants will always limit monopolistic behavior.

9. Market theories are said to have the happy consequence of getting individuals to think in more focused and analytical ways. Has this happened to you? Give examples to illustrate.

This is purely a subjective question based upon the student's own reflection of how much he or she has learned to this point.

10. Give an example of a prisoner's dilemma situation other than the two mentioned in this chapter.

Take two major league baseball owners, each of whom would like to restrain the runaway escalation of player salaries, but who are prevented from discussing individual players' situations with one another. Assuming that both would also like to win their respective pennants, each will be forced to assume that the other will pay whatever it takes, and, thus, salaries will continue to rise.

11. How are oligopoly and monopolistic competition alike? How are they different?

In both market structures market power exists among some or all suppliers -- in the oligopoly it's because of the small number of suppliers, in monopolistic competition, it's because of product differentiation. As a result, neither market will achieve the allocative efficiency of a perfectly competitive market, and producers in both markets may realize real economic profits. One significant difference between the two is the extent and nature of entry barriers. In oligopoly, they are typically significant -- that's the main reason why there are so few firms. In a monopolistically competitive market, there are no barriers, per se; however, if consumers have developed brand loyalty, there may be significant de facto barriers which will make it very difficult for new competitors to take on established firms.

12. In Exhibit 23-5, what is the highest dollar amount marginal cost can rise to without changing price? Explain.

MC can rise to $18. If it went any higher, then MC does not equal MR at 20 units, and the oligopolist would have to reduce output to produce efficiently, which would move him upward and leftward along his demand curve.

■ LECTURE SUPPLEMENTS

"Crocs of Gold," *The Economist*, March 25, 1995, p. 76.

This is one example of monopolistic competition which your students should be familiar with, and it shows some of the problems which firms can run into when trying to create some monopolistic power.

Lacoste originated the line of clothing which featured a crocodile on the shirt as a logo for the firm's product. The firm was founded by the French tennis star, Rene Lacoste, who was known on the court as "*le crocodile*". Lacoste allowed Crocodile to use its emblem in Hong Kong before Lacoste decided to move into the Asian market. Lacoste wants to keep Crocodile from moving into China, but Crocodile has its own ideas. This creates conflict between the parent and the franchise, and aids counterfeiters who keep all the profits for themselves.

This article provides a good example of the problems franchises can encounter.

"The Puzzling Infirmity of America's Small Firms," *The Economist*, February 18, 1995, pp. 63-64.

Monopolistically competitive and oligopolistic firms are usually larger than perfectly competitive firms. Monopolistically competitive and oligopolistic firms try to generate monopoly power which compensates for some of the diseconomies of scale which may be produced by their larger size. So are smaller firms more efficient?

The article shows that the number of small firms in the United States may be shrinking instead of expanding. During the 1980s, many small firms took over some of the activities of larger firms, either through high-tech products, flexible manufacturing techniques, or cost cutting. But during the 1990s, "downsizing" and greater emphasis on entrepreneurial activities within the firm have made large firms more competitive, relatively speaking. Whereas smaller firms thrive on research and introducing new products, they falter on marketing. As technologies converge, consolidations become inevitable.

The article also discusses how Thermo Electron is trying to get its employees to become more like employees of a small, entrepreneurial firm while maintaining the benefits of a larger company. Use this article to discuss whether small is beautiful or not, which leads to the next article.

"Small Isn't Beautiful in Sweden," *The Economist*, **February 18, 1995, p. 64.**

The problems small firms face in Sweden have little to do with the market and everything to do with government regulation. Heavy taxes and strict labor laws make it difficult for medium-sized firms to be profitable. Small firms which don't face the stringent rules have grown, and larger firms which can spread the fixed costs of these government regulations over many employees remain in business, but medium-sized businesses with between 20 and 200 employees represent a small portion of the private-sector workforce.

This article would provide a good starting point for discussing how government regulations influence the size and behavior of firms in the United States as well as in other countries.

CHAPTER 24

Government and Product Markets:
Antitrust and Regulation

Chapter 21 introduced students to the theory of perfect competition and the workings of the perfectly competitive market. Chapters 22 and 23 dealt with markets that are not perfectly competitive -- specifically, with the cases of monopoly, oligopoly, and monopolistic competition. One of the great debates in economic theory and policy concerns whether or not the government should intervene into these non-competitive market structures; and, if so, what form that intervention should take. Chapter 24 addresses this debate, looking at the rationale for government intervention, and the various ways that government intervenes in the market, as well as the recent trend towards reducing government intervention in certain markets. Specifically, Chapter 24 discusses the evolution of *antitrust law* -- law aimed at dealing with the anti-competitive tendencies of monopolies and other highly concentrated industries; regulation of monopolies; regulating non-monopolistic markets; and, the rationale and recent record for *deregulation*.

■ CHAPTER OBJECTIVES

Upon completing this chapter, your students should be able to:

- state the purpose of *antitrust law* and trace its development from the *Sherman Act* to the current reforms;

- explain the derivation of both *concentration ratios* and the *Herfindahl index* and their importance to antitrust law;

- define *natural monopoly*, and describe the different methods of regulating natural monopolies;

- discuss some of the problems associated with regulating natural monopolies, particularly the *regulatory capture theory*;

- contrast regulatory capture theory and the *public interest theory of regulation*; and,

- assess the recent track record of *deregulation*.

■ KEY TERMS

- antitrust law
- trust
- Herfindahl index
- horizontal merger
- vertical merger
- conglomerate merger

- natural monopoly
- regulatory lag
- capture theory of regulation
- public interest theory of regulation
- public choice theory of regulation

■ CHAPTER OUTLINE

I. **ANTITRUST** -- In Chapter 22 we learned that a monopoly produces less output, charges a higher price, and causes a welfare loss to society, relative to the perfectly competitive solution for an industry with the same revenue and cost considerations. As a result, many economists feel that government should take some action to restrict the activities of monopolies (and cartels, since they function as monopolies), and the formation of new monopolies and cartels. In this section we look at **antitrust law** -- *legislation passed for the stated purpose of controlling monopoly power and promoting competition.* The second section of this chapter will discuss regulation.

A. **Major Developments in Antitrust Law** -- Beginning with the 1890 *Sherman Act*, there have been seven major pieces of legislation that constitute U.S. antitrust policy.

1. **The Sherman Act (1890)** -- The origin of the term "antitrust" comes from the era of the Sherman Act. At the time that the Act was passed, firms often combined to form **trusts** -- *combinations of firms that come together to act as a monopolist.* The purpose of the Sherman Act was to "bust" such trusts, and was laid out in two provisions: (1) "*Every contract, combination . . ., or conspiracy, in restraint of trade or commerce among the several states, or with foreign nations, is hereby declared illegal;*" and, (2) "*Every person who shall monopolize, or attempt to monopolize, or combine or conspire with any other person or persons to monopolize any part of trade or commerce . . . shall be guilty of a misdemeanor.*"

2. **The Clayton Act (1914)** -- made the following business practices illegal when their effects *"may substantially lessen competition or tend to create a monopoly"*:

    a. **Price Discrimination** -- charging different customers different prices for the same product, where the price difference is not related to cost differences;

    b. **Exclusive Dealings** -- selling to a retailer on the condition that the retailer not carry any rival products;

    c. **Tying Contracts** -- agreements whereby the sale of one product is conditioned upon the purchase of some other product(s);

    d. **The Acquisition of Competing Companies' Stock, if the Acquisition Reduces Competition**; and,

e. **Interlocking Directorates** -- an agreement whereby the directors of one company sit on the board of directors of a competing firm. The Clayton Act prohibited interlocking directorates *under all circumstances*, regardless of their effect on competition.

3. **The Federal Trade Commission Act (1914)** -- In the same year that the Clayton Act was passed, Congress established the **Federal Trade Commission (FTC)** and empowered it to combat *"unfair methods of competition in commerce"* -- that is, methods considered to be "too aggressive."

4. **The Act (1936)** -- Passed in an attempt to decrease the failure rate of small businesses by protecting them from competition from large chain stores, the Act *prohibited suppliers from offering special discounts to large chain stores unless they also offered those discounts to everyone else.*

5. **The Wheeler-Lea Act (1938)** -- empowered the Federal Trade Commission (FTC) to deal with *false and deceptive trade practices.*

6. **The Celler-Kefauver Antimerger Act (1950)** -- designed to close a "loophole" in the Clayton Act by *banning anticompetitive mergers that occurred as a result of one company acquiring the physical assets of another company.*

B. **Unsettled Points in Antitrust Policy** -- Several important points remain unsettled in determining what firms should be subjected to antitrust scrutiny and how their competitive situation should be assessed.

1. **Does the Definition of the Market Matter?** -- Should a market be defined broadly or narrowly? Should only actual competitors be considered, or should potential competitors also be included? The way a market is defined and the number of competitors (real and potential) will significantly affect whether or not a particular firm or merger is found to be a monopoly or an attempt at monopolization.

2. **Concentration Ratios** -- Recall from Chapter 23, that a *concentration ratio* measures the percentage of total sales, revenues, profits, etc., accounted for by the four, eight, or twenty largest firms in the market. For many years, the four-firm concentration ratio was the "measuring stick" by which the competitiveness of an industry was measured. The problem with concentration ratios is that they ignore two key considerations: (1) the presence of foreign competition; and, (2) the degree to which market power is dispersed beyond the four (or eight) biggest firms -- that is, the total number of firms in the market and their ability to compete with the biggest firms.

3. **The Herfindahl Index** -- In 1982, the Justice Department replaced the four- and eight-firm concentration ratios with the Herfindahl index, which is *equal to the sum of the squared market shares of each firm in the industry* -- that is:

$$\text{Herfindahl index (HI)} = (S_1)^2 + (S_2)^2 + (S_3)^2 + \ldots + (S_n)^2,$$

where S_1 through S_n are the market shares of firms 1 through n.

Exhibit 24-1 compares the Herfindahl index to the four-firm concentration ratio. *The Justice Department considers any HI value less than 1,000 to be representative of an unconcentrated industry. Furthermore, any merger in a previously unconcentrated industry that raises the HI value by less than 200 points is allowable.*

C. **Mergers** -- There are three basic types of mergers.

    1. **Horizontal Merger** -- is a merger between firms that are selling similar products in the same market.

    2. **Vertical Merger** -- is a merger between companies in the same industry, but at different stages of the production process.

    3. **Conglomerate Merger** -- is a merger between companies in different industries.

D. **Antitrust and Mergers** -- The government looks most carefully at proposed horizontal mergers because these mergers are more likely to increase concentration and reduce competition than vertical or conglomerate mergers. See *the Economics In Our Times* feature" Antitrust Decisions: A Mixed Bag" for a review of several antitrust decisions. Do you agree with the government's decisions?

II. REGULATION

A. **The Case of Natural Monopoly** -- Recall from Chapter 22, if economies of scale are so pronounced in an industry that only one firm can survive, that firm is called a *natural monopoly*. Consider Exhibit 24-2. The profit-maximizing level of output for the natural monopolist is Q_1, but at Q_1 we have a problem: resources are allocated inefficiently. Q_2 represents the level of output necessary to achieve resource allocative efficiency. The question is: How can we achieve that level of output? There are two basic options: (1) The firm currently producing Q_1 could increase its output to Q_2; or, (2) another firm could enter the industry and produce the difference between Q_1 and Q_2.

    The problem, of course, is that, if the firm is a natural monopoly, it is not in its best interest to increase output to Q_2, nor will any firm be able to enter the industry and make up the difference between the monopoly's output and the efficient level of output for any length of time. Furthermore, as Exhibit 24-3 shows, the natural monopolist will charge a higher-than-competitive price (P_1). As a result, many people will argue that natural monopolies should be regulated. But how?

B. **Ways of Regulating the Natural Monopoly**

    1. **Price Regulation** -- One possibility is to regulate price. Specifically, we want to make the price the monopolist charges approximate the competitive price as much as possible. In order to do this, we may use **marginal-cost pricing**, which requires the monopoly to *charge a price equal to its marginal cost*. In Exhibit 24-4, this price is shown as P_1. The problem with marginal-cost pricing is that it *usually results in the monopolist suffering a loss* -- a result that cannot be sustained for long.

    2. **Profit Regulation** -- A second possibility is to limit the monopolist to zero economic profit, either by taxing all economic profits away, or by using **average-cost pricing**, which *requires the monopolist to charge a price equal to average total cost*. In Exhibit 24-4, this price is shown as P_2. The problem here is that the monopolist has no

incentive to minimize costs, since it will be allowed to pass all costs on to customers, and gains no additional benefit by being cost-efficient.

3. **Output Regulation** -- The third possibility is for government to mandate a quantity of output it wants the natural monopoly to produce. In this way, the government can assure a particular level of output, and the monopolist can gain additional economic profits by lowering its costs.

C. **Problems with Regulating a Natural Monopoly** -- Regulation of natural monopolies runs into three potential snags: distorted incentives, poor information, and time lags.

1. **Distorted Incentives** -- To reiterate, any regulation -- price, profit, or output -- that guarantees zero economic profit for the natural monopoly will eliminate the monopolist's incentives to reduce costs. Furthermore, the owners of regulated monopolies will have an incentive to use time and otherwise-productive resources in the pursuit of influencing their regulators -- which, as we saw with rent-seeking, is highly inefficient.

2. **Information Problems** -- Each of the types of regulation we discussed requires information. Three problems arise here: (1) Cost information is not easy to come by, even for the firm itself; (2) what cost information is available can be "rigged" by the firm; and, (3) regulators have little incentive to obtain accurate information, since their jobs do not depend on it.

3. **Time Lags** -- Lastly there is the **regulatory lag** -- the period of time between when a monopoly's costs change and when the regulatory agency adjusts prices for the monopoly. The lag time may be months, as such changes require public hearings, and public hearings require prior notification and information dispersal. During the time between cost change and price change, the monopoly is liable to be operating at an even-less efficient level, and may be suffering an economic loss.

D. **Regulating Industries That Are Not Natural Monopolies** -- Not all regulated industries are natural monopolies -- in fact, most are not. Some non-natural monopolies are regulated in order to ensure service to customers, some because the service is considered too essential to be determined by market price, some to protect existing firms from "cut-throat" competition. The sensibility of such regulation is part of the next section. For an example of how cabs are regulated in London, see *The Global Economy* feature, "On the Streets of London Town."

E. **Theories of Regulation** -- Finally, we look at two theories of regulation: the *regulatory capture hypothesis*, and the *public interest theory of regulation*.

1. **The Capture Theory of Regulation** -- *no matter what the motive for the initial regulation, eventually the agency responsible for the regulation will be "captured" (controlled) by the industry that is being regulated.* As a result, the regulatory measures enacted will be affected by this relationship. There are several reasons to support the capture theory. First, regulatory agencies are often staffed by former employees of the regulated firm(s). Second, regulated industries will generally be disproportionately represented at regulatory hearings, since consumers/taxpayers often do not make the effort to attend. Third, regulated firms will expend substantial resources lobbying their regulators.

258

2. **The Public Interest Theory of Regulation** -- holds that *regulators are seeking to do, and will do through regulation, what is in the best interest of society at large.* An alternative to both theories is the **public choice theory of regulation**. This theory says that regulators are seeking to do, and will do through regulation, what is in *their* best interest. Specifically, they will do what enhances their power and the size and budget of their regulatory agency.

F. **Social Regulation** -- *Social regulation* is concerned with the conditions under which goods and services are produced and the safety of these items for the consumer. The most important government agencies which provide this regulation are the Occupational Safety and Health Administration (OSHA), the Consumer Product Safety Commission (CPSC), and the Environmental Protection Agency (EPA). Opponents of social regulation say that the economic costs of social regulation are high, but proponents say that the benefits of regulation exceed their costs.

G. **The Costs and Benefits of Regulation** -- If the EPA imposes pollution controls on a firm which in turn fires a worker because of the extra costs the EPA has imposed upon them, the worker may oppose this regulation. But if the pollution would have caused the worker cancer, the costs of continuing on the job would have been high. Economists are not necessarily for or against regulation, but analyze the costs and benefits of regulation.

H. **Some Effects of Regulation are Unintended** -- While regulations may solve some problems, they can unintentionally create other problems. For example, if the government mandates greater fuel efficiency to reduce the United States' dependence on oil, this can reduce the cost of traveling and may encourage people to travel more, increasing the amount of pollutants which cars emit. Similarly, deregulation of the airlines has reduced airfares, but it has also made flying more complicated. See the *Economics In Our Times* feature, "Phoenix to New York, with a Change in Dallas" for an explanation why.

I. **Deregulation** -- Using the capture and public choice theories of regulation, economists began arguing that regulation actually promoted and protected market power instead of reducing it. The solution? Deregulate.

J. **A Question for Economist George Stigler** -- George Stigler is closely associated with the capture theory of regulation. But the theory raises an important question. Does it follow that where deregulation exists, the broadly based public interest has somehow come to outweigh the special interests? Not necessarily, as the example of the SEC's regulation of commission rates shows, they were beneficiaries of this deregulation.

K. **Deregulation and Technology** -- Technology can change the need for deregulation. Local cable provision of telephone service is a natural monopoly. Long distance service is not a natural monopoly. So AT&T charged a high price for access to local telephone service. In 1982, AT&T agreed to the Justice Department's request to break itself up.

III. **ECONOMICS ON THE INTERNET** -- Sources for information on antitrust and regulation from the Department of Justice and the Federal Trade Commission are highlighted in this section.

■ ANSWERS TO CHAPTER QUESTIONS

1. Why was the Robinson-Patman Act passed? The Wheeler-Lea Act? The Celler-Kefauver Antimerger Act?

The Robinson-Patman Act was passed in an attempt to decrease the failure rate of small businesses by protecting them from competition from large chain stores. The Act prohibited suppliers from offering special discounts to large chain stores unless they also offered those discounts to everyone else. The Wheeler-Lea Act empowered the Federal Trade Commission (FTC) to deal with false and deceptive trade practices. The Celler-Kefauver Antimerger Act was designed to close a "loophole" in the Clayton Act by banning anticompetitive mergers that occurred as a result of one company acquiring the physical assets of another company.

2. Explain why defining a market narrowly or broadly can make a difference in how antitrust policy is implemented.

If a market is defined narrowly, there is a greater probability that a given firm will be said to be dominant in the market. Since the stated objective of antitrust policy is to promote competition, and to reduce domination of a market by a single firm, the more narrowly a market is defined, the more likely antitrust action will be taken against a firm.

3. What is one difference between the four-firm concentration ratio and the Herfindahl index?

The four-firm concentration ratio ignores the relative concentration which exists among the four largest firms and smaller firms while the Herfindahl index attempts to measures this.

4. How does a vertical merger differ from a horizontal merger? Why would the government look more carefully at one than at the other?

Whereas a vertical merger occurs between firms at different stages of production, horizontal mergers occur between firms at the same stage of production. Horizontal mergers are more likely to increase concentration and reduce competition within an industry than a vertical merger, so the government looks more closely at horizontal mergers.

5. What is the implication of saying that regulation is likely to affect incentives?

It implies that a firm's behavior without regulation is likely to be different than it is with regulation. For example, if government were to regulate a natural monopoly by mandating that it could earn only zero economic profits -- and it was not allowed to earn more, or less -- then we would expect that the firm would have less reason to keep its costs down.

6. Explain price regulation, profit regulation, and output regulation.

All three are methods for regulating natural monopolies. Price regulation has the firm set price equal to marginal cost to achieve allocative efficiency; however, the firm may be unable to make a profit at this price. Profit regulation has the firm set price equal to average total cost; however, the firm loses its incentive to reduce cost when average-cost pricing is used. Output regulation mandates the quantity which the natural monopoly produces; however, the firm might lower the quality of the product as a way of increasing its profits.

7. Why might profit regulation lead to rising costs for the regulated firm?

Under profit regulation, the firm is allowed to use its average total costs after allowing for some return on capital. If average total costs rise, the firm is allowed to raise its price. Consequently, the firm does not have an incentive to lower its costs, and costs may rise.

8. What is the major difference between the capture hypothesis (or capture theory of regulation) and the public interest theory of regulation?

The public interest theory of regulation holds that regulators not only seek to benefit the public interest with regulation, but that this will be the effect of their intent. The capture hypothesis says that no matter what the intent of the regulators (good, bad, or indifferent), the result of setting up regulations and regulatory agencies is that the special interests -- or those who are supposedly the ones to be regulated -- will end up controlling the regulatory agency. In conclusion, the public interest theory of regulation holds that the public interest will be served through regulation; the capture hypothesis holds that the interests of the regulated will be served. Thus the two theories reach different conclusions as to the beneficiary of the regulation.

9. George Stigler and Claire Friedland studied both unregulated and regulated electric utilities and found no difference in the rates charged by them. One could draw the conclusion that regulation is ineffective when it comes to utility rates. What ideas or hypotheses presented in this chapter might have predicted this?

Two, in particular, can be mentioned. First, the chapter noted that regulators do not have complete information about the costs of the regulated firm. Consequently the regulated firm may be able to present a cost picture (to the regulators) that is most likely to give it what it wants. Second, the capture hypothesis would have predicted this outcome. If the regulators are "captured" or controlled by the regulated firm, then regulation will likely give the regulated firm what it wants.

10. The courts have ruled that it is a *reasonable restraint of trade* (and therefore permissible) for the owner of a business to sell his business and sign a contract with the new owner saying he will not compete with her within a vicinity of, say, 100 miles, for a period of, say, 5 years. If this is a reasonable restraint of trade, can you give an example of what you would consider an unreasonable restraint of trade? Explain how you decide what is a reasonable restraint of trade and what isn't.

Clearly, the distinction between a "reasonable" restraint of trade and an "unreasonable" one must rest on the restraints overall effect on the competitiveness of a market. In the case of a single owner signing a "no-compete" agreement (as such things are often called), the negative effect on

261

the degree of competition within the industry is likely to be negligible. On the other hand, a restraint such as an organized boycott of a group of producers and/or consumers would likely have much more effect on the overall competitiveness of the industry, and will be more likely to be considered "unreasonable."

As far as the students' definitions are concerned, there is no single "right" answer; however, the rationale for the answer and the example should be consistent and sensible.

---

11. In your opinion what is the best way to deal with the monopoly power problem? Do you advocate antitrust laws or regulation, or something else we didn't discuss? Give reasons for your answer.

There is no correct answer here, only good ones and bad ones (as to the quality of the reasons given for the answer).

12. It is usually asserted that public utilities such as electric companies and gas companies are natural monopolies. But an assertion is not proof. How would you go about trying to prove (disprove) that electric companies and the like are (are not) natural monopolies? (Hint: You might consider comparing the average total cost of a public utility that serves many customers with the average total cost of a public utility that serves relatively few customers.)

Ideally, we would conduct an experiment which would allow one or more competing firms to enter the market, and then determine whether the market is capable of sustaining them all, or whether there is, in fact, room for only one firm. In real life, such an experiment would be costly and potentially disruptive to residential and business customers. So, perhaps the best way to determine if a firm is a natural monopoly is to compare it to a similar market -- where the product, number of customers, and cost structure closely approximates the market in question -- and see whether that market enables more than one firm to produce at the minimum efficient scale.

13. Discuss the advantages and disadvantages (as you see it) of regulation.

The primary advantage of regulation is that it can reduce market failures which exist such as the presence of externalities, public goods, monopoly power, and so forth. The government can subsidize positive externalities and tax negative externalities, or the government can provide these goods directly, for example, providing free flu shots or banning the production of a lethal chemical. Because public goods are non-excludable, private firms would be unable to collect enough revenue to provide the good, so the government must provide the good, using their power to collect taxes to fund the good. In the case of monopoly power, in the absence of public regulation, an inefficient level of the good would be produced, reducing economic welfare. The government can remedy this situation either by regulating a natural monopoly or by preventing firms from merging and increasing their market power.

Theory and practice often differ, and this leads to the disadvantages of regulation. The capture theory of regulation shows that government regulators may respond more readily to the demands of the regulated interest group than to the public as a whole because relatively speaking, the interest group receives greater benefits from the government's intervention than individual consumers are hurt. Interest groups will demand, and may receive, regulation which benefits them, without clearly considering the impact on the rest of society. There is evidence for government regulators both making choices which primary benefit the regulatees, and making choices which benefit society as a whole.

14. Calculate the Herfindahl Index and the four-firm concentration ratio.

Firms	Market Share
A	17 %
B	15
C	14
D	14
E	12
F	10
G	9
H	9

The four-firm concentration ratio for this industry would be 60% and the Herfindahl Index would be 1312.

■ LECTURE SUPPLEMENTS

"Microsoft's Divorce Court," *Time* **(145), May 8, 1995, p. 84.**

There are, of course, many articles relating to the government's intervention in Microsoft's attempt to buy out Intuit, and any would be suitable for the course.

The gist of the Microsoft-Intuit case was that Microsoft wanted to buy out Intuit which produces the best selling money management software which is available, Quicken. Microsoft has put out their own software, Microsoft Money, but it has not been as successful as Quicken. Microsoft has established themselves in the software business, providing the operating system for the vast majority of IBM-compatible computers, and expanding into the "office suite" business where they currently make up 90 percent of the market with their Microsoft Office software.

Realizing the potential that the Internet and electronic banking offer, Microsoft is trying to move into those areas, but is facing stiff competition from Intuit. Microsoft's solution? If you can't beat 'em, buy 'em. However, the government thought otherwise.

There are similarities between the way the Justice Department is treating Microsoft today and the way the Justice Department went after IBM in the 1970s. IBM also had a near-monopoly in the mainframe computer field, built primarily through technological innovation and marketing aggressiveness. The Justice Department finally gave up their battle after Reagan was elected, and ironically, this is when IBM began to face problems. They failed to realize the impact personal computers would have on the market and fell behind.

The Microsoft case should provide an excellent example of the role of the government in regulating monopoly. Is Microsoft being hounded by the government because it is successful, or does it use its operating system to create monopoly wealth for itself? As long as Microsoft continues to be successful, the battle between it and the Justice Department will probably continue.

"Thoroughly Modern Monopoly," *The Economist*, **July 8, 1995, p. 76.**

This article looks at how firms in the technology industry are able to create monopolistic power for themselves and the role which the Justice Department can play in keeping these firms from using their power at the expense of consumers. As the article shows, there is good reason to believe that high-tech companies have a tendency to become monopolistic for sound, economic reasons.

Networks provide one possible cause of market failure. If networks cannot communicate with one another, then they are no longer networks, so a single standard is needed to insure that networks can exist. This fact will bias the market toward a single firm and standard rather than allowing consumers to choose among hundreds of competitors.

Every computer needs an operating system, and as Microsoft has shown, this gives the firm which provides the operating system a competitive advantage in providing the software for word processing, spreadsheets and other applications. Whoever establishes the industry standard is going to have tremendous power within the market, as Microsoft has illustrated.

On the other hand, the essence of technology is innovation, and innovation means cost reduction. Intel is certainly the standard for semiconductors which run computers, but they are constantly innovating and lowering prices to insure that their competitors do not catch up with them.

Herein lies the problem. How much of a trade-off is there between some monopoly power by creating a successful product or standard and the winds of innovation which force firms to continually adapt to the changing market? And as always, the most important question is, how can we be assured that regulators will be able to better choose which standards will succeed than the market? The article concludes by suggesting that this final question would suggest that trustbusters should probably rely upon the market to do the regulating for them.

"Off-Line," *The Economist*, **May 27, 1995, p. 59.**

This article looks at antitrust enforcement in both America and in Europe. Just as the United States Department of Justice had intervened in the Microsoft-Intuit merger, the German government intervened in the proposed merger between Deutsche Telekom and France Telecom to carry out a joint venture named Atlas. As the article shows, since 1992, investigations by the Department of Justice in restraint of trade has increased, and the article reviews the government's decision to stop the Microsoft-Intuit merger.

The article compares the German government's decision not to stop a joint venture between British Telecom and MCI with the decision to stop the Atlas joint venture, explaining why one was allowed to proceed and the other was not. The article provides a good look at why government officials make the decisions which they make and contrasts the current attempts at trust-busting with those which occurred around the turn of the century in the United States.

CHAPTER 25

Agriculture: Farmers' Problems, Government Policies, and Unintended Effects

This chapter focuses on the issues facing the U.S. agricultural sector. Agriculture has no monopoly power, and it is a perfectly competitive industry. Nevertheless, the government plays a very active role in this industry. Beginning with a theoretical discussion of the problems facing the typical farmer -- high productivity, income- and price-inelastic demand, and unstable prices -- the chapter then turns to the various types of policies that the federal government has enacted over the years to assist farmers, and assesses their impact on three groups: farmers, consumers, and taxpayers.

■ CHAPTER OBJECTIVES

Upon completing this chapter, your students should be able to:

- identify the major economic problems facing farmers and describe their effects on farmers and consumers, on price and output;

- describe the relationship between inelastic demand and price instability and understand the tremendous amount of uncertainty involved in both farming and making agricultural policy;

- calculate a *parity price ratio*, and use it to determine whether farm prices are rising, falling, or holding steady, relative to other prices;

- explain why farmers, as a group, might prefer bad weather to good weather;

- define *price supports*, *supply restrictions*, and *target prices*, describe how they work, and assess their impact on farmers, consumers, and taxpayers; and,

- discuss the three types of supply-restricting policies that have been used (or are currently in use), by the U.S. government.

■ KEY TERMS

- income elasticity of demand
- parity price ratio
- price elasticity of demand
- price support
- target price

■ CHAPTER OUTLINE

I. **AGRICULTURE: THE ISSUES** -- From the perspective of some farmers, there are three issues of major concern: high productivity in the agricultural sector, income inelasticity for certain foodstuffs, and price inelasticity for certain foodstuffs. Related to these three issues is the problem of price instability in the agricultural sector.

   A. **Agriculture and High Productivity** -- Since the turn of the century, the productivity of the American farmer has increased more than four-fold -- more than the economy-wide increase in productivity during that same period. As a result, the supply curve of farm products has shifted rightward, lowering relative prices; but, because the demand for many foodstuffs is inelastic, lower prices have meant lower total revenues for farmers, rather than the higher revenues one might expect. [See Exhibit 25-1]

   B. **Agriculture and Income Inelasticity** -- Recall, from Chapter 18, that the income elasticity of demand measures the change in quantity demanded brought about by a change in income. If the change in income is proportionally greater than the change in quantity demanded -- that is, if $|E_Y| < 1$ -- we say that demand is income inelastic. Studies estimate that the income elasticity of foodstuffs in the U.S. is less than 0.2 -- meaning that a 10% increase in income increases food purchases by less than 2%.

   If we put the income inelasticity of demand for food together with high productivity, we see that the supply of food has been increasing significantly faster than the demand for food, reducing prices. [See Exhibit 25-2] In fact, if we look at the prices that farmers pay, relative to the prices that they earn for their products -- the **parity price ratio** -- Exhibit 25-3 shows us that agricultural prices have fallen relative to other prices over most of this century.

   C. **Agriculture and Price Inelasticity** -- Finally, the demand for many agricultural products is price inelastic, meaning that a decrease in price will result in lower total revenues to farmers. If market demand is inelastic, and supply is subject to severe shifts from season to season -- owing largely to unpredictable weather -- it follows that (1) price changes are likely to be large, and (2) total revenue is likely to be highly volatile. [See Exhibit 25-4]

   The instability of price and total revenue (farmers' gross income) increases the uncertainty associated with farming. Typically, farmers argue that they have no idea what prices will be when they bring their products to market from season to season. As a result, they argue, it is almost impossible to make rational planting decisions.

   D. **Price Variability and Futures Contracts** -- There is one way farmers can reduce their uncertainty over future prices -- *futures contracts*. The futures contract passes the risk of future price fluctuations from the farmer to the speculator who sells the contract. No matter what happens to the price of the commodity between the purchase of the futures contract and the delivery date, the farmer's price is guaranteed. Although the futures contract protects the farmer against a fall in the price of wheat or some other commodity, the farmer can no longer benefit from any increase in wheat prices.

E. **Can Bad Weather Be Good for Farmers?** -- An interesting sidelight to this discussion is the case of good and bad weather and their effects on the individual farmer and all farmers, as a whole. For an individual farmer, concerned with total revenue in a market where price is set by market forces, good weather is always preferable to bad weather, for good weather will increase his/her production and total revenue, given the market price. For farmers as a whole, however, bad weather may be preferable to good weather, as bad weather may reduce supply sufficiently to raise price; and, if demand is price inelastic (as we have assumed), total revenues will rise.

F. **The Changing Farm Picture** -- Because of the problems directly and indirectly related to high productivity, income inelastic demand, and price inelastic demand, the U.S. farm picture today is significantly different than it was in years past. The *number of farms is down significantly* since 1900, and both *farm population and farm employment are also down sharply* since the 1940s.

II. **AGRICULTURE POLICIES: EFFECTS ON FARMERS, TAXPAYERS, AND CONSUMERS** -- Farmers could solve many of their problems if they could control the supply of and/or the prices of their products. But farmers have been unable to control supply and price by themselves, and so they have turned to the government for help. The result has been a variety of farm-relief policies, which have generally fallen into one of three categories: *price supports, supply restrictions,* and *target prices.*

A. **Price Supports** -- An agricultural **price support** is *a government-guaranteed minimum price* -- a price floor, that is, *where the government guarantees to purchase all unsold quantities of the good at the guaranteed price.* Look at Exhibit 25-5. If the minimum price is set above the equilibrium price, a surplus will result -- quantity supplied will be greater than quantity demanded -- which government will have to buy and store, and consumers will buy less of the good than at the equilibrium price.

So, *the consequences of a price support above equilibrium are: (1) a surplus; (2) fewer private exchanges (less quantity demanded); (3) higher prices paid by consumers; and, (4) government purchase and storage of the surplus product (for which taxpayers pay).*

B. **Restricting Supply** -- Prices of agricultural products can also be increased indirectly by restricting supply. *The objective of any supply restriction is to shift the supply curve leftward,* as shown in Exhibit 25-6, *and raise price against a given demand curve.* The U.S. government has used three types of supply restrictions: (1) assigning acreage allotments; (2) assigning market quotas; and (3) paying farmers not to produce.

1. **Acreage Allotment Program** -- The **acreage allotment program** *limits the number of acres that can be used to produce a particular crop.* The allowable total acreage is distributed among eligible farmers, often on the basis of the farmers' historical production of that crop. The idea is to reduce the amount of the crop grown by reducing the land that is used to grow it. In fact, one of the common problems encountered by acreage allotment programs is that farmers take their least-productive land out of production and farm the remaining land more intensively, so

that the actual reduction in output (if any) is nowhere near what the government wanted.

2. **Marketing Quota System** -- Under a **marketing quota**, government does not restrict land usage, but instead sets *a limit on the quantity of a product that a farmer is allowed to bring to market*.

    a. **Soil Bank Program** -- The **soil bank program**, initiated in 1956, *paid farmers to take their land out of production*. As under acreage allotment, farmers tend to take their least-productive land out of production and farm their remaining land more intensively. In effect, farmers are paid not to grow food. You might ask your students whether they think economic professors should be paid not to teach.

    b. **Target Prices and Deficiency Payments** -- Another way the government tries to aid farmers is by setting a **target price**. This is different from a price support, because the government doesn't guarantee the target price, it only *guarantees to pay farmers any difference between the target price and the actual market price*. That is, if the target price is $6 and the equilibrium price is $4, farmers will sell the equilibrium level of output to consumers at $4, and the government will pay farmers a *deficiency payment* of $2 per unit, as described in Exhibit 25-7. As a result, the target price system doesn't create or have to deal with large surpluses; but, of course, farmers will tend to increase output by more than if there were no support, thus driving the market price down, and causing deficiency payments to rise.

C. **Agricultural Prices, Land Prices, and Rent** -- The benefits of the government's agricultural policies will be included in the price of land because ownership of the land grants the farmer the right to receive the government's price supports. Consequently, the landowner who rents land to a farmer would receive the benefits of the price supports, not the person who actually did the farming.

D. **Do Agriculture Policies Have Any Unintended Effects?**

    1. **Agricultural Payments for the "Rich?"** -- Approximately two-thirds of all agricultural program payments go to the largest 18 percent of farms. The average farm payment recipient is no longer poor.

    2. **Financial Barriers to Becoming a Farmer** -- By making farming more profitable, agricultural policies increase the price of farm land, making it more difficult for non-wealthy individuals to become farmers.

    3. **Discouraging Environmentally Beneficial Practices** -- Farmers plant the crops which receive the highest subsidies, and by doing so, they may ignore the importance of crop rotation, reducing the fertility of the land they farm.

E. **The Politics of Corn** -- This *Economics In Our Times* feature provides a very good explanation of why agricultural policies continue despite their apparent economic inefficiency. The average farmer receives $10,000 in benefits while the program costs the average taxpayer $1.33. Farmers can better afford to fight to save these programs than individual taxpayers can afford to fight to repeal them. *The Global Economy* feature, "Farmers Around the World" shows that U.S. farmers aren't the only ones receiving government aid. In fact, farmers in all other industrialized countries (except Australia and New Zealand) receive greater support from their governments than farmers do in the United States.

III. **ECONOMICS ON THE INTERNET** -- If you want to know how the price subsidy program works, you can use the Internet sites which are provided to get information on this and other agricultural data.

■ ANSWERS TO CHAPTER QUESTIONS

1. What is the connection between inelastic demand and price instability?

If demand is highly inelastic, a large decrease in supply brings about a large rise in price. Similarly, if demand is highly inelastic, a large increase in supply brings about a large fall in price. In short, for any given change in supply, the more inelastic demand is, and the larger the change in price.

2. Why don't all supply-restricting agricultural policies work as intended?

Supply-restricting policies that seek to limit the number of acres farmers can farm often do not limit supply to the desired level because farmers tend to increase the productivity of their remaining acreage.

3. Some people argue that unless small family farms are assisted through price supports, target prices, or supply-restricting policies, they will soon disappear and large (corporate) farms will control food production in this country. Some go even further and say that without government assistance to small farmers, agriculture will cease to be a perfectly competitive market and will become an oligopolistic market. Today, 5 percent of all farms have annual sales over $200,000 and are considered large farms. If the agriculture industry comes to be dominated by these large farms, is it likely that agriculture will become an oligopolistic market?

One of the characteristics of oligopoly is *few sellers.* There are approximately 2.1 million farms in the United States today. Five percent of this is 105,000 farms. Even if there were only 105,000 farms in the agriculture industry, it is doubtful that agriculture could be considered an example of oligopoly. The number of sellers would still be too large.

4. How might government reduce the amount of farm payments in the federal budget and still assist farmers?

In order to reduce the amount of farm payments in the federal budget, government must reduce or eliminate the price support and target price programs, both of which end up costing taxpayers something (in the price support program taxpayers have to pay for the purchase and storage of the surplus, and in the target price program taxpayers make the deficiency payments to farmers). In their place it could put a supply-restricting policy that forces farmers to take certain acreage out of production. If the supply-restricting policy is in fact successful in shifting the supply curve leftward, this would result in higher prices for agricultural products, which would be paid for by consumers. Higher prices paid for by consumers are not registered in the federal budget.

5. Critics of present-day agricultural policies argue that government does for farmers what they can't do for themselves: restrict supply and push prices up. Do you agree or disagree? Why?

It depends on which policy we are discussing. But, as a rule, yes, that is exactly what the government is often trying to do: restrict supply and increase prices received by farmers.

6. Some people contend that the majority of Americans realize that they subsidize farmers through various government programs, but they don't mind doing this because they know they are preserving a way of life. This argument assumes that America wouldn't be the same -- would in some way be diminished -- without family farms and that it is worth paying taxes to preserve them. What do you think of this argument? How would you go about determining how much truth there is in it?

The average American probably has very little idea of the extent of agricultural price supports and other programs which drive up food prices; and, if they did, they would probably scream bloody murder.

Probably the best way to determine just how much Americans are willing to pay to maintain the family farm is for the government to be forthright about the extent of its agricultural supports and their effects on prices. More to the point, consumers should be informed that they could buy the same foodstuffs at a price of $X or $X + $Y, where $Y is a price premium that helps to maintain the family farm. By determining the relative demand for the food at $X and at $X + $Y, we could see just how supportive the average American is of the family farm, and how far he/she is willing to go to express that support.

7. Do you think the number of farmers in the United States will increase, decrease, or stay roughly the same in the next 20 years? Why?

It all depends on agricultural productivity, in both the U.S. and abroad, and on population growth. If U.S. population growth remains fairly slow and agricultural productivity continues to rise, then the number of farmers needed will continue to decline, as long as demand for U.S. food from abroad does not increase significantly.

8. What is parity, and why is it important to farmers?

Parity is the ratio of an index of prices that farmers receive to an index of prices that farmers pay. Since 1910-1914, this ratio has consistently fallen. Measured in terms of output, rather than dollars, and ignoring productivity improvements, this means that farmers' purchasing power has consistently declined during the twentieth century.

9. How can good weather be desirable for an individual farmer, but not for farmers as a group?

270

Individual farmers desire good weather because only then will the farmer have a crop which can be harvested and brought to market. However, demand for food is price inelastic. As the price of food rises, the quantity demanded falls by a smaller percent than the increase in the price of food. A decrease in the supply of farmers' output produces an increase in the total revenue which farmers as a group receive. When there is a decline in output because of bad weather, some farmers have no crops left and suffer; however, farmers who were not directly affected by the bad weather will be able to sell their crops at a handsome profit.

10. List and explain the effects on consumers and on taxpayers of each of the following programs: (a) price supports, (b) target prices, and (c) acreage allotments.

Price supports (through the purchase of surplus crops) and target prices (through deficiency payments) are designed to directly increase the price that farmers receive for their crops. Acreage allotments reduce the amount of land devoted to specific crops in order to reduce the quantity supplied and thus increase the price of crops. Under the acreage allotment program, farmers might be paid to reduce the amount of planted land. In all three cases, taxpayers provide the funds to raise the price of agricultural goods. In all three cases, consumers have to pay higher prices for their food. The methods are different, but the results are the same.

■ LECTURE SUPPLEMENTS

"Farm Subsidies Face Almost Certain Cuts in the GOP Congress," *The Wall Street Journal*, **February 16, 1995, page A1, column 6.**

This article can provide students with a good introduction to how and why the government subsidizes farmers, and the problems that these subsidies create. First, explain to your students how the farm subsidy program works. In short, during the Great Depression, the government wanted to raise the income of farmers, so the government raised the price that farmers receive above the market clearing level. The result is excess supply which the government reduces both through export subsidies which increase demand, and subsidies to farmers who leave land idle in order to reduce the supply.

The article provides a chart showing the cost of the USDA's Commodity Credit Corp. which has spent as much as $25 billion in one year (1986) to support farmers. As in the article on rent controls, you should ask your students why the government is helping farmers. The ostensible reason is to keep farmers from going bankrupt or to live in poverty; however, most of the subsidies go to rich farmers, not poor ones. Since the subsidies are tied to production, the more a farm produces, the greater its subsidy. And even though subsidies cannot exceed $50,000 per person, each partner in a farm is eligible. In theory, a farm which had 1000 partners could receive $50,000,000 from the government.

The way the system works is that participating farmers are allowed to use their crops as collateral for loans from the government. If the market price slips below the per-bushel loan rate, farmers can repay their loan in kind rather than with money. This insures that prices do not fall below the government supported level. The government also sends farmers "deficiency" checks when prices fall below a certain level, and pays farmers to set aside some of their land and not grow food. (Ask your students if they think teachers should be paid not to teach!) Moreover, some crops are covered by price supports, but others are not, and only one-third of farmers receive any subsidies.

For detailing just how government restrictions on supply and demand work in the real world, this is an excellent article to use. Your students will not only learn a lot from this article, but also understand the costs of intervening in markets.

271

"Ploughshares into Carving Knives," *The Economist,* **October 7, 1995, pp. 28-29.**

This article can be used to update your students on the current debates in Congress over agricultural subsidies. The Republican Congress is attempting to cut some government expenditures, and one area which they have decided to attack is the agricultural subsidy program. The problem is the inevitable trade-off between economics and politics. Cutting agricultural subsidies may increase economic efficiency, but it is not necessarily politically prudent.

Even though the government is going to cut agricultural subsidies by 25 percent, biases show up in where the cuts come. The Chairman of the House Agriculture Committee, Pat Roberts, wants to change the current system with his Freedom to Farm Act which would convert the crop subsidies into straight cash welfare payments, cap them, and ratchet them down over seven years. Truth in advertising at last.

Farm states don't like these changes, and they have tried to undo them. Congress will probably abolish acreage set-aside policies, and scale back the programs in which the government buys up the farmers' crops. The article also discusses how scaling back the farm subsidies would affect different farmers. Wheat farmers in Kansas would be more adversely affected than farmers in Washington state because Kansas farmland grows wheat efficiently, but not much else. Cotton farmers oppose the plan because the Freedom to Farm Act would cap the maximum payment to farmers at $50,000 a year, much less than the $250,000 a year which some farmers now receive by using various loopholes. So politics is driving the debate over this plan for very solid financial reasons.

"Carter-Era Law Keeps the Price of Electricity Up In Spite of a Surplus," *The Wall Street Journal,* **May 17, 1995, p. A1, column 1.**

Although not about agriculture, this article can be used to show that the government's policies on agricultural subsidies can be applied to other areas of the economy just as easily. In this case, it is energy which is receiving the subsidies. When the United States was facing an energy crisis back in the 1970s, the government introduced numerous subsidies to find alternatives to petroleum as a source of energy to make sure the United States could survive when oil hit $100 a barrel.

The government addressed this problem by passing the Public Utility Regulatory Policies Act of 1978 (PURPA) which provided a system of generous payments to independent power producers and compelled utilities to buy the power. It is estimated that these power plants will receive $37 billion between now and the year 2000 over and above market prices. The problem is that the United States does not have a shortage of electric generating plants, but a surplus.

You won't be surprised to learn that the independent power producers are lobbying to protect their lucrative power contracts, and they want the government to allow the utilities to keep electricity prices high so they can pass their extra costs on to consumers. They say it would be unfair to abruptly subject the industry to competition.

The parallels between the alternative energy providers and farmers should be obvious, and would be instructive in class.

CHAPTER 26

Factor Markets: With Emphasis
on the Labor Market

Chapter 26 is the first of three chapters to focus on the theory and workings of *factor markets*. Studying factor markets serves two purposes: first, we begin to get a better grasp of what underlies the firm's cost curves; and, second, in and of themselves, they provide an interesting study of resource allocation and pricing in a market situation. Chapter 26 begins with some general information on factor markets, the various degrees of market power that firms have as suppliers of goods and demanders of factors, and the appropriate profit-maximizing behavior of firms in the factor market. The chapter then turns specifically to the labor market, and discusses the function of the (idealized) labor market, under the assumptions of perfect competition and perfect information. The chapter concludes with a discussion of the role of information in the labor market, with specific reference to its effects on hiring, promotion, and discrimination.

■ CHAPTER OBJECTIVES

Upon completing this chapter, your students should be able to:

- explain the impact of derived demand on factor markets;

- define *marginal revenue product (MRP)* and *marginal factor cost (MFC)*, and explain why firms maximize profits by hiring/buying inputs at the point where MRP = MFC;

- state and explain the *least-cost rule* for hiring combinations of two or more inputs;

- identify the factors which will affect the demand for labor and the supply of labor;

- describe how the equilibrium wage rate is determined in a competitive labor market;

- explain why wages may differ between jobs;

- understand the factors which influence the elasticity of demand for labor; and,

- use *marginal productivity theory* to determine the appropriate wage for labor in a competitive market.

■ KEY TERMS

- derived demand
- marginal revenue product
- factor price taker
- value marginal product
- least-cost rule
- elasticity of demand for labor
- marginal productivity theory
- screening

■ CHAPTER OUTLINE

I. FACTOR MARKETS

A. Derived Demand -- A firm hires factors of production for one specific purpose: to produce the firm's product. As a result, the firm's demand for factors is closely related to the demand for the firm's output in the product market-- that is, the firm's demand for factors is **derived demand**, dependent upon the demand for the firm's product. *If the demand for the product rises, the firm's demand for factors rises; if demand for the product falls, the firm's demand for factors falls.*

B. Marginal Revenue Product -- Exactly how many additional (fewer) factors should the firm hire/buy if the demand for its product changes? To answer this question, we need two concepts. The first is **marginal revenue product (MRP)** -- *the additional revenue generated by employing an additional unit of a factor;* that is,

$$MRP = \Delta TR / \Delta \text{ quantity of the factor.}$$

Alternatively, we can calculate MRP using the concept of marginal revenue, such that

$$MRP = MR \times MPP_X,$$

where MPP_X, the *marginal physical product* of factor X, is the additional quantity of output produced by using one more unit of factor X. There are two ways of calculating marginal revenue product, as illustrated in Exhibit 26.1

1. **MRP = Δ TR/ Δ quantity of the factor** -- as shown in Exhibit 26-1a.

2. **MRP = MR x MPP** -- as shown in Exhibit 26-1b.

C. The MRP Curve is the Factor Demand Curve -- See Exhibit 26-2.

D. Value Marginal Product (MPP) -- is equal to the price of the product times the marginal physical product of the factor, or

$$VMP = P \times MPP.$$

E. An Important Question: Is MRP = VMP? -- Yes for price takers and no for price searchers. Yes, MRP equals VMP for a perfectly competitive firm because price equals marginal revenue for a perfectly competitive firm. No, VMP > MRP for monopolists, monopolistic competitors and oligopolists because P > MR for these firms.

F. **Marginal Resource Cost (MFC)** -- is the additional cost incurred by employing an additional factor unit. It is calculated as

$$MFC = \Delta TC / \Delta \text{ quantity of the factor.}$$

Marginal factor cost for a price taker is shown in Exhibit 26-4.

G. **How Many Units of a Factor Should a Firm Buy?** -- The firm should continue to buy/hire units of a factor as long as MRP > MFC -- that is, as long as the new factor adds more to the firms revenues than it takes away in additional cost. The firm maximizes profits by buying/hiring just enough factors so that, for the last factor unit added

$$MRP = MFC.$$

H. **When There Is More Than One Factor, How Much of Each Factor Should the Firm Buy?** -- Suppose a firm requires two factors, labor and capital. In order to cost-minimize the firm should purchase those factors such that the MPP-to-price ratio for one factor equals the MPP-to-price ratio for the other factor. In other words,

$$\frac{MPP_L}{P_L} = \frac{MPP_K}{P_K}$$

where L = labor and K = capital. This is the **least-cost rule** which shows the firm how it can spend its money on labor and capital most effectively.

You should notice that the least-cost rule for the firm is similar to the way consumers allocate their money to choosing consumer goods (as discussed in Chapter 17). For consumers, the rule was

$$\frac{MU_A}{P_A} = \frac{MU_A}{P_A}$$

The application is different, but the methodology is the same.

A good example of this principle is provided in the *Economics In Our Times* feature, "Why Jobs Don't Always Move to the Low-Wage Country." The feature shows that even though Mexican workers may receive lower wages, their productivity may also be lower, and that firms which can hire highly productive workers in the United States will not move their factories to Mexico.

II. **THE LABOR MARKET** -- We now turn to the market for a specific factor of production -- labor -- and apply our basic concepts to that market while building a specific theory of the demand for and supply of labor, the optimal level of employment, and the equilibrium wage.

A. **Shifts in the Firm's MRP (or Factor Demand) Curve** -- Based upon our earlier discussion, recall that
$$MRP = MPP \times MR;$$

and, if we assume that the firm is a product price taker, MR = P, so

$$MRP = P \ x \ MPP.$$

From this, we can see that there are two things that can change MRP; and, thus, the firm's demand for factors: (1) the price of the product; and, (2) the MPP of the factor.

1.   **Changes in Product Price** -- *An increase in the price of the product will shift the MRP curve to the right; a decrease in the price of the product will shift the MRP curve to the left.* [See Exhibit 26-6]

2.   **Changes in Factor Productivity** -- *An increase in the productivity (MPP) of a given factor, relative to other factors, will shift the MRP curve for that factor to the right; a decrease in the MPP of a factor, relative to other factors, will shift the MRP curve to the left.*

B. **Market Demand for Labor** -- Given that background, let's look specifically at the demand for labor. Exhibit 26-7 shows the derivation of the market demand curve for labor. Notice that it is not simply a horizontal summation of the MRP curves of each individual firm in the market. Instead, the market demand curve must take into account the effect of wage increases on the supply and price of the output produced by the firms in the market. Since MRP reflects the price of those products, as supply and price adjust to higher wages, the MRP will also adjust, so that the market demand curve for labor tends to be much steeper than any individual firm's demand for labor.

C. **The Elasticity of Demand for Labor** -- This difference boils down to the difference between the elasticity of a single firm's demand for labor, and the elasticity of the entire market's demand. The **elasticity of demand for labor (E_L)** is *the percentage change in the quantity demanded of labor divided by the percentage change in the price of labor (wage rate).* That is,

$$E_L = \frac{\text{percentage change in quantity demanded of labor}}{\text{percentage change in wage rate}}$$

There are three main determinants of the elasticity of demand for labor.

1. **Elasticity of Demand for the Product that Labor Produces** -- Since the firm's demand for labor is largely dependent upon the demand for the product it produces, it shouldn't be surprising that there is a relationship between E_L and E_d. Specifically, *the greater the elasticity of demand for the product, the greater the elasticity of demand for labor; the lower the elasticity of demand for the product, the lower the elasticity of demand for labor.*

2. **Ratio of Labor Costs to Total Costs** -- The second major determinant is the *percentage of total costs for which labor costs are responsible.* The **labor cost-total cost ratio** measures this relationship. *The greater the labor cost-total cost ratio, the greater the elasticity of demand for labor; the lower the labor cost-total cost ratio, the lower the elasticity of demand for labor.*

3. **Number of Substitute Factors** -- Finally, the availability of substitute factors will affect the elasticity of demand for labor. The more substitutes, the more sensitive employers will be to changes in the wage rate. Thus, *the more substitutes for labor,*

the greater the elasticity of demand for labor; the fewer substitutes for labor, the lower the elasticity of demand for labor.

D. **The Supply of Labor** -- *As the wage rate rises, the quantity supplied of labor rises, ceteris paribus.* The upward-sloping market labor supply curve is illustrated in Exhibit 26-8. Even though the single price-taking firm faces a horizontal labor supply (MFC) curve, the market as a whole faces an upward-sloping labor supply curve. The upward slope of the curve reflects that individuals must receive sufficient wages to cover their opportunity cost of employment, and that opportunity cost rises as the quantity of labor-hours employed increases.

E. **Change in the Supply of Labor** -- There are two main factors which will affect the market labor supply curve: wage rates in other markets; and, the nonmoney aspects of a job.

   1. **Wage Rates in Other Labor Markets** -- The wage rate offered in other labor markets will serve as a check on the wage rate in a particular labor market. To the extent that workers can find employment in other markets, then the wage rate will have to accurately reflect their opportunity cost of employment. *If wage rates rise in other labor markets, the market labor supply curve will shift left; if wages fall in other labor markets, the market labor supply curve will shift to the right.*

   2. **Nonmoney or Nonpecuniary Aspects of a Job** -- Other things held constant, people prefer "enjoyable" jobs, to ones that involve dirty, heavy, socially unacceptable, or dangerous work. *An increase in the overall "unpleasantness" of a job will cause a leftward shift in the labor supply curve; an increase in the overall "pleasantness" of a job will cause a rightward shift in the labor supply curve.*

F. **Putting Supply and Demand Together** -- Exhibit 26-9 illustrates a typical labor market with an upward-sloping labor supply curve and a downward-sloping labor demand curve. The equilibrium of labor supply and labor demand determines the equilibrium wage rate and quantity of labor-hours employed in that market at any point in time. As with other markets we have studied, market forces will work to remedy a shortage of labor caused by a lower-than-equilibrium wage rate (W_3), and to remedy a surplus created by a higher-than-equilibrium wage rate (W_2).

G. **Why Do Wage Rates Differ?** -- Assume the following conditions hold: (1) the demand for every type of labor is the same; (2) there are no special nonpecuniary aspects to any job; (3) all labor is ultimately homogeneous and can be costlessly trained (and retrained) for different types of unemployment; and, (4) all labor is mobile at zero cost. In such a world, as Exhibit 26-10 illustrates, there would be no long run difference in wages rates between labor markets. However, in the "real" world, none of these assumptions hold universally.

H. **Why Demand and Supply Curves Differ in Different Labor Markets**

   1. **Differential Demand for Labor** -- The demand for labor may be quite different between markets. For one thing, *the demand for labor is largely conditioned on the demand for the product it produces*; and, to the extent that product demand varies from producer-to-producer, market-to-market, the demand for labor to produce that product will also vary. Secondly, worker productivity will vary between workers as

277

workers' abilities, skills, and degree of effort are different. To the extent that the *wage paid is also a function of the individual worker's productivity (MPP)*, different MPPs will yield different MRPs, which will cause wage differentials.

2. **Supply Factors** -- Factors on the labor supply "side" of the equation will also cause wage differentials between labor markets. First, there is the problem of *nonpecuniary aspects* of a given job -- some jobs are more "unpleasant" than others, and the wage paid reflects that fact. Second, labor supply reflects *available skills*, and some jobs require sufficiently technical skills and/or training that the supply of potential workers is limited. Thirdly, *training costs* to acquire certain skills may be sufficiently high that they restrict the supply of labor. Finally, *labor immobility* will create wage differentials if there is a mismatch between job location and worker location.

I. **Why Did You Choose the Major That You Chose?** -- Demand and supply play a role. There is greater demand for accountants than for history majors, and accountants receive higher salaries, so many students will choose accounting over history.

J. **Marginal Productivity Theory** -- Here are some things we now know:

1. **MFC = W** -- If the firm is a factor price taker, MFC = P (of the factor); so, in the case of labor, where the wage rate (W) is the price of the factor, we get MFC = W.

2. **MRP = MFC** -- Profit-maximizing firms hire the factor quantity at which MRP = MFC. For an unusual application of this principle, see *The Global Economy* feature, "How Much Is a Royal Family Worth?"

3. **MRP = W** -- Given points 1 and 2, a profit-maximizing factor price taker must pay labor a wage such that W = MRP.

4. **If the Firm is a Product Price Taker, MRP = VMP.**

5. **If the Firm is Both a Product Price Taker and a Factor Price Taker, Then W = VMP.**

This is the essence of **marginal productivity theory** -- *if a firm sells its product and purchases its factors in perfectly competitive markets* (and is, therefore, both a product price taker and a factor price taker), *it pays factors a price equal to their MRP or VMP, which are equal.*

III. **LABOR MARKETS AND INFORMATION** -- Finally, we turn to a brief discussion of certain observed behavior in the "real" world, and attempt to assess and explain it in light of marginal productivity theory.

A. **Employee Screening: Or, Does Your GPA Matter?** -- Employers typically do not know how productive a potential employee will be until they are actually hired and incorporated into the production process. What an employer wants, but lacks, is perfect information about a potential employee's future performance so that MPP and VMP may be estimated, in order to make a rational salary or wage offer. In order to try to minimize the risk of making a bad hiring decision, employers **screen** potential employees based upon certain criteria that they have found to be good indicators of success in the past.

B. **Promoting From Within** -- Sometimes employers promote from within their company, because they have better information on their own employees than on potential employees. What may look like discrimination to outsiders may simply be a reflection of the costs of acquiring relevant information on employees inside and outside the company.

C. **Is It Discrimination or Is It an Information Problem?** -- Oftentimes, what is called "discrimination" is, in fact, simply a problem of either lower relative productivity or of costly information. Suppose that Company A hires and promotes one type of person more than other types of people. Is it discrimination? It depends. If that types of person is relatively more productive, they should be hired and promoted disproportionately. What if a very highly-qualified minority candidate applied for a job and the firm turned him/her down? Is it discrimination? Again, it depends. If the firm turned the applicant down because they had never seen anyone like him/her, and the cost of acquiring the information necessary to assess his/her potential was considered prohibitive, the company could rationalize its action on the basis of overly-costly information. This isn't to suggest that there are not legitimate discrimination problems out there. Rather, it is to say: Not everything that looks like discrimination is necessarily discrimination, some of it has to do with relative productivity and some of it has to do with poor information.

IV. **ECONOMICS ON THE INTERNET** -- Several good sources of information dealing with labor and labor productivity are provided.

■ ANSWERS TO CHAPTER QUESTIONS

1. The supply curve is horizontal for a single price taker in a factor market; however, the industry supply curve is upward sloping. Explain why.

This is similar to the case we found in perfect competition in Chapter 21. There we noted that the firm's demand curve was horizontal, but that the market (or industry) demand curve was downward-sloping. In factor markets, we are simply talking about the supply side of the market instead of the demand side. The firm's supply curve is flat because it can hire additional factor units and not drive up the price of the factor because it buys a relatively small portion of the factor. For the industry, however, higher factor prices must be offered in order to entice workers from other industries. The difference in the two supply curves -- the firm's and the industry's -- is basically a reflection of the different sizes of the firm and the industry.

2. What forces and factors determine the wage rate for a particular type of labor?

The best way to answer this question is to ask you to visualize a two-dimensional diagram with a downward-sloping demand curve for labor and an upward-sloping supply curve of labor. The wage rate in a competitive market is determined by the forces of supply and demand. But these forces are what they are because of different factors.

On the demand side is the price or marginal revenue of the product that labor produces. This is related to the demand for and supply of the product. Also on the demand side is the marginal physical product of labor. This, in turn, is dependent upon a number of factors: the other factors labor works with; labor; a person's innate and learned abilities; and the degree of effort a person applies to the job.

The supply of labor in a particular labor market depends upon the wage rates in other labor markets; the nonmoney or nonpecuniary aspects of a job; the number of persons who can do a job; the costs of moving across labor markets; and training costs necessary to join the particular labor market.

3. What is the relationship between labor productivity and wage rates?

As labor productivity increases, so do wage rates. This is due to the fact that an increase in labor productivity (MPP) causes the demand for labor to rise.

4. What might be one effect of government legislating wage rates?

We learned in this chapter that wage rates are determined by the demand for and supply of labor. If either the supply of or demand for a type of labor changes, and government doesn't permit the wage rate to respond, we can expect to see either surpluses or shortages of labor in the particular labor market. Whether there is a surplus or shortage depends upon whether the legislated wage is above (surplus) or below (shortage) the equilibrium wage.

5. Using the theory developed in this chapter, explain the following: (a) why a worker in Ethiopia is likely to earn much less than a worker in Japan; (b) why the army expects recruitment to be up during economic recessions; (c) why basketball stars earn relatively large incomes; (d) why jobs that carry a health risk offer higher pay than jobs that do not, *ceteris paribus*.

a. Workers in Japan produce goods that are, as a rule, in much greater demand on the world market that those goods produced by workers in Ethiopia. As a consequence, the demand for labor will be higher in Japan, driving up wages. Additionally, Japanese workers are considerably more productive, owing largely to superior training and better tools and production techniques; thus, their MPP is higher, which raises their MRP, which should also result in higher wages.

b. During recessions, people buy less goods and services. As a result, labor demand falls, reducing the level of employment, and increasing the level of unemployment. With a larger pool of unemployed workers looking for work and a decent wage, the armed forces have a much better chance of recruiting otherwise disinterested prospects than if the labor market were tight and the economy were booming.

c. Basketball stars have natural abilities and developed skills that make them unique. As a result, they are in short supply, and firms wishing to hire them must pay exceptionally high wages in order to attract one or more.

d. Health risks would be considered a nonpecuniary aspect of a job. The greater the health risk, the greater the "unpleasantness" of the task, and the higher the wage that must be paid (*ceteris paribus*) to attract a worker to take a "risky" job over a less "risky" one.

6. Discuss the factors that might prevent the equalization of wage rates for identical or comparable jobs across labor markets.

Labor immobility, poor information, differing skills, varying degrees of productivity, and different supply and/or demand conditions for the products of labor may all create wage differentials for the same job across labor markets. First, if the supply of eligible workers is geographically concentrated, the wage those workers are paid in the areas where they are in great supply will be lower than the wage they are paid in areas where they are scarce.

Second, workers and/or employers may not realize that two jobs are sufficiently identical that they should pay the same wage. Workers and/or employers may not be aware of the wages that are being paid for similar work elsewhere.

Third, not all workers have the same skills and/or training. Thus, even if the job is the same, a worker with more experience, superior skills, and/or more or better training may be paid more on the assumption that she/he will be more productive at the same job than the average worker.

Fourth, not all workers are equally productive. Since marginal productivity theory tells us that workers should be paid a wage equal to their MRP, differing levels of productivity means differing MRPs and different wages.

Fifth, and finally, if the same work is capable of producing goods with different demands and/or if the work may be done for suppliers with different degrees of market power (in the product market), then the MRP of labor will vary, even if the MPP is the same. As a result, a wage differential will also exist.

7. Prepare a list of questions that an interviewer is likely to ask an interviewee in a job interview. Try to identify which of the questions are part of the interviewer's screening process.

Typical "screening" questions include: "Where did you get your degree?" "What is/was your major field of study?" "How much full-time work experience have you had?" "What was your G.P.A.?" "What salary are/were you making in your current/previous job?" And so on.

8. Explain why the market demand curve for labor is not simply the horizontal summation of firms' demand curves for labor.

See Exhibit 26-7. As the wage rate rises, a firm's costs of production increase, shifting its supply curve leftward and raising the product price. As P increases, so does the MRP of labor (recall, MRP = MPP x P). Therefore, a change in the wage rate changes the MRP curve, resulting in a market labor demand curve that is steeper than the labor demand curves of individual firms, as shown in Exhibit 26-7c.

9. Discuss the firm's objective, its constraints, and how it makes its choices in its role as buyer of resources.

As a buyer of resources, the firm's objective is to minimize cost while fully utilizing its factors. Its constraints are the price, productivity, and availability of those factors. The firm will try to achieve its objective by purchasing combinations of factors such that the ratio of marginal physical product (MPP) to price of the last unit of each input "hired" will be equal. For example, in a two-input world,

$$\frac{MPP_L}{P_L} = \frac{MPP_K}{P_k}$$

where L = labor and K = capital.

10. Explain the relationship between each of the following: (a) elasticity of demand for a product and the elasticity of demand for labor that produces the product; (b) labor cost-total cost ratio and the elasticity of demand for labor; (c) the number of substitutes for labor and the elasticity of demand for labor.

a. If the demand for the product that labor produces is highly elastic, a small percentage increase in price will decrease quantity demanded of the product significantly, which will, in turn, decrease the quantity of labor demanded significantly. Therefore, the higher the elasticity of demand for the product, the higher the elasticity of demand for labor; and, likewise, the lower the elasticity of demand for the product, the lower the elasticity of demand for labor.

b. The higher the percentage of total cost accounted for by labor, the more elastic the demand for labor, since an increase in wage rates will raise total cost more under such circumstances, increasing price and reducing quantity demanded of the product.

c. The more substitutes available for any good or service, the more elastic the demand for that good or service, since a price increase can be responded to by looking to the substitutes.

11. Fill in the appropriate numbers in the lettered spaces.

(1) Units of Factor X	(2) Quantity of Output	(3) MPP_X	(4) Product Price = Marginal Revenue	(5) Total Revenue	(6) MRP_X
0	15	0	$ 8	F	L
1	24	A	8	G	M
2	32	B	8	H	N
3	39	C	8	I	O
4	45	D	8	J	P
5	50	E	8	K	Q

The answers are:

Units of Factor X	Quantity of Output	MPP$_X$	Product Price = Marginal Revenue	Total Revenue	MRP$_X$
0	15	0	$ 8	$120	$ 0
1	24	9	8	192	72
2	32	8	8	256	64
3	39	7	8	273	56
4	45	6	8	360	48
5	50	5	8	400	40

■ LECTURE SUPPLEMENTS

G. Pascal Zachary, "Service Productivity Is Rising Fast, and So Is Fear of Losing Jobs," *Wall Street Journal*, **June 8, 1995, p. A1, column 6.**

This articles gives several examples showing how technological improvements are putting at risk service-related jobs. For example, Kansas City Power & Light Co. has installed a device which automatically reads electric usage and can broadcast the data every few minutes, eliminating the need to have meter readers. Of course, having technology eliminate jobs is as old as the Industrial Revolution, just think of all the people who used to run elevators. The question is whether the current round of layoffs stemming from technological change is different.

Some individuals say that this time it is different, for several reasons. First, whereas in the past technological innovations might affect one industry, such as farming or machine tools, the innovations in semiconductors and other technologies are no respectors of jobs and are applicable to thousands of occupations. Second, not only are these changes widely applicable, but the pace of change in the electronic industry is extremely rapid. Microprocessors double their performance every eighteen months or so.

Nevertheless, the productivity improvements provide large benefits to consumers, and as always, technological innovations which destroy jobs, also create new ones.

Matt Murray, "Amid Record Profits, Companies Continue to Lay off Employees," *Wall Street Journal*, **May 4, 1995, page A1, column 1.**

This article can be used to discuss the current spate of downsizing which has been striking corporate America during the past few years. To some, these changes may seem like a contradiction. If firms are increasing their profits, they should be hiring new workers rather than laying off existing workers, but such is not the case.

Of course, there were layoffs during the 1990-91 recession, but most workers assumed these would be discontinued once economic recovery set in. This did not occur. Instead of expanding their operations when profits role in, extra cash is used more often to buy back shares or buy up other firms, not to hire additional employees.

Firms blame heightened competition on the need for layoffs. They are not laying off employees to avoid bankruptcy, but to get even higher margins on their investments and equity.

The layoffs hit individuals who are hard-working, dedicated employees, not just the shirkers, and fewer people feel secure in their jobs nowadays.

Gene Epstein, "Full-Time Work Giving Way to Part-Time? Statistics, and Reporting, Paint a Wrong Picture," *Barron's,* **April 24, 1995, p. 44.**

One complaint which is often heard today is that in the past, firms provided full-time jobs to employees, but today they hire them part-time to keep down there costs. Is this true? Have full-time jobs become a thing of the past?

According to Mark E. Schweitzer and Max Dupuy of the Cleveland Federal Reserve, the answer is no. First, their research showed that the growth in full-time jobs outpaced the growth in part-time jobs both before and after the 1990-91 recession. Second, most part-time workers would not accept full-time jobs if they were offered one. Third, while part-time jobs generally pay less than full-time, there are still many part-time positions that pay more than the average for full-time.

They argue that commentators often misinterpret their data to come to these results. They found that since the 1950s, the proportion of workers who are involuntarily part-time employed has barely changed, but the proportion of workers who are voluntarily part-time employed has tripled. Although the median wage for part-timers was $6.50 an hour in 1993 versus $10 for full-timers, 27 percent of part-time workers earned more than the median full-time workers. As always, real world facts are more complicated than the simple conclusions some analysts draw.

CHAPTER 27

Wages, Unions, and Labor

Chapter 26 introduced students to the labor market, the factors that affect the supply of and demand for labor, and how the equilibrium wage and level of employment are determined in a perfectly competitive labor market. Chapter 27 examines a significant "barrier" to competition in the labor market: *labor unions*. The chapter begins with a description of the various types of labor unions, followed by a brief history of the U.S. labor movement. We then turn to a more theoretical analysis, looking at the possible objectives of labor unions, and the various methods they may employ to pursue those objectives. Finally, we assess the possible effects of unionization -- both "good" and "bad" -- on union members, nonunion workers, the labor market, and the economy as a whole.

■ CHAPTER OBJECTIVES

Upon completing this chapter, your students should be able to:

- distinguish between *craft (trade) unions*, *industrial unions*, *public employee unions*, and *employee associations*, with regards to their membership and basic function(s);

- identify the possible objectives of labor unions, with respect to employment and wages, and the various methods that may be used to pursue those objectives;

- define *collective bargaining* and describe the role collective bargaining and *strikes* play in pushing union objectives;

- define *monopsony*, and find the optimal level of employment and wage for a monopsonist facing an unorganized (non-unionized) labor supply;

- describe the effect(s) of unionization on the wages of union and nonunion labor;

- understand the relationship between union wages and product prices, for both those goods that are products of union labor and those that are not; and,

- present arguments as to the effect of unions on efficiency and productivity.

■ KEY TERMS

- craft (trade) union
- industrial union
- Public Employee Union
- employee association
- right-to-work laws

- closed shop
- union shop
- collective bargaining
- strike
- monopsony

■ CHAPTER OUTLINE

I. **THE FACTS AND FIGURES OF LABOR UNIONS**

   A. **Types of Labor Unions** -- Economists often distinguish between three types of labor unions: *craft (trade) unions*, *industrial unions*, and *public employee unions*. In addition, we include *employee associations* in our discussion.

   1. **Craft or Trade Union** -- a union whose membership is made up of individuals who practice the same craft or trade, such as the plumbers' or musicians' unions.

   2. **Industrial Union** -- a union whose membership is made up of workers who work for the same firm, or in the same industry, but do not necessarily practice the same trade. Examples include the UAW (auto workers) and UMW (mine workers). For an industrial union to be successful, it must unionize all firms in the industry; otherwise, nonunion firms and workers will compete with union firms and workers.

   3. **Public Employee Union** -- a union whose membership is made up of local, state, and/or federal government employees, such as teachers' and police unions.

   4. **Employee Association** -- an organization whose members belong to a particular profession and band together to promote that profession, such as the American Bar Association or the American Medical Association.

   B. **A Few Facts and Figures** -- Union membership as a percentage of the labor force rose from 5.6 percent in 1910 to a peak of 25 percent in the mid-1950s. In 1993, membership was down to 15.8 percent. [See Exhibit 27-1]

II. **HISTORY OF THE LABOR MOVEMENT** -- National union movements began in the U.S. after the Civil War, suffered some legal setbacks in the late-1800s and early-1900s, and then began to boom in the 1930s, 1940s, and early-1950s, as a result of changing economic conditions and favorable federal legislation. Here we outline a few of the major steps in the evolution of the U.S. organized labor movement.

   A. **The Knights of Labor** -- The first large-scale labor union was the Knights of Labor, organized in 1869. The Knights of Labor cut across craft and industry lines, welcoming (almost) anyone who worked for a living. Its main objectives were the establishment of workers' cooperatives, improving wages, reducing the typical work day to eight hours, and replacing the capitalist economic structure with socialism.

B. **The American Federation of Labor** -- Half of the best-known labor organization today (AFL-CIO), the American Federation of Labor (AFL) was formed by Samuel Gompers in 1886 to serve skilled craft workers. Gompers' feeling was that skilled workers would suffer if unskilled workers were admitted to the union and included in wage bargaining. Unlike the Knights of Labor, the AFL concentrated on basic economic issues, such as better pay and improved working conditions for its members, choosing to leave the political debates to others.

C. **The Courts In the Early Days** -- In the early days of the labor movement, courts treated unions as illegal conspiracies, often prosecuting union leaders and holding them liable for damages. The passage of the Sherman Antitrust Act made things worse, allowing government prosecutors to charge unions under the "conspiracy to monopolize" section of the Act, and allowing judges to issue injunctions to prevent strikes, pickets, and boycotts.

D. **The Norris-LaGuardia and Wagner Acts** -- The two biggest legal breakthroughs for the union movement came in 1932, with the passage of the **Norris-LaGuardia Act**, which *declared that workers should be able to organize and choose their leaders free of restraint from employers*; and, in 1935, when the **Wagner Act**, or the **National Labor Relations Act (NLRA)**, *required that employers bargain in good faith with workers, prohibited employers from interfering with their employees' attempts to unionize, and established the **National Labor Relations Board (NLRB)** to investigate unfair labor practices.*

E. **The Congress of Industrial Organizations (CIO)** -- The other half of today's powerful AFL-CIO, the Congress of Industrial Organizations (CIO) was founded by John L. Lewis, to provide a force to unionize major production industries -- such as automobiles, steel, and rubber -- across craft lines. The AFL, at the time, was adamant about maintaining the integrity of craft unions, so Lewis (of the United Mine Workers) and other like-minded leaders broke off and formed their own union. It was not until 1955 that, under the leadership of George Meany, the AFL and CIO re-joined.

F. **The Taft-Hartley Act** -- The congressional sentiment that made the Wagner Act possible began to shift after World War II, in response to a few particularly damaging strikes in 1946, leading to the passage of the Taft-Hartley Act in 1947. The **Taft-Hartley Act** *gave states the power to pass **right-to-work** laws that prohibited unions from requiring employers to make union membership a pre-condition for employment. The Act also outlawed certain union practices aimed at forcing nonunion employees to join the union, and gave the President the power to issue an injunction to halt a strike that could threaten the national interest.*

G. **The Landrum-Griffin Act** -- The wave of strong anti-Communist sentiment in the 1950s, kindled by the recollection of the role organized labor played in the early years of the Bolshevik revolution in the Soviet Union, led to even more restrictive legislation. The **Landrum-Griffin Act** of 1959 was passed with the express intent of *policing the internal affairs of labor unions. The Act set-up election guidelines for union officials and prohibited ex-convicts and "known communists" from holding union office.*

II. **OBJECTIVES OF LABOR UNIONS** -- Labor unions usually seek one of three objectives: to maximize members' employment, to maximize the total wage earnings of its members, or to maximize the wage rate earned by whatever members are employed.

A. **Employment for All Members** -- One possible objective is to maximize employment. Suppose the demand for labor is as illustrated in Exhibit 27-1. If the union chose to maximize employment, it would have to choose wage rate W_1.

B. **Maximizing the Total Wage Bill** -- A second possible objective is to maximize the total earnings of union members, by maximizing the value:

wage rate x number of labor hours worked.

In order to do this, the union would seek wage rate W_2 in Exhibit 27-2.

C. **Maximizing Income for a Limited Number of Members** -- A third possible objective is to maximize the income of a limited number of members, which is brought about by seeking the maximum wage rate at which that group can be employed, given demand conditions in the labor market. In Exhibit 27-2, the union would maximize the wage rate for this group by seeking W_3.

III. **Practices of Labor Unions** -- Labor unions try to meet their objectives by affecting one or more of the following: the elasticity of demand for labor, the demand for labor, and the supply of labor.

A. **Elasticity of Demand for Union Labor** -- As Exhibit 27-3 illustrates, the lower the elasticity of demand for labor, the smaller the cutback in labor for any given wage increase. Obviously, from the union's perspective, a lower elasticity of demand for union labor is desirable. In order to affect the elasticity of demand for union labor, unions focus on two key issues:

1. **Availability of Substitute Products** -- The greater the availability of substitutes for the products of union labor, the greater will be the elasticity of demand for those products; and, as a result, the greater the elasticity of demand for union labor. Consequently, unions will often seek to reduce the availability of substitutes for the products they produce.

2. **Availability of Substitute Factors** -- The fewer the substitute factors for union labor, the lower the elasticity of demand for union labor. There are two basic types of substitutes for union labor: nonunion labor and "labor-saving" machines. Labor unions often lobby for legislation that will reduce the availability and/or increase the effective cost of nonunion labor, and they usually oppose machines that can be substituted for labor.

B. **The Demand for Union Labor** -- Another means for promoting union objectives is to increase the demand for union labor. All other things held constant, this will improve wages and union employment. In order to boost demand, unions pursue the following:

1. **Increasing Product Demand** -- The greater the demand for the product of labor, the greater the demand for labor. Consequently, unions occasionally urge the public to buy the products they produce.

2. **Increasing Substitute Factor Prices** -- If union action leads to a rise in the relative price of other factors, the demand for union labor will rise. In this regard, unions have

288

often lobbied for an increase in the minimum wage -- the price of unskilled (and usually nonunion) labor.

3. **Increasing Marginal Physical Product** -- If unions can increase the productivity of their members, the demand for labor will rise. With this in mind, unions prefer skilled labor to unskilled labor, and will often support training programs for members.

C. **The Supply of Union Labor** -- A third approach is to decrease the supply of nonunion labor. Such an approach focuses on the use of union membership as a condition of hiring and/or continued employment. In the past, craft unions, in particular, were successful at turning many businesses into **closed shops**, where all employees had to belong to the union. While the Taft-Hartley Act prohibited union membership as a pre-condition to hiring, **union shops** still exist, where individuals do not have to join the union before being hired, but are required to join within a certain period of time in order to stay on the job.

Today unions argue for union shops and for the repeal of legislation barring closed shops. They also argue against right-to-work laws, which make even union shops illegal in the states that have passed such laws.

D. **Affecting Wages Directly: Collective Bargaining and Strikes**

1. **Collective Bargaining** -- Besides increasing wage rates indirectly through changes in the demand for and supply of their labor, unions can directly affect wage rates through **collective bargaining** -- *the process whereby wage rates are determined by the union bargaining with management on behalf of its members*. In collective bargaining, union members act as a single unit in order to increase their bargaining power. On the other side of the market, employers may also try to band together to improve their position, as well.

2. **Strikes** -- From the viewpoint of the union, collective bargaining is unlikely to be successful unless the union can *strike*. A **strike** occurs when union employees refuse to work at a certain wage or under certain working conditions. The purpose of a strike is clearly to convince management that the union can control the supply of labor. Often, the extent to which this can be done will depend on the union's ability to keep nonstriking and nonunion employees from working at the disputed wage and/or working conditions.

3. **Labor Supply under Collective Bargaining** -- If the union is able to control the supply of labor and act as its collective bargaining agent, then employers will face a labor supply curve like the one shown in Exhibit 27-4. Here, the union specifies a minimum acceptable wage rate, such as W_2, implying that *no one* will work for less; and then negotiates upward from there, depending upon how much labor the employer needs. The union wants to make the heavy supply curve the relevant supply curve for the firm, but if the firm can hire nonunion workers, the union's bargaining strength will be reduced.

III. EFFECTS OF LABOR UNIONS

A. **The Case of Monopsony** -- A single buyer in a factor market is known as a **monopsonist**. Because the monopsonist is the sole buyer of factor (labor) services -- and, therefore, faces the market supply curve for the factor -- it cannot buy (hire) additional units of the factor without increasing the price (wage) it pays for the factor. For the monopsonist, marginal factor cost (MFC) increases as it buys additional units of a factor. More specifically, as Exhibit 27-5 illustrates, MFC rises *faster* than the price of the factor -- that is, the MFC curve lies *above* the supply curve.

Suppose that the labor supply is not organized, as Exhibit 27-5b shows, the monopsonist will hire the quantity of labor such that MFC = MRP, and pay the corresponding wage rate -- but, since MFC > W, the firm's MRP of labor will be greater than W. Now, suppose that the labor supply was organized and represented by a union. In this case, the union would present the monopsonist with a labor supply curve like that depicted in Exhibit 27-5c. Here MFC = W over much of the supply curve. Successful collective bargaining would force the firm to pay W_3 for labor rather than W_1. Both the wage rate and the number of workers working have increased. Real world examples of monopsony are rare. The best example is the "company town" in which one firm hires a large proportion of the labor within that town.

B. **Unions' Effects on Wages** -- We can take a quick look at Exhibit 27-5c and see the difference between the equilibrium wage and level of employment with and without unions in a non-monopsonist situation, as well. By comparing the labor supply curves to the MRP curve, we see that a union should reduce employment and raise wages relative to the nonunionized, non-monopsonistic result.

Most empirical studies show that some unions have increased members' wages substantially, while others have not. Data from a study by Weiss, Freeman and Medoff are provided in Exhibit 27-6. The relevant question, it seems, is not so much the effect on the average wage, as the creation of a **union-nonunion wage gap** -- that is, a *differential between the wages earned by union workers and their nonunion counterparts for similar labor.* As Exhibit 27-7 illustrates, changes in the labor supply and wage conditions in the unionized sector can bring about changes in supply and wages in the nonunion sector, which will lead to the creation of a wage gap between the two sectors.

C. **Unions' Effects on Prices** -- The effects of unions don't stop at wages and employment. Higher union wages mean higher production costs, which in turn mean higher prices for the products that union labor produces. Conversely, lower nonunion wages, also brought about by union activity, lower production costs for nonunion employers, and thus reduce the prices of the products that nonunion labor produces.

D. **Unions' Effects on Productivity and Efficiency: Two Views**

1. **The Traditional or Orthodox View** -- The traditional view holds that unions reduce labor productivity and efficiency. First, they argue, labor unions often have unnecessary staffing requirements ("featherbedding") and insist that only certain people do certain jobs. Because of this, the economy operates below its potential, and inefficiency results. Second, strikes disrupt production and thus prevent the economy from realizing its productive potential. Third, unions drive an artificial wedge between the wages of comparable labor in the union and nonunion sectors, causing a misallocation of labor resources and reducing resource allocative efficiency.

2. **A New View: The Labor Union as a Collective Voice** -- Some studies show that, in some industries, union firms have a higher rate of productivity than nonunion firms.

Some economists argue that this indicates that unionization makes workers feel more confident, less intimidated, and more secure in their work, causing them to be happier, more productive employees. One consequence, economists predict, is that union employees should be less likely to quit their jobs. And, in fact, empirical evidence suggests that unionization does reduce job quit rates.

IV. **ECONOMICS ON THE INTERNET** -- This section shows how to access information on wages and salary of labor using the University of Michigan Gopher, how to get information on labor and unions through the Yahoo WWW site, and how to join the labor economics Usenet newsgroup through the Sam Houston State University Internet site.

■ ANSWERS TO CHAPTER QUESTIONS

1. What is the difference between a craft (trade) union and an industrial union?

A craft (trade) union is made up of individuals who practice the same craft or trade. An industrial union is made up of individuals who work in the same firm or industry but do not all practice the same craft or trade.

2. What do the Norris-LaGuardia, Wagner, and Taft-Hartley Acts say?

The Norris-LaGuardia Act declared that workers should be able to organize and choose their leaders free of restraint from employers. The Wagner Act, or the National Labor Relations Act (NLRA), required that employers bargain in good faith with workers, prohibited employers from interfering with their employees' attempts to unionize, and established the National Labor Relations Board (NLRB) to investigate unfair labor practices. The Taft-Hartley Act gave states the power to pass right-to-work laws that prohibited unions from requiring employers to make union membership a pre-condition for employment. The Act also outlawed certain union practices aimed at forcing nonunion employees to join the union, and gave the President the power to issue an injunction to halt a strike that could threaten the national interest.

3. What view is a labor union likely to hold on each of the following issues: (a) easing of the immigration laws; (b) a quota on imported products; (c) free trade; (d) a decrease in the minimum wage?

a. A labor union is likely to be against any easing of the immigration laws. Less stringent immigration laws would increase the availability of substitute factors (for labor) -- an outcome that is not in the best interest of union labor.
b. A labor union is likely to be for a quota on imported products, especially if it will be applied to products similar to those produced by workers in the union.
c. A labor union is likely to be against free trade for the same reason that it is for quotas.
d. A labor union is likely to be against decreasing the minimum wage. A decrease in the minimum wage decreases the price of a substitute factor for union labor -- something that is not in the best interest of union labor.

4. Most actions or practices of labor unions are attempts to affect one of three factors. What are these three factors?

The activities or practices of labor unions are, for the most part, attempts to affect the elasticity of demand for labor (in order to "soften" the wage-employment trade-off), the demand for labor (in order to increase union wage rates), and the supply of labor (in order to increase union wage rates).

5. Explain why the monopsonist pays labor a wage rate less than labor's marginal revenue product.

First, the supply curve of labor the monopsonist faces is the industry supply curve; thus if it wants to hire additional labor, it must offer a higher wage rate. Second, as a result, the marginal factor cost is greater than the wage rate -- that is, MFC > wage rate. Third, since the monopsonist hires the amount of labor at which MRP = MFC, it follows that the wage rate will be less than MRP.

6. It has been suggested that organizing labor unions is easier in some industries than others. What industry characteristics make unionization easy?

All other things held constant, the lower the elasticity of demand for the product that labor produces, the easier unionization efforts will be. The reasoning is straightforward: With low elasticity of demand, an increase in wage rates results in a smaller percentage fall in employment than with high price elasticity of demand. Since employees thinking about becoming unionized care whether they keep their jobs, they will be less likely to unionize the more jobs that must be traded for any given wage rate increase.

7. What is the effect of labor unions on nonunion wage rates?

Both theory and empirical research show that labor unions increase the wage rates of their members and decrease the wage rates of nonunion labor. We explain this theoretically by noting that labor unions either collectively bargain for higher wage rates or decrease the supply of their labor in order to achieve higher wage rates indirectly. In either case, if the unions are successful, fewer persons will be working in the union sector of the labor market. They will shift over to the nonunion sector, thus pushing up the supply of nonunion labor, and pushing down the nonunion wage rate.

8. Some persons argue that a monopsony firm exploits its workers if it pays them less than their marginal revenue products. Others disagree. They say that as long as the firm pays the workers their opportunity costs (which must be the case or the workers would not stay with the firm), the workers are not being exploited. This suggests that there are two definitions of exploitation: (a) paying workers below their marginal revenue products (even if wages equal the workers' opportunity costs) and (b) paying workers below their opportunity costs. Keeping in mind that this may be a subjective judgment, which definition of exploitation do you think is more descriptive of the process and why?

The first definition -- paying workers less than their marginal revenue product -- seems to be more descriptive of the "exploitation" that most people see occurring in monopsony situations. As stated, if the monopsonist were paying workers less than their opportunity costs, then the workers would leave. However, if the firm is a monopsonist, it can get away with paying workers less than their MRP, because the firm hires at MFC = MRP, but MFC > W; therefore, MRP > W.

9. A discussion of labor unions will usually evoke strong feelings. Some persons argue vigorously against labor unions, others argue with equal vigor for labor unions. Some persons see labor unions as the reason why the workers in this country enjoy as high a standard of living as they do; others see labor unions as the reason the country is not as well off economically as it might be. Speculate on why the topic of labor unions generates such strong feelings and emotions and often such little analysis.

The worker-management relationship in the United States is considerably more adversarial than in most other developed economies. Unions may add to this adversarial feeling. As a result, most people take sides -- either supporting labor or management -- and allow the emotions of the issue to cloud their judgment and analysis.

10. What forces may lead to the breakup of an employer (monopsony) cartel?

The most important force would be the entry of one or more new firms into the labor market. Additionally, the existence of a labor union doesn't "break up" a monopsony, *per se*, but it will decrease the monopsony's ability to choose its wage rate and level of employment.

11. Fill in the appropriate numbers in the lettered spaces.

(1) Workers	(2) Wage Rate	(3) Total Labor Cost	(4) Marginal Factor Cost
1	A	$12.00	$12.00
2	$12.10	24.20	E
3	12.20	C	F
4	B	D	12.60

The answers are:

Workers	Wage Rate	Total Labor Cost	Marginal Factor Cost
0			
1	$12.00	$12.00	$12.00
2	12.10	24.20	12.20
3	12.20	36.60	12.40
4	12.30	49.20	12.60

293

■ LECTURE SUPPLEMENTS

Heidi Hartmann, Roberta Spalter-Roth, and Nancy Collins, "What Do Unions Do For Women?" *Challenge*, **July-August 1994, pp. 11-17.**

When you think of union workers, you usually think of men, but there are many women who are members of unions. What role do women play in unions, and how have unions helped women in their jobs. This article explores this question, giving a wealth of statistics on the role that women play in unions, and discusses how their role can be improved.

There is some truth to the stereotype of the male union worker. In 1990, 22 percent of male workers were members of unions while only 14.2 percent of female workers were union members. The absolute number of female union workers has increased, in part because the number of women in the work force has increased. Relative to men, women are more likely to be in white-collar jobs than men, more likely to be college-educated, and women do better under collective-bargaining agreements and union membership than when no unions are present. Furthermore, women of color gain more from union membership than white women, members at the low end of pay scale gain more from union membership than those at the high end, there is a smaller wage gap between male and female workers in unions than in non-union industries, and job tenure tends to be longer for union workers.

Still, the authors have some recommendations. Specifically, they feel that unions need to train more women for leadership positions, women's voices need to be better represented in unions, and women need to be more actively involved in determining issues and formulating organizing and bargaining strategy. If you are interested in this topic, this is an excellent survey article.

"Getting Their Dues," *The Economist*, **March 25, 1995, pp. 68, 73, 74.**

This article provides a good overview of the current state of unions in the United States. Between 1979 and 1992, unions lost one-fifth of their members, almost 4.6 million. One reason is that during the 1980s, recessions led to sharp layoffs, and workers sided with management to protect their jobs, and when the economy was booming, firms tried to circumvent unions by offering generous non-wage benefits and grievance procedures usurping the traditional role of the union.

In the 1990s, on the other hand, the keywords are restructuring, downsizing, delayering, re-engineering, and outsourcing. As a result, some workers are returning to unions to help protect them from managers who pursue these policies. Workers are becoming insecure, and the number of strikes and union members has actually started to increase. Unions are also becoming better at marketing themselves, trying to shed the image of ideological groups who hire someone's brother-in-law to organize for an image of hiring professionals who seek practical gains. Unions are trying to preserve existing jobs and insure that if workers are laid off, they will receive retraining from their former employers.

"Adapt or Die," *The Economist*, **July 1, 1995, pp. 54, 56.**

This article argues that to survive, unions should go back to their roots and concentrate more on craft unions and less on industrial unions. In almost every country in the world, union membership declined between 1970 and 1990, Sweden providing the most notable exception.

There are several reasons for these changes. Research has shown that union membership is closely correlated with plant size, and average plant size has fallen in OECD countries. Unions are less common in service industries, and the service sector has grown as a percentage of the work force during the past twenty years. Unions are more successful in countries which have centralized wage systems. As these have broken down, union membership has declined. Finally, people are less willing to join institutions of any kind, whether they be church or unions, than was true in the past. As Dennis McShane of the British parliament puts it, "Capitalism changed and unions didn't change with it." The article shows several ways in which craft unions have strengthened their membership during the past years.

CHAPTER 28

The Distribution of Income and Poverty

One of the most emotionally- and politically-charged issues in economics is the distribution and redistribution of income. The emotional fervor evident in a debate about how to increase the income of the nation can rarely approach a similar debate on how that income should be distributed among the various members of society. Income distribution is an area where the boundary between normative and positive economics is thin and often breached, as will happen now and again in this chapter. Given the highly emotional nature of this subject, Chapter 28 makes a determined effort to avoid making judgments, choosing instead to present the facts and their various interpretations, to describe some of the causes of income inequalities and the views various parties hold toward them, and to discuss a few prominent normative theories on income distribution from the perspectives of both proponents and critics. The second half of the chapter turns to the particular income distribution problem that is largely responsible for its political and emotional volatility: *poverty*. We begin with two definitions of poverty -- one absolute and the other relative. The chapter then briefly discusses some causes of poverty, before concluding with a discussion of three ways of addressing the issue of poverty: the current welfare system, the *negative income tax*, and the market-oriented approach.

■ CHAPTER OBJECTIVES

Upon completing this chapter, your students should be able to:

- describe various ways of determining who is "rich" and how rich they are;

- distinguish between *ex ante* and *ex post income distributions*, and describe how *transfer payments* and *in-kind transfers* affect these distributions;

- determine an individual's income, given the necessary information about labor income, *asset income*, transfer payments, and taxes;

- draw a *Lorenz curve* and calculate a *Gini coefficient* for an economy, and explain what each tells us about the distribution of income in a society;

- identify the key causes of income inequality (and poverty) and briefly describe how each one can create a "gap" between one group of people and another;

- present the *marginal productivity*, *absolute income equality*, and *Rawlsian normative standards of income distribution*, and the key points of proponents and critics of each;

- understand some of the problems of defining and measuring poverty, and of accurately determining the cause(s) of any individual's poverty; and,

- discuss the three anti-poverty programs presented in the chapter: the current welfare system, the *negative income tax*, and the market-oriented approach.

■ KEY TERMS

- ex ante distribution (of income)
- ex post distribution (of income)
- transfer payments
- in-kind transfer payments
- Lorenz curve
- Gini coefficient
- human capital

- wage discrimination
- veil of ignorance
- poverty income threshold (poverty line)
- guaranteed income level
- implicit marginal tax rate
- negative income tax

■ CHAPTER OUTLINE

I. **SOME FACTS ABOUT INCOME DISTRIBUTION**

A. **Who Are the Rich and How Rich Are They?** -- By many interpretations, the lowest fifth (lowest 20%) of family income groups is considered to be poor, the top fifth is considered to be rich. If we want a more restrictive definition of "rich," we can look at the top five percent. In 1992, the lowest 20% of families in the U.S. earned 4.4% of the total money income, and the highest 20% earned 44.6%, or almost ten times as much. In that same year, the top 5% earned 17.6% of the total money income, almost four times as much as the bottom 20%. [See Exhibit 28-1]

B. **The Income Distribution Over a Period of Time** -- Exhibit 28-2 shows the income shares of family groups in the U.S. in 1929 and 1992. As we can see, the top 20% of families earned 54.4% of total money income in 1929, as opposed to 44.6% in 1992; and, the bottom 20% earned only 3.9% of total income in 1929, as opposed to 4.4% in 1992. From this, we can see that income distribution has become somewhat more equal since 1929.

C. **Income Distribution Adjusted for Taxes and Transfer Payments** -- Government can change the distribution of income through the use of taxes and transfer payments. Economists distinguish between the *ex ante* and *ex post distributions of income.*

   1. **Ex Ante Income Distribution** -- the distribution of earned income before taxes and transfer payments are accounted for.

   2. **Ex Post Income Distribution** -- the distribution of individual income, which includes all earned income adjusted for *transfer payments* and taxes. **Transfer payments** are payments to persons (from the government) that are not made in return for any goods or services currently supplied. **In-kind transfer payments** are made through the provision of a specific good or service, rather than cash. *Cash transfer payments and in-kind transfers increase people's ex post income, while taxes reduce that income.*

3. **The Effect of Age on the Income Distribution** -- It is important to distinguish between individuals who are temporarily poor due to career changes or lay-offs, and those who are poor for long periods of time, and to understand how income changes over the course of one's life. As a whole, people's income tends to be low up until the mid-20s, to rise during their late-20s, 30s, and 40s, to peak sometime in the late-40s or early-50s, and remain fairly level until retirement, at which point it will drop significantly. Owing to this, one could argue that the appropriate income comparison would be to look at lifetime income, rather than income at one particular point in time. As Exhibit 28-3 shows, John and Stephanie's relative income distributions of income are unequal during the ten years which are covered; however, over time they have an equal distribution of income.

D. **A Simple Equation** -- Including taxes and transfers, we get the following simple equation:

individual income = labor income + asset income + transfer payments - taxes,

where **asset income** consists of such things as interest earned on savings, return on capital investment, and the like, and where transfer payments includes both cash and in-kind transfers.

Many economists argue that the value of transfer payments and in-kind transfers, minus taxes paid, is such as to significantly improve the income distribution picture for the poor, and to create a more even *ex post* distribution of income than the *ex ante* distribution would suggest.

II. **MEASURING INCOME INEQUALITY** -- There are two commonly used measurements of income inequality: the *Lorenz curve* and the *Gini coefficient*.

A. **The Lorenz Curve** -- a graphical representation of the distribution of income, *expressing the relationship between cumulative percent of families and cumulative percent of income* -- that is, you can look at a particular point on the graph and see what percent of income is earned by what percent of the population, starting with the poorest families and working our way "up" the income ladder. [See Exhibit 28-5]

The Lorenz curve for one economy may look substantially different from that of another, depending upon how evenly income is distributed among their populations. If there were **perfect income equality**, the Lorenz curve would be a 45° line, as is shown for reference in Exhibit 28-4b. If there were **perfect income inequality**, the Lorenz curve would lie on the horizontal axis up to the point where 99.9% of the families had been included, and then become a vertical line, such that the entire income of the economy would be held by one person/family. The Lorenz curve for the United States (in 1992) lies somewhere between these two extremes.

B. **The Gini Coefficient** -- measures the degree of inequality in the income distribution as the difference between the **line of perfect income equality** (or 45°-line) and the actual Lorenz curve for an economy. Specifically, the Gini coefficient is calculated as:

area between line of perfect income equality and actual Lorenz curve
entire triangular area under the line of perfect income equality

Exhibit 28-6 illustrates both the line of perfect income equality and an actual Lorenz curve. The Gini coefficient is computed by dividing the shaded area by the area 0AB.

The Gini coefficient is a number between 0 and 1. A Gini coefficient of 0 would indicate that there is no difference between the actual Lorenz curve and the line of perfect income equality; therefore, *if the Gini coefficient = 0, the economy has a perfectly equal income distribution*. A Gini coefficient of 1 would mean that the area between the actual Lorenz curve and the line of perfect income equality is equal to the area of the triangle under the line of perfect income equality -- that is, the Lorenz curve is as far away from the line of perfect income equality as possible; therefore, *if the Gini coefficient = 1, the economy has a perfectly unequal distribution of income*, or *perfect income inequality*.

It follows then, that *the larger the Gini coefficient, the greater the degree of income inequality; the smaller the Gini coefficient, the less the degree of income inequality*.

C. **Limitations of the Gini Coefficient** -- While the Gini coefficient can tell us a great deal about the overall distribution of income in a society, it cannot tell us about what is happening to specific groups. For instance, if the Gini coefficient is .10 in Country A and .20 in Country B, we cannot necessarily conclude that the top 20% have a smaller percentage of the income in A, or that the bottom 20% are worse off in B. [See Exhibit 28-7]

III. **WHY INCOME INEQUALITY EXISTS** -- Recall our earlier definition on individual income, where individual income = labor income + asset income + transfer payments - taxes. Obviously, and most generally, income inequality exists because people do not receive the same labor income, asset income, and transfer payments, or pay the same taxes. If we want to reduce income inequality, we can increase transfer payments and/or lower taxes to those with lower labor and asset incomes; and decrease transfer payments and/or increase taxes to those with higher labor and asset incomes. The real question, to begin with, is: Why do different people have different labor and asset incomes in the first place?

A. **Factors Contributing to Income Inequality**

1. **Innate Abilities and Attributes** -- Individuals are not all born with the same innate abilities and attributes. Intelligence, creativity, strength, size, and appearance vary widely from person to person. To the extent that the market rewards some innate abilities and attributes more than others, the possessors of those desired qualities will tend to have higher incomes than others.

2. **Work and Leisure** -- Individuals must choose between work and leisure. Those who choose to work more (enjoy less leisure time), *ceteris paribus*, will earn more income than those who choose to work less (enjoy more leisure time).

3. **Education and Other Training** -- Education and training develop an individual's **human capital** -- education, skills, and anything else that increases individual productivity. Individuals who "invest" in developing their human capital will tend to be rewarded more once they enter the labor market than others without comparable training and skills, *ceteris paribus*.

4. **Risk Taking** -- Individuals differ as to the degree of risk they are willing to take. Individuals who are willing to take risks have a greater earning potential than those who do not; they also have the potential of losing more than less risk-oriented individuals.

298

5. **Luck** -- There are times when good and bad luck (unexplainable consequences) influence income; though luck isn't likely to have as much long term impact, on average, as the other factors discussed here.

6. **Wage Discrimination** -- exists when individuals of equal ability and productivity, as measured by their marginal revenue products, are paid different wage rates. There are all sorts of reasons for wage discrimination -- some legitimate, others not. For instance, as seen in Chapter 26, labor immobility may cause substantial wage discrimination between employees holding similar jobs in different locations. On the other hand, if the wage differential is due to the employees race, gender, or age, then the discrimination has no economic rationale.

B. **Income Differences: Some Are Voluntary, Some Are Not** -- Even in a world of no discrimination, differences in income would still exist. Some individuals would have more marketable skills than others, some would decide to work longer and harder than others, and some would undertake more education and training than others. In short, some degree of income inequality exists because people make different choices. On the other hand, some income differences are due to factors unrelated to innate ability or choices, such as luck, inheritance (a particular form of luck, where you happen to choose the right ancestors), or discrimination. It is these latter sources of income differences that trouble most people, and which motivate much of the existing and proposed actions to redistribute income. But how? One possibility lies in the notion of *comparable worth*, discussed in the *Economics In Our Times* feature "Comparable Worth: Or, What is a Truck Driver Really Worth?"

IV. **NORMATIVE STANDARDS OF INCOME DISTRIBUTION** -- The "proper" distribution of income has attracted the interest of economists, political philosophers, sociologists, and others, for hundreds of years. Here we discuss three of the more well-known products of the debate over the normative standard of income distribution.

A. **The Marginal Productivity Normative Standard** -- The marginal productivity theory of income (discussed in Chapter 26) states that, in a competitive setting, people tend to be paid their marginal revenue products. The **marginal productivity normative standard of income distribution** holds that *people should be paid their marginal revenue products*. [See Exhibit 28-8a]

Proponents of this position argue that it is just for people to be rewarded on the basis of their contribution to the productive process, no more and no less. They also argue that paying people their MRPs give them an incentive to become more productive. Critics respond that some persons are innately more productive than others, and that rewarding innate qualities is unfair, because the individual did not pick or develop them.

B. **The Absolute Income Equality Normative Standard** -- Exhibit 28-8b illustrates the viewpoint of those who advocate that *all individuals receive the same percentage of total income, no more and no less*.

Proponents of this position argue that an equal income distribution will maximize total social utility. Specifically, they argue: (1) All individuals receive the same marginal utility from the same amounts of income; and, (2) additions to income are subject to the law of diminishing marginal utility; therefore, (3) redistributing income from the rich to the poor will increase total social utility, since the poor will gain more utility than the rich will lose for any dollar transferred from rich to poor. Critics respond that it is impossible to know if all individuals receive the same marginal utility from an additional dollar of income; therefore, redistributing income on that basis will not necessarily maximize total utility -- and may, in fact, reduce total utility.

C. **The Rawlsian Normative Standard** -- In *A Theory of Justice*, philosopher John Rawls argues that individuals' feelings about income distribution are affected by their circumstances -- that is, those who are well-off tend to view the current system more favorably than those who are not. In order to control for this, Rawls suggests that people be subjected to a **veil of ignorance**, which will blind them to their current situations. Behind this veil, Rawls argues, individuals will tend to opt for a more equal distribution of income than if they knew their situation with certainty, since most individuals tend to be risk-averse and will want to protect against ending up extremely poor. The **Rawlsian normative standard** -- *the income distribution that individuals would choose from behind the veil of ignorance* -- is illustrated in Exhibit 28-8c.

Critics of Rawls argue that individuals behind the veil may not reach a consensus, as people have different feelings about risk. Furthermore, they argue, greater income equality may very likely mean less total income to be shared. As a result, individuals behind the veil will weigh the relative benefits to a more equal distribution against the harms of less total income to be divided.

D. **Justifying Government Welfare Assistance** -- This *Economics In Our Times* feature can be used to discuss economic justifications for government welfare assistance. One problem that redistributing income creates is the free-rider problem. I benefit from someone else reducing the poverty around me whether I contribute or not. *The Global Economy* feature "Monks, Blessings, and Free Riders" illustrates one way the free-rider problem has been reduced in Thailand.

V. **POVERTY**

A. **What is Poverty?** -- There are two basic views of *poverty*. One view holds that poverty should be defined in absolute terms -- for instance, any individual earning less than $X per year is in poverty. The other view holds that poverty should be defined in relative terms -- that is, as a certain percentage of average individual (family) income.

1. **A Relative Standard** -- Viewing poverty in relative terms means that poverty will always exist -- unless there is absolute income equality. Given any unequal distribution of income, people with lower incomes (no matter how high) will be considered poor, while people with higher incomes (no matter how low) will be considered rich.

2. **An Absolute Standard** -- The U.S. government defines poverty in absolute terms. Specifically, the Department of Agriculture annually determines the minimum-necessary level of income, called the **poverty line**. Anyone receiving an income below the poverty line is considered to be poor. In 1992, the poverty line for a family of four was $14,335.

B. **Limitations of Official Poverty Statistics** -- We need to be aware of certain shortcomings of the official poverty statistics gathered and published by the U.S. government. First, they are *based solely on money income* -- that is, they exclude in-kind transfer payments. Second, they are *not adjusted for unreported or illegal income*. Third, they *ignore regional differences* in the cost of living. Fourth, they *exclude a part of the population* that cannot be "found," because they are homeless or illegal aliens. As a result, the official poverty figures may well be distorted.

Whether they are too high or too low depends upon the relative magnitudes of in-kind benefits and unreported income, as compared to "missing" people and geographical differences.

C. **Who Are the Poor?** -- The poor are made up of all religions, races, genders, ages, and ethnic backgrounds. In absolute numbers, there are more poor whites than any other racial group, but that is simply because there are more whites in the total population than any racial group. In terms of their percentages of the total population, a disproportionate number of *blacks and Hispanics* are living in poverty, as are those *under 16 years of age*, *families with seven or more members*, families with *low levels of education*, and *families headed by single females*.

D. **People Don't Always Agree on the Causes of Poverty** -- The causes of poverty are much the same as the causes of income inequality. The relative importance of these causes, however, varies from case to case; as does the degree of "choice" involved in the particular person's situation. Is Christine poor because she chose not to complete her education and get pregnant outside of marriage, or were these choices the result of growing up in a dysfunctional family? Is Christine's poverty fate or choice?

E. **Proposed and Existing Ways of Fighting Poverty**

1. **The Current Welfare System** -- The current welfare system aids the poor in two ways: by providing cash benefits, through such programs as Aid to Families with Dependent Children (AFDC) and unemployment compensation; and by providing in-kind benefits, such as food stamps, public housing, and Medicaid.

   Critics of the current welfare system say that it is too costly, that it provides benefits to many who are undeserving, and that it creates a disincentive to work, since most programs within the current system reduce benefits as quickly as (or, in some cases, more quickly than) income rises. The problem with such a set-up, they argue, is it often makes it better for the individual to stay on public assistance than to work.

2. **The Negative Income Tax** -- One proposal aimed at reducing the work disincentive effect of the current welfare system is the negative income tax. The negative income tax ensures all families a **guaranteed income level**, below which no family (that reports its income) will be allowed to fall below. As income is earned, benefits are reduced, and eventually income is taxed, at the **implicit marginal tax rate**. For example, if the implicit marginal tax rate were 50 percent, an increase in family income of $1000 would cause government payments to the family to fall by $500. Plus, by combining welfare administration and tax collection, the negative income tax should reduce administrative costs and paperwork.

3. **The Market-Oriented Program** -- In both the current welfare system and the negative income tax, government is actively involved in trying to reduce or eliminate poverty through the use of taxes and transfer payments. The market-oriented program suggests that government should concentrate its efforts to breaking down existing barriers to employment, thereby indirectly assisting the poor by enabling them to find work.

■ ANSWERS TO CHAPTER QUESTIONS

1. "The Gini coefficient for country A is .35, and the Gini coefficient for country B is .22. From this it follows that the bottom 10 percent of income recipients in country B have a greater percentage of the total income than the bottom 10 percent of the income recipients in country A." Do you agree or disagree? Why?

The Gini coefficient gives us a measurement of the degree of income inequality overall; it does not tell us the percentage of income that is received by a specific income group nor can we deduce this from the Gini coefficient. It is possible for the bottom 10 percent of income recipients in a country with a lower Gini coefficient to receive a lower percentage of total income than the same group receives in a country with a higher Gini coefficient.

2. Would you expect greater income inequality in country A, where there is great disparity in age, or in country B, where there is little disparity in age? Explain your answer.

All other things held constant, we would expect more income inequality in country A where there is great disparity in age. We know that most persons' income starts off low, rises in their twenties, thirties, and forties, takes a slight downturn in their late forties or early fifties and then levels off. In a country where the disparity in age is great, the income distribution will reflect the fact that many people are in different stages of their life-cycle earnings pattern (and the more "different stages" there are, the greater the income inequality). In a country where there is little disparity in age, the income distribution will reflect the fact that most people are in the *same* stage of their life-cycle earnings pattern (and the fewer "different stages" there are, the less the income inequality).

3. What is a major criticism of the absolute income equality normative standard?

The standard holds that redistributing income from those with more income to those with less would increase total utility because a person with more income receives less utility from the last dollar he receives than does the person with less income. However, there is no proof of this.

4. Would the work-disincentive effect of the negative income tax be less with a 10 percent implicit marginal tax rate than with a 50 percent implicit marginal tax rate, *ceteris paribus*?

Yes, it would. With a 10 percent implicit marginal tax rate, instead of a 50 percent rate, the individual would keep more of his income from working and would thus be more inclined to work.

5. A good welfare system is said to be one that takes care of the deserving without encouraging people to become undeserving. In other words, it helps the people who deserve to be helped, but doesn't distort incentives to the degree that the undeserving put

themselves into situations where they can cash in on people's generosity. Discuss the current welfare system, the negative income tax, and the market-oriented program with this thought in mind.

The two main problems with the current welfare system, according to most economists, are that it errs on the side of being "too inclusive" -- that is, it would rather provide benefits to someone who is undeserving than not provide benefits to someone who is deserving -- and that it tends to discourage work, because many recipients would lose more in benefits than they would gain in after-tax income if they went off the welfare roles and into the work force.

The market-oriented approach tends to err in the opposite direction -- it would rather exclude those that are deserving than include any that are undeserving -- even to the point of eliminating welfare programs all together, and relying on the market to provide jobs for everyone capable of working, and on private benevolence to take care of those who cannot work.

The negative income tax tries to resolve some of the "distorted" incentives of the current welfare system, while avoiding the "heartlessness" of the market-oriented approach. The negative income tax would qualify everyone for some guaranteed minimum level of income; and, if properly enforced, would pay no benefits to anyone earning income above a certain level. Further, it would make it beneficial for families on income-assistance to work, as their benefits would be reduced at a substantially slower rate than their income would increase.

Thus, the negative income tax provides a stronger work incentive than the current welfare system (though not as strong as the market-oriented approach), and is more concerned with providing assistance to the truly deserving than the market-oriented approach (though no more so than the current system).

6.   In what ways does the Rawlsian technique of hypothesizing individuals behind a veil of ignorance help or not help us decide whether we should have a 55 mph speed limit or a higher one, a larger or smaller welfare system, and higher or lower taxes placed on the rich?

Were we able to place people "behind" the veil of ignorance, we could survey them to determine their preferences on each of these issues. Then, given people's responses -- unbiased by their current state of affairs, since the veil of ignorance "blinds" them to their current state -- we could see what the public feels and wants done on these issues.

7.   Welfare recipients would rather receive their benefits in cash than in-kind, but much of the welfare system provides benefits in-kind. Is there any reason for not giving recipients their welfare benefits the way they want to receive them? Would it be better to move to a welfare system that only provides benefits in cash?

The notion behind in-kind benefits is that it allows the government to "target" its assistance to those needs -- such as housing, medical care, and nutritional requirements -- that policymakers see as being the most important. If the government were to provide all benefits in cash, it would have no control over how those benefits were spent -- so that there might still be a number of people without decent housing, or whatever, despite receiving their welfare benefits.

A second reason is that in-kind benefits bypass the difficult process of assessing cash value to certain basic needs. For instance, by assuring some minimum level of medical assistance, the government avoids having to calculate some "medical budget" for welfare recipients in a world where health costs are constantly changing. Related to this, the government can pay for only those benefits received, so that it doesn't provide unneeded assistance; thus, both the idea of "targeting" benefits, and the desire to keep costs down are somewhat appeased this way.

8. Critics of the market-oriented program of reducing poverty often remark that is does too little and that it does not really address the root causes of poverty, such as discrimination. Do you agree or disagree? Why?

This is basically an opinion question. One point to be made is that the market-oriented program assumes perfect information and perfectly competitive markets. As such, there can be no market failures, such as lack of information, and any willful discrimination that occurs is considered to be too costly to sustain. The problems, it seems, are that not all markets are perfectly competitive, nor is information perfect (or costless). As a result, there may be some institutional causes of poverty that will go unaddressed by a market-oriented approach. Although there may be economic benefits for reducing discrimination, there may be social costs which are more important than the economic costs.

9. What is the effect of age on the income distribution?

More young people are poor than other age groups. As the population ages, the distribution of income could improve because lower-income young people represent a smaller proportion of the population.

10. What are some of the unintended effects of comparable worth?

If the market-clearing wage rate for a secretary is $7 per hour, but the comparable worth board sets the wage at $12 per hour, there will be an increase in the supply of individuals for secretary positions. A surplus will occur at the $12 rate and the employer will have to ration jobs. As a result, people who would be working as secretaries at $7 per hour may be unable to find a job when the wage rate is $12 per hour and highly qualified individuals begin competing against them for the positions which are available.

■ LECTURE SUPPLEMENTS

Dorothy J. Gaiter, "Black Women's Gains in Corporate America Outstrip Black Men's," *Wall Street Journal*, March 8, 1995, page A1, column 6.

This article looks at the current condition of black professional women, a group which grew by 125 percent between 1982 and 1992 and number about 200,000. This is nearly twice the number of professional black males. The compounded annual growth rate of employment in professional jobs grew by 8.4 percent for black women between 1982 and 1992, but by only 4.2 percent for black males. This article is a good source of information, and it explores the economic and social impacts of these changes on both corporate America and the black community.

Gene Epstein, "Decade of the Woman, In 1980s, Females' Pay Rose more than Men's," *Barron's,* **October 31, 1994, p. 47-48.**

This article provides information based upon the research of Stephen J. Rose with the Joint Economic Committee of the Congress. Using longitudinal data from the University of Michigan data base, he was able to compare how individuals' working conditions changed over time. The research covered a 12 year period tracking people who were between 22 and 46 at the beginning of the period and between 34 and 58 at the end. The data covered workers during the 1960s, 1970s, and 1980s.

The data showed that the percentage of men who gained ground declined across all levels of educational attainment, and more lost ground in the 1980s than gained. Normally, as people age, their income goes up, but this was not true for men in the 1980s on average. On the other hand, a higher percentage of men saw their incomes gain by more than 40% in the 1980s than in the 1970s.

For women, the results were very different. For every educational group, women held their own or increased their wages. The primary reason for this improvement was that women increased the number of hours they worked from 870 in the 'Seventies to 1200 in the 'Eighties.

Another important finding was that the number of hours worked by men fell more significantly among blacks than among whites. The decline in hours worked translated into lower incomes. Whereas two out of three black men saw positive career advancement in the 1970s, fewer than one in two experienced normal wage growth in the 1980s. This article should provide a good number of topics for class discussion.

Gene Epstein, "Still Trickling," *Barron's,* **July 17, 1995, pp. 36-37.**

This article looks at poverty rates in the United States. Drawing from a paper by Cleveland Federal Reserve economist Elizabeth Powers, the article tries to explain why the poverty rate failed to decline during the 1980s despite economic growth. Up until the 1980s, there was a close correlation between increases in GDP and declines in the poverty rate, but during the 1980s, this relationship broke down. Why?

Powers provides a couple explanations. First, the number of female-headed households grew in the 1980s. Second, wage inequality grew in the 1980s. The increase in poverty rates cannot be blamed on cutbacks in welfare under the Reagan administration because state and local government increased their spending just as the Federal government began to cut spending. She also feels that employment among those near the poverty level was more volatile in the 1980s than in the 1970s, increasing the likelihood that they would be thrown below the poverty level in any given year.

One of the most important factors, however, is the way poverty is measured. It is based upon cash income rather than one's standard of living. Income poverty, as calculated by the Commerce Department, excludes in-kind transfers such as Medicaid and food stamps. Dale Jorgensen and Daniel Slesnick put together a consumption poverty rate which they felt was more accurate than the Commerce Department's income poverty rate. They found that the consumption poverty rate is generally below the income poverty rate, and that the consumption poverty rate had declined during the 1980s. Their reasoning for this finding was that the income poverty rate excluded assets such as homes and cars which are left out of income measurements of poverty, but which are consumed each year. Second, they hypothesized that some people underreport their income to the government. Third, and most importantly, they took into consideration the permanent income hypothesis. Older people are disproportionately represented under the poverty line because the income poverty rate does not impute the rental value of their homes into their incomes. This article should provide some good insights into the difficulties of measuring poverty, and as always, reveals that the facts are always more complicated than they appear to be.

305

CHAPTER 29

Interest, Rent, and Profit

Chapter 29 concludes our study of factor markets by turning to the markets for capital, land, and entrepreneurial skill -- the remaining factors of production. More specifically, this chapter develops the theories of *interest*, *rent*, and *profit* as payments to nonlabor factors of production. Combining this material with the previous two chapters will give the students a well-developed look at the factors of production, the means by which they are priced and purchased/hired, and their impact on production costs and the prices of goods and services.

■ CHAPTER OBJECTIVES

Upon completing this chapter, your students should be able to:

- state the basic premise of *loanable funds theory* with regard to the rate of interest and identify the primary sources of the supply of and demand for loanable funds;

- describe the relationships between the rate of interest and an individual's *rate of time preference*, and between the rate of interest and *roundabout methods of production*;

- understand the relationship between interest as the price of loanable funds and interest as the rate of return on capital;

- identify some sources of interest rate differentials between loans;

- distinguish between *nominal* and *real interest rates* and describe the importance of each in determining the levels of saving and investment in the economy;

- define *present value* and understand its relationship to firms' investment decisions;

- explain the concept of *rent* in economics and the condition(s) necessary for a factor to receive *pure economic rent*; and,

- discuss the various theories of *profit*, where it comes from, and what it signifies.

■ KEY TERMS

- loanable funds
- positive rate of time preference
- roundabout method of production
- nominal interest rate

- real interest rate
- present value
- economic rent
- pure economic rent

■ CHAPTER OUTLINE

I. **INTEREST** -- The word interest is used in two ways in economics. On the one hand, interest refers to the *price that borrowers pay for the use of loanable funds*. Interest can also refer to the *rate of return earned by capital as an input of production*. Over time, there is a tendency for the price of loanable funds and the rate of return on capital to approach one another -- so that, even though we can define interest two different ways, we end up with one interest rate.

A. **Loanable Funds: Demand and Supply** -- According to the theory of loanable funds, *the interest rate is determined by the equilibrium of the supply of and demand for loanable funds.*

1. **The Supply of Loanable Funds** -- The primary source of loanable funds is personal saving. Savers are paid a rate of interest for the use of their money, and the amount of money saved is directly related to the interest rate. *The supply of loanable funds curve is upward sloping, showing that the supply of loanable funds increases as the interest rate increases, and decreases as the interest rate decreases.*

2. **The Demand for Loanable Funds** -- The demand for loanable funds is composed of the demand for consumption loans by individual's, investment loans by business, and the deficit-financing needs of the government. We will concentrate here on borrowing by households and businesses.

a. **The Demand for Loanable Funds: Consumption Loans** -- Consumers demand loanable funds because they have a **positive rate of time preference** -- that is, *consumers prefer to consume today, rather than wait until later.* As a result, consumers are willing to pay for the privilege of consuming now; and, therefore, they demand loanable funds to fill the gap between their current consumption desires and the funds they have to spend. In this sense, the interest rate on consumer loans is the (extra) price consumers pay to consume today instead of later.

b. **The Demand for Loanable Funds: Investment Loans** -- Firms demand loanable funds so they can invest in capital goods and finance **roundabout methods of production** -- where the firm first directs its efforts to produce capital goods and then uses those capital goods to produce finished goods. Because capital goods improve productivity and make finished good production more lucrative, firms are willing to borrow the funds necessary to produce them.

Adding the demand for consumption loans to the demand for investment loans, we get the total demand for loanable funds. *The demand for loanable funds curve is* downward sloping, and shows that there is an inverse relationship between the interest rate and the willingness of consumers and firms to borrow funds.

Exhibit 29-1 illustrates both the supply of and demand for loanable funds. The **equilibrium interest rate** is *the interest rate at which the quantity demanded of loanable funds equals the quantity supplied of loanable funds.*

B. **The Price of Loanable Funds and the Rate of Return on Capital Goods Tend to Equality** -- Over time, the price of loanable funds and the rate of return on capital goods tend toward equality. For instance, if the rate of return on capital was higher than the price of loanable funds, firms would borrow additional funds -- increasing the demand for loanable funds and the price of loanable funds -- in order to buy additional capital -- increasing the supply of capital and reducing the rate of return on capital.

C. **Why Do Interest Rates Differ?** -- The supply and demand analysis in Exhibit 29-1 suggests that there is an interest rate; but, in fact, there are many. Why? Three important factors stand out: risk, the length of the loan, and loan processing costs.

   1. **Risk** -- Any time a lender makes a loan, there is a possibility the borrower will not repay it. As a rule, *the greater the risk associated with a loan, the higher the interest rate; the lower the risk, the lower the interest rate.*

   2. **Term of the Loan** -- Lenders require interest rate premiums to give up their money for long periods of time. As a result, *the longer the term of the loan, the higher the interest rate; the shorter the term of the loan, the lower the interest rate.*

   3. **Cost of Making the Loan** -- All loans have processing costs associated with them, due to running credit histories, collecting payments, keeping records, and the like. *The more it costs to process and administer a loan, the higher the interest rate; the lower the cost of making the loan, the lower the interest rate.*

D. **Nominal and Real Interest Rates**

   1. **The Nominal Interest Rate** -- the interest rate determined by the forces of supply and demand in the loanable funds market -- it is *the interest rate in current dollars, unadjusted for expected inflation.* The nominal interest rate will change if the demand and/or the supply of loanable funds changes.

   2. **The Real Interest Rate** -- *the nominal interest rate adjusted for expected inflation* -- that is,

      real interest rate = nominal interest rate - expected rate of inflation.

      It is the real interest rate, not the nominal interest rate, that matters to lenders and borrowers, for the real interest rate is the better reflection of the opportunity costs of borrowing and lending. Exhibit 29-2 shows how expected inflation can affect the nominal and real interest rates.

E. **Present Value: What is Something Tomorrow Worth Today?** -- Is a dollar worth the same today as it will be worth tomorrow? How much will that dollar buy today compared to tomorrow? These questions introduce the concept of **present value**, which *measures* *the current value of some future dollar amount.* Specifically, the present value (PV) of some future sum can be calculated using the formula:

$$PV = A_n / (1+ i)^n$$

where A_n is the actual sum in a particular year in the future, i is the interest rate, and n refers to the number of years until the "payoff." If there is a future income stream, the formula would be

$$PV = \Sigma\, A_n / (1+ i)^n$$

F. **Deciding Whether to Purchase a Capital Good** -- Businesses often consider present value when making investment decisions. *If the present value of the revenues generated by the investment exceeds the cost of purchasing the capital good, the firm will borrow and invest; if the cost of purchasing the capital good exceeds the present value of the revenues generated by the investment, the firm will not borrow and invest.* Tying this back into the interest rate, *as the interest rate falls, present value increases, and firms will buy more capital goods; as interest rates increase, present value falls, and firms will buy less capital goods.* For an individual application of the idea of present value, use the *Economics In Our Times* features, "How Do you Know If You Should Buy the Car?" and "The Medical Degree Goes to Court."

G. **Interest Rates, Present Values, and your Wage Rate: Is There a Link?** -- Yes. As interest rates fall, the present value of capital goods rises, and business firms buy more capital goods. This investment increases the marginal productivity of labor which increases the demand for labor and ultimately the interest rates that labor is paid.

II. **RENT** -- While most people think of rent as something you pay to use someone else's property, in economics we are concerned with the concept of **economic rent** -- *payments in excess of opportunity costs* -- and with a subset of economic rent called **pure economic rent**, where the factor in question is in perfectly fixed supply and has no alternative use; and, therefore, *opportunity costs are zero.* Exhibit 29-3 illustrates such a situation.

A. **David Ricardo, the Price of Grain, and Land Rents in New York and Tokyo** -- All of the early theoretical work on economic rent focused on payments to land, which was seen as being in perfectly inelastic supply. Prevailing wisdom argued that land prices were excessively high, since land was in fixed supply, and that that was increasing the price of grain. Ricardo took a longer look, and concluded that the prevailing wisdom had things backwards: he argued that *land prices were high because grain prices were high*, creating more demand for land -- the demand for land was a derived demand based upon the demand for grain. In large cities such as New York and Tokyo, the prices of goods are higher than in the suburbs because the higher cost of land must be passed on to consumers.

B. **The Supply Curve of Land Can Be Upward Sloping** -- While the total supply of available land world-wide, with the notable exception of the Netherlands, is basically fixed, any given parcel of land may have multiple, competing uses. The supply curve for land with competing uses is upward-sloping, suggesting that potential users will have to bid against one another for the right to use the land and to acquire additional land for their use. In this case, economic rent is less than before, but still positive. [See Exhibit 29-4]

C. **Economic Rent and Other Factors of Production** -- The concept of economic rent applies to any factor of production that is receiving a payment in excess of its opportunity cost. The extent of that economic rent often depends upon the perspective from which the factor is viewed. Two individuals may receive the same wage rate at McDonald's, but their economic rents will differ if the opportunity cost of working at McDonald's differs.

D. **Economic Rent and Baseball Players; The Perspective from Which The Factor Is Viewed Matters** -- If we compare the salary of a baseball player to his potential salary as a high school coach, we get a significantly different picture of economic rent than if we compare his salary with one team to his potential salary with another team.

E. **Artificial and Real Rents** -- Individuals and firms compete for *artificial* and *real rents*.

1. **Artificial Rent** -- an economic rent that is artificially contrived by government that would not otherwise exist; for instance, monopoly rents created by granting a patent or exclusive license. Because of legal protection, firms will devote resources in an effort to secure these artificial rents -- resources that would otherwise be used in productive pursuits. As a consequence, competition for artificial rents is socially wasteful and causes significant inefficiencies.

2. **Real Rent** -- an economic rent that is not artificially created, and where there are no barriers to competing for it. Because of the lack of barriers, competition for real economic rents is socially productive, leading resources to be allocated more efficiently.

F. **Do People Overestimate Their Worth to Others, or Are They Simply Seeking Economic Rent?** -- If someone demands a higher salary than we think they should receive, we may think they are arrogant, but they may just be trying to gain some economic rent.

III. **PROFIT** -- Again, remember the distinction between accounting profits and economic profits. Accounting profits are total revenues minus total costs. Economic profits are the difference between total revenue and total costs where total costs include both explicit and implicit costs.

A. **Theories of Profit** -- Several different theories address the question of the source of profits. We discuss three of them here.

1. **Profit and Uncertainty** -- Uncertainty exists when a potential occurrence is so unpredictable that a probability cannot be estimated for it. Because uncertainty exists, expected profits may or may not materialize. Between the time a firm purchases its inputs and sells its output, unanticipated changes may make the firm's plans either overambitious or underambitious. In short, unanticipated changes create winners and losers, profit-makers and loss-takers.

2. **Profit and Arbitrage Opportunities** -- The way to make a profit, so it goes, is to "buy low and sell high." In the case of productive endeavors, we can interpret this as buying inputs at the lowest possible costs, combining those factors to make a product, and then selling that product at the highest price possible. If doing this results in profit, we would say it was a result of being alert to an arbitrage opportunity.

3. **Profit and Innovation** -- In this theory, profit is the return to the entrepreneur as innovator: the person who creates new profit opportunities by devising a new product, production process, or marketing strategy.

B. **What Do a Microwave Oven and an Errand-Runner Have in Common?** -- Both save people time, and since time is money, people are willing to pay for this good or service.

C. **American Entrepreneurs and European Taxes** -- In Europe, consumers pay a value-added-tax (VAT) when they buy products. Americans who buy goods in Europe and take the goods back to the U.S. can receive a refund of the VAT. One entrepreneurial firm, Advance Ross, simplifies the refund process and keeps a portion of the refund for their service.

D. **Monopoly Profits** -- As discussed earlier, monopolies can earn profits above normal profits, owing to high barriers to entry. In contrast to the temporary profits that exist where there are no barriers to entry, monopoly profits can exist for a long time. Recall, also, that these monopoly profits may be competed for, capitalized, or may be eliminated if the market is sufficiently contestable (see Chapter 22).

E. **Profit and Loss as Signals** -- In addition to being entries on a balance sheet, profit and loss both acts as signals. For example, when a firm makes an economic profit, other firms view this as a signal that the profit-making firm is selling a good that buyers value more than the factors that make that good. This causes new firms to enter the market, shifting resources to production of the profit-making good. In short, resources follow profit. The process is similar in the case of a loss, except that resources shift away from a loss. Thus, resources move to where they are most valued, thereby promoting resource allocative efficiency; and, over time, the prices of those profit-making goods will respond to the increase in supply, eliminating the economic profit once the proper amount of resources have been shifted into their production. Some individuals may see profits as evidence of exploitation, but most economists see profits, rent and interest as economic tools which aid in the efficient reallocation of resources.

IV. **ECONOMICS ON THE INTERNET** -- Several sources for information on loanable funds, interest rates, profits, wages and salary disbursements, proprietor's income, personal dividend income, personal interest income, and so forth are provided.

■ ANSWERS TO CHAPTER QUESTIONS

1. **What type of people are most willing to pay high interest rates?**

We expect that individuals who have a stronger preference for present over future consumption will be the most willing to pay high interest rates. That is, persons with a higher positive rate of time preference will be more willing to pay a higher interest rate than persons with a low positive rate of time preference.

2. Some persons have argued that in a moneyless (or barter) economy, interest would not exist. Is this true?

This is not true because interest can be viewed as the manifestation of a positive rate of time preference. Individuals living in a moneyless or barter economy are just as inclined to a positive rate of time preference as individuals living in a money economy. Whereas individuals living in a money economy pay their interest in money, individuals living in a moneyless economy would pay their interest in goods and services (two chickens next week for one chicken this week).

3. In what ways are a baseball star who can do nothing but play baseball and a parcel of land similar?

One might begin by saying that the opportunity cost of each is zero and, therefore, any payment is pure economic rent. However, this is only one way of looking at the question. It could also be said that the baseball star has the opportunity of playing for a team other than the one he currently plays for, and that the land can be used for something other than its present use. Looking at things this way, each would then have opportunity costs, and therefore any payment each received would not be *pure* economic rent (although some economic rent may be received).

4. What is the overall economic function of profits?

Profits direct resources. If a good is linked to profits, there is an inclination for resources to flow into the production of that good. Negative profit, or loss, also directs resources. If a good is linked to losses, there is an inclination for resources to flow out of the production of that good.

5. "The more economic rent a person receives in his job, the less likely he is to leave the job, and the more contented he will be on the job." Do you agree or disagree? Explain your answer.

To the extent that one's job satisfaction is largely determined by pay, and pay is judged relative to the opportunity cost of doing the job, then this is probably a true statement. Of course, there are many non-pay factors that must be considered, and their importance in determining whether or not the worker will be content on the basis of his/her economic rents will depend on whether they are fully incorporated into the worker's notions of opportunity cost.

6. It has been said that a society with a high savings rate is a society with a high standard of living. What is the link (if any) between saving and a relatively high standard of living?

Higher savings make it possible to fund greater amounts of investment, thus increasing productive capacity and allowing the economy to grow more and more rapidly. Further, to the extent that greater savings may lower interest rates, consumers will be able to borrow more freely and pursue their positive rate of time preference, making them feel more "well-to-do."

7. Make an attempt to calculate the present value of your future income.

This will, of course, depend greatly on the student's assessment of his/her future earning potential. The proper method is to treat future income as a stream of payments, such that

$$PV = \frac{Y_1}{(1+i)^1} + \frac{Y_2}{(1+i)^2} + \frac{Y_3}{(1+i)^3} + \ldots + \frac{Y_n}{(1+i)^n}$$

where Y_1 = expected (annual) income in year 1, and so on.

8. What do you think each of the following events would do to individuals' rate of time preference, and thus to interest rates: (a) a technological advance that raises longevity; (b) an increased threat of war; (c) growing older?

a.   If individuals feel more certain about their prospects for the future, they may be less inclined toward current consumption, reducing their rate of time preference and their demand for consumer loans; thus, reducing the interest rate.
b.   By the same logic, if individuals feel less certain about their future prospects, they will likely increase their desire for current consumption, increasing their rate of time preference and their demand for loanable funds; thus, increasing the rate of interest.
c.   Same as b.

9. "As the interest rate falls, firms are more inclined to buy capital goods." Do you agree or disagree? Explain your answer.

Yes. A reduction in interest rates raises the present value of potential investments, making more of them "economical." As a result, firms will increase their demand for capital goods and for the loanable funds with which to purchase them.

10. Compute the following:
a.   The present value of $25,000 each year for 4 years at a 7 percent interest rate.
b.   The present value of $152,000 each year for 5 years at a 6 percent interest rate.
c.   The present value of $60,000 each year for 10 years at a 6.5 percent interest rate.

a.   PV = $84,680.29.
b.   PV = $640,279.30.
c.   PV = $431,324.82.

■ LECTURE SUPPLEMENTS

Robert W. Brown, "An Estimate of the Rent Generated by a Premium College Football Player," *Economic Inquiry* **(31) October 1993, pp. 671-684.**

This article provides a good application of the concept of economic rent which your students should be able to identify with, and allow them to see a topic which is close to them in a new way.
There are several economic problems here. First, the National Collegiate Athletic Association (NCAA) limits the payments athletes can receive for their services. Second, colleges are effectively

monopsony employers so players will not be paid their marginal revenue product. The combination of monopsony and a price ceiling insures that colleges are able to capture the economic rent generated by their football players (as well as those in basketball and other sports). The question is, how much rent will the college capture?

To estimate this, Robert Brown estimates the marginal revenue product of a top college football player and compare this with how much a college football player is paid. Although technically a salary cannot be paid, football players do receive scholarships which have a market value of between $5,000 and $20,000 a year. Since no salary is paid, Brown had to impute the value of the MRP by looking at the NFL draft data as a means of measuring performance, and then working backward from this data. His conclusion? A premium college player can generate over $500,000 in annual revenues for his team.

"Copy to Come," *The Economist*, January 7, 1995, pp. 51-52.

Profits exist because of some barrier to entry. Either someone can process information about the market more efficiently than others, someone is more willing to take risks than others, or they have protection from competition through copyrights, patents, trademarks and other means. What if firms didn't have this protection? This article shows what can happen.

China is awash with fake products causing American firms to lose billions of dollars every year. The problem is not just that stray individuals are copying American and other foreign products and putting their names on it, but that firms and factories which are owned by the Chinese government are doing so. Many of the 29 plants which press 75 million pirated compact discs each year are state-owned. One plant is run by a foreign defense ministry official. There are fake Coca-Cola cans, fake McDonald's hamburger restaurants, and even fake Chrysler Jeeps. There is little enforcement of copyright laws in China, and when enforcement occurs, the fines are rarely large enough to discourage others from counterfeiting.

If entrepreneurs cannot keep the benefits of their discoveries, there will be little incentive for innovation and investment. Although counterfeiting may generate short-term profits for some, it is not a generator of dynamic growth.

"Of Politics, Pensions and Piggy Banks," *The Economist*, July 1, 1995, p. 72.

Savings are important because they provide the funds for investment, and the level of savings within a country influences the interest rate which in turn allocates capital. Countries with higher savings will have lower interest rates and higher rates of growth. One reason that east Asian countries have achieved high rates of growth is their high savings rates. This article asks the question, Why do east Asian countries have high savings rates, but Latin American countries do not?

Remember, savings come from two sources: the public sector and the private sector. How much each saves depends on factors such as the age profile of the population (older people save more than the young), relative wealth levels (rich people can save more), fiscal policy, tax rates, and so forth. There is also a question about cause and effect, do high growth rates generate higher savings while low growth rates generate low savings rates?

Sebastian Edwards tried to untangle these threads by looking at 36 countries. He concluded that one of the most important contributors to high savings is rapid economic growth. A second important factor is demography and the dependency ratio. Countries with high dependency ratios saved less. Countries with high urbanization saved less, probably because farmers face greater uncertainty and must save money as insurance against a failed crop. Edwards found that while a under-developed financial sector tended to reduce savings rates, government savings did not completely crowd out private savings. He found that government savings were higher when the country grew rapidly, but that political instability had a strong impact on the savings rate. This article provides some very useful information.

CHAPTER 30

Market Failure: Externalities, the Environment, and Public Goods

A **market failure** *occurs when the market does not provide the optimal amount of a particular good, despite the rational behavior of the participants in the market.* In Chapters 22 and 23 we saw one class of market failure -- the *structural market failure,* where the structure of the market itself insures that the optimal quantity of the good will not be produced. In this chapter, we turn to two other types of market failures: *externalities* and *public goods.* The first two sections of Chapter 30 develop the theory of externalities -- negative and positive -- and the ways in which external costs and/or benefits may be "controlled." The third section analyzes some important environmental issues from an economic perspective. The fourth section introduces the student to the notion of public goods, the *free rider problem,* and the role of the government in providing public goods. Finally, we discuss some interesting "real world" cases involving externalities and/or public goods, in light of the theory developed in the preceding pages.

■ CHAPTER OBJECTIVES

Upon completing this chapter, your students should be able to:

- define *negative externalities* and *positive externalities,* and explain how they are a source of *market failure;*

- discuss the various methods presented here for dealing with externalities and assess their strengths and weaknesses;

- understand the basic premise(s) of the *Coase theorem* and its significance to the theory of externalities and the appropriate responses to external costs and benefits;

- compare and contrast the workings of pollution standards and *market environmentalism,* or "selling the right to pollute;"

- define *public good,* with particular attention to the notions of *nonrivalry in consumption* and *nonexcludability;* and distinguish between a public good and a government-provided good;

- explain the *free rider problem* and its relationship to public goods; and,

- describe some "real world" externality and public good problems, and the ways in which society has chosen to deal with them.

■ KEY TERMS

- market failure
- externality
- negative externality
- socially optimal output
- positive externality
- internalizing externalities
- transaction costs

- Coase theorem
- public good
- Coase theorem
- nonrivalrous in consumption
- rivalrous in consumption
- excludability
- free rider

■ CHAPTER OUTLINE

I. **EXTERNALITIES** -- Sometimes, when goods are produced and consumed, that production/consumption affects people not directly involved in the market exchange. These "spillover" effects are called **externalities**, because the costs or benefits that occur are external to the party (-ies) that caused them.

A. **Negative Externalities** -- When a person's or group's actions cause harmful side effects that are felt by others, we say a **negative externality** has occurred. Examples of negative externalities include air, water, and noise pollution. As a consequence, the costs of the transaction to society (**social costs**) are not fully reflected in the costs to the purchaser(s)/producer(s) of the good or service (**private costs**). That is, private costs are unequal to social costs. What is the result?

Look at Exhibit 30-1. Since the market participants only take private costs into account, they produce output level Q_1, where *marginal private costs* (MPC) intersects the demand curve. As a consequence, the **socially optimal level of production**, Q_2, where **marginal social costs** (MSC) intersects the demand curve for the product, is not achieved. Instead, the failure of market participants to account for externalities results in an *over production* of the good.

Notice that the shaded triangle in Exhibit 30-1, and reproduced in Exhibit 30-2, illustrates the extent of the market failure -- it represents the net social cost of not producing at the socially optimal level of output.

B. **Positive Externalities** -- When a person's or group's actions cause a beneficial side effect that is felt by others, we say a positive externality exists. Examples of positive externalities include the rewards to society from education, the pride people feel when their local football team does well, and so on. Here, the benefits of the transaction to society (social benefits) are greater than the benefits to the individual producers and/or consumers themselves (private benefits). That is private benefits are unequal to social benefits.

In Exhibit 30-3, marginal social benefit (MSB) is greater than the marginal private benefits to consumers reflected in the demand curve. However, since the market participants only consider private benefits, they produce the level of output, Q_2, where the demand (MPB) curve intersects the supply (MPC) curve. As a consequence, the *socially optimal level of production*, Q_1, where **marginal social benefits** *(MSB) intersects the demand curve for the product*, is not achieved. Instead, the failure of market participants to account for externalities results in an *underproduction* of the good.

II. **INTERNALIZING EXTERNALITIES** -- An externality is **internalized** if the parties that generated the externalities incorporate the external costs and/or benefits of their actions into their own private cost-benefit calculations. This can be achieved by several means.

A. **Persuasion** -- Many negative externalities occur simply because the parties that create them do not consider the effects of their actions on others. By informing the parties responsible for an externality of the consequences of their actions, and persuading them to alter their behavior, we may get them to consider social costs (not just private costs) in their cost-benefit calculations.

B. **Assigning Property Rights** -- Some economists argue that many negative externalities occur because no one "owns" the air, oceans, etc. As a result, they continue, there is no one to take action against polluters for infringing on their property rights. If we could only assign *property rights* -- that is, determine legal ownership of these natural resources -- we could reduce negative externalities. The absence of land ownership on grazing lands in the western United States in the 19th century led to overgrazing, reducing the quality of the land.

C. **Voluntary Agreements** -- Externalities may also be internalized through voluntary agreements between the creator(s) of the externality and the third party (-ies) affected by it. In order for such an agreement to be reached, however, the **transactions costs** associated with making the agreement, must be lower than the expected benefits of the agreement. One example of transaction costs is illustrated in the *Economics In Our Times* feature, "Lowering 'Transaction Costs' in the Big Apple. The feature shows how a "key number" can be used to lower the costs of postal workers delivering the mail.

   The importance of transaction costs brings us to the **Coase Theorem**. The Coase theorem holds that, *if transaction costs are trivial or zero, resource allocative efficiency is unaffected by the assignment of property rights* -- that is, as long as it is cheap for affected parties to come together with externality-makers and reach some agreement, then they will do so, regardless of any legal decisions made as to who owns what. The Coase Theorem is important because it shows that under certain conditions the market can internalize externalities, and it provides a benchmark for analyzing externality problems.

   For some examples of externalities in the home and how individuals can resolve these problems, see the *Economics In Our Times* feature, "Externalities in the Home".

D. **Taxes and Subsidies** -- Taxes and subsidies are often used to "correct" a market failure caused by externalities. Specifically, a tax is used to adjust for a negative externality, and a subsidy to promote an activity with positive externalities.

   Look back at Exhibit 30-1. Here a negative externality exists. The objective of a corrective tax, then, would be to shift the supply curve such that the equilibrium level of output falls from the current Q_1 to the socially optimal Q_2. Of course, as Exhibit 30-4 reminds us, we must be careful not to "overtax," such that we reduce output more than is socially optimal.

E. **Beyond Internalizing: Setting Regulations** -- A final way to deal with externalities, particularly negative externalities, is for government to apply regulations directly to the activity that generates the externality. For instance, if steel mills emit air pollutants through their smoke-stacks, the government may regulate smokestack emissions.

   Critics of the regulatory approach often complain that, once enacted, regulations are difficult to remove -- even if they are no longer productive. In addition, regulations are often applied across the board, when circumstances dictate otherwise. Finally, regulations are expensive to create and enforce, and require the reallocation of otherwise-productive resources; thus, reducing the economy's ability to produce.

   F. **Pigou versus Coase** -- Is assigning property rights, or introducing taxes/subsidies the most efficient way of dealing with externalities? The text recounts the night when Coase successfully defended his ideas and the Coase theorem was born.

III. **THE ENVIRONMENT** -- The classic negative externality is pollution, and pollution in all of its forms, along with other environmental issues, have become the focus of increasing economic scrutiny in the past decade. Economists make three points concerning pollution: (1) pollution is a negative externality, (2) no pollution is sometimes worse than some pollution, and (3) the market can be used to deal with the problem of pollution.

   A. **Is No Pollution Worse Than Some Pollution?** -- Eliminating a negative externality often causes more economic harm than the externality itself. Thus, as with most other negative externalities, the **optimal level of pollution** is not zero but, rather, that amount of pollution where the *marginal social benefit of pollution equals its marginal social cost*.

   B. **Two Methods to Reduce Pollution** -- There are a number of alternative means for reducing pollution: setting government pollution standards and employing *market environmentalism* (using market forces to clean up the environment). Let's see how these two approaches work and how they differ.

      1. **Government Sets Pollution Standards** -- One alternative is for the government to set emission standards that limit the amount of pollution that a given polluter may generate. Exhibit 30-5 explores the costs of this alternative for three firms. Each firm must lower their pollution to a certain level, and the cost of reducing pollution will vary from one firm to the next.

      2. **Market Environmentalism at Work: Government Allocates Pollution Permits and Then Allows Them to Be Bought and Sold** -- The basic idea is that, for a given area, a certain amount of pollution is "acceptable." That "acceptable" amount of each given type of pollution is then parceled into permits which would-be polluters "bid" for in an "auction." The idea is that this allows polluters to compare the (internalized) cost of polluting to the revenues which could be earned by producing the additional output that would generate that pollution. It also allows producers to pass on the cost of pollution (more specifically, the cost of buying pollution rights) to their customers. If one firm can reduce their pollution more cheaply than another firm, they can buy the other firm's pollution rights and profit from the transaction. The same level of pollution is achieved as under the regulations discussed above, but the firms which are the most efficient at producing pollution carry out these activities rather than having all firms reduce pollution. Exhibit 30-5 can be used to show how this process would work.

IV. **PUBLIC GOODS** -- Another source of non-structural market failure is in the provision of **public goods** -- goods that, once produced and provided to one person, give benefits to more than one person. As a rule, the market underproduces public goods, if it produces them at all. Two factors characterize public goods: *nonrivalry in consumption* and *nonexcludability*.

A. **Nonrivalry in Consumption** -- *Consumption of the good by one person does not reduce its consumption by others.* Consider national defense -- once produced, national defense protects all persons within the geographic region, and its consumption by one person does not reduce its value to anyone else.

By contrast, a good has **rivalry in consumption** if its consumption by one person does reduce its consumption by others. For example, if I take a bite from an apple, there is less apple left for the next person.

B. **Nonexcludability** -- It is impossible, or prohibitively costly, to exclude someone from obtaining the benefits of the good once it has been produced. Consider a sunset, once it is "produced" in the Western sky, it is impossible (or "prohibitively costly") to exclude someone from viewing it.

By contrast, a good is **excludable** if it is possible, or not prohibitively costly, to exclude someone from obtaining the benefits of the good once it has been produced. For example, if I charge an enforceable price for my good, then I may exclude anyone unwilling or unable to pay that price from consuming my good.

C. **Nonrivalry Does Not Necessarily Imply Nonexcludability** -- There is a tendency to believe that nonrivalry and nonexcludability go hand in hand. In fact, there are many goods that are nonrivalrous in consumption which can be excludable; just as there are many examples of goods that are excludable, but nonrivalrous. Only a public good, by definition, is both nonrivalrous and nonexcludable.

D. **The Free Rider** -- When a good is nonexcludable, it is possible for individuals to benefit from the good without paying for it. Persons who do so are called **free riders**; and, it is because of free riders that the market will fail to produce the appropriate quantities of public goods, if it produces them at all. The reason being: no rational producer will supply a good for which no one has to pay in order to consume (unless, perhaps, the cost of production is zero).

The free-rider problem is the basis for accepting the public provision of goods. We need to be careful, though, that we do not assume that all **government-provided goods** -- any good or service provided by the government -- are public goods. The government provides many goods and services that are not public goods, because they are either rivalrous in consumption, excludable, or both.

The *Economics In Our Times* feature, "The Economics of Recycling" provides an application of the idea of free riding. To one individual, the hassle of collecting recyclable glass bottles and plastic containers may not exceed the amount which that person would receive when the bottles and containers are turned in, so he/she doesn't recycle. But this person still receives the benefits of others who recycle, making him/her a free rider.

V. **SOME EXTERNALITY AND PUBLIC GOODS ISSUES** -- This last section simply walks through a number of interesting issues in economics and applies to them the theory and understanding of externalities and public goods developed in the preceding pages.

A. **Acid Rain** -- Acid rain is a rain, or mist, that carries a mixture of sulfur-dioxide (SO_2) gases and nitrous-oxide (NO) emissions which, when they fall to earth, cause damage to forests, lakes, and rivers. The problem with acid rain is that no consensus has been reached on what causes it and who is responsible for the emissions that form it. As a result, it is impossible to internalize its costs, leaving taxes and regulation as the only viable options; and, even then, we aren't really sure who to tax and/or what to regulate.

B. **Traffic Congestion** -- In most cases, roads are provided by government and are assumed to be public goods. However, some economists argue that roads are not public goods. First, while they are nonrivalrous at some times, they are quite rivalrous at other, "rush" hours. Second, there are means by which roads may be made excludable -- perhaps not perfectly so, but somewhat excludable nonetheless. Given that, is traffic congestion an unnecessary consequence of a government-provided good misperceived to be a public good, and therefore, inadequately "priced?" In Hong Kong, the government has begun experimenting with a system which bills drivers for using heavily-traveled roads during peak travel hours.

C. **Smoking Sections in Restaurants** -- While many states now require designated smoking and non-smoking areas in restaurants -- in fact, some localities have banned smoking in restaurants altogether -- such did not used to be the case. Consider two diners, one a smoker, the other not. How can the non-smoker persuade the smoker to desist, so as not to ruin the non-smoker's enjoyment of her meal? While it is possible to use persuasion and/or to make a voluntary agreement, the time, effort, frustration, and embarrassment involved may be considered prohibitive by most people. As a result, non-smokers have opted for legal regulations to try to make their point. In effect, smoking rights have been redefined. In the past, it was assumed that individuals had the right to smoke in restaurants, and nonsmokers had to negotiate for the right to smoke-free areas. Now, nonsmokers have the right to smoke-free areas, and smokers have to negotiate for the right to smoke.

D. **Is Charitable Giving Subject to Free Riding?** -- If an individual gets some satisfaction out of seeing the needy receive assistance, is it possible to do so without actually giving one's own money? The likely answer is yes. To the extent that no single individual (on average) gives enough money to significantly affect total charitable giving, one has an incentive to become a free rider, enjoying the benefits of a "social conscience" without the burden of actually paying anything.

E. **Free Riders and the Size of the Group: Can Committees Get Too Big?** -- The previous example is just one case of a larger principle: *The larger the size of a group, and the smaller or less significant the individual's contribution to the total group effort, the greater the likelihood of free riding.*

F. **Economics 22,300 Miles High, or You Can See for Miles and Miles** -- One last example is the increasing congestion of space -- more specifically, geostationary (or, in some cases, geosynchronous) orbitary space -- by telecommunications, weather, and other types of satellites. This is complicated by the fact that sovereign nations, many of whom have differing legal and economic systems, are involved. Up to now, the use of space has been "first-come, first-served." However, as more and more nations and companies express the desire and attain the capability to move into the "neighborhood," negative externalities are bound to arise -- for example, signal interference or collision risk.

1. **Why Space Congestion Exists** -- The reason is simple, no one owns outer space. The United Nations has designated outer space as communal property, but communal property is not always used efficiently.

2. **Assigning Property Rights to Space** -- One solution is to sell property rights to space slots. This would encourage the efficient allocation of space slots.

3. **To Whom Do the Space Slots Go?** -- How to initially distribute the space slots would remain a problem. Should they be auctioned to the highest bidder, or distributed in a lottery, allowing the winners to sell the slots to others?

VI. **ECONOMICS ON THE INTERNET** -- A Usenet newsgroup which discusses environmental concerns is provided.

■ ANSWERS TO CHAPTER QUESTIONS

1. Give an example that illustrates the difference between private costs and social costs.

A manufacturer of chemicals incurs a cost of $100,000 to produce a certain quantity of chemicals. In the process of producing the chemicals, the manufacturer emits pollution into the air that eventually results in higher medical bills for the people who live nearby. If we consider only the costs of the manufacturer -- the $100,000 -- we are speaking of private costs. If we consider this private cost plus the cost to the persons affected by the pollution -- that is the $100,000 plus the increase in the medical bills -- we would be speaking of social costs.

2. Consider two types of divorce laws. Law A allows either the husband or the wife to obtain a divorce without the other person's consent. Law B permits a divorce only if both parties agree to the divorce. Will there be more divorces under law A or law B, or will there be the same number of divorces under both laws? Why?

The Coase theorem tells us that there would be the same number of divorces under both laws. To see this, consider a situation where (1) the husband wants a divorce but the wife does not, and (2) the husband wants the divorce more than the wife does not want the divorce. Under law A, there will be a divorce. The wife would not be able to change her husband's mind because he wants the divorce more than she doesn't want the divorce.

What about under law B? Will there be a divorce under law B? At first sight, most persons would say no. They would argue that since both must agree to the divorce under law B and the wife does not want the divorce, there will be no divorce. But consider, once again, that the husband wants the divorce more than the wife doesn't want the divorce. With trivial or zero transaction costs, the husband will offer the wife more than she requires to agree to the divorce. For example, if the husband is willing to pay $5,000 to obtain a divorce, and the wife is willing to pay $3,000 to stop the divorce, then it is possible for the husband to pay the wife something more than $3,000 and less than $5,000 to win her agreement to the divorce. Under law B, there will be a divorce. We conclude that under both divorce laws a divorce will result.

3. People have a demand for sweaters, and the market provides sweaters. There is evidence that people also have a demand for national defense, yet the market does not provide national defense. What is the reason the market does not provide national

defense? Is it because government is providing national defense and therefore there is no need for the market to do so, or because the market won't provide national defense?

The market isn't providing national defense because it won't provide national defense. National defense is a public good; it is nonrivalrous in consumption and nonexcludable. Because it is a public good, it is subject to the free rider problem; that is, its benefits can be received without making payment. Given this, rational producers won't supply a good that no one is likely to pay for.

4. Education is often said to generate positive externalities. How might it do this?

It is often argued that an educated person is a more informed voter, a better citizen, and a more productive worker who is likely to generate more jobs. If this is true, then education not only directly benefits the persons acquiring it, but others, too.

5. Give an example of each of the following: (a) a good rivalrous in consumption and excludable; (b) a good nonrivalrous in consumption and excludable; (c) a good rivalrous in consumption and nonexcludable; (d) a good nonrivalrous in consumption and nonexcludable.

a. A hamburger
b. An opera being staged in a theater
c. Fish in the ocean
d. National defense

6. Some individuals argue that with increased population growth, negative externalities will become more common and there will be more instances of market failure and more need for government to solve externality problems. Other individuals argue that as time passes, technological advances will be made and used to solve negative externality problems. They conclude that over time there will be fewer instances of market failure and less need for government to deal with externality problems. What do you believe will happen? Give reasons to support your position.

There is no right or wrong answer, only good or bad rationale. Basically, increased population means an increased likelihood of infringing on someone else's utility function. On the other hand, increased technology means that we may be able to reduce the extent of our externalities.

7. Name at least five government-provided goods that are not public goods.

The list will vary from person to person, but here are five: (1) education, (2) electricity generation, (3) mail service, (4) personal security, and (5) low-cost housing.

8. One view of life is that life is one big externality. Just about everything that someone does affects someone else either positively or negatively. To permit government to deal with externality problems is to permit government to tamper with everything in life. There

is no clear dividing line between externalities government should and should not become involved in. Do you support this position? Why?

Again, this is basically an opinion question intended to make the student think about "real world" problems in the context of economic theory and economic analysis. Most students will probably argue for some government intervention -- some externalities are bad enough or good enough to warrant action -- the problem is determining which externalities are "deserving" of government attention and which are not.

9. Economists sometimes shock noneconomists by stating that they do not favor the complete elimination of pollution. Explain the rationale for this position.

At some point, the marginal cost of pollution abatement is greater than the marginal social cost of pollution. To expend otherwise-productive resources to reduce pollution beyond that level would be an inefficient allocation of available resources.

10. Why is it cheaper to reduce, say, air pollution through market environmentalism than through government standards and regulations?

Government standards and regulations make all polluters reduce their pollution to a certain level regardless of how much it costs firms to reduce their pollution. It may cost one firm $100,000 to reduce their pollution down to an acceptable level, and cost another firm $25,000. If the second firm bought the first firm's pollution rights and was able to further reduce their pollution for another $25,000, society would get the same reduction in pollution for $50,000 rather than $125,000. The result is the same, but the cost to society of achieving this goal is substantially lower using market environmentalism than using government standards and regulations.

■ LECTURE SUPPLEMENTS

Scott Kilman, "Iowans Can Handle Pig Smells, but This Is Something Else," *The Wall Street Journal*, May 4, 1995, p. A1, column 4.

This is a good little article on negative externalities. Technology now allows farmers to have megafarms of thousands of genetically uniform pigs whose activities are regulated daily until they are sent from the metal-and-concrete building in which they live to that great pigpen in the sky. However, hogs are not known for their aromatic contributions to the environment. The simple fact is, pigs stink.

Pigs always have smelled, but packing thousands of them into a closed area creates a level of malodorous odor which would not be achieved with just a few hogs. The stench stings the eyes up close, and can waft for a mile across the countryside. Moreover, the megafarms are driving down the price of hogs causing smaller farms to get out of the hog business. The combination of these factors has caused individuals to go to their county Board of Supervisors and try to redress the problem. Ask your students how they would deal with this externality, and see if their response is similar to the people living in Iowa.

David Gardiner and Paul R. Portney, "Does Environmental Policy Conflict with Economic Growth?" *Resources*, **Spring 1994, pp. 19-23."**

If you need an article which raises issues concerning the conflicts between environmental policy and economic growth, this is a good place to start.

The "traditional" point of view is that environmental regulation impedes economic growth; however, the article looks at an opposing point of view which holds that not only can environmental regulation provide health and ecosystem protection, but it can stimulate the economy and enhance U.S. competitiveness at the same time. The two articles by David Gardiner and Paul Portney echo this point of view.

They point out that when decision makers adopt an either/or model of the economy-environment interaction, less-than-optimal outcomes can result for both the economy and the environment. In fact, the economy and environment are interrelated, and the relationship between them is more complex than most decision makers aver. Gardiner gives several examples of cases where firms both reduced their pollution and cut costs simultaneously. Environmental regulations do not necessarily lead to plant closures, and air pollution has been reduced in the United States without a significant impact on growth.

Pomeroy contends that the impact of environmental regulations has been small, and that regulations should pass a cost-benefit test before being introduced. Pomeroy believes that there have been costs to environmental regulations, but the difficulty lies in comparing the out-of-pocket costs which are immediately visible, and the opportunity costs which are not so readily apparent.

"Hertz Is a Little Worried About Putting You in the Driver's Seat," *Wall Street Journal*, **July 28, 1995, p. B1, column 3.**

This article can be used to analyze the problem of moral hazard and how firms deal with it. The source of moral hazard should be obvious. Because a rented car is not an individual's property, they are less likely to treat the car with the care and consideration which they treat their own car. The article provides several examples of the problems Hertz faces in renting their cars and the ways which Hertz deals with this moral hazard problem.

CHAPTER 31

Public Choice: Economic Theory
Applied to Politics

Chapter 30 discussed two major sources of market failure -- situations in which the market fails to produce the optimal quantity of output. To a large degree, this chapter is about **government failure** -- *situations in which government enacts policies that produce inefficient and/or inequitable results as a consequence of the rational behavior of the participants in the political process.* Chapter 31 develops the theory of *public choice*, using economic rationale to study the "market" for political outcomes -- both elections and policies -- and the participants in that market: politicians, voters, special-interest groups, and bureaucrats. Chapter 31 is a great companion to the preceding chapter, in that it can be used to look at the decisions to tax, subsidize, and regulate (or not to) *externalities*, as well as to produce *government-provided* and *public goods*.

■ CHAPTER OBJECTIVES

Upon completing this chapter, your students should be able to:

- define *government failure* and explain how *public choice* theory can be used to analyze government failures, as well as "successful" political decisions;

- understand the premise that institutional arrangements have a strong impact on individual behavior within those institutions;

- describe the rationale behind the median voter model, and how and why politicians will change their positions and rhetoric under this model;

- explain the concept of *rational ignorance* and its importance to the shaping of the American political process and the policy outcomes of that process;

- discuss the role of *special-interest groups* in American politics and why they seem to "win" on so many issues, despite representing only a small minority of the affected voters; and,

- show how the incentives which bureaucrats face influences the decisions which they make, and determine what bureaucrats try to maximize.

■ KEY TERMS

- government failure
- median voter model
- rational ignorance

- special-interest groups
- logrolling
- government bureaucrat

■ CHAPTER OUTLINE

I. **PUBLIC CHOICE THEORY** -- **Public choice** is the branch of economics that deals with the application of economic principles and tools to public-sector decision making. In so doing, public choice theory makes a basic assumption that people are people, and that the difference between "economic" behavior and "political" behavior is one of institutions, and not of fundamentally-different human characteristics.

The same types of people who are employers, employees, and consumers in the market sector are the politicians, bureaucrats, special-interest group members, and voters in the public sector. According to public choice theory, the differences between the behavior of people in the market sector and people in the public sector arise from different institutional arrangements in the two sectors, not from different motives or character traits.

II. **THE POLITICAL MARKET**

A. **Moving Toward the Middle: The Median Voter Model** -- During most U.S. political elections, voters complain that the candidates are "too much alike" -- they have similar backgrounds, and they campaign on more or less the same slate of issues. Why does this happen? Exhibit 31-1 illustrates that political office-seekers are faced with a distribution of voters that is largely made-up of people "in the middle" -- or, to use the political term: moderates. Given this, a rational office seeker will modify his/her positions and/or rhetoric in order to appear more "mainstream," and thus attract the moderate voter.

B. **What Does the Theory Predict?** -- Given this process of modifying positions and appealing to the *median* voter, we see a pattern emerging which describes many U.S. election campaigns.

1. **Candidates Will Label Their Opponents As Either "Too Far Right " or "Too Far Left"** -- Given the importance of attracting the median voter, a rational campaigner will paint his/her opponent(s) as being "too liberal" or "too conservative" for the average voter's tastes.

2. **Candidates Will Call Themselves "Middle-of-the-Roaders" Not Right- or Left-Wingers** -- At the same time, the rational campaigner will label him-/herself as a "moderate," who is on the side of, and in agreement with, the average voter.

3. **Candidates Will Take Polls, and If They Are Not Doing Well in the Polls and Their Opponent Is, They Will Modify Their Positions to Become More Like Their Opponent** -- Polls tell candidates how well their message is getting across. A rational candidate who finds that he/she is not appealing to a majority of voters will modify his/her positions accordingly, in order to improve his/her standing.

4. **Candidates Will Speak in General, Instead of Specific, Terms** -- Voters agree more on *ends* than on *means*. As most campaigns indicate, candidates and voters on both sides of the political spectrum share concern over a number of issues, it is their proposed solutions that differ. Thus, by concentrating on stating the problems -- the "ends" -- rather than the more politically-volatile solutions -- the "means" -- the rational candidate will appeal to a broader base of support.

C. **Simple Majority Rule: The Case of the Statue in the Square** -- *This Economics In Our Times* feature makes an important point. All of the "dollar votes" which citizens cast have the same impact on the political decision which is made, and the majority rules. Majority rule ignores the fact that some people may feel very intensely about a political decision, but their vote has the same impact as someone who has little interest in the outcome of the vote.

III. VOTERS AND RATIONAL IGNORANCE

A. **The Costs and Benefits of Voting** -- Voters are rational, utility-maximizing individuals, just as they are in their roles as consumers and employees/producers. This means that the rational voter must weigh the benefits of voting against the costs of doing so, in order to determine whether or not it is "worth it" to vote; and, if so, how much time and effort to spend becoming informed about the candidates and issues.

 The benefits of voting vary from person to person. At a somewhat esoteric level, many people benefit from exercising their "civic duty," may feel patriotic for their participation in the democratic process, and may feel that they have more right to criticize government and demand more from government. More tangibly, many people will vote for a particular candidate because they feel his/her election will "pay off" to them or to some group(s) about whom the voter is concerned. The costs of voting are even more tangible. They include: the time spent traveling to and from the polling place; the time spent waiting at the polling place; the cost of transportation; and, in some cases, lost wages.

B. **Rational Ignorance** -- Even if a person decides to vote, there is another list of costs involved with becoming informed about the candidates and issues. To the extent that *the costs of becoming informed outweigh the benefits*, voters practice what is called **rational ignorance**, choosing not to acquire additional information. If your students don't believe in this concept, have them take the quiz in the *Economics In Our Times* feature, "A Simple Quiz You Are Likely to Fail (But That's Not Bad)."

IV. SPECIAL-INTEREST GROUPS -- While voters are the "consumers" of political decisions, one subset of voters, so-called *special-interest groups*, play an unusually large role in shaping the outcomes of the political process -- both elections and policies. **Special-interest groups** are made up of people who share some common interest(s) and, as a result, have strong preferences for or against particular government services, activities, or policies.

A. **Informational Content and Lobbying Efforts** -- Because of their intense feeling about their particular issue(s), members of special-interest groups tend to be better informed than average voters, and participate more actively in the political process. The reason: the benefits of participating (or the costs of not participating) are perceived to be much higher than for the average voter, thus the cost-benefit calculation favors participation. As a result, the desires of special-interest groups tend to be represented disproportionately in the outcomes of elections and of the policy process.

B. **Congressional Districts as Special-Interest Groups** -- In addition to issue-oriented special-interest groups, geographical location will often play a role in the issues that voters are interested in and the degree to which they participate in the political process. For instance, suppose that a piece of legislation is before Congress that would significantly benefit or harm a particular congressional district. The Congressperson from that district would have an incentive to take his/her constituents' opinions into account, and the voters in that district will let their voices be heard if the proposal is important enough.

But, there's a problem: no single Congressperson has enough power to pass or defeat legislation by themselves. As a result, Congresspersons must seek the support of their colleagues on legislation that is important to them, and offer their own support on other legislation in return. Such a process is called **logrolling**, *the exchange of votes to gain support for (or opposition to) legislation.* It is the widespread use of logrolling -- somewhat necessitated by the size and distribution of power in the Congress -- that is largely responsible for the abundance of so-called "pork barrel" legislation.

C. **Public-Interest Talk, Special-Interest Legislation** -- Students should recognize that when special interest groups favor policies which will help the general public, they may have a hidden agenda. Farmers may want to propose a bill to set aside wetlands to preserve the environment, but the hidden agenda may be to obtain subsidies for idle lands.

V. **GOVERNMENT BUREAUCRACY** -- The next group in our discussion of the political market is the thousands of departments, agencies, and offices that carry out the task of governance on a daily basis, administering the programs of the legislature, as well as formulating their own policies within the boundaries allowed by the legislature. In particular, we are concerned about the individuals that staff the bureaucracy -- the **government bureaucrats**.

A. **Government Bureaus: Some Facts And Their Consequences** -- In order to understand the forthcoming predictions about bureaucratic behavior, we should first present some basics about the government bureaucracy.

1. **Funding** -- Bureaus are funded by legislative appropriation. Often, a bureau's funding for coming years will depend on how much it spends during the current year.

2. **Motive** -- A government bureau has no profit-motive to entice it to be cost-efficient.

3. **Control** -- There are no transferable ownership rights in a government bureau -- no "stockholder," if you will. The bureau is solely responsible to the elected officials that created, staff, and fund it.

4. **Competition** -- Many government agencies compete in a monopolistic situation, having no real competition for the services they provide (inside government or out).

5. **Life Span** -- Bureaus are often created by specific legislation. If that legislation is repealed, or expires, the bureau will soon follow.

Given these observations, many economists argue one or more of the following points about bureaucratic behavior:

1. **No Surplus Funds** -- If funding next year depends upon spending this year, bureaus are unlikely to end the year with surplus funds; otherwise, their appropriations will be cut next year, and that might cut jobs and will certainly cut prestige.

2. **Not Cost-Efficient** -- Since government bureaus don't attempt to maximize profits, they are unlikely to be as cost-efficient as a firm.

3. **Less Oversight** -- No one has a monetary incentive to watch over the bureau because no one "owns" the bureau, in the sense that there are no stockholders. As a result, there is no one to ensure that the bureau operates efficiently.

4. **Less "Customer-Oriented"** -- Government bureaus and bureaucrats are not as likely to try to please their "customers" as private firms would be, since (in many cases) they have no competition, real or potential, to force them to do so.

5. **Self-Promotion** -- Government bureaus are likely to lobby for the continued existence and expansion of the programs they administer.

B. **A View of Government** -- The purpose of this presentation is not to present government bureaucrats as uncaring, self-centered individuals, but to show how the incentives which bureaucrats face produce the behavior which results. Although these ideas are theoretical, the facts do tend to support the theory. If you teach at a large university, ask your students whether this theory would apply to the university bureaucrats.

VI. **ECONOMICS ON THE INTERNET** -- Several good sources for data on political economy are provided, and a Usenet newsgroup at the Sam Houston State University Gopher is given.

■ ANSWERS TO CHAPTER QUESTIONS

1. Some observers maintain that not all politicians move toward the middle of the political spectrum to obtain votes. They often cite Barry Goldwater in the 1964 presidential election and George McGovern in the 1972 presidential election as examples. Are these exceptions to the theory developed in this chapter?

That is not necessarily the case. It is correct that Goldwater was perceived as being to the far right of middle, and that McGovern was perceived as being to the far left of middle, but we do not know if both candidates thought they were in the middle of the political spectrum. In short, both Goldwater and McGovern may have thought they were gravitating toward the middle of the political spectrum, but were wrong on where the middle of the spectrum was.

It is interesting to note what their respective political parties did in the next presidential election. In 1968, the Republicans, having suffered a defeat with Goldwater in 1964, chose a presidential candidate who was closer to the middle of the political spectrum than Goldwater: Richard Nixon. In 1976, the Democrats, having suffered a defeat with McGovern in 1972, chose a presidential candidate who was closer to the middle of the political spectrum than McGovern: Jimmy Carter.

2. Would voters have a greater incentive to vote in an election in which there were only a few registered voters or many registered voters? Why?

All other things held constant, a voter would have a greater incentive to vote in an election the smaller the number of registered voters. The reason is that the smaller the number of voters, the greater the likelihood that one's vote will affect the outcome. The greater the number of voters, the smaller the likelihood that one's vote will affect the outcome.

3. Many individuals learn more about the car they are thinking of buying than about the candidates running for the presidency of the United States. Explain why.

If an individual learns about the car he is thinking of buying, this information can be extremely useful. Since the individual who buys the car has to live with his choice, he wants to make certain it is a good one. If he decides incorrectly, money has been wasted. When it comes to the presidential candidates, however, the individual knows that he will not decide the election, and that no amount of information that he has on the candidates will matter to the decision at hand.

4. If the model of politics and government presented in this chapter is true, what are some of the things we would expect to see?

First, we would expect to see a higher voter turnout in warm weather than in cold, rainy weather, *ceteris paribus*. The reason is that cold, rainy weather increases the costs of voting.

Second, we would expect to see congressional representatives from nonfarm states voting for farm subsidies. If we didn't see this, we would question the existence of logrolling.

Third, we would expect to see government bureaus spending any excess funds before the end of the fiscal year. Excess funds cannot be divided up among the government bureaucrats themselves, so from their point of view it is better to spend the money than leave it unspent and return it to the legislature. Returning it to the legislature might result in a smaller budget the next year.

Fourth, we would expect to see the programs, ideas, and policies of representatives elected by large majorities copied by other representatives. What they are copying is success. The representative who wins an election by a large majority is presenting other representatives, or other individuals running for office, with information as to where the middle of the political spectrum *is* in a particular voting distribution.

5. It has often been remarked that Democratic candidates are more liberal in the Democratic primaries and that Republican candidates are more conservative in the Republican primaries than either is in the general election, respectively. Explain why.

In the party primaries, the median Democratic voter is to the "left" of center, and the median Republican voter is to the "right" of center. As a result, a rational candidate, wishing to appeal to the median voter in whatever election he/she is running, will adjust his/her rhetoric and positions accordingly. Thus, since the median voter in the Democratic primary is to the left of the median voter on the presidential election, we would expect Democratic hopefuls to appear more "liberal" in the primaries than in the general election. And, since the median voter in the Republican primary is to the right of the median voter in the presidential election, we would expect Republican hopefuls to appear more "conservative" in the primaries than in the general election.

6. What are some ways of reducing the cost of voting to voters?

Some simple ways would be to: provide more thorough information on the candidates and their positions on issues important to voters; increase the period of time during which voters may vote; allow people to cast their votes via telephone or home computer link (assuming we can protect against computer sabotage); require employers to let employees off work, with pay, in order to go vote; and, provide free public transportation to voting places.

7. What are some ways of making government bureaucrats and bureaus more cost conscious?

Probably the best proposal would be to reward bureaus that spend their budgets efficiently, rather than punishing them by reducing their appropriations if they fail to spend all of their budgeted funds. Additionally, Congress could make budget appropriations -- and, perhaps, salaries -- subject to performance reviews, rather than simply adding to last year's levels.

8. Some individuals see national defense spending as benefiting the special interests -- in particular, the defense industry. Others see it as directly benefiting not only the defense industry but the general public as well. The issue here is that while some individuals see "special interest" only, others see special interest and public interest. This difference in view often leads to political arguments. Does this same difference in view exist for issues other than national defense? Name a few.

Sure. The investment tax credit is seen by some as a "break" for big business, allowing them to get out of paying their "fair" share of the tax burden, while others see it as a way of promoting investment, expanding productive capacity, and enabling the economy to grow. On the other side of the political spectrum, many people view environmental legislation and nuclear plant bans as a threat to their jobs and their standard of living, while others see protecting the environment as being essential to maintaining the well-being of every American and ensuring the integrity of the Earth's ecosystem. The Republicans have passed legislation to lower the capital gains tax. The rationale for this is that it will spur investment and economic growth. Assuming that many republicans have capital gains in the stocks they own, this reduction would provide them with direct benefits by reducing their tax burden if they sell their shares.

9. Evaluate each of the following proposals for reform in terms of the model presented in this chapter: (a) linking all spending programs to a visible tax hike; (b) a balanced budget amendment that stipulates that the Congress cannot spend more than total tax revenues;

(c) a budgetary referenda process whereby the voters actually vote on the distribution of federal dollars to the different categories of spending (X percentage to agriculture, Y percentage to national defense, and so on) instead of the elected representatives deciding.

a. By linking all spending programs to a visible tax hike, voters will better be able to see the cost of proposed legislation -- making it less difficult for them to become informed, and enabling them to make more rational choices and to hold elected officials more accountable.

b. Requiring a balanced budget may well restrict the tendency to vote for new spending programs simply to collect political favors (logrolling), and force politicians to more carefully consider the economics of their decisions. It could also help to reduce the growth of bureaucratic spending, or at least force any increases to be considered on their merits, and not simply passed.

c. Having voters decide on the distribution of funds could serve two purposes. First, it would encourage voters to become more informed about the programs government conducts, because the cost of ignorance is much higher if you have to make a decision, rather than delegating that responsibility to someone else. Second, it would likely reduce the extent of "special-interest" spending, since the cost to special-interest groups of effectively lobbying 200 million voters would be much greater than the cost of lobbying 535 Senators and Congresspersons.

■ LECTURE SUPPLEMENTS

Gary S. Becker, "End Affirmative Action As We Know It," *Business Week*, **August 21, 1995, p. 16.**

Whether you agree or disagree with Gary Becker, this article will certainly generate some in-class debate. Becker argues that policies which set aside job opportunities and college slots for individuals who are less qualified than others but come from a particular minority group is not only inefficient, but is opposed by the majority of Americans. One form of discrimination should not be replaced with another. Instead, he proposes affirmative action policies which would raise minorities' human capital so they could gain the skills needed to compete in the market.

How do you do this? Kids from poor families should be given tuition vouchers they can use to get a decent education. Becker emphasizes that the most effective policies are ones which change the attitudes and skills of young persons. Policies should also aim at cracking down on crime and keeping families intact. Consequently, students arrive at college unprepared. This is shown in the University of California at Berkeley where 59 percent of blacks graduate within six years, 64 percent of Hispanics, 84 percent of whites, and 88 percent of Asians. Affirmative action programs also generate resentment and stereotyping of the beneficiaries. Use this article to analyze the economic impact of affirmative action and how to deal with it.

Richard B. Schmitt, "While Congress Debates, States limit Civil Lawsuits," *Wall Street Journal*,**" June 16, 1995, p. B1, column 5.**

This article looks at a political-economic problem which continues and has no simple answer. Tort laws provide damages to those who are harmed by others actions. These cases end up in court, and the awards which are provided for "pain and suffering" or to penalize the person who caused the harm can run into the millions of dollars. The impact of these tort rulings can be subtle, but widespread. When I was growing up, every swimming pool had a diving board which provided me many hours of fun and enjoyment. Today, diving boards are almost non-existent because one kid fell off a diving board into an empty pool, sued the manufacturer, and won several million dollars. The manufacture of diving boards soon ground to a halt.

This article looks at the ways in which different states are currently acting to limit the damages which can be awarded under tort laws. Although the Federal government is moving to limit damages, some states are moving faster. The political-economic issue here is how individuals use two different branches of government, the judicial and the legislative, to achieve economic goals. If one branch produces "inefficient" results in which awards given by tort cases reduce economic efficiency, individuals turn to the legislature to control the decisions which courts are allowed to make. In a sense, the two branches of government are competing to provide political services, and if the courts provide inefficient results, individuals will seek legislative solutions where judicial solutions fail. This, of course, is one of the primary ideas behind the economics of the law literature, and this article could be used to discuss its issues.

Daniel Pearl, "Telecommunications, Like Politics, Is Local the Locals are Saying," *Wall Street Journal*, **August 3, 1995, p. A1, column 6.**

The telecommunications bill which has been moving through Congress provides a good example of how laws are more often battlegrounds between competing industries and corporations, and politicians pay scant attention to the interest of individuals. Cable companies, entertainment companies, telephone companies, and others all want a slice of the information superhighway, and the battle over this market starts in the U.S. Congress. By using the telecommunications bill to restrict or increase access to different telecommunications markets, corporations can win half the market battle before it even begins.

As the article points out, in January 1995, House GOP leaders met privately with top network and phone executives to find what they wanted. Consumers were largely ignored. As the article shows, individual consumers care about what happens to the telephone and cable services they receive, but compared with the giant telecommunications companies, their impact is minimal. This is why many individuals want more local control over cable companies because they are on a more equal footing at the local level. This article shows how politicians, without necessarily being venal, inevitably favor the interests of those who have economic and political clout over consumers who rarely have this clout.

CHAPTER 32

International Trade

Chapter 32 begins the final section of the text. This chapter, along with the three that follow, looks at the theory of international trade and finance, the implications of international economic conditions and policies on domestic economic conditions and policies, and the major economic challenges faced by developing countries and by planned economies. Chapter 32 focuses on the theory of international trade: why nations trade, how they determine what to trade, and how and why some nations restrict free international trade. Specifically, we are dealing here with the exchange of (real) goods and services. Chapter 33 will turn to exchange of another kind: currency exchange, both as a facilitator of international trade and as an end to itself. We are also dealing, specifically, with the exchange of (real) goods and services between countries, and, as we will see in this chapter and the next, there are some clear distinctions between intra-national and international trade.

■ CHAPTER OBJECTIVES

Upon completing this chapter, your students should be able to:

- understand why nations trade and how they determine what and how much to trade;

- distinguish between *absolute advantage* and *comparative advantage*, and describe their importance to decisions about international exchange;

- discuss the concepts of *consumers' surplus* and *producers' surplus*;

- describe the effects of permitting and prohibiting imports and exports on domestic consumers and producers;

- define *tariff* and *quota*, explain how each works, and describe their effects on prices, quantity consumed, quantity imported, producers' surplus, consumers' surplus, and government revenues;

- assess the various arguments for trade restrictions, being able to explain both the rationale behind each argument, as well as the shortcomings of each; and,

- know some of the ways in which governments have recently acted to liberalize trade.

■ KEY TERMS

- absolute advantage
- comparative advantage
- consumers' surplus
- producers' surplus

- tariff
- quota
- dumping
- "voluntary" export restraint

■ CHAPTER OUTLINE

I. **INTERNATIONAL TRADE THEORY** -- How important is trade to most nations' economies? Why do nations trade? How do nations determine what to trade and how much?

   A. **What Does the United States Export and Import?** -- What does the U.S. export and import? In 1994, major U.S. exports included automobiles, computers, aircraft, agricultural products, scientific instruments, coal, and plastic materials. In 1994, major U.S. imports included petroleum, automobiles, clothing, iron and steel, office machines, footwear, fish, coffee, and diamonds. Exhibit 32-1 shows the major categories of U.S. exports and imports for 1994. Exhibit 32-2 shows the countries and regions of the world where U.S. exports are purchased.

   B. **Why Do People in Different Countries Trade With One Another?** -- As we have seen before, mutually beneficial exchange between two or more people allows for specialization, division of labor, and significant gains in efficiency and total output. The economic rationale for international trade are much the same. Different countries have different natural resources, labor conditions, skills, and institutions; and, by specializing in the production of those goods for which each country is best suited and trading for other needs, all countries may be made better off by international exchange than by attempting to be self-supporting.

   C. **How Do Countries Know What to Trade?** -- To explain how countries find which goods they are "best suited" to produce and trade, we turn to the principles of *absolute advantage* and *comparative advantage*.

   1. **Absolute Advantage** -- Exhibit 32-3 presents hypothetical data for two countries -- the U.S. and Japan -- and two goods -- clothing and food. Notice that, with the same amount of resources, the U.S. can produce more food than Japan; and that, with the same amount of resources, Japan can produce more clothing than the U.S. Such a situation indicates that the U.S. has an absolute advantage in the production of food, while Japan has an absolute advantage in the production of clothing. A country has an **absolute advantage** in the production of a good if, *using the same amount of resources as another country, it can produce more of a particular good*. Put differently, we also say a country has an absolute advantage in the production of a particular good *if it can produce the same amount of the good using fewer resources*.

      a. **Output With and Without Specialization** -- Now, look at Exhibit 32-4. Column 1 shows the output of food and clothing for both the U.S. and Japan assuming no specialization and no trade. Column 2 offers a comparison, showing the possible output of food and clothing if the U.S. were to specialize in the production of food (the good in which it has an absolute advantage) and Japan were to specialize in the production of clothing (the good in which it has an absolute advantage). As can be seen, the total output of both goods rises as a result of specialization and trade.

b. **The Terms of Trade** -- After they have specialized in the production of the goods in which they have their respective absolute advantages, the U.S. and Japan must agree on the **terms of trade** -- that is, how much food will trade for how much clothing. While there are several possible answers, the terms of trade must be such that both countries benefit by the exchange -- that is, the cost to the U.S. of purchasing clothing from Japan must be less (in food traded) than from producing it in the U.S. (in terms of lost food output); and, the same for Japan and the cost of food relative to clothing.

Based upon an opportunity cost ratio of 3 units of food foregone for every 1 unit of clothing produced in the U.S. (that is, 3F = 1C) and a ratio 1 unit of clothing foregone for every 1 unit of food produced (that is, 1F = 1C); then, the terms of trade must be somewhere between 1F = 1C and 3F = 1C. Column 3 in Exhibit 32-4 assumes a "mid-point" solution of 2F = 1C.

c. **The Gains From Trade** -- Column 4 of Exhibit 32-4 shows the amount of food and clothing consumed in Japan and the U.S., each, assuming specialization and trade at the stated terms of trade. Column 5 consolidates this information, and shows that both the U.S. and Japan gain from trade, in that they have more goods to consume than they would have had if they had chosen not to specialize.

2. **Comparative Advantage** -- Exhibit 32-5 paints a somewhat different picture. Here the U.S. is better than Japan at producing both food and clothing -- that is, it has an absolute advantage in the production of both goods. Now what do we do?

a. **The Law of Comparative Advantage** -- Suppose that neither country specializes. This situation is represented by the data in Column 1 of Exhibit 32-6. Now, suppose that the two countries decide to specialize and trade. How do they decide who should produce what? The general answer is stated in the **law of comparative advantage**: *Countries specialize in the production of the good in which they have a comparative advantage.* A country has a **comparative advantage** in the production of a good when *it can produce the good at a lower opportunity cost than another country*.

While the U.S. can produce more of both clothing and food, Japan gives up less food to produce clothing than does the U.S.; therefore, we say Japan's opportunity cost of producing clothing is less than the United States' costs.

b. **The Gains From Trade** -- Suppose the U.S. and Japan agree to specialize in the production of the good in which each has the comparative advantage. Column 2 of Exhibit 32-6 shows the appropriate levels of food and clothing output. Assuming the same terms of trade established previously, Column 3 shows the flow of food from the U.S. to Japan, and of clothing from Japan to the U.S. Column 4 shows total consumption in the U.S. and Japan. And, as Column 5 summarizes, both countries are better off specializing and trading, despite the fact that the U.S. has an absolute advantage in the production of both goods.

D. **How Do Countries Know When They Have a Comparative Advantage?** -- Countries do not plan their comparative advantages and trade accordingly, but the market provides

336

price incentives to entrepreneurs when their country has a comparative advantage. If beef is cheaper in the United States than in England, the U.S. will export beef to England using its comparative advantage.

II. **TRADE RESTRICTIONS** -- Of course, only rarely will two countries sit down, determine where each one has a comparative advantage, and agree to export the good(s) in which each country has a comparative advantage and import the good(s) in which each country has a *comparative disadvantage*. Instead, the process of determining comparative advantage and of adjusting international production and trade accordingly takes time.

A. **Why Are There Trade Restrictions In the Real World?** -- While trade benefits all people *on average*, certain individuals will be hurt by trade -- some fairly severely. If the group(s) harmed by international trade have sufficient economic and/or political clout, they are often able to get the government to restrict imports, even though doing so hurts the economy as a whole.

B. **Consumers' and Producers' Surplus** -- In order to understand the effects of trade and trade restrictions on consumers and producers we should first understand the concepts of *consumers'* and *producers' surplus*.

1. **Consumers' Surplus** -- *the difference between the actual price buyers pay for a good and the maximum price they are willing and able to pay for it*. It is a dollar measure of the benefit gained by being able to purchase a unit of a good for less than one is willing to pay for it. [See Exhibit 32-7a]

2. **Producers' Surplus** -- *the difference between the price sellers receive for a good and the minimum price for which they would be willing and able to sell the good*. It is a dollar measure of the benefit gained by being able to sell a unit of output for more than one is (minimally) willing to sell it. [See Exhibit 32-7b]

C. **How Is Trade Restricted?** -- Two of the most commonly used methods to restrict free trade are the *tariff* and the *quota*.

1. **Tariffs** -- *a tax on imports*. The primary effect of a tariff is to raise the price of the imported good to the domestic consumer. Exhibit 32-8 illustrates this. The effect of a tariff is to redistribute some of the consumers' surplus (from free trade) to domestic producers, and some to the government. The real cost of tariffs is that they result in a so-called **"deadweight loss"** equal to *the difference between lost consumers' surplus and the gains by producers and government*. Tariffs provide both a redistribution *and* a deadweight loss. In Exhibit 32-8, consumers lose areas 1 + 2 + 3 + 4. Producers gain area 1, and the government gains area 3. The deadweight loss is shown by the sum of areas 2 and 4.

2. **Quota** -- *a legal limit on the amount of a good that may be imported*. Quotas actually come in two varieties: the *strict quota*, which sets an actual quantitative limit on imports; and, the *variable quota*, which limits imports to a fixed percentage of total domestic sales. A quota, like a tariff, raises the price paid by domestic consumers, as is shown in Exhibit 32-9. The principal difference here is how the effects of the price increase are distributed. As with the tariff, part of the consumers' surplus lost due to the quota (and higher prices) is transferred to

337

domestic producers (area 1); and, like the tariff, there is a "deadweight loss" associated with the quota (the sum of areas 2 and 4); but, unlike the tariff case, area 3 is transferred to foreign producers, rather than to the government.

D. **The Politics of Quotas** -- If quotas make consumers worse off, why do they exist? The answer is that the benefits of the quota are concentrated on one industry, but the costs of the tariff are widely distributed. A tariff may profit 100 producers $400,000 each, but cost each of 20 million consumers only $2. To producers, lobbying for the quota is a worthwhile "investment," but to an individual consumer, it is cheaper to pay the $2 than to lobby against the quota.

E. **Japanese Protectionism, Japanese Consumers** -- One study found that protectionism costs Japanese consumers severely, raising the price of some consumer items several hundred percent over the free trade price.

F. **If Free Trade Results in Net Gain, Why Do Nations Sometimes Restrict Trade?** -- Groups which propose limits on trade argue that the restrictions are in the public interest, but in most cases, the primary interest is their own, not that of the public as a whole.

G. **Arguments for Trade Restrictions** -- Despite the conclusions of the preceding analysis that free trade benefits both producers and consumers on net more than trade restrictions would, trade is often not free. There are several arguments for trade restriction, some of which have economic merit, others of which do not.

1. **The National-Defense Argument** -- It is often argued that certain industries -- such as steel, aircraft, petroleum, chemicals, and the like -- are of vital strategic importance and must be maintained in order to maintain national security, even if the industry is not economically competitive. The main problem with such an argument is identifying those industries that are truly vital to national security.

2. **The Infant-Industry Argument** -- A long-accepted argument for trade restriction is that "infant" industries ought to be protected against import competition until they gain sufficient expertise and achieve an adequate scale to compete on "even ground" with their established foreign competitors. The main problem here is that, once enacted, protectionist legislation is hard to undo, and may even cause the protected industry to become dependent on protection.

3. **The Antidumping Argument** -- **Dumping** is *the sale of goods abroad at a price below their cost of production, and below the price charged in the domestic market.* Critics of dumping argue that it is an unfair trade practice, often used to drive rightful competitors out of the market and then raise prices and reap monopoly profits. Whether or not the latter part of the argument is true, most countries (including the U.S.) have anti-dumping laws on their books. The principal defense of dumping is that it allows consumers access to lower-priced goods.

4. **The Foreign-Export-Subsidies Argument** -- Some governments subsidize firms that export goods and services. By offering below-market (interest rate) loans, offsetting shipping and customs costs, providing tax breaks, and the like, the government is lowering the production and distribution costs of the exporter and allowing them an "unfair" advantage against unsubsidized competitors. Much like the

defenders of dumping, many argue that if foreign governments want to subsidize exports and drive down prices paid by foreign customers, that benefits consumers.

5. **The Low-Foreign-Wages Argument** -- It is sometimes argued that American products cannot compete with foreign products because American producers pay their workers higher wages than foreign producers pay their workers. What this argument overlooks are two factors: first, higher productivity in the U.S.; and, second, higher cost of living -- both of which suggest that U.S. wages should be higher.

6. **The Saving-Domestic-Jobs Argument** -- Last, but not least, is the argument that imports -- fair or unfair -- displace domestic output and create domestic unemployment. The response is that, as long as the jobs are being lost due to more efficient foreign production, the job loss is a signal that resources can be better allocated elsewhere.

   Americans are not the only ones to make this argument. As *The Global Economy* feature "Jobs in Japan" shows, many Japanese feel that American firms place them at an unfair disadvantage. Japanese firms offer lifetime employment to some of their employees, and "poaching" employees from other firms is unlawful. Japanese firms' relative inflexibility in hiring and firing labor puts them at a competitive disadvantage relative to the Untied States.

H. **What Price Jobs?** -- If tariffs and quotas save jobs, an important economic question to ask is, how much does it cost consumers to save these jobs? Studies have shown that the cost is very high. It cost $77,714 to protect each $8,340 domestic footwear job in 1977, and the **"voluntary" export restraints** (which work the way quotas do) saved 44,000 domestic jobs at a cost of $193,000 per job.

III. **Liberalizing Trade** -- There have been several recent attempts to liberalize trade.

A. **North American Free Trade Agreement (NAFTA)** -- NAFTA went into effect on January 1, 1994 and will phase out most tariffs between the United States, Canada and Mexico. Opponents of NAFTA argued that it would cause unemployment in the United States by encouraging firms to produce in Mexico where wages are lower. Proponents of NAFTA argued that the higher productivity of American workers would reduce this job loss, and NAFTA would allow American firms to specialize and use their comparative advantage to raise living standards in the U.S. As Mexicans' incomes increased, they would demand more American goods.

B. **Asia-Pacific Economic Cooperation (APEC)** -- was established in 1989 as a mechanism to achieve freer trade and investment among Pacific Rim countries. Member countries aim to eliminate all trade barriers by the year 2020.

C. **European Union (EU)** -- has fifteen members in western Europe. The EU has eliminated most economic barriers to the movement of people, goods and services, and its members hope to have a single currency by the end of the century.

D. **World Trade Organization (WTO)** -- This is the successor organization to the *General Agreement on Tariffs and Trade (GATT)* which was created in 1947 to coordinate tariff reductions among member countries. The WTO was set up under the *Uruguay Round* of negotiations which concluded in 1993, and it has the responsibility for settling trade disputes among member nations. Almost all the countries in the world are members of the WTO.

IV. **ECONOMICS ON THE INTERNET** -- Sites for gaining access to information on GATT and NAFTA are provided in Chapter 15. This chapter provides sites for information on the Maastricht Treaty for the European Union as well as a good source for information on trade data.

■ ANSWERS TO CHAPTER QUESTIONS

1. A production possibilities frontier is usually drawn for a country. One could, however, be drawn for the world. Picture the world's production possibilities frontier in your mind. Is the world positioned at a point on the curve or below the frontier? Give a reason for your answer.

The world is positioned at a point below the frontier. We know this because we live in a world where countries impose tariffs and quotas. As the chapter explained, both tariffs and quotas come with net losses; that is, without tariffs and quotas (with free trade), there would be net gains that are not received with tariffs and quotas. In short, the countries of the world would produce and consume more if no restrictions existed. Thus we conclude that in a world where tariffs and quotas do exist, the world must be positioned at a point below its production possibilities frontier.

2. Using the data in the table, answer the questions that follow: (a) In which good does Canada have a comparative advantage? (b) In which good does Italy have a comparative advantage? (c) What might be a set of favorable terms of trade for the two countries? (d) Prove that both countries would be better off in the specialization-trade case than in the no specialization-no trade case.

Points on Production Possibilities Frontier	CANADA		ITALY	
	Good X	Good Y	Good X	Good Y
A	150	0	90	0
B	100	25	60	60
C	50	50	30	120
D	0	75	0	180

a. Canada has a comparative advantage in the production of good X. In Canada, the opportunity cost of producing 1 unit of X is 1/2Y. In Italy, the opportunity cost of producing 1 unit of X is 2Y. Since Canada can produce good X at a lower opportunity cost than Italy can, Canada has a comparative advantage in the production of good X.

b.   Italy has a comparative advantage in the production of good Y. In Italy, the opportunity cost of producing 1 unit of Y is 1/2X. In Canada, the opportunity cost of producing 1 unit of Y is 2X. Since Italy can produce good Y at a lower opportunity cost than Canada can, Italy has a comparative advantage in the production of good Y.

c.   In Canada, 1X = 1/2Y, and in Italy, 1X = 2Y. A favorable set of terms of trade would be anything between these two extremes; for example, 1X = 3/4Y, or 1X = 1Y, or 1X = 1-3/4Y. To see this, pick any of these terms of trade, say, 1X = 1Y. At present, Italy has to give up 2Y to get 1X; it would prefer to give up only 1Y to get 1X. At present, Canada gives up 1X and only gets 1/2Y; it would prefer to give up 1X and get 1Y instead.

d.   Suppose that in the no specialization-no trade case, Canada is producing and consuming at point B on its production possibilities frontier, and Italy is producing and consuming at point C on its production possibilities frontier. This means the situation is as follows:

No Specialization - No Trade

Canada	Italy
Produces 100 units of X	Produces 30 units of X
Consumes 100 units of X	Consumes 30 units of X
Produces 25 units of Y	Produces 120 units of Y
Consumes 25 units of Y	Consumes 120 units of Y

Now suppose the countries agree to the terms of trade 1X = 1Y and trade (in absolute amounts) 40C for 40Y. Canada specializes in the production of good X; Italy in the production of good Y. Now Canada is in this situation: It produces 150 units of X, trades 40 units to Italy, and receives 40 units of Y in exchange. It consumes 110 units of X (150 - 40 = 110) and 40 units of Y (received in trade). Italy is in this situation: It produces 180 units of Y, trades 40 units to Canada, and receives 40 units of X in exchange. It consumes 140 units of Y (180 - 40 = 140) and 40 units of X (received in trade). Thus both countries consume more of both goods in the specialization-trade case than in the no specialization-no trade case.

Specialization - Trade

Canada	Italy
Produces 150 units of X	Produces 180 units of Y
Consumes 110 units of X	Consumes 140 units of Y
Consumes 40 units of Y	Consumes 40 units of X

3.   "Whatever can be done by a tariff can be done by a quota." Discuss.

To a large degree, this is true. For example, if a tariff raises the price of imported goods from P_1 to P_2, a quota can raise the price by exactly the same amount. And, if a tariff and quota both raise the price of imports by the same amount, both will reduce consumers' surplus and increase producers' surplus by the same amount. A difference between a tariff that produces a price of P_2 and a quota that produces a price of P_2 is that the tariff will raise tariff (tax) revenues for the government and the quota will not.

4. Consider two groups of domestic producers: those that compete with imports and those that export goods. Suppose the domestic producers that compete with imports convince the legislature to impose a high tariff on imports, so high, in fact, that almost all imports are eliminated. Does this policy in any way adversely affect domestic producers that export goods? How?

Yes, it does. To simplify, suppose there are only two countries in the world, the United States and Mexico. If the United States imposes a high tariff on Mexican goods so that Americans no longer buy Mexican goods, this will drastically reduce the number of dollars Mexicans will have to buy American goods. In turn, this will affect American producers who produce goods for export. The point is simple: If a nation does not import goods from foreigners, foreigners will not have the purchasing power to buy that nation's export goods.

5. Suppose the U.S. government wants to curtail imports, would it be likely to favor a tariff or a quota to accomplish its objective? Why?

It would most likely favor a tariff over a quota. A tariff raises revenue for the government, a quota does not. (As an aside, the average U.S. tariff rate has been approximately 10 percent in the past decade.)

6. Suppose the land mass known to you as the United States of America had been composed, since the nation's founding, of separate countries instead of separate states. Would you expect the standard of living of the people who inhabit this land mass to be higher, lower, or equal to what it is today? Why?

Lower. The flow of goods, services, and factors across the 50 states would be substantially lessened if they were 50 separate countries, since each country would have political pressures to protect its indigenous industry and work force. Since the flow of goods, services, and factors is reduced, the distribution of resources would be less optimal than with unrestricted trade, resulting in a lower level of real output, and a lower standard of living.

7. Even though Jeremy is a better gardener and novelist than Bill is, he (Jeremy) still hires Bill as his gardener. Why?

As long as Bill can allow Jeremy to become more productive by devoting all of his time to writing novels than by splitting his time between writing and gardening, then Jeremy is making a wise choice. It all has to do with comparative advantage -- while Jeremy has an absolute advantage in both tasks, Bill is "less worse" at gardening than at novel writing, and thus has a comparative advantage there that, if exploited, will allow both men to be better off than if they each acted separately and performed tasks.

8. Suppose that tomorrow a constitutional convention were called and you were chosen as one of the delegates from your state. You and the other delegates must decide whether it will be constitutional or unconstitutional for the federal government to impose tariffs and quotas or restrict international trade in any way. What would be your position?

The answer to this question will depend upon how the student weighs the economic arguments against trade restrictions against the political arguments for it. There is no "right" answer; but, be sure that the student believes what he/she says, and can support it with sound reasoning.

9. Some economists have argued that since domestic consumers gain more from free trade than domestic producers gain from (import) tariffs and quotas, consumers should buy out domestic producers and rid themselves of costly tariffs and quotas. For example, if consumers save $400 million from free trade (through paying lower prices) and producers gain $100 million from tariffs and quotas, consumers can pay producers something more than $100 million but less than $400 million and get producers to favor free trade, too. Assuming this scheme were feasible, what do you think of it?

In a sense, this is like the "voluntary agreement" introduced in Chapter 30. As long as both parties benefit more from the agreement than they would from disagreement, then this is an economically-sound policy. Consumers will gain more from free trade, even after "paying-off" domestic producers, than producers would gain from restricted trade; and, producers should favor the proposal, for they are guaranteed a gain greater than they would get with restricted trade, when they cannot even be sure that trade would otherwise be restricted to protect them.

■ LECTURE SUPPLEMENTS

"Legal changes Keep Electric Golf Cart Going to Court," *The Wall Street Journal*, **May 24, 1995, p. A1, column 4.**

If there ever was a classic example of how trade barriers can triumph over economic efficiency, the case of the Melex golf cart would probably win the prize. The golf cart can drive 54 holes on one battery charge, but it has driven for 21 years through a series of lawsuits which would have strained the Energizer bunny. The Polish manufacturer has been charged with dumping the Melex golf cart on American markets, and the lawsuit has outlasted five U.S. Presidents, Poland's martial law, and the Soviet empire.

In the late 1960s, an American entrepreneur searched Eastern Europe for a low-cost production facility and discovered the huge PZL-Mielec military aviation complex in Poland. The entrepreneur proposed that PZL build the golf cart, later dropped out, and PZL decided to build the golf cart on their own. Initial sales were quite good in the United States, but in the 1980s, the U.S. pressured it to raise prices, Japanese imports flooded the market, and martial law was imposed. At this point, the lawyers took over, and Melex and American golf cart manufacturers have been battling it out in court ever since. If you want to talk about non-tariff barriers, this is a very good place to start.

"Japan's Protection Racket," *The Economist*, **January 7,1995, p. 58.**

How much do barriers to imports cost Japanese consumers? A lot, as this article shows. Although few of the goods have tariffs imposed upon them, non-tariff barriers keep foreign goods out of the hands of Japanese consumers.

To measure the cost of these non-tariff barriers, three Japanese economists calculated the implied non-tariff barrier rate for such common goods as rice, radios and TVs, wheat, cosmetics and so forth. The results will amaze you. The implied non-tariff barrier rate for milled rice is 737 percent; for cosmetics, 659 percent; for radios and TVs, 607 percent; and for clothing, 282 percent. The way the three economists calculated these rates was by comparing the dockside price of imports with the price of Japanese goods at the factory gate. They estimated that the cost to Japanese consumers totaled around $110 billion a year in 1989, or about 3.8 percent of GDP. There are a couple shortcomings in their measurements. The three economists do not allow for quality differences, and exchange rates can affect the degree of protection. But the result is clear. Trade barriers push up the price of Japanese goods and make imports more expensive.

"Big MacCurrencies," *The Economist*, April 15, 1995, p. 74.

Once a year, *The Economist* calculates their Big Mac index which compares the price of Big Macs in almost forty countries to see how much individual currencies are overvalued or undervalued. The idea is that the Big Mac is the same in every country. By comparing the price of Big Macs in each country, and using the Purchasing Power Parity Theorem, you can calculate how much currencies have deviated from their PPP equilibrium. Of course, this is not an exact science. There are many other factors which can affect the price of Big Macs because they, unlike oil or gold, are not perfectly fungible and freely traded between countries. Nevertheless, the index does give an idea of which countries' currencies are overvalued (Denmark, Japan and Switzerland were the most significantly overvalued) or undervalued (China, Hong Kong and Poland) relative to the dollar. This should prove a light-hearted introduction to Purchasing Power Parity theorem for your students.

CHAPTER 33

International Finance

Chapter 32 presented the *real* side of international transactions, in that it concentrated on the flow of goods and services, essentially leaving money out of the process. In Chapter 33, we turn to the *monetary* side of international exchange where currencies are traded for one another in order to purchase foreign goods and service, to make overseas investments, and for speculative purposes. The chapter first discusses the *balance of payments* and what it does and does not tell us, then turns to the determination of *exchange rates*. This latter discussion is broken down into three sections: the theory of *flexible exchange rates*, the theory of *fixed exchange rates*, and the history of international monetary systems from the *gold standard* of the 1870s to the present system of *managed flexible exchange rates*. The chapter concludes with an assessment of the strengths and weaknesses of the current international monetary system.

■ CHAPTER OBJECTIVES

Upon completing this chapter, your students should be able to:

- distinguish between the *merchandise trade balance* and the *balance of payments* and explain what each tells us about the state of U.S. international transactions;

- identify the main accounts of the balance of payments statement -- the *current account*, the *capital account*, and the *official reserve account* -- and their various components;

- define the *exchange rate* and describe how exchange rates are determined under both a *flexible exchange rate system* and a *fixed exchange rate system*;

- explain *currency appreciation* and *depreciation*, and identify the factors that can cause each;

- understand the *purchasing power parity (PPP) theory* and its implications for exchange rates and expected changes in exchange rates;

- describe how a currency can become *overvalued* or *undervalued*, and discuss the options available under a fixed exchange rate system for dealing with an over- or under-valued currency;

- present the main theoretical arguments for and against a fixed exchange rate system and a flexible exchange rate system;

- trace the major developments in international monetary relationships, beginning with the *gold standard*, and working through the *Bretton Woods system* up to the current system of *managed flexible exchange rates*, or *"managed float;"* and,

- assess the strengths and weaknesses of the current international monetary system, in light of the theoretical and historical background developed in this chapter.

■ KEY TERMS

- balance of payments
- debit
- credit
- current account
- foreign exchange market
- merchandise trade balance
- merchandise trade deficit
- merchandise trade surplus
- current account balance
- capital account
- capital account balance
- exchange rate
- flexible exchange rate system

- appreciation
- depreciation
- purchasing power parity (PPP) theory
- real interest rate
- fixed exchange rate system
- overvaluation
- undervaluation
- devaluation
- revaluation
- International Monetary Fund (IMF)
- Special Drawing Right (SDR)
- managed float

■ CHAPTER OUTLINE

I. **THE BALANCE OF PAYMENTS** -- Countries keep track of their level of domestic production by calculating their gross domestic product (GDP); similarly, they keep track of the flow of their international exchange (real and monetary) by calculating their *balance of payments*. The **balance of payments** is *a periodic statement of the money value of all transactions between residents (and the government) of one country and residents (and governments) of all other countries.*

Balance of payments accounts record both *debits* and *credits*. *Any transaction that involves an outlay of domestic currency (in exchange for foreign currency) is recorded as a* **debit**. *Any transaction that involves the receipt of foreign currency (in exchange for domestic currency) is recorded as a* **credit**. Exhibit 33-1 summarizes the various debit and credit items that make up the balance of payments, and a hypothetical U.S. balance of payments account is provided in Exhibit 33-2. Notice that these items are grouped into three accounts: the *current account*, the *capital account*, and the *official reserve account*.

A. **The Current Account** -- *includes all payments related to the purchase and sale of goods and services, as well as unilateral transfers of funds from one country to another.* There are three major components of the current account: exports of goods and services, imports of goods and services, and net unilateral transfers abroad.

1. **Exports of Goods and Services** -- Americans exports goods and services, and they receive interest income on foreign investments. All three activities involve supplying foreign currencies in exchange for U.S. dollars (since payment to

Americans must be made in U.S. dollars); thus, they are recorded as *credits* -- that is, they increase the value of the current account.

2. **Imports of Goods and Services** -- Americans import goods and services, and foreigners receive interest income on assets they own in the U.S. These activities involve supplying U.S. dollars in exchange for foreign currencies (since payment to foreigners must be made in their own currencies); thus, they are recorded as *debits* -- that is, they reduce the value of the current account.

3. **Note: The Merchandise Trade Balance** -- If we look at the difference between the value of U.S. goods exported (item 1.a. in Exhibit 33-2) and foreign goods imported by the U.S. (item 2.a. in Exhibit 33-2), we have the **merchandise trade balance** which is equal to merchandise exports minus merchandise imports.
   If the value of a country's merchandise exports (goods exported) is greater than the value of its merchandise imports (goods imported), the country is said to have a **merchandise trade surplus** -- or, shortened for the media, a *trade surplus*. *If the value of a country's merchandise exports is less than the value of its merchandise imports*, the country is said to have a **merchandise trade deficit** -- or, a *trade deficit*. Exhibit 33-3 shows the U.S. merchandise trade balance from 1980 through 1993.

4. **Net Unilateral Transfers Abroad** -- A **unilateral transfer** is *a one-way money payment from citizens or the government of one country to citizens or the government of some other country.* If Americans make a unilateral transfer to some foreign country, it shows up as a debit on the current account; if foreigners make a unilateral transfer to the U.S., it shows up as a credit on the current account. *The value of total U.S. transfers to foreign citizens and countries minus total foreign transfers to U.S. citizens and the U.S. government equals net unilateral transfers abroad.*

5. **The Current Account Balance** -- *the summary statement of the value of goods and services exported and imported, plus net unilateral transfers abroad.*

B. **The Capital Account** -- *includes all payments related to the purchase and sale of assets and to borrowing and lending activities.* Its major components are the outflow of U.S. capital and the inflow of foreign capital.

   1. **Outflow of U.S. Capital** -- American purchases of foreign assets and U.S. loans to foreigners are outflows of U.S. capital. As such, they give rise to supplying dollars in exchange for foreign currencies; thus, they are a *debit* to the capital account.

   2. **Inflow of Foreign Capital** -- Foreign purchases of U.S. assets and foreign loans to Americans are inflows of foreign capital. As such, they give rise to supplying foreign currencies in exchange for dollars; thus, they are a *credit* to the capital account.

   3. **The Capital Account Balance** -- *the summary statistic for capital flows and is equal to the difference between U.S. capital outflows and foreign capital inflows.*

C. **Official Reserve Account** -- All governments possess official reserve balances in the form of foreign currencies, gold, reserve holdings in the International Monetary Fund (IMF), and special drawing rights (SDRs). Countries with a deficit in the current and capital accounts (combined) may draw down these official reserves, resulting in a credit to the official reserve account. Countries with a surplus in the combined current and capital accounts will accumulate additional official reserves, resulting in a debit to the official reserve account.

For the purposes of calculating the official reserve account and the balance of payments, we distinguish between *U.S. official reserve assets* (a *debit* item) and *foreign official assets in the U.S.* (a *credit* item). The rationale is that U.S. holdings of other currencies constitute an exchange of dollars for those currencies -- hence, a debit to the balance of payments; whereas, foreign holdings of U.S. dollars constitute an exchange of foreign currencies for dollars -- hence, a credit to the balance of payments.

D. **Statistical Discrepancy** -- In addition to the current, capital, and official reserve accounts, the balance of payments also includes a statistical discrepancy to account for unreported transactions.

E. **What the Balance of Payments Equals** -- The balance of payments is the summary statistic for the following:

> Exports of goods and services
> Imports of goods and services
> Net unilateral transfers abroad
> Outflow of U.S. capital
> Inflow of foreign capital
> Increase in U.S. official reserve assets
> Increase in foreign official assets in the United States
> Statistical discrepancy

Alternatively, the balance of payments is the summary statistic for the current account balance, capital account balance, official reserve balance, and the statistical discrepancy. By definition, the balance of payments will always equal zero. However, as we have seen, none of its components need equal zero. And, it is the values of these components -- particularly the current account -- that attract the interest of economists and policy makers.

II. **FLEXIBLE EXCHANGE RATES** -- When a U.S. buyer wants to buy something from a U.S. producer, the buyer simply exchanges the required number of dollars with the producer in order to receive the good. If, on the other hand, a U.S. buyer wants to purchase a good from a seller in France, the process is slightly more complicated. In this instance, the U.S. buyer must first convert her dollars into French francs, and then exchange francs for the good in question. While the second half of the transaction is familiar, the first part -- trading dollars for francs -- is somewhat new.

How do we trade dollars for francs, yen, pounds, etc? The market in which currencies are exchanged in called the **foreign exchange market** and the price for which any two currencies are bought and sold is called the **exchange rate** between those two currencies. In this section, we focus on how exchange rates are determined in a world where the forces of supply and demand are allowed to act relatively freely -- a **flexible exchange rate system**. In the next section, we will discuss many of the same issues within the context of a *fixed exchange rate system*.

A. **The Demand and Supply of Currencies** -- Where do currency supply and demand come from? Our analysis of the balance of payments answers the question fairly well, when combined with the statement in the paragraph above. Americans wish to buy foreign goods and services, to invest in foreign assets and lend money abroad, to make gifts to foreigners, and, in addition, some people hold currencies themselves for their "investment value" -- all of these desires require exchanging dollars for foreign currencies; thus, we see both sides of the coins: the demand for currencies comes from the desire to spend money abroad and to speculate on exchange rate changes, and the supply of currencies is provided by those people demanding some other currency.

Exhibit 33-4 shows the currency supply and demand relationship when an American wants to purchase British goods, and Exhibit 33-5 shows the effect of a British buyer wanting to purchase American goods. Notice that the supply of dollars is equal to the demand for pounds, and the demand for dollars equals the supply of pounds. Notice, also, that the demand for a currency is inversely related to the exchange rate, while the supply of that currency is positively related to the exchange rate. The reason: the higher the value of the pound, the more expensive British goods become, so American consumers demand less British goods and, as a result, less British currency. It is important to understand that *a demand for British pounds creates a supply of U.S. dollars*, and vice versa. This impact can be seen in Exhibit 33-4 and Exhibit 33-5.

B. **The Equilibrium Exchange Rate** -- Assuming fully flexible exchange rates, *the equilibrium exchange rate between the dollar and the pound (or between any two currencies, for that matter) is determined by the equilibrium of the supply of and demand for pounds (in the dollar-pound market)*. At the equilibrium exchange rate, the quantity supplied of pounds exactly equals the quantity demanded of pounds -- there are no shortages or surpluses. At any other exchange rate, however, either an excess demand for pounds or an excess supply of pounds will exist. [See Exhibit 33-6]

Also, note that the exchange rates are the reciprocals of each other. This fact allows you to calculate cross-currency conversion rates, as explained in *The Global Economy* feature, "The Economics of Currency Conversion."

C. **Changes in the Equilibrium Exchange Rate** -- A change in the demand for pounds, or in the supply of pounds, or both, will change the equilibrium dollar price per pound -- that is, the dollar-pound exchange rate. If the dollar price per pound rises -- say, from $1.50 = £1 to $1.80 = £1 -- the pound is said to have *appreciated* and the dollar to have *depreciated*. A currency has **appreciated** in value *if it takes more of a foreign currency to buy it than before*. A currency has **depreciated** in value *if it takes less of a foreign currency to buy it than before*. What factors can cause changes in the supply of and/or demand for a currency? We discuss three here.

1. **A Difference in Income Growth Rates** -- An increase in a nation's income will usually cause an increase in the consumption of both domestic and foreign goods. Thus, as national income rises, imports tend to rise, increasing the demand for foreign exchange. An interesting result, here, is that *the currency of the country experiencing relatively more income growth will depreciate, while the currency of the country experiencing relatively less income growth will appreciate.* [See Exhibit 33-7]

2. **Differences in Relative Inflation Rates** -- A relative increase in the U.S. price level will make British goods relatively less expensive for Americans, and American goods relatively more expensive for British consumers. As a result, the American demand for British goods and for British pounds will increase, while the British demand for U.S. goods and dollars will decline. *The result is a depreciation in the value of the dollar and an appreciation in the value of the pound.* [See Exhibit 33-8]

349

How much will the dollar depreciate? According to the **purchasing power parity (PPP) theory**, *changes in the relative price levels of two countries will affect exchange rates such that one unit of a nation's currency will continue to buy the same amount of foreign goods as it did before the change in the relative price levels.* So, for instance, if the price level in the U.S. rose 10 percent more than in Great Britain, then the value of the dollar would fall by 10 percent, relative to the pound. While this theory is not, by any means, a completely accurate reflection of the "real world," over time, it proves to be a fairly good gauge of long run exchange rates.

3. **Changes in Real Interest Rates** -- In addition to goods and services, capital -- in the form of both investment and lending -- flows between countries, and the primary determinant of the flow of capital between countries is the relative real interest rates available in different countries. Suppose that real interest rates rise in the U.S. What will happen? Foreigners will increase their demand for dollars, in order to take advantage of the more lucrative lending opportunities in the U.S., and will therefore supply more of their own currencies. As the demand for dollars and the supply of foreign currencies rises, the exchange rate between the dollar and these currencies will change such that the dollar appreciates, while the currencies of the prospective foreign investors will depreciate (relative to the dollar).

III. **FIXED EXCHANGE RATES** -- The major alternative to the flexible exchange rate system is the **fixed exchange rate system**, wherein *exchange rates are fixed or "pegged," by international agreement, and they are not allowed to fluctuate freely in response to the forces of supply and demand.*

A. **Fixed Exchange Rates and Overvalued/Undervalued Currency** -- Generally, we call the dollar price of the pound, for instance, set by a fixed exchange rate agreement as the *official price*. Look at Exhibit 33-9. If the official price happens to be above equilibrium, as is the case with Official Price 1, the pound is said to be **overvalued** and the dollar **undervalued**. If, on the other hand, the official price is below equilibrium, such as Official Price 2, the pound will be *undervalued* and the dollar *overvalued*. If the exchange rate is not in equilibrium, that means there will be either an excess supply of pounds (excess demand for dollar) if the official price is too high, or an excess supply of dollars (excess demand for pounds) if the official price is too low. What can be done?

B. **What is So Bad About an Overvalued Dollar Anyway?** -- The answer is that an overvalued dollar makes American goods more expensive (for foreigners to buy), which in turn can affect the U.S. merchandise trade balance. Fewer exports because of an overvalued dollar would lead to a trade deficit.

C. **Government Involvement in a Fixed Exchange Rate System** -- Since the fixed rate scheme prevents supply and demand from "correcting" for the disequilibrium exchange rate, one solution is for the central bank(s) of the U.S. and/or Britain to intervene. Suppose that the agreed-upon exchange rate is Official Price 1, in Exhibit 33-9. Here we have a persistent excess supply of pounds (excess demand for dollars). In order to maintain the fixed exchange rate, the central bank could buy the surplus of pounds. This would show up as an addition to the U.S. official reserve holdings, and would reduce the value of the U.S. balance of payments. Alternatively, the Bank of England could sell dollars in order to fill the shortage existing in the market. This would reduce British official

350

reserve holdings and, thus, the balance of payments deficit that must exist at Official Price 1. Finally, some combination of the two actions might be taken.

D. **Options Under a Fixed Exchange Rate System** -- A nation that has a persistent deficit or surplus in its combined current and capital accounts has several options under a fixed exchange rate system.

1. **Devaluation and Revaluation** -- Suppose the U.S. and Great Britain have agreed upon an official price that results in a persistent surplus in the United States' combined current and capital accounts, and a persistent deficit in Britain's combined accounts. At some point U.S. and/or British authorities will tire of constantly intervening in the foreign exchange markets to maintain an artificially high dollar price per pound, and the two countries will agree to re-"peg" the value of the pound, so that the new official price is lower than it was before. This *reduction in the official price of a currency* is called **devaluation**. As a consequence of devaluing the pound, the official price of the dollar rises. This is called **revaluation**.

   For a good example of how a devaluation can affect the balance of trade, see *The Global Economy* feature, "The Peso, Mexican Workers in the *Maquiladoras*, and Mexico's Balance of Trade."

2. **Protectionist Trade Policy (Quotas and Tariffs)** -- Another way of attacking, specifically, a persistent trade deficit is to erect quotas and tariffs to restrict the flow of imports into the country. This may reduce the trade deficit, but it can also provide direct benefits to special interests, redistributing income and reducing economic welfare.

3. **Changes in Monetary Policy** -- A third alternative is to change domestic monetary policy in order to support the exchange rate, or official price, of the country's currency. Specifically, if the official price of the dollar is such that the U.S. runs persistent deficits, the Fed might enact tight monetary policy to cause a relative price level decline and to raise real interest rates (at least in the short run). In so doing, the Fed will promote U.S. exports, discourage foreign imports, and encourage foreign capital inflows into the U.S., *ceteris paribus*.

E. **Promoting International Trade** -- Which are better, fixed or flexible exchange rates?

1. **The Case for Fixed Exchange Rates** -- Proponents of fixed exchange rates argue that they promote international trade whereas flexible rates stifle international trade. Fixed exchange rates provide a great deal of certainty. Barring a major policy change -- such as an official devaluation or revaluation -- exchange rates remained relatively constant day-in and day-out. To the extent that exchange rates are known, then the disadvantages that occur due to uncertainty accrue as advantages to certainty. Furthermore, flexible exchange rates break up the world market, creating numerous mini-economies instead of one giant economic trade area which would exist with fixed rates. On the other hand, fixing exchange rates runs the risk of artificially maintaining a disequilibrium exchange rate, resulting in inefficiencies in the currency market, and creating the potential for policies which either restrict international trade or force countries to sacrifice their domestic economic goals in order to maintain their official exchange rate.

2. **The Case for Flexible Exchange Rates** -- Flexible exchange rates reduce the likelihood of a persistent disequilibrium exchange rate, and the accompanying problem of persistent balance of payments deficits, which then often lead to restrictive trade policies which harm both the deficit and surplus countries. Flexible exchange rates also allow countries to divorce domestic economic policy from exchange rate policy, allowing them to pursue desired domestic policy goals, rather than sacrifice those goals in order to maintain a fixed exchange rate.

   The biggest risk of flexible exchange rates is the uncertainty they create. If exchange rates change on a frequent basis, potential buyers and sellers of currencies will be faced with anticipating changes in exchange rates and, consequently, in the factors that affect exchange rates. Despite the uncertainty which flexible exchange rates provide, there is a solution: futures contracts. A futures contract can guarantee you a fixed exchange rate in the future. To see how, look at the *Economics In Our Times* feature, "The Future Sometimes Looks Brighter With Futures, Or, How to Lock in the Price of the Yen without Really Trying."

F. **The Value of the Dollar and American Real Estate** -- When the dollar depreciates, this makes American assets relatively inexpensive to foreign investors. This change causes some people to make two complaints.

   1. **Foreign Investment in the United States Unfairly Drives Up Real Estate Prices for the American Buyer** -- This is true, but those who sell real estate benefit from the higher prices.

   2. **Foreign Investment Will Result in Foreign Control of American Businesses** -- The fear here is that when foreigners buy American companies, they will run them differently; however, both foreigners and Americans have the same goal: profit maximization. This goal will limit the differences in how Americans and foreigners run the corporation.

G. **The Gold Standard** -- For much of recorded economic history, the countries of the world have operated on some form of **gold standard**, *where they (1) define the value of their currencies in terms of ounces of gold, (2) stand ready to freely convert gold into money and money into gold, and (3) link their domestic money supplies to the available supply of gold.* Since the gold exchange value of all countries' currencies were fixed in terms of gold, the effect was that of a fixed exchange rate system.

   How did the gold standard work? Any imbalance of trade between two countries was settled by transferring gold from the deficit country to the surplus country, expanding the money supply in the surplus country, driving up prices and reducing the attractiveness of the surplus country's goods to foreign purchasers. At the same time, the deficit country's money supply shrinks by the amount of the outflow of gold, reducing prices and increasing the attractiveness of the deficit country's goods to foreign purchasers. Consequently, consumers in the surplus country begin to buy more of the deficit country's goods, while consumers in the deficit country buy less of the surplus country's goods. The process continues until the trade imbalance is resolved.

IV. Where We've Been, Where We Are

A. **The Crack-up of the Gold Standard** -- From the 1870s to the 1930s most major nations of the world tied their currencies to gold and, for most of the period, the system worked fairly well. But, after World War I, things began to change. Some countries began to issue money beyond their gold reserves, thus reducing the ability of the inflow and outflow of gold to resolve trade imbalances. Attempts to restore the gold standard in the 1920s led to a series of competitive devaluations, where each country tried to "one-down" its trading partners, in an effort to boost export demand and restrict imports. Meanwhile, other countries began to grumble that the discipline of the gold standard was too strict, in that it forced them to use domestic monetary policy to meet international obligations, rather than to attend to domestic economic problems and priorities. The Great Depression and the bitter trade wars of the mid-1930s finally spelled the end of the old international monetary regime; and it was not until after the end of World War II that a new, fairly uniform international monetary system would arise.

B. **The Bretton Woods System** -- In 1944 negotiators from the U.S., Great Britain, and the other allied nations met in Bretton Woods, New Hampshire to map out a new international monetary system. Under the **Bretton Woods system**, nations were expected to maintain fixed exchange rates (within a narrow range) by buying and selling their own currency and other countries' currencies.

A nation experiencing a trade deficit could borrow international reserves from the newly-created **International Monetary Fund (IMF)**, under the assumption that, over time, the nation would generate a trade surplus sufficient to pay off the loan. The IMF was funded by imposing a quota on member nations, based upon each nation's national income and the value of its foreign trade. Each member nation contributed 25 percent of its quota in gold and/or U.S. dollars, and the remaining 75 percent in its own currency. It is from these contributions that countries may borrow international reserves to fund a trade deficit. In an effort to expand its supply of reserves so that it could better assist countries in resolving short-term trade imbalances, the IMF created **special drawing rights (SDRs)** in the 1960s.

Nations experiencing persistent trade imbalances were required to resort to official currency devaluation and revaluation under the rules of the Bretton Woods accords. This led to two problems. First, currency speculators aware of a country's persistent trade imbalance often made those imbalances worse by selling overvalued currencies and buying undervalued currencies. By so doing, currency speculation would widen the gap between the equilibrium exchange rates of deficit and surplus countries and their official exchange rates. A second problem related to the requirement of devaluation and revaluation is that many countries considered official devaluation to be tantamount to economic defeat, and were thus very resistant to using devaluation. As a result, currencies persisted in being overvalued, reducing the system's ability to resolve trade imbalances to promote efficient international exchange.

The problems of the Bretton Woods system came to a head in the late-1960s and early-1970s when the United States, previously fairly insulated from the problems of currency speculation and from persistent trade imbalances, began to experience both, and found itself unable to respond because of the special role the dollar played in the system. Furthermore, the U.S. became concerned about its obligation to exchange official dollar reserves for gold, particularly as its trade deficit worsened and more and more dollars were released into the world economy. On August 15, 1971, President Nixon announced that the U.S. would no longer convert official dollar reserves into gold, and that the dollar would no longer be fixed at $35 per ounce of gold. The Bretton Woods system was dead.

C. **The Current International Monetary System** -- After a failed attempt to re-establish fixed exchange rates in the early-1970s, the post-Bretton Woods international monetary system has been a **managed flexible exchange rate system**, or **managed float**, where *exchange rates are primarily set by the forces of supply and demand in international currency markets, but where central bank intervention to manipulate exchange rates occurs from time to time.* Proponents of the current international monetary system stress the following three advantages over previous regimes:

1. **It Allows Nations to Pursue Independent Monetary Policies** -- Under previous systems, nations have had to sacrifice domestic monetary policy goals in order to maintain the official exchange rate. With the managed float, domestic monetary policy can concentrate on domestic concerns, like output, the price level, and so on, and the exchange rate will adjust as needed.

2. **It Solves Trade Problems Without Trade Restrictions** -- With a fixed exchange rate system, nations were often forced to enact trade restrictions to resolve trade imbalances. With the managed float, exchange rate changes should solve all but the most serious trade imbalances.

3. **It Is Flexible and Therefore Can Easily Adjust to Shocks** -- Fixed exchange rate systems have a hard time adjusting to widespread supply shocks, like the 1973-74 OPEC oil embargo. Under a system of floating exchange rates, much of the effect of supply shocks can be sorted out through exchange rate changes, lessening the impact on domestic economies and trade balances.

Opponents of the current international monetary system stress the following disadvantages:

1. **It Promotes Exchange Rate Volatility and Uncertainty and Results in Less International Trade than Would Be The Case Under Fixed Exchange Rates** -- Under a flexible exchange rate regime, exchange rates are highly volatile and, therefore, make it risky for importers and exporters to conduct business; as a result, international trade is less than it would be under a fixed exchange rate system.

2. **It Promotes Inflation** -- Under the current system, a nation with a merchandise trade deficit does not have to concern itself with maintaining exchange rates or trying to solve its deficit through changes in its domestic money supply. Opponents of the current regime argue that this frees nations to "solve" their trade imbalances by allowing their price levels to rise, resulting in more inflation than would be the case under a fixed rate system.

3. **Changes in Exchange Rates Alter Trade Balances in the Desired Direction Only After a Long Time; in the Short Run, a Depreciation in a Currency Can Make the Situation Worse Instead of Better** -- Finally, opponents argue that currency depreciation will often make a trade deficit worse before it makes it better. This is because imports will not respond quickly to a change in import prices. They point to something called the **J-curve**, which shows a short-run decline in net exports following a depreciation -- a decline that is remedied only over a period of time.

V. **ECONOMICS ON THE INTERNET** -- If you need information on balance of payments, exchange rates, and stock markets around the world, consult the addresses provided in this section.

354

■ ANSWERS TO CHAPTER QUESTIONS

1. The following foreign exchange information appeared in a newspaper:

	U.S. $ EQUIVALENT		CURRENCY PER U.S. $	
	THURS.	FRI.	THURS.	FRI.
France (franc)	.204084	.20534	4.9	4.8700
Japan (yen)	.012032	.012092	83.11	82.70
German (mark)	.72271	.7303	1.3837	1.3693

(a) Between Thursday and Friday, did the dollar appreciate or depreciate against the French franc? (b) Between Thursday and Friday, did the dollar appreciate or depreciate against the Japanese yen? (c) Between Thursday and Friday, did the dollar appreciate or depreciate against the West German mark?

a. On Thursday it took 20.4084 cents to buy a French franc, and on Friday it also took 20.534 to buy a franc. Since it took more dollars (cents, actually) to buy a franc on Friday than on Thursday, the dollar depreciated relative to the franc. Looking at it from France's point of view, it took 4.90 francs to buy a dollar on Thursday, and 4.87 francs to buy a dollar on Friday. Since it took fewer francs to buy a dollar on Friday than on Thursday, the franc appreciated relative to the U.S. dollar.
b. On Thursday it took 83.11 Japanese yen to buy a dollar, and on Friday it took 82.7 yen to buy a dollar. Since it took fewer yen to buy a dollar on Thursday than on Friday, the yen appreciated and the dollar depreciated.
c. On Thursday it took 72.271 cents to buy a West German mark, and on Friday it took 73.03 cents to buy a mark. Since it took more dollars and cents to buy a mark on Friday than on Thursday, the dollar depreciated and the mark appreciated. (Note: Foreign exchange rates are published daily in the *Wall Street Journal.*)

2. Suppose the United States and Greece are on a flexible exchange rate system. Explain whether each of the following events will lead to an appreciation or depreciation in the U.S. dollar and Greek drachma: (a) U.S. real interest rates rise above Greek real interest rates. (b) The Greek inflation rate rises relative to the U.S. inflation rate. (c) Greece puts a quota on imports of American radios. (d) Americans learn on the nightly news that terrorists at the Athens airport boarded a plane that they subsequently skyjacked with American citizens aboard. As a result, American tourism to Athens (Greece) drops off substantially.

a. If the U.S. real interest rates rise above Greek real interest rates, Greeks will seek out the higher real return. This increases the demand for U.S. dollars. The drachma price for a dollar rises. The U.S. dollar appreciates and the Greek drachma depreciates.
b. An increase in the Greek inflation rate relative to the U.S. inflation rate decreases the demand for drachmas and increases the supply of drachmas. As a result the dollar price of a drachma falls. The drachma depreciates, the U.S. dollar appreciates.
c. If Greece puts a quota on American radios, the demand for U.S. dollars falls. As a result, the drachma price of dollars falls. The U.S. dollar depreciates, the drachma appreciates.
d. If American tourism to Athens drops off, the demand for drachmas falls. As a result, the dollar price of drachmas falls. The U.S. dollar appreciates, the drachma depreciates.

3. Give an example that illustrates how a change in the exchange rate changes the relative price of domestic goods in terms of foreign goods.

Suppose the exchange rate between the U.S. dollar and the English pound is $1.50 = £1. At this exchange rate an American X with a price tag of $1.50 equals one English Y with a price tag of one pound. That is, 1X = 1Y. If the exchange rate changes to $3 = £1, an American can either buy 1X with $1.50 or 1/2Y. That is, 1X = 1/2Y. In conclusion, the depreciation of the dollar makes U.S. goods relatively cheaper. This means it makes English goods relatively more expensive.

4. Suppose the media report that the United States has a deficit in its current account. What does this imply about the U.S. capital account balance and official reserve account balance?

It could imply many things. Since we know that current account balance + capital account balance + official reserve balance + statistical discrepancy = 0, we could have any of the following situations (to make things simple, we shall assume the statistical discrepancy = 0):

A minus in parentheses (-) signifies a deficit, a plus in parentheses (+) indicates a surplus.

    (1) Current account (-) = capital account (+), and official reserve account = 0.

    (2) Current account (-) = capital account (+) + official reserve account (+).

    (3) Current account (-) + capital account (-) = official reserve account (+).

    (4) Current account (-) + official reserve account (-) = capital account (+).

Looking at things this way suggests that perhaps we need to look at a current account deficit along with the capital account and official reserve account balances to see how things stack up. For example, is (1), where the current account deficit is exactly matched by the capital account surplus, the same or different (better or worse?) from (4), where the current account deficit is less than the capital account surplus?

5. Suppose that Great Britain has a merchandise trade deficit and France has a merchandise trade surplus. Since the two countries are on a flexible exchange rate system, the franc appreciates and the pound depreciates. It is noticed, however, that soon after the depreciation of the pound, England's trade deficit grows instead of shrinks. Why might this be?

It could be because it takes time for the British to switch from buying (now) higher-priced French goods to buying lower-priced British goods. That is, in the short run, the percentage increase in the price of French goods (due to the depreciation of the pound) is greater than the percentage decrease in the quantity of French goods purchased by the English. As a result, the English spend more on imports. This is the first part of the J-curve phenomenon.

6. **What are the strong points of the flexible exchange rate system? What are the weak points? What are the strong points of the fixed exchange rate system? What are the weak points?**

The arguments for and against flexible and fixed exchange rates are laid out in sections III.E.1 and III.E.2. of this chapter in this Instructor's Manual and the corresponding text sections.

7. **Individuals do not keep a written account of their balance of trade with other individuals. For example, John doesn't keep an account of how much he sells Alice and how much he buys from Alice. Additionally, neither cities nor any of the 50 states calculate their balance of trade with all other cities and states. However, nations do calculate their merchandise trade balance with other nations. If nations do it, should individuals, cities, and states do it? Why?**

No. Given the definition in the chapter, the primary purpose of maintaining balance of payments accounts is to track the exchange of national currencies. Since individuals, cities, and states within a country all use the same currency, there is no need for a balance of payment accounts.

Furthermore, the merchandise accounts, in particular, also consider the flow of real purchasing power across national boundaries -- and, one would guess, out of one economy and into another. Specifically, imports represent the outflow of real purchasing power, while exports represent an inflow of real purchasing power. However, between people and places within the same country, the flow of goods and services from one place to another does not represent the loss (outflow) or gain (inflow) of any real purchasing power to the economy as a whole, merely a redistribution of purchasing power within the economy.

8. **Since every nation's balance of payments equals zero, does it follow that each nation is on equal footing when it comes to international trade and finance with every other nation? Explain your answer.**

Not exactly, for while every nation's balance of payments may equal zero, its current and capital account balances most likely will not equal zero. If this is the case, then some countries will find themselves with current account deficits -- meaning that they are buying more goods and services from other countries than they are selling to other countries and/or are making more transfers to other countries than they are receiving from those countries. Now, while these countries' capital accounts will likely be in surplus to offset the current account deficit, all that means is that foreigners are buying more domestic capital than domestic citizens are buying foreign capital. While such a situation may be good to a point -- in that it increases the availability of funds for investment -- beyond that point it means that an increasing amount of the domestic capital stock is owned by foreigners. To put it bluntly, countries with current account deficits are buying more foreign goods and services and paying for them by selling domestic capital to those foreigners who benefit twice -- once with the gain in net exports and again with the returns to capital.

9. **Suppose your objective is to predict whether the British pound and the U.S. dollar will appreciate or depreciate on the foreign exchange market in the next two months. What information would you need to help you in making your prediction? Specifically, how**

would this information help you predict the direction of the foreign exchange value of the pound and dollar? Next, explain how a person who could accurately predict exchange rates could become extremely rich in a short time.

One would want to know what was happening to the various factors that affect flexible exchange rates, specifically: relative changes in real income, changes in relative price levels, and differences in real interest rates (and, thus, in the factors that affect real interest rates). Also, one would want to know if the central banks of either the U.S. or Great Britain planned any "intervention" into the foreign exchange markets to intentionally adjust exchange rates. Given that information, then, one could predict any changes in exchange rates based upon the observed relationships between these variables and exchange rates.

If one could predict exchange rate changes with a high degree of accuracy, one could purchase the currency that is expected to appreciate while its price is still (relatively) low and then sell it after it appreciates, when its price is relatively higher. Futures contracts provide significant leverage, and they often require only 5 percent of the amount of currency you control. With this amount of leverage, you could pyramid your profits very quickly. When George Soros correctly guessed that the British government would devalue the pound in September 1992, he made $1 billion in a week, but when he incorrectly guessed that the Japanese yen would depreciate in February 1994, he lost $600 million. C'est la bourse!

■ LECTURE SUPPLEMENTS

"A Much Devalued Idea," *The Economist*, **March 25, 1995, p. 86.**

Do currency devaluations deliver strong growth with low inflation? After the September 1992 Eurocurrency crisis, Britain, Spain, Sweden and Italy all devalued their currencies. This made the four countries more competitive and gave a big boost to manufacturing output and to exports. Despite the devaluations, inflation is not notably higher in any of the four countries than the European countries which did not devalue.

As the article points out, the exact impact of devaluation will depend upon the significance of trade in GDP, the responsiveness of wages, and the timing of the economic cycle. Devaluations will only work if workers accept real wage cuts and there is excess capacity available. In the United States, imports represent a smaller portion of GDP than in Europe, and U.S. labor markets are more flexible than European markets, reducing the overall impact of a depreciation.

The article argues that even though these economies have not suffered the adverse impacts of the devaluation, these effects may soon appear. Recession and monetary policy muted the inflationary impacts of the devaluations in 1993 and 1994, but this could change. This article provides a good case study.

"Fixed and Floating Voters," *The Economist*, **April 1, 1995, p. 64.**

This article looks at the issue of whether the world should return to a system of fixed exchange rates, have greater international co-ordination of exchange rates, or keep the floating exchange rate system which has existed since the Bretton Woods system broke down in 1973.

The advantage of floating rates is that they allow a country to adjust monetary policy without worrying about the exchange rate; however, floating rates are volatile and make it easier for countries to pursue loose monetary policies. The article looks at a book by Barry Eichengreen which says that the success of a managed exchange-rate system will depend on three factors.

The system must be flexible enough to cope with economic shocks, it must provide governments with the credibility they need to defends the system, and it must be stronger than the speculators who would try to profit under the exchange-rate regime.

Eichengreen points out that financial innovations have made capital controls all but impossible, and raising interest rates to defend a currency can be politically unpopular. He concludes that any fixed exchange-rate system is doomed, so only two solutions remain--floating rates or a single world currency. The article also mentions John Williamson's proposal for target bands for currencies which allow a 10 percent band around a fixed exchange rate. Recent evidence suggests that these bands would probably not be very effective.

"After a Devaluation, Two African Nations Fare Very Differently," *Wall Street Journal*, **May 10, 1995, p. A1, column 1.**

This article looks at the impact of a devaluation on two African countries, the Ivory Coast and Cameroon. In 1994, the CFA franc, which is shared as a currency by 14 former-French colonies, was devalued by 50 percent against the French franc. This was the first devaluation of the CFA franc in 46 years. The goal was to revive exports and local production while reducing imports, a move made necessary by a 40 percent plunge in real per-capita income in the franc zone.

The impact of the devaluation depends upon whether individuals are exporters or consumers of imports. The price of imports doubled overnight, and consumers were immediately hurt. Eventually, exports, chiefly of commodities began to grow, and foreign investors began looking at the Central West African countries once more. This is a classic example of how the J-curve works.

CHAPTER 34

International Economic Development

Chapter 34 looks at the problem of economic development which, according to the World Bank, is the most important challenge facing the human race. The goal of development is to transform underdeveloped countries into productive, efficient societies which can provide a higher standard of living to all their citizens. This chapter looks at the role economic development plays in different nations, including the impact of poverty on life in those countries and how per capita GDP differs between developed and underdeveloped countries. The chapter also looks at the role that natural resources, human capital, physical capital, and other productive inputs can play in generating economic development.

■ CHAPTER OBJECTIVES

Upon completing this chapter, your students should be able to:

- know the degree that per capita GDP incomes differ between developed and developing countries;

- understand the impact which the lack of development has on infant mortality levels and how much poverty there is in developing countries;

- explain how natural resources, capital formation, labor productivity, technological advances, and the property rights structure affect economic development;

- differentiate between physical capital and human capital and explain how each can contribute to economic development;

- discuss how improvements in labor productivity can raise the standard of living in developing countries; and,

- identify the major reasons economists cite to explain why less developed countries are poor.

■ KEY TERMS

- developed country (DC)
- less developed country (LDC)
- infant mortality rate

- dependency ratio
- vicious circle of poverty

■ CHAPTER OUTLINE

I. Economic Development

A. How Countries Are Classified -- Economists do not refer to countries as being "rich" or "poor", but as being **developed countries (DCs)** or **less-developed countries (LDCs)**. The GDP of the country determines whether a country is developed or less-developed. Exhibit 34-1 compares the GDP for a number of different countries in 1993. The 10 poorest countries had an average GDP per capita of $160, while the 10 richest countries had a GDP per capita of more than $20,000

   If one country has a GDP per capita of $20,000, and another country has a GDP per capita of $4,000, this does not necessarily mean that individuals in the first country can buy five times as many goods on average as people in the second country. There are several reasons for this. First, exchange rates change daily, and can move by 10 or 20 percent in a month. Second, goods have different costs in different countries. Services (such as haircuts) will be much cheaper in low-income countries than in high-income countries. For this reason, comparing per capita GDP based upon purchasing power parity rather than nominal exchange rates would provide a more accurate measure of relative purchasing power.

B. The Situation in Many less Developed Countries -- Less-developed countries face additional problems which accompany low per-capita GDPs. LDCs generally have a higher infant mortality rate than developed countries, and the calorie intake level for the average person is lower. Also, they often lack access to safe drinking water and adequate medical services. Approximately 23 percent of the world's population, or 1.25 billion people, were living in poverty in the early 1990s with sub-Saharan Africa having the highest concentration of poverty.

II. FACTORS THAT AFFECT ECONOMIC DEVELOPMENT

A. Natural Resources -- Although natural resources may be used to improve a nation's standard of living, some countries with an abundant supply of natural resources have relatively low rates of economic growth. *Natural resources are neither necessary nor sufficient to generate economic growth.* Ghana has natural resources, but a low growth rate, while Hong Kong has few natural resources, but a high growth rate.

B. Capital Formation -- This includes both physical and human capital formation. Physical capital allows individuals to be more productive, but these machines required the sacrifice of current consumption to invest in them, and they require an investment in human capital in order that skilled workers can use the machines efficiently. The evidence shows that *countries with high rates of savings and investment attain high rates of growth.*

C. Labor Productivity -- refers to the amount of output a worker produces in some time period, or more simply, *GDP per hours worked.* Workers with higher levels of physical and human capital to work with are more productive and have a higher standard of living.

D. Technological Advances -- make it possible to obtain more output from the same amount of resources. The higher standard of living which people of the twentieth century have, relative to previous generations, is due largely to the technological advances which have occurred since the onset of the Industrial Revolution. LDCs may not use high-tech innovations because it is cheaper to use labor given the relative costs of capital and labor.

E. **Property Rights Structure** -- Without a property rights structure which insures that individuals will get to keep the fruits of their labor, they will have little incentive to make the investments necessary to raise the standard of living within that country.

   It should be remembered that a small improvement in the growth rate can go a long way. A country with a 3 percent growth rate will, using the *Rule of 72*, double its per capita GDP in 24 years, but a country with a 4 percent growth rate will only take 18 years.

F. **A Conclusion** -- If everyone knows these five factors can generate economic development, why do some countries remain underdeveloped? The answer is that the presence of barriers to development, such as a low savings rate, can prevent a country from pursuing the development path it would like to follow.

III. **Obstacles to Economic Development** -- There are five important obstacles to economic development.

A. **Rapid Population Growth** -- LDCs have higher population growth rates for several reasons. First, in the absence of a social security/pension system, individuals have more kids so that someone will take care of them when they are older. *Their kids become their old-age insurance.* Second, the mortality rate has fallen faster than the birth rate has declined causing population to grow more rapidly. Developed countries faced this problem when they began developing. The high rate of growth increases the number of young relative to the working population, increasing the **dependency ratio**. This places an added burden on the working-age population.

B. **Low Savings Rate** -- Capital formation requires investment which in turn requires savings, but if the standard of living is barely above the subsistence level, it will be difficult to save money. LDCs are poor because they can't save and invest, but they can't save and invest because they are poor. This is referred to as the **vicious circle of poverty**. [See Exhibit 34-2]

C. **Cultural "Differences"** -- Individuals in some countries may be unwilling to change either because tradition rules their lives, or because they are fatalistic and do not believe that their standard of living can improve. They believe that fate and luck determine life's outcome, not individual initiative.

D. **Political Instability and Government Expropriation of Private Property** -- If political instability or the threat of government expropriation is high, individuals will be less likely to invest in new economic ventures because they will not be able to enjoy the fruits of their labor.

E. **High Tax Rates** -- Alvin Rabushka found a negative correlation between tax rates and rates of economic growth. Hong Kong had the lowest marginal tax rate, but the highest growth rate in per-capita GDP during the period he studied.

F. **Foreign Aid** -- is discussed in this *Economics In Our Times* feature. Foreign aid comes in the forms of long-term loans, *soft loans*, the sale of surplus products in local currency, and technical assistance. However, factors other than development influence which countries receive foreign aid and the form in which the foreign aid is provided. Israel and

Egypt are the largest recipients of U.S. foreign aid for military reasons. Countries often tie aid to the purchase of domestic goods, or require that the aid be spent on infrastructure which may be a secondary need for a developing country (such as colleges rather than elementary schools). Even if the aid is assigned to a particular goal, such as education, this frees up money which can be spent on other projects, such as a new palace or mosque.

G. **Vietnam Fights Poverty** -- This *Global Economy* feature looks at the ways Vietnam has promoted economic growth and development. The country has encouraged more foreign investment, made progress in education and health, freed agricultural markets, and it is trying to limit population growth.

H. **Population Pressures in India** -- India's high rate of population growth provides a severe obstacle to its economic development. Solutions include introducing more free enterprise, providing family planning services, raising the status of women, but as long as children are seen as a form of old-age insurance, these changes will come slowly.

IV. **ECONOMICS ON THE INTERNET** -- The National Bureau of Economic Research Gopher provides excellent data on worldwide economic development. Also provided are sources for agricultural situations across countries, and a Usenet newsgroup relating to international economic development.

■ ANSWERS TO CHAPTER QUESTIONS

1. Why is it better to compare GDP per capita figures that have been adjusted using the purchasing power parity exchange rate than the nominal exchange rate?

Although incomes are lower in LDCs than in DCs, so are the prices of goods, and especially services. If you are paid $1 an hour and a haircut costs 50 cents, you are better off than if you live in a country where you are paid $5 an hour and a haircut costs $7.50. By adjusting exchange rates for their purchasing power parity values, you can get a more accurate comparison of the standard of living between countries which might have substantial differences in the cost of goods and services. Moreover, exchange rates change daily, and sudden changes in the exchange rate can bias inter-country comparisons.

2. If Country X has a GDP per capita that is three times as great as Country Y, it follows that everyone in Country X is three times better off than everyone in Country Y. Do you agree or disagree? Explain your answer.

Disagree. This statement ignores the distribution of income within those two countries. To provide an extreme example, if one person in Country X receives two-thirds of the income in a particular country, then the per-capita GDP of the remaining people in Country X would be the same as the per-capita GDP in Country Y. Income distributions vary between LDCs. Korea has a much better distribution of income than Brazil, and comparisons between the two countries based only on GDP per capita would be insufficient.

3. In the early 1990s, what percentage of the world's population lived in poverty?

Approximately 23 percent, representing 1.25 billion persons.

4. If, before you had read this chapter, someone had asked you why the LDCs were poor and what they should do to promote economic development, what would you have said? What would you say now? Is there much difference between the two views? To what do you attribute the difference?

It is hard to say what students thought before they read this chapter, but we can point out the factors to explain why LDCs are poor which they should know after having read this chapter. These factors include rapid population growth, a low savings rates, cultures which are traditional or fatalistic, discouraging individual initiative, the presence of political instability and government expropriation of private property, and high marginal tax rates.

5. Some people argue that the LDCs will not grow and develop without foreign aid from developed countries. Other people argue that foreign aid actually limits development (they see it as a handout that distorts the incentive to produce) and propose in its place a reliance on foreign trade. In the real world, there is some of both. Do you think, however, that an increase in the aid-to-trade ratio (amount of foreign aid received divided by the amount of foreign trade) would decrease, increase, or leave unchanged the economic development of an LDC? What about a decrease? Explain your answer.

There is no clear-cut answer to this question. First, you must assume that the foreign aid is used efficiently. If it is wasted, then no amount of foreign aid can help the country develop. Assuming the foreign aid is used efficiently, and that the aid is used to provide public goods such as infrastructure (roads), education, and other inputs which can aid economic development, then an increase in the aid-to-trade ratio could increase economic development. However, there are so many other variables affecting economic growth, and the variables are interrelated with one another to such a high degree that it is difficult to provide a definitive answer.

Ceteris paribus, an increase in the aid-to-trade ratio should increase economic development, but all else is not equal. In the long run, other factors such as export promotion, providing stable property rights, high savings rates, and other factors discussed in this chapter will play a much more important role in economic development than a change in the aid-to-trade ratio.

6. Give an example to illustrate how an increase in the amount of capital that workers work with will raise labor productivity.

Let's divide your students into two groups. One group has access to non-electric typewriters. The other group has access to computers with word-processing software. Which group do you think will be more efficient and have higher labor productivity?

7. What is the vicious circle of poverty?

LDCs are poor because they can't save and invest, but they can't save and invest because they are poor. This is referred to as the vicious circle of poverty. It refers to the fact that the presence of poverty in and of itself may make it difficult for individuals to escape poverty.

8. **Why don't LDCs use all the technology that currently exists?**

There are two primary reasons. First, technology is not free. Countries must set aside current resources to make the investments in the technology which can raise productivity, but if the country is poor and has a low savings rate, making this investment will be difficult. Second, given the relative opportunity costs of labor and capital, it may be more efficient to have a good produced by cheap labor than expensive technology.

9. **Explain how a country's property rights structure may influence its economic development.**

Economic growth requires investment in capital. If you live in Sarajevo, you would be unlikely to build a factory because the factory could be destroyed at any moment. Investment under these circumstances is extremely risky and unlikely to occur. If expropriation is likely, investment will also be discouraged. For example, the Chinese government in Beijing recently told McDonald's that they would have to close their restaurant near Tiananmen Square because they were going to allow a Hong Kong developer build a new mall where the restaurant was located. McDonald's objected that they had a twenty-year lease on the site, but to no avail. McDonald's will be more cautious about building restaurants in the future, knowing that their investment can be usurped at the whim of the Beijing government.

10. **What is the dependency ratio and how might it influence economic development?**

The dependency ratio is the ratio of working to non-working (either young or elderly) individuals within a country. A high growth rate increases the number of young relative to the working population. This makes it more difficult for the working population to save money which can be invested because what money they do have must be devoted to supporting their dependents. A high dependency ratio can act as a barrier to economic growth.

■ LECTURE SUPPLEMENTS

"Developing Countries Pass Off the Tedious Job Of Assisting the Poor," *The Wall Street Journal*, **June 5, 1995, p. A1, column 1.**

Who helps the poor in poor countries? This article looks at El Salvador and shows how the system works, or doesn't work as the case may be. In El Salvador, Virginia Hernandez works for a nongovernment organization (NGO) and has been trained to deal with simple medical problems that people face. The reason for the increasing importance of NGOs is that foreign aid from developed country governments has been declining. Some NGOs are large, well-known organizations, such as CARE or Save the Children, but most are smaller organizations few people have heard of. NGOs collect trash, operate national parks, provide primary medical care, education, and vocational training, work on environmental projects, and provide small loans to would-be entrepreneurs.

One reason for the increasing importance of NGOs is the end of the cold-war. Governments on both sides of the ideological divide no longer try to buy their way into the hearts and minds of developing countries. NGOs also are less bureaucratic than governments and can get to the poor and disadvantage more quickly. As foreign aid is cut, NGOs will play an increasingly important role in helping the poor in developing countries.

"Spreading Capitalism, New Entrepreneurs are Remaking China," *The Wall Street Journal*, July 20, 1995, page A1, column 1.

Chinese capitalism would have been an oxymoron twenty years ago, but today it is a fact. When China decided to free up its internal markets, some Chinese made the most of the opportunity, and as the article puts it, there are many "bicycle-to-Benz" stories in China today.

Entrepreneurs in China carry out more foreign trade than the state sector, and in some cases, are competing with China head on. In fact, the private sector has grown so large that the changes are probably irreversible. Any serious effort to suppress the private sector would almost certainly result in economic collapse and social instability. It may be that instead of the government withering away as Marx had predicted, it will be the state sector which withers away. Currently, there are over 25 million non-state economic enterprises. If you want your students to read about the originator of Wahaha-brand baby food and other entrepreneurs, share this article with them.

Matt Moffett, Paul Carroll and Jonathan Friedland, "As the Crunch Eases, Latin Economies Stay on the Free Market Path," *Wall Street Journal*, May 12, 1995, page A1, column 1.

Most Latin American countries are pursuing a more market-oriented path during the 1990s than they did during the 1970s and 1980s, primarily because of the success which Chile and East Asian countries have had with economic liberalization, and the lack of success which Latin American countries had with their own import substitution policies of the 1960s and later. This article looks at Argentina, Brazil and Mexico to report how these countries are staying on the free-market path despite the economic setbacks which occurred during the previous year.

The peso devaluation in December of 1994 had an adverse impact on all Latin American countries as the crisis shook confidence in Latin America as a whole. Despite the problems this crisis created, Latin American countries are not returning to the protectionist policies of the past. If anything, Argentina is using the effects as a reason to further loosen the regulatory reins which had been imposed upon the economy in the past. Other countries continue to privatize the economy, and push ahead with economic reforms. As the article points out, this response is in sharp contrast to the changes which Latin American countries made in the wake of the 1982 debt crisis. Use this article to analyze how Latin American countries are changing their economies and pursuing free-market policies.

Anne O. Krueger, "Lessons from Developing Countries About Economic Policy," *The American Economist*, 38 (1), Spring 1994, pp. 3-9.

This article looks at how economists' views on development policy have evolved over the past several decades. In the past, it was assumed that government could analyze the problems which their country faced, find policies which optimized social welfare, and introduce those policies to the benefit of all. Countries set up five-year plans which detailed how these changes would be instituted. The emphasis was on government controls over the private sector through import substitution policies, industrialization, government control over agriculture, finance and other activities, credit controls, labor market regulation, and so forth.

Initially, these policies appeared to work, but over time their benefits seemed to dwindle. Inflationary pressures began to appear, administration became more difficult, attempts to control firms which sought to get around government regulations distorted resource allocation, and so forth. In some cases, policies proved politically unsustainable, in others, they led to a high level of corruption. Inevitably, some policies created interest groups which had a vested interest in maintaining these policies despite the inefficiencies they produced. When support for policies diminished, politicians tried to "buy" support for their policies through increasing expenditures for special interest groups, but this often made matters worse. Only when the situation became desperate was real reform introduced. In short, the unintended consequences of policies soon took over.

CHAPTER 35

Capitalism and Socialism: Two Views of the World, Two Economic Systems

Up until now, this book has described the workings of an economy which practices mixed capitalism. Under mixed capitalism, both the private and public sectors play a role in the economy, but the majority of economic decisions are left to the private sector. This system is practiced in most industrialized countries. There are alternatives to mixed capitalism, and this chapter explores those alternatives. The book looks at two sets of ideas which offer alternatives to mixed capitalism: extreme versions of capitalism which would minimize the role of the government in the economy, and the works of Karl Marx who plays a major role in socialist economic ideas. Finally, the book looks at how the ideas of Karl Marx influenced the economy of the Soviet Union, and how Russia is transforming its economy now that the Communist Party no longer rules the country.

■ CHAPTER OBJECTIVES

Upon completing this chapter, your students should be able to:

- know what the two major economic systems, capitalism and socialism, are by explaining the differences between the two;

- understand the visions that stand behind the capitalist view of the world and the socialist view of the world;

- explain what libertarianism is, what changes they would make in a mixed capitalist economies, and critics' views of libertarianism;

- identify the two major intellectual strands in Marx's thinking, explain how these two strands shaped Marx's vision of the economic system he helped to create, and be able to discuss the criticisms of Marx's vision;

- describe how command-economy socialism works, using the Soviet Union as an example; and,

- know how Russia is transforming its economy from one of command-economy socialism to a mixture of socialism and capitalism, and discuss the problems this transition is causing in Russia.

■ KEY TERMS

- mixed capitalism
- economic system
- vision
- pure capitalism
- command-economy socialism

- labor theory of value
- dialectic
- surplus value
- Gosplan

■ CHAPTER OUTLINE

I. **TWO VISIONS SHAPE TWO ECONOMIC SYSTEMS** -- The two systems are **capitalism** and **socialism**. *Each provides a vision of the way the world works.*

   A. **Economic Systems** -- refers to the structure society uses to answer the three economic questions. The two major systems are capitalism and socialism, but most countries use some combination of the two producing a *mixed economy* with some economies closer to capitalism and others closer to socialism.

   B. **Different Visions Shape the Different Economic Systems** -- A *vision* is a sense of how the world works. One person may see government officials as constantly trying to better the well-being of citizens while another sees government officials as representatives of special-interest groups who make donations to politicians' campaigns in exchange for his support.

   C. **What Shall We Call the Two Different Visions?** -- In calling the two competing visions socialism and capitalism, we make no judgments about the superiority of one or the other. We are primarily trying to *understand* the visions, not *judge* them.

   D. **The Two Visions as They Relate to the Market**

      1. **Prices** -- The capitalist thinker sees prices as a mechanism which *rations goods and services, conveys information, and serves as an incentive to respond to information.* A freeze in Florida reduces the orange crop. Orange prices rise, conveying information about a change in scarcity of oranges causing both producers and consumers to respond. The socialist thinker *views price as being set by greedy businesses with vast economic power*, not a result of the impersonal interaction of supply and demand. If the price of oranges rises suddenly, the government should restrict the price increase to prevent orange growers from exploiting consumers.

      2. **Competition** -- A capitalist thinker *views competition as being omnipresent* in the market, whereas the socialist thinker *views the market economy as being largely controlled by big business interests which dictate prices* and may use manipulative advertising to influence their buying decisions.

      3. **Private Property** -- The capitalist thinker *places a high value on private property because it encourages individuals to make efficient use of the resources they own.* The socialist thinker believes that *large private property owners have greater political power and use this power to take advantage of those who have little property.* For this reason, it is better to have government ownership than private ownership.

4. **Exchange** -- The capitalist thinker sees an exchange as a *mutually beneficial action between consenting market participants* whereas the socialist thinker would often see one person as benefiting from the exchange more than the other person.

E. **The Two Visions As They Relate to Government** -- The socialist thinker sees government decision makers as promoting the best interest of society as a whole who will make every effort to obtain the information needed to make the right decision. The capitalist thinker finds this naive, and believes that the government is more likely to respond to producers who have the political power to lobby Congress than to consumers who do not lobby. The reason is that the goal of government decision makers is to get elected, and for this reason, they may favor special-interest groups at the expense of the rest of society.

F. **The Two Visions As They Relate to Unintended Consequences and Deliberate Actions** -- A capitalist thinker sees market equilibria as *evolving naturally from the decisions of thousands of individuals who act independently of one another*. The socialist thinker places *a greater emphasis on planning outcomes than allowing them to evolve naturally*. The socialist would try to determine the price which would benefit the greatest number of people then set the price at that level, whereas the capitalist would allow market forces to determine the price. The capitalist believes that *many good inventions and results (such as money) can evolve through the interaction of individuals without any single individual planning the outcome*.

G. **The Two Visions in a Nutshell** -- In short, the capitalist vision holds that free markets are a marvelous system for determining people's needs and allocating resources to meet those needs. The socialist vision holds that markets lead to exploitation and that government-decision makers can act in the best interest of society and keep one group within society from exploiting the other.

II. PURE CAPITALISM

A. **Arguing the Pure Capitalism Case** -- Supporters of pure capitalism are usually referred to as *libertarians* who favor a very limited role for government in society, or even no government. At best, government should protect property, enforce contracts, and provide national defense. Everything else could be provided by the private sector. Here are some libertarian views on various topics:

1. **Professional Licensing** -- limits the supply of physicians and other professionals in order to raise the price of their services and exists largely because of government.

2. **Minimum Wage Laws** -- restrain free trade and should be eliminated.

3. **The U.S. Postal Service** -- should not be allowed to have a monopoly. Competition against the postal service should be allowed.

4. **Restraints on Price** -- such as price floors and price ceilings restrain trade and should be eliminated.

5. **Discretionary Fiscal and Monetary Policies** -- often have negative effects on the economy. The free market is inherently stable and discretionary intervention is not needed.

6. **The Federal Reserve** -- is an "engine of inflation" which responds to political pressures. A monetary rule or gold standard would be preferable.

7. **Antitrust Policy** -- often stifles competition rather than promoting it, attacking firms such as IBM or Microsoft because they are big, not because they inhibit competition. Management in firms which may be harmed by a proposed merger will use the Department of Justice to try and stop the merger regardless of whether the merger enhances competition or not.

8. **Quotas and Tariffs** -- serve narrow special-interest groups and should not exist.

9. **Social Security** -- combines compulsory savings and a redistribution program. If someone wants to save for their retirement that is their choice. The government should not have the right to impose a savings program on individuals and redistribute the money to others.

10. **Welfare** -- is a forced redistribution program which can make people dependent on welfare rather than helping them overcome poverty. Voluntary charity is preferable.

B. **A Critique of Libertarianism**

1. **Libertarians do not see the merit of using government's taxing, subsidy, and regulatory powers to adjust for third-party effects** -- Where externalities exist, the market will fail to allocate resources efficiently which may require some government adjustment to the market mechanism.

2. **Libertarians do not seriously consider complex changes** -- Some goods are too complex to be obtained through the market, such as national defense or public education, so society turns to the government for their provision.

3. **Libertarians do not see the stabilizing effects of government monetary and fiscal policies** -- Libertarians claim discretionary policy is ineffective while critics claim there are benefits.

III. **Karl Marx and Socialism** -- Here we will discuss **command-economy socialism**.

A. **The Basics of Marx's Thought** -- Two ideas are of prime importance, the labor theory of value and Hegel's dialectic.

1. **The Labor Theory of Value** -- holds that *all value in produce goods is derived from direct and indirect (or embodied) labor.* Machines have value because labor contributed to their construction. Any good could be broken down into the labor hours which were put into the final good or the machines used to produce the good, and the sum of the labor hours should determine the price of the good. The difference between the value of labor embodied in the good and the price the firm charges is the **surplus value** which the capitalist exploits from the worker.

2. **Dialectic** -- Knowledge and progress occur through action and reaction, described by Hegel as the thesis, antithesis and synthesis. The **dialectic** can be used to explain the stages of economic development.

B. **Marx on Economic Development** -- Marx thought economies passed through a number of stages in their path to economic development which culminated in pure communism. These stages were

1. **Primitive Communism** -- was the first stage of economic development in which goods were owned in common and there was no surplus value nor exploitation.

2. **Slavery** -- began at some point and allowed one person to exploit the other. At this point, class conflict begins.

3. **Feudalism** -- existed between lords and serfs creating a situation which was similar to slavery.

4. **Capitalism** -- created a system which was similar to that between the master and slave, or between lord and serf, but created large increases in productivity and output. Eventually, class warfare would break out between the capitalists/bourgeoisie and the workers/proletariat.

5. **Dictatorship of the Proletariat, or Socialism** -- would occur once workers overthrew the bourgeois state. Capital and land would be owned by the proletarian government and exploitation of the workers would cease.

6. **Pure communism** -- would result once the proletarian government had withered away. Individuals produce according to their abilities and receive according to their needs; selfishness and greed are largely a thing of the past; and there is no need for a formal government apparatus.

B. **The Critics of Marx**

1. **The Labor Theory of Value is Faulty** -- Labor is not the sole source of value, but land, capital and entrepreneurism also contribute to value.

2. **There is No Large Reserve Army of the Unemployed** -- Massive unemployment under capitalism has been the exception, not the rule.

3. **Most Workers Earn an Above-subsistence Wage** -- Competition for workers by firms puts upward pressure on wages, improvements in working conditions, shorter working hours, fringe benefits, and so forth.

4. **Marxist Revolutions Have Not Appeared in the Places Marx Expected** -- According to Marx, worker revolutions would occur in advanced capitalist nations, but instead they have occurred in developing countries.

IV. **Historical Example of Command-Economy Socialism** -- Here is how command-economy socialism worked in the Soviet Union.

A. **The Public and Private Sectors under Command-Economy Socialism** -- The government owned almost all the factors of production. The private sector was very small.

B. **Gosplan** -- had the responsibility of drafting the economic plan for the Soviet economy in the form of general five-year plans and more specific one-year plans. Gosplan outlined what each of the Soviet Union's 200,000 Soviet enterprises were to produce each year.

C. **Allocating Resources: A Major Problem Under Command-Economy Socialism** -- There are numerous mistakes the planning agency could make in specifying their plan. The agency could misspecify the number of inputs needed to produce an output, not respond to productivity changes which occur over time, or inadvertently create bottlenecks in the production process.

D. **The Case against Central Economic Planning** -- One criticism is that planners cannot process information as efficiently as the market. Wrong plans waste resources, but the cost of being wrong to planners is small. Firms which make wrong production decisions are penalized by smaller profits, forcing them to respond. Second, planners see individuals as pieces on a chess board which can be moved around to achieve his or her goal, but individuals may have goals other than those of the planner.

E. **The Next Step: Supply and Demand** -- Soviet planners usually set price below the equilibrium level. This created shortages and forced people to stand in line to obtain goods when and if they were available. Planners correctly determining the market-clearing price was the exception rather than the rule.

V. **Russia Today**

A. **Antoly Chubais and Reading Hayek** -- Hayek won the Nobel Prize for his criticisms of central planning and his advocacy of the market and prices as the most efficient method for allocating resources in society. With Hayek as his inspiration, Chubais went about the difficult task of privatizing the socialist economy by giving every Soviet citizen a voucher which could be used to buy shares in the privatized Soviet firms or invest in a mutual fund which could buy shares in the privatized Soviet firms. Shareholders could then influence the privatized firms to respond to market incentives.

B. **The Transition to a Market Economy Is Not Painless** -- Russian GDP halved between 1989 and 1994, more than during the Great Depression in the United States in the 1930s, though the actual reduction in Russian GDP is probably smaller than this. With a decrease in GDP came an increase in unemployment. As prices were decontrolled, the price of necessities shot up, reducing purchasing power.

C. **Subsidies and Inflation** -- Russia continues to subsidize many of the nation's industries. This creates a budget deficit which is paid for by increases in the money supply generating inflation as high as 20 to 40 percent per month.

D. **Russia's Private Sector** -- represents 62 percent of the country's official GDP.

E. **Property Rights and Economic Growth** -- Russia does have a high savings rate which should help it to invest, but much of the savings goes into foreign accounts, in part because the lack of strong property rights discourages domestic investment. In some cases, Mafia-style gangs influence property rights as much as the government does.

F. **Will Russia Continue on Its Current Economic Path?** -- Unless there is a sudden political change, the answer is yes. Capitalism is seen as a superior economic system, or to paraphrase Winston Churchill, "Capitalism is the worst economic system in the world, except for its alternatives."

G. **Poland and Economic Reforms** -- This *Global Economy* feature discusses the changes which Poland has gone through in transforming its economy from a command economy to a capitalist economy. Instead of gradual reform, the Polish government under the Balcerowicz Plan sought radical economic reform through "shock therapy". Entrepreneurs, responding to market incentives, now provide goods and services which were scarce under Communism.

VI. **ECONOMICS ON THE INTERNET** -- Sites which provide information on different political and economic systems are provided. Also, two sites which contain information on emoticons are provided.

■ ANSWERS TO CHAPTER QUESTIONS

1. What does the socialist thinker say about (a) prices, (b) competition, (c) private property, and (d) exchange? What does the capitalist thinker say about (a)-(d)?

See I.D. in the outline for this chapter for a detailed description of what the socialist thinker and the capitalist thinker say about each of these issues.

2. Discuss the differences between the socialist and capitalist visions of government.

The capitalist vision holds that free markets are a marvelous system for determining people's needs and allocating resources to meet those needs. The socialist vision holds that markets lead to exploitation and that government-decision makers can act in the best interest of society and keep one group within society from exploiting the other. These are the **basic** differences between their visions. For more specific differences, see section I. in the outline for this chapter.

3. Discuss the differences between the socialist and capitalist visions as each relates to the effects of deliberate actions.

The socialist thinker relies on deliberate actions to direct economic activities whereas the capitalist thinker relies more on the interaction of thousands of individuals and the results which evolve from these interactions. A capitalist thinker sees market equilibria as evolving naturally from the decisions of thousands of individuals who act independently of one another. The socialist thinker places a greater emphasis on planning outcomes than allowing them to evolve naturally. The socialist would try to determine the price which would benefit the greatest number of people then set the price at that level, whereas the capitalist would allow market forces to determine the price. The capitalist believes that many good inventions and results (such as money) can evolve through the interaction of individuals without any single individual planning the outcome.

4. A capitalist thinker would be much less likely to support controls on prices than would a socialist thinker. Why?

The capitalist thinker sees prices as a mechanism which rations goods and services, conveys information, and serves as an incentive to respond to information. A freeze in Florida reduces the orange crop. Orange prices rise, conveying information about a change in scarcity of oranges causing both producers and consumers to respond. The socialist thinker views price as being set by greedy businesses with vast economic power, not a result of the impersonal interaction of supply and demand. If the price of oranges rises suddenly, the government should restrict the price increase to prevent orange growers from exploiting consumers.

5. Discuss the criticism that have been made of libertarian thought.

There are three primary criticisms. First, Libertarians do not see the merit of using government's taxing, subsidy, and regulatory powers to adjust for third-party. Second, Libertarians do not seriously consider complex changes. Third, Libertarians do not see the stabilizing effects of government monetary and fiscal policies.

6. Some people argue that capitalism and socialism are usually evaluated only on economic grounds, where capitalism has a clear advantage. But in order to evaluate the two economic systems evenhandedly, other factors should be considered as well--justice, fairness, the happiness of the people living under both systems, the crime rate, the standard of living of those at the bottom of the economic ladder, and much more. Do you think this is the proper way to proceed? Why or why not?

Clearly, non-economic factors should be considered in evaluating the two systems. However, it is difficult to separate to what degree non-economic factors result from the economic system, and to what degree they result from the political system. Individuals in eastern Europe and the Soviet Union have gotten rid of both the political and economic system which existed under Communism. In China, citizens have yet to be given a choice about their political system.

Differences over the impact which capitalism and socialism have on non-economic factors can explain why mixed economies are spread over the spectrum in their emphasis on socialism and capitalism. Anglo-American countries tend to favor more capitalism while Scandinavian countries tend to favor more socialism, relatively speaking. Countries do consider non-economic factors in choosing their economic systems.

7. The *convergence hypothesis*, first proposed by a Soviet economist, suggests that over time the capitalist economies will become increasingly socialistic and that the socialistic economies will become increasingly capitalistic. Do you believe the convergence hypothesis has merit? What real-world evidence can you cite to prove or disprove the hypothesis.

I would generally disagree with the convergence hypothesis. While it is certainly true that over time western European countries have become more socialistic and eastern European countries have become more capitalistic, it would be hard to say that the two have met in the exact middle. It would be more accurate to say that capitalist economies have taken five baby-steps toward socialism and socialist economies have taken ten giant-steps toward capitalism. In almost every country in the world today, the trend is more toward the capitalist vision than toward the socialist vision.

8. State the case against central planning.

There are two primary criticisms. First, planners cannot process information as efficiently as the market. Wrong plans waste resources, but the cost of being wrong to planners is small. Firms which make wrong production decisions are penalized by smaller profits, forcing them to respond. Second, planners see individuals as pieces on a chess board which he can move around to achieve his or her goal, but individuals may have goals other than those of the planner.

9. Give an arithmetical example that illustrates the concept of *surplus value*.

Assume that a worker needs to work 4 hours to produce $20 worth of goods, but the employer requires the worker to labor for 10 hours to earn $20. The difference between the value produced by the worker, 6 hours worth of output, is the surplus value which the capitalist exploits from the worker.

10. Describe the six stages of economic development according to Marx.

The six stages are private communism, slavery, feudalism, capitalist, the dictatorship of the proletariat, and pure communism. A description of each can be found in section III.B. of the outline.

11. How were prices determined in the Soviet Union under command-economy socialism?

Prices were set by central planners, not the market. In most cases, the government-set price differed from the market-clearing price creating surpluses of goods when the price was above the market-clearing price, and shortages of goods when the price was below the market-clearing price.

12. What are some of the economic hardships likely to arise when a country makes a move away from command-economy socialism and toward capitalism?

Under command-economy socialism, factories were geared toward producing what the plan required them to produce, responding to government incentives. Under capitalism, firms respond to supply and demand as dictated by the market. Many firms and factories which operated under command-economy socialism would be unable to produce the goods which are demanded in a market economy. New factories would need to be built, and individuals would have to change their job skills to meet the change in demand. During the transition, GDP will decline and unemployment will increase. The government's tax base and system will change, and initially budget deficits will occur because spending will change more slowly. If the government monetizes the deficit, high inflation can result. Finally, the price of necessities will rise as price controls are removed, reducing individuals' purchasing power. On the other hand, shortages will be eliminated, and now entrepeneurial individuals will have the opportunity to make profits.

■ LECTURE SUPPLEMENTS

William Easterly and Stanley Fischer, "What We Can Learn from the Soviet Collapse," *Finance and Development*, **December 1994, pp. 2-5.**

If you would like to explore in more detail the collapse of the Soviet economy and the reasons behind the collapse, use this article. Soviet growth was very satisfactory up until the 1960s, but deteriorated after that. Reasons for this deterioration include heavy defense expenditures, low morale, and too heavy a reliance on capital accumulation as a source of growth (as opposed to productivity improvements). The Soviet Union began with a low capital/labor ratio, but increased this ratio consistently until the 1960s at which point the marginal productivity of new investment was almost zero. The primary reason for this result was that new machines and production techniques were dictated from above rather than allowing workers and local managers to adjust to changing technology and demand as occurs in capitalist countries. Planners focused on the quantity of investment, but rarely the quality of investment. They conclude that the diminishing returns which resulted were an inherent part of the central planning system and in the long run was inescapable.

"Eastern Europe's Capitalism," *The Economist*, **May 20, 1995, pp. 65-68.**

This is a survey article which looks at the problems and successes eastern European countries have had in making their transition to capitalist economies. This article would prove a valuable supplement to this chapter.

As the article shows, the transition to capitalism has not been easy. The result is not mixed capitalism, but mutant capitalism in which the state still plays a large vestigial role in firms which are nominally private, and workers and managers still wield a disproportionate amount of power relative to their shareholder/owners. Most firms are in a form of economic limbo in which they still have ties to the state whether they are public or private firms, but having to respond to the market in order to survive.

The article looks at how firms have been privatized, where the bosses of the firms come from, the impact of the changes on workers, the difficulties which the local stock markets are having in becoming efficient allocators of capital and prices, the problems which cross-ownership and skewed incentives create, the inevitable conflicts of interest, and other topics. I think your students will find this article interesting.

For a more in depth look at the central European countries (Hungary, the Czech Republic, Slovakia, Slovenia, and Poland) which have emerged from years of Communist rule and are now opening up their economies, see the survey in the November 18, 1995 issue of *The Economist*.

"Tired of Capitalism? So Soon," *The Economist*, **January 21, 1995, pp. 61-62.**

This article also looks at the transition in eastern Europe and Russia. In particular, it focuses on the declining interest in privatizing state-owned businesses. Privatization sought to remove companies from state ownership as quickly as possible, to collect money for the state, and to spread ownership throughout society. Whereas the Czech republic privatized first and left the task of reorganizing the firms to their new owners, Hungary sought to reorganize firms before selling them off to the public. The Czech republic privatized rapidly, Hungary and Poland did so more slowly, and though Russia launched the biggest privatization program of all, it is currently a mess. But in countries where capital and entrepreneurs are scarce, the transition to creating firms which respond to market incentives has been difficult, and many firms rely on state subsidies to keep them from going bankrupt. But as the article points out, markets breed entrepreneurs, and governments breed bureaucrats. To slow privatization will not create more entrepreneurs to run the newly privatized firms. The article which follows this one, "King of the Castle?" looks at how a London metals-trader ended up dominating Russia's huge aluminum industry.

Appendix A

Transparency Acetates
to accompany

Economics, Third Edition

TRANSPARENCIES

Arnold, ECONOMICS, 3/E

Transparency Acetate #	Chapter/ Exhibit #	Title
1	Ex 1-1	A Summary Statement of Scarcity and Related Concepts
2	Ex 1-3	Building and Testing a Theory
3	Ex 2-1b	Production Possibilities Frontier for Grades
4	Ex 2-2	More Hours of Study and a Shift in the Production Possibilities Frontier
5	Ex 2-3b	Production Possibilities Frontier (Constant Opportunity Cost)
6	Ex 2-4b	Production Possibilities Frontier (Changing Opportunity Costs)
7	Ex 2-7	Political Debates, Economic Growth, and the PPF
8	Ex 2-8	Efficiency, Inefficiency, and Unemployed Resources within a PPF Framework
9	Ex 3-1	A Circular-Flow Diagram and Two Markets
10	Ex 3-2b	Demand Schedule and Demand Curve
11	Ex 3-3	Deriving a Market Demand Schedule and a Market Demand Curve
12	Ex 3-4	Shifts in the Demand Curve
13	Ex 3-5	Substitutes and Complements
14	Ex 3-6	A Change in Demand Versus a Change in Quantity Demanded
15	Ex 3-7	Keeping the Law of Demand Straight

Appendix B

Answers to Study Questions

The Economics Reader

1. Identities in Economics

STUDY QUESTIONS:

1. Thomas Schelling quotes Peter Bauer as saying that there are no more than five things that economists know that are true, important, and not obvious. List three things that you think economists know that are: a) true, b) important, and c) not obvious.

   Answers will vary.

2. Schelling states that "There are not just free lunches but banquets awaiting the former socialist countries that can institute enforceable contracts, copyrights, and patents, or eliminate rent-free housing and energy subsidies." What does he mean by this?

   One interpretation is that once former socialist countries institute certain changes, there are gains (benefits) to be had—at practically zero cost.

3. According to Schelling, what do economists do?

   They try to find ways to move the economy from below the production possibilities frontier to the frontier.

2. Unintended Consequences in Economic Analysis

STUDY QUESTIONS:

1. How might an understanding of the "law of unintended consequences" change one's view of government legislation or programs?

   A person may no longer be in favor of a piece of government legislation or program if there are negative unintended consequences.

2. Identify some action in your life that has had an unintended consequence.

   Answers will vary.

3. List and explain Robert Merton's five sources of unintended (or unanticipated) consequences.

   The five sources are: 1) ignorance, 2) error, 3) imperious immediacy of interest (a person wants an intended consequence so much that she ignores any unintended effects), 4) basic values, 5) the self-defeating prediction (the prediction causes the change of history).

4. According to Martin Feldstein, what is an unintended consequence of Social Security?

   Workers save less for their old age.

3. Primary and Secondary Consequences in Economic Analysis

STUDY QUESTIONS:

1. According to Hazlitt, what is the difference between a bad economist and a good economist?

   The bad economist sees only what immediately strikes the eye (the primary consequence); the good economist looks beyond (to the secondary consequences, too).

2. According to Hazlitt, what error did classical economists commit?

   They considered only the long-run effects on the community.

3. Are there any political arguments currently being made that you think focus exclusively on the primary consequences of a policy proposal or program (to the neglect of the secondary consequences)? Give an example.

   Answers will vary.

4. What should we learn from Hazlitt's story of the broken window?

   One suggested answer is that there are often effects (to actions) beyond those we can readily and easily see.

4. The Scientific Method

STUDY QUESTIONS:

1. What is the difference between inductive and deductive reasoning? Give an example to illustrate each.

   Inductive reasoning is going from specific examples to general conclusions. Deductive reasoning is the reverse: it goes from the general to the specific. Examples will vary.

2. Pirsig says that "an experiment is never a failure because it fails to achieve predicted results." What does he mean by this?

   The objective of an experiment is not to achieve a particular result, but to establish the truth.

3. A motorcycle mechanic has to employ both mental and physical labor. What is the nature of the mental labor?

   He or she has to figure out—perhaps by way of the scientific method—what is the cause of a certain motorcycle problem.

4. In applying the scientific method, it is important to state only what you know, nothing more and nothing less. Why is this so important? Give an example to illustrate your answer.

   If you state more than you know, you may lead yourself down the wrong path. If you state less than you know, you omit accurate and potentially useful information. Examples will vary.

5. Efficiency

STUDY QUESTIONS:

1. When economics professors tell their students that peoples' wants are infinite or insatiable, there is often a student who will disagree. "This is not true," she says. "Our wants are few: only food, shelter, and clothing." What is at the core of the disagreement between the professor and the student?

The student is talking about biological wants; the economics professor about economic wants.

2. According to Blinder, how do economists view economic systems?

As devices for delivering goods and services to people.

3. According to Blinder, how do we know if something is inefficient (or wasteful)?

If activities can be rearranged so that some people are made better off, but no one is made worse off, then we have uncovered an inefficiency.

4. Blinder says that the gains to winners of deregulation outweighed the losses to losers so that the winners could, in principle, have compensated the losers and still had something left over for themselves—but, in fact, no compensation was made. Do you think it should have been (assuming there is a costless way to do this)? Why or why not?

Answers will vary.

6. Price

STUDY QUESTIONS:

1. According to Robert Frank, how does Disneyland's current pricing structure cut down on the amount of money that parents have to spend on rides at Disneyland?

   If Disneyland charged a high enough price to eliminate the long lines of certain rides, parents would end up paying more in dollars (and less in wait time) to have their children ride, say, 10 rides than if it leaves the current pricing structure in place (which reduces the dollar cost of the rides for the parents but increases the wait time).

2. Why might vacationers care less about waiting in line than non-vacationers?

   When a person is on vacation, she is not at work earning an income, thus the opportunity cost of waiting in line (in terms of foregone earnings) is likely to be lower for a vacationer.

3. Do you agree with Lawrence White that the long lines at Disneyland validate consumers' decisions to go to Disneyland in the first place? Why or why not?

   Answers will vary.

7. Decisions Made at the Margin

STUDY QUESTIONS:

1. If health is more important than recreation, why will some people spend more money in a week on a skiing trip than on purchasing high-quality, nutritious food to eat?

   Health may be more important than recreation when the decision is between either one or the other: good health or recreation. But on the margin, recreation may be more important.

2. In the essay, Rhoads says that "Marginalism suggests that our real concern should be with proportion, not rank." What does this mean?

   We should be concerned with how much more of X we obtain relative to the amount of X we already have, and how much more of Y we obtain relative to the amount of Y we have, instead of with whether X is more important or less important than Y in total.

3. A student chooses to skip his economics class and read a book. Does it follow that the student values reading the book more than attending the class?

   Yes, on the margin, but not necessarily in total.

4. Health care is a necessity. Do you agree or disagree?

   It depends on how much health care we are talking about relative to the amount of health a person currently possesses. If Smith is relatively healthy, a little more health care may mean little and therefore is not necessary (to a good life). However, if Smith has relatively poor health, a little more health care may mean much and therefore may be necessary (to a good life).

8. The Exchange Equation and E=mc^2

STUDY QUESTIONS:

1. According to Friedman, who first carefully and precisely stated the exchange question?

   Simon Newcomb.

2. What determines velocity?

   Velocity is determined by how *useful* the public finds its cash balances and how much it *costs* to hold them.

3. Do you think that Friedman believes that truisms can provide us with useful insights?

   Yes. Friedman says that the exchange equation is a truism, yet he goes on to imply that it is useful when answering questions about the economy.

9. A New Way to Measure the Economy

STUDY QUESTIONS:

1. According to Cooper and Bernstein, how is the new measure of Real GDP different from the old measure of Real GDP?

   The old measure was a fixed-weighted version of Real GDP, the new measure is a chain-weighted version of Real GDP.

2. Suppose Real GDP in 1995 is 118.3. What does this mean?

   It means that Real GDP has risen 23.5 percent [(125-100/100) x 100] between the base year and 1995.

3. In the article, we read that "GDP has been grossly overstating the contribution of one of economy's fastest-growing segments [computers], especially in recent years." Explain.

   Quality-adjusted computer prices have been falling in recent years, but with a fixed-weighted measure of Real GDP computers are weighted at their previously higher prices. This process of weighting currently "lower-priced" items at their formerly higher prices overstates the contribution of computers to the economy.

4. If the components of GDP—such as consumption, investment, government purchases, and net exports—and GDP itself, are each an index number, will the sum of the components equal the GDP index?

   No. It is different, though, if we measure GDP, and its components, in dollars. Then, the components of GDP sum to total GDP.

10. What Killed Health Reform?

STUDY QUESTIONS:

1. According to Wiener, who were the main organized supporters of health care reform?

   The unions and elderly advocacy groups.

2. Wiener argues that health care advocates were not as organized or as wealthy as health care opponents. If they had been, he suggests, the outcome might have been different. Do you agree or disagree? Explain your answer.

   Answers will vary.

3. Does Wiener express your view of why health care reform failed? Explain your answer.

   Answers will vary.

4. Wiener says that Americans are "schizophrenic about health care." What does he mean?

   Americans believe that the U.S. health care *system* needs major reform, but they are quite content with their own health care.

5. According to Wiener, how much was spent to defeat health care?

   $150 million

11. Social Security and Redistribution

STUDY QUESTIONS:

1. What is Goldstein's rationale for proposing that the federal government play a bigger role in funding of education and other transfer programs for the young?

   Since Social Security is a federal program, and some states are net winners while others are net losers in the program, these net gains and net losses can be offset by federal education funding. If they weren't offset by federal funding, they wouldn't be offset at all—which, we assume, Goldstein believes is unfair.

2. The Social Security program is a pay-as-you-go system. What does this mean?

   The workers of today pay the taxes that are received as benefits by today's retirees.

3. Social Security is said to be an intergenerational transfer system and an interstate transfer system. What does this mean?

   Social Security transfers funds from workers (who tend to be young) to retirees (who tend to be old), and it transfers funds (on net) from states with younger populations to states with older populations.

12. Democracy and Economic Development

STUDY QUESTIONS:

1. According to Jagdish Bhagwati, which is more important to economic prosperity: democracy or free markets?

   Free markets. He argues that free markets—irrespective of the political system—produce economic prosperity.

2. Bhagwati mentions *glasnost* and *perestroika*. What is the definiton of each?

   Glasnost is a policy of open and frank discussion of economic and political realities. Perestroika is the actual program of economic reform.

3. Do you think democracy is the best route from being a less developed country to being a developed country? Explain your answer.

   Answers will vary.

4. According to Bruce Bartlett and Roman Lyniuk, how do economic liberties lead to political rights?

   Economic freedom leads to economic growth; growth creates wealth and a power structure outside of the government; in time, an independent middle class demands political power.

5. According to Bruce Bartlett and Roman Lyniuk, what is "perhaps the best example of markets-first-and-then-democracy?

   Chile

13. Technology on Location

STUDY QUESTIONS:

1. With whom do you agree more, Peters or Gilder? Explain your answer.

   Answers will vary.

2. Peters implies that economic creativity and business growth is strengthened in cities. What is his explanation for this?

   There is a richness and exuberant variety in cities that somehow stimulates creativity. This cannot be matched by the Internet.

3. Gilder says that "cities are great consumer[s] of time" while Peters says that "they are savers of human time, they allow humans to intersect with more different stuff per hour." What does each mean by his statement?

   Gilder means that since there are so many different things to do in a city, these different things will consume your time. You will go to the bookstores, the ballparks, the museums, the restaurants, etc. Peters looks at it from a slightly different perspective, implying that since in a city there are so many things to do in a limited space (so many things per square mile), you don't have to waste time going between one thing and another. It is a short distance between the ballpark and the bookstore, between the museum and the restaurant.

4. What is Moore's Law?

   It says that the number of transistors on a chip—and hence the cost effectiveness of computers—essentially doubles every 18 months.

14. A Bit of History: The Debate on NAFTA

STUDY QUESTIONS:

1. In a brief statement, summarize the main arguments of Michael Kantor and Richard Gephardt regarding the passage of NAFTA.

   Answers will vary, but a few essential elements are: 1) Kantor generally discusses the benefits of free trade: how NAFTA will help both the United States and Mexico. 2) Gephardt stresses the decline in wages for Americans if NAFTA is passed. He also says that it is better to wait and restructure the NAFTA agreement than to proceed with the one in hand.

2. According to Kantor, how many cars did the Big Three automakers export to Mexico before NAFTA?

   1,000 cars.

3. Which person do you agree with the most: Kantor or Gephardt? Why?

   Answers will vary.

4. Give a few examples of non-tariff barriers.

   Domestic content requirements, restrictions on investment, performance requirements, import-licensing requirements, citizenship requirements.

15. Immigration

STUDY QUESTIONS:

1. According to George Borjas in his article "Know the Flow," what is incorrect about the Urban Institute's 1994 study on the costs and benefits of immigration?

    According to Borjas, "The Urban Institute's claim that immigrants create a $27 billion net surplus for the United States assumes that immigrants do not increase the cost of any program other than the ones included in the Institute's calculations (mainly welfare and education)." Borjas maintains that immigrants may benefit from more programs and impose more costs on others than the Urban Institute accounts for. Borjas states, "Because we do not know by how much immigrants raise the cost of freeways, national parks, and even defense, accounting exercises that claim to estimate the fiscal impact of immigration should be viewed suspiciously."

2. According to Borjas, what percentage of the U.S. growth in population is accounted for by immigration?

    40 percent

3. According to Julian Simon in his interview with *Forbes*, what is the "*commonality of immigration?*"

    Immigrants are young and willing to try anything.

4. According to Julian Simon, what should the immigration policy of the United States be?

    The U.S. ought to jump the number of visas to 1 million a year. If, in three years, there are no problems, then jump it again. And then again.

5. Discuss what you see as the advantages and disadvantages of Gary Becker's proposed auction of immigration permits.

    Answers will vary.

16. The Flat Tax

STUDY QUESTIONS:

1. According to Hall and Rabushka, their flat tax is not really flat? Why?

   There are exemptions for the certain low income groups. For example, a family earning $25,000 pays no individual tax; one earning $50,000 pays $4,655; etc.

2. Do you favor a flat income tax (even one with exemptions at certain low income levels) or a progressive income tax? Give reasons for why you choose one over the other.

   Answers will vary.

3. Robert Kuttner briefly discusses the "good social purposes" of the current tax system. Do you believe that it is the function of a tax system to simply raise revenue, or to undertake "good social purposes," too? Explain your answer.

   Answers will vary.

4. Do you think Milton is correct about the flat tax not being politically feasible? Explain your answer.

   Answers will vary.

17. Affirmative Action

STUDY QUESTIONS:

1. Do you agree with Kahlenberg that affirmative action should be based on class instead of race? Explain your answer.

   Answers will vary.

2. In his essay Kahlenberg quotes Michael Kingsley as saying that any preference system, whether race- or class-based is "still a form of zero-sum social engineering." What do you think the term "zero-sum social engineering" means?

   Answers will probably vary, but one reasonable interpretation (from the reading) is "zero-sum" refers to one person benefitting to the degree that costs are incurred by another, and "social engineering" refers to choosing to benefit one over another. Putting the full term together, zero-sum engineering refers to choosing to benefit one person over another where the gains to the one are exactly offset by the losses to the other.

3. What do you see as the merits and/or demerits of what Sowell says about affirmative action?

   Answers will vary.

4. Do you agree with Sowell that even a totally nondiscriminatory society could have gross underrepresentation of some groups?

   Answers will vary, but a reasonable answer is that it depends on how "discrimination" and "group" are defined. Let's say that discrimination is defined as having a smaller percentage of persons working for, say, a company than the percentage of the group (which we assume has been defined) in the general population, and that group refers to race. If, then, blacks have a lower median age than whites, and, say, age is a proxy for what an employer is seeking, then it is possible for one group to be underrepresented relative to the other—even if no discrimination was intended.

18. Congressional Term Limits

STUDY QUESTIONS:

1. Are you in favor or against term limits? State your reasons.

   Answers will vary.

2. Some proponents of term limits have said that with term limits pork-barrel, special-interest politics will play a smaller role in government. Others have argued that if this is the objective, the best way to increase the likelihood that politicians do not cater to special-interest groups is to guarantee them their positions for life. What are your thoughts on the subject? If the objective is to have pork-barrel, special-interest politics play a smaller role in government, what is the best way to proceed?

   Answers will vary.

3. Senator Thompson says that term limits have the "overwhelming support of the American people." Assuming this is true at this time, is this a good reason for Congress to pass term limits? Why or why not?

   Answers will vary.

4. Ornstein argues that with term limits, Congress will be weakened because its expertise and experience will be weakened. Do you agree or disagree? Explain your answer.

19. Capitalism and Socialism

STUDY QUESTIONS:

1. Heilbroner says that "whether socialism in some form will eventually return as a major organizing force in human favors is unknown." What do you think? Explain your answer.

   Answers will vary.

2. According to Hessen, "the emergence of capitalism is often mistakenly linked to a Puritan work ethic." What, according to Hessen, explains the link between capitalism and the work ethic.

   Hessen: "A better explanation of the Puritans' diligence is that by refusing to swear allegiance to the established Church of England, they were barred from activities and professions to which they otherwise might have been drawn—land ownership, law, the military, civil service, universities—so they focused on trade and commerce."

3. According to Heilbroner, why did socialism fail?

   Bureaucrats under socialism do not have the motivation to act on information.

4. According to Hessen, how does capitalism differ from perfect competition?

   Hessen: "Neither rivalry nor product differentiation occurs under perfect competition, but they happen constantly under real flesh-and-blood capitalism."

TEXT IS PRINTED ON 10% POST CONSUMER RECYCLED PAPER

0–314–09034–7